T0260647

Cyber Operations

A Case Study Approach

Jerry M. Couretas
Journal of Defense Modeling and Simulati
Hampton Hill Circle
United States

Library of Congress Cataloging-in-Publication Data applied for:
Hardback ISBN 9781119712091

Cover Design: Wiley
Cover Image: © Yuichiro Chino/Getty Images

Set in 9.5/12.5pt STIXTwoText by Straive, Pondicherry, India

Dedication

The development of this book had many hands. Mr. Ed Waltz was key to the early discussions, feedback, and support for this work. In addition, I would like to thank Adam Gordon and Pat Adrounie for reviewing each of the chapters during the writing phase. I would also like to thank Aileen Storry, my editor at Wiley, whose patience was key in completing this project.

I would like to dedicate this book to Monica, Sophie, and Ella for the time and patience that they provided. In addition, I would also like to thank my parents, Gus and Mary, for providing an example of persistence and faith.

Contents

Preface

The goal of this book is to help the reader understand cyberattacks. And case studies are one way to untangle the teams, targets, and tools that compose a cyber operation. While current cyber operations' reporting can be a challenge to "unpack," this book defines the terms, describes the operations, and profiles some of the key players that scan our critical infrastructure, broadcast fake news, and influence our elections.

One excuse for challenges in understanding cyberattacks is that cyber is "new." Cyber is not new. We have had cyberattacks in their current form since at least the 1980s, with the former Soviet Union using German hackers to steal US Star Wars missile defense system secrets (Stoll, 2005). In addition, intelligence operations that include the now-key cyber actions of denial, data theft, and disinformation have been around for millennia.

There are shifting definitions of "cyber" due to overlaps between changing technology and operation types. For example, a cyberattack in the early 2000s would likely have been theft or website defacement. By 2020, a cyberattack was more likely to be a system locked down by ransomware with a payment required in Bitcoin to regain system access.

We will track the relatively short history of cyber operations in terms of the technologies developed, the operations performed, and the effects achieved. A shortened version is provided in Table P.1.

As shown in Table P.1, the use of cyber spans from simple data exfiltration to information operations to delaying a nation-state nuclear program (e.g., 2010 STUXNET). In addition, cyber operations developed in phases from hackers to hacktivists to cyber teams. This development occurred in time phases, supported by web technology and social media development, with the 2010 STUXNET and WikiLeaks attacks proving the ability to deliver strategic effects via cyber. This was also the same time frame when multiple political transitions seemed to have led to increased cyber operations' investment. Using Table P.1's timeline, we will

Table P.1 Technical and Operational Cyber Timeline.

Technical Development	First(s) of a Kind in terms of Cyberattack
1960s to early 1990s	1960s: Research network (i.e., ARPANET) set up between universities and government labs
	1980s: Soviet Union uses ARPANET for espionage to attempt to extract US Star Wars missile defense system secrets
	1989: Morris worm – used to shut down ARPANET
	1990s: Russian Federation launches Operation Moonlight Maze
1993: Windows NT Released	
1994: Netscape Browser released	
2000: The Onion Router (ToR) anonymous connection capability released	
	2003: China starts Operation Titan Rain/Byzantine Hades intrusion set (i.e., extract US F-35 data)
	2007: Estonia DDoS attack
	2008: Georgia cyber/kinetic attack
2009: Bitcoin paper released	2009: Reveton requires ransomware payment in Bitcoin (Shea, 2023)
	2010: STUXNET
	2011: ISIS emerges from the Internet as a "state"
	2011–2013: Silk Road used the Internet to sell drugs using ToR for communications and Bitcoin for payment
2012: Nation-State Cyber Operations Professionalize	2012: Russia (Operation Dragonfly) and China (Operation Night Dragon) probe US energy pipelines
	2012: Iran attempts to use cyber to induce an energy and banking crisis through Operations Al Shamoon and Al Ababil, respectively
	2014: ISIS live streams the capture of Mosul on Twitter
	2016: DPRK attempts to steal $1 billion from the Bank of Bangladesh
2016: Nation-state tools compromised and released to the wild (Shadow Brokers)	
	2017: NotPetya malware results in $10 billion remediation cost

Table P.1 (Continued)

Technical Development	First(s) of a Kind in terms of Cyberattack
	2017: WannaCry malware results in $100 million remediation cost
	2021: SolarWinds supply chain attack used to compromise approximately 20,000 organizations
2022+	Russia attacks Ukraine leading with cyber wiper attack
	China probing US critical infrastructure
	Iran monitoring and suppressing protests
	DPRK continuing to exfiltrate digital wallets

describe nation-state and independent/hacker cyber actors in terms of operations, effects, and environment (Figure P.1).

As shown in Figure P.1, Section I starts with tactical operations' examples (e.g., ISIS, Russia) (Chapter 1). We will then provide an example of ISIS using the web as a maneuver space to move from a Phase I to a Phase III insurgency (Chapter 2). Chapter 3 is a background on cybercrime, including the Shadow Brokers and the proliferation of ransomware. Chapters 4 through 8 describe nation-state operations, including those in Russia, China, the DPRK, and Iran. And Chapter 9 is a review of independent cyber operators, including current operations' development from hacktivists and the global effects felt from WikiLeaks in 2010.

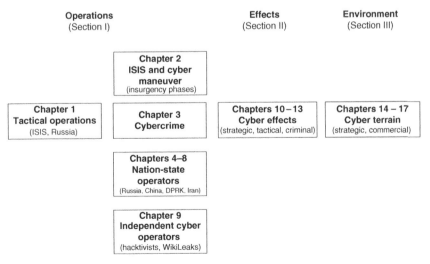

Figure P.1 Cyber Case Studies Book Organization.

Section II discusses effects in terms of strategic, tactical, and criminal. Strategic effects cause a nation-state level change of plans. And STUXNET is a good example. In addition, we will look at tactical effects, especially those employed by Russia in the Ukraine. We will also look at criminal cyber operations, many stemming from the Shadow Brokers tool release (e.g., ransomware), along with potential strategic effects stemming from criminal attacks (e.g., critical infrastructure shut down, etc.).

Section III is a review of cyber terrain and is designed to discuss the current composition of the Internet and which systems really have the ability to change our way of life (e.g., voting machines, critical infrastructure, ... , developing crypto currencies). Section III includes tool examples, from operational command and control frameworks to example firing paths used in actual operations.

Section I

Cyber Operations Introduction

Cyber attacks can produce nightmare scenarios. For example, a 2015 Lloyd's of London study, "Business Blackout," showed a possible 93 million Americans, across 11 states and the District of Columbia, being without power due to a cyber attack, costing an estimated $243 Billion, $1 Trillion in the most stressing scenario (Trevor Maynard, 2015). This is a factor of 25 times more than the $10 billion NotPetya attack in 2017 that brought global trade to a standstill (Greenberg, 2017).

In addition to catastrophic scenarios, we now have ransomware gangs, criminals, attacking critical infrastructure targets, and holding them hostage. For example, Russian ransomware gangs became famous for attacking critical infrastructure in Brazil (JBS Foods), Costa Rica (Government IT), and the United States (Colonial Oil, NEW Cooperative) in 2021. These critical infrastructure targets are considered strategic due to the life sustaining necessity of keeping these services available.

In the following Section I chapters, we will cover cyber operations in terms of their phased development. This includes a brief history of ISIS operations, and then Russia, in an overview of the use of cyber operations for tactical and strategic effects (Chapter 1). Chapter 2 includes a look at ISIS using cyber as a maneuver space in transitioning through the phases of an insurgency, maturing to a Phase III insurgent with a firm base in Raqqa, Syria. And Chapter 3 includes a review of criminal cyber, including the development of ransomware.

Nation-state operations are introduced in Chapter 4, including a description of the research, development, and clandestine operational resources applied to their cyber operations. This is followed by chapters on Russia, China, North Korea, and Iran in order to compare/contrast the different countries' policy implementations of cyber operations. This Section's examples span the current history and development of cyber operations. This progression spans from early hactivism to current political uses of social media platforms. Section I also includes examples from

Cyber Operations: A Case Study Approach, First Edition. Jerry M. Couretas.
© 2024 John Wiley & Sons, Inc. Published 2024 by John Wiley & Sons, Inc.

simple, experimental hacks, to nation-state operators performing cyberspace espionage and information operations (IO) (Table I.1).

As shown in Table I.1, cyber operations have often included nation-state interest, with "The Cuckoo's Egg" (Stoll, 2005) documenting the Former Soviet Union (FSU) use of hackers to attempt to steal U.S. military secrets near the end of the Cold War (Chapter 4). The near success described in "The Cuckoo's Egg," in the late 1980s, likely inspired Russian operators to continue their cyber collection pursuits, eventually succeeding with Operation Moonlight Maze in the mid-1990s.

Table I.1 Cyber Operations Development – 1980s to Present Day.

Time Period	Stage	Examples
1980s to late 1990s	Hacking and Experimentation	• 1988 Morris Worm • 1989 Cuckoo's Egg – example of Russian KGB collecting on U.S. Star Wars program (Former Soviet Union) • 1998 Moonlight Maze (Russian Federation) • 1998 Honker Union Hackers (1998 Indonesia, 2001 U.S. White House web page) (China)
Early 2000s to mid-2010s	Development	• 2002 Titan Rain (China) • 2007 Estonia Denial of Service (DoS) (Russia) • 2008 Georgia Multi-Domain (Russia) • 2010 Stuxnet attack on Iran's nuclear program • 2010 Wikileaks (State Department Cables) • 2011 DigiNotar (Iran) • 2011–2016 ISIS emergence from the Internet • 2014 Ukraine Denial of Service (DoS) (Russia)
≥mid-2010s	Implementation	• 2014 – present Ukraine cyber kinetic attack (Russia) • 2014 Mosul Offensive broadcast live on Twitter (ISIS) • 2014–2018 "Big Data" exfiltrations (China) • 2016 U.S. Presidential election attack (Russia) • 2016 Bangladesh Bank (DPRK) • 2017 NotPetya (Russian Federation) • 2017 WannaCry (DPRK) • 2019 Great Cannon (China)
≥mid-2020	Proliferation	• 2021 Colonial Pipeline Attack, JBS Foods . . . • 2022 Counter Protest (Iran)

During this hacking and experimentation period of networked computers, we will also looked at potentially damaging hacks (Chapter 9). For example, the Jester Worm (1997), the Slammer Worm (2003), and the Sobig Worm (2003) were examples of critical infrastructure denial capabilities. These hacks produced effects that included shutting down telephony systems, nuclear reactors, trains, telephones, and air traffic control systems.

While hackers have provided worst-case scenarios by literally shutting off critical parts of our infrastructure, nation-states have also leveraged their hackers to develop cyber capabilities. For example, while Russia (Chapter 5) started with the use of cyber for espionage, China (Chapter 6) developed a little differently. Starting in the late 1990s, China's hackers self-organized to deface Indonesian Government web sites (in 1998) in order to protest attacks on ethnic Chinese (Nuttall, 1998). Similarly, in 1999, Chinese hackers attacked U.S. Government web sites in order to protest the bombing of the Chinese embassy in Serbia (Messmer, 1999). Chinese hackers also attacked U.S. Government web sites in 2001 to protest a PRC plane colliding with a U.S. spy plane (Tang, 2001). China then matured this capability for wide scale collection a few years later, in the form of Operation Titan Rain from 2003 to 2007.

And, while China was conducting its first widespread cyber collection campaign (i.e., Operation Titan Rain) Russia incorporated cyber into all-domain operations, initially using Denial of Service (DoS) in Estonia (2007), and expanding the use of cyber to include information operations in Georgia (2008). Russia subsequently developed the Gerasimov doctrine (2013) and then integrated cyber kinetic operations in their 2014 annexation of Crimea (Greenberg, 2019).

As introduced in Chapter 4, and elaborated on in Chapters 5 through 8, there are approximately 50 nation-state-level advanced persistent threat (APT) teams that are currently accounted for (Mandiant). Within this number are crypto currency operators, ransomware group members, tool suppliers, and other support folks working for foreign intelligence services who are contributing to the cause. Independent cyber operators, discussed in Chapter 9, can also provide strategic effects. For example, we reviewed Wikileaks' publishing classified U.S. military documents, State Department cables, Panamanian corporate charters, and Democratic National Committee e-mails – each of which led to geopolitical change.

1.1 Phases of Cyber Operations

As discussed in the preceding chapters, cyber operations to date have transitioned in roughly three phases over the development from hackers to nation-state and professional ransomware cyber operations. This includes Internet development (1980s–2002), operations experimentation (2003–2012), and professional cyber operations (2013 to present).

I.1.1 1980s–2002

Even before the roll out of personal computers, hacking was a game of wits between the hacker and machine. Early incarnations of the Internet (e.g., Arpanet) included thousands of networked computers. It was only a matter of time before a determined hacker would test the limits of this new, networked, cyber world. The popular movie "WarGames" (Badham, 1983) raised awareness about the dangers of computers and led to policy makers writing the Computer Fraud and Abuse Act (Congress, 1986). It was only a few years later, in 1988, that this law was used to prosecute Robert Tappan Morris for the damages that his "Morris Worm" perpetrated on the early Internet.

Due to the government's use of the pre-Internet to connect government and university computers, one of the first documented cyber operations included the KGB experimenting with the use of West German hackers to steal information on the U.S. Star Wars missile defense system in the 1980s.

In 1984, Judge Greene broke up the AT&T monopoly, decentralizing telecommunications initially into seven regional companies. This led to opportunities for developing operating system and routing companies to enter a new market space. A few years later Microsoft went public (1986). In addition, Cisco, one of the first big Internet routing companies, went public in 1990. These are the companies that provide the building blocks for the current Internet.

At the same time that telecommunications, personal computers, and networking were rapidly changing, the geopolitical order was also put in flux with the fall of the Soviet Union (1991). This included changes in the military/political landscape. While Russia started working its way toward a non-Soviet system, client states (e.g., DPRK, Iraq) lost their super power sponsorship.

1991 was also the year that the United States, along with a coalition, expelled Saddam Hussein's Iraq from Kuwait after a surprise invasion. This war included the use of "smart bombs" and cruise missiles, computer-based weapons fielded for the first time. The United States suffered few casualties, while winning decisively against Iraq's Soviet Russian trained and equipped army. This was at least partially due to the employment of new information-related capabilities.

China watched the Gulf War closely and processed their lessons learned as the need to strike first, before an adversary builds a decisive position that predetermines a victorious engagement (Chapter 6). China's offensive cyber ops tempo for the last two decades may very well be their longer term, slow motion, "first strike." The late 1980s were also the time period when China began to open up to foreign business and send scholars overseas for education, including post-doctoral appointments to U.S. national laboratories.

The 1990s and early 2000s were characterized by hactivists, cyber operators using the web with a political axe to grind. One of the more famous hactivist groups was from mainland China (Chapter 9), protesting the treatment of ethnic Chinese during riots in Indonesia (1998) and the crashing of a Chinese fighter that was harassing a U.S. intelligence aircraft in the South China Sea (2001). One form of protest for these Chinese hactivists web site defacement, including the U.S. White House.

I.1.2 2003–2012

The latter 1990s included the disintegration of Soviet Russian institutions, minimizing Russia as a threat in the minds of Western policy makers. This was until U.S. government cyber operators discovered the Russian Federation's Operation Moonlight Maze (1996–1999), a cyber exfiltration that resulted in the loss of 5 GB of data (Doman, 2016), an extraordinary amount at that time. As a newly organized Russian Federation, and intelligence service, Turla (i.e., FSB) performed Operation Moonlight Maze against U.S. military targets (Chapter 5).

The Iraq insurgency (2004–2008) included a novel development in al Qaeda and al Qaeda in Iraq (AQI) using cyber operations to support their recruiting, financing, and communications. A plethora of videos and documents that spanned from recruitment sermons, weapons manuals, and executing infidels developed into a rich cyber footprint that characterized AQI. This included using cyber to coordinate and to participate in physical attacks (Chapter 1). The web also provided a maneuver space for AQI's gestation into ISIS just after Coalition Forces left Iraq's Anbar province. This was also during the Arab Spring (2011), which included Syria's partial disintegration. ISIS emerged from the web with a physical entity with a capital in Raqqa, Syria (2013). Uncannily, ISIS' development followed classic insurgency phases, using cyberspace for the initial phases (Chapter 2).

The first decade of the twenty first century, prior to 2012, also included nation-states experimenting with cyber. For example, Russia tested tactical cyber with denial of service operations in Estonia (2007) and information operations in Georgia (2008) (Chapter 5). And China collected a surprising amount of data on U.S. defense programs during Operations Titan Rain and Byzantine Hades (Chesaux, 2019) from 2003 to 2007 (Chapter 6). In 2009, Iran (Chapter 8) used cyber to suppress Twitter in order to quash dissent to the re-election of political hard liner Mahmoud Ahmadinejad.

In 2010, STUXNET was outed as a first in the use of cyber to deny a nation-state nuclear development program. This unexpectedly effective use of cyber occurred just before new leaders ascended in China, DPRK, and Iran; with each of these countries having an already proven cyber capability. The early 2010s were also when Russia stepped up its cyber game with the formation of the Internet Research Agency (IRA).

By 2009, cyber had proven itself for both strategic/espionage and tactical effects. Operation Aurora (2009), for example, included China exfiltrating key Google technologies. 2009 was also the year that China was found to be probing U.S. energy infrastructure via Operation Night Dragon (Chapter 6).

In 2009, Iran debuted as a cyber actor to perform its first denial attack against the Green Movement on Twitter. The Green Movement was protesting election results that favored political hardliner Mahmoud Ahmadinejad being re-elected. Then, the 2010 STUXNET revelation resulted in a spate of Iranian cyber attacks. For example, DigiNotar (2011) was the compromise of a Dutch certificate authority so that the MOIS could access 300,000 gmail accounts in order to provide information on the internal and external communications of Iranian citizens. Operation Newscaster (2011) was a set of fake Facebook personas that imitated journalists and was used by Iran to get access to policy makers that could influence thinking on Iran. Operation Cleaver (2012) was an Iranian cyber penetration operation that directly preceded Operation Al Shamoon I (2012), a cyber denial attack that destroyed 30,000 disk drives at Saudi Aramco and the penetration of the U.S. Navy's e-mail system (NMCI) (2012). 2012 was also the year that Iran executed a denial attack on the U.S. financial system (Operation Ababil).

These early stages of cyber operations also saw major outing attacks. For example, Wikileaks (Chapter 9) released secret U.S. military and State Department data that potentially influenced the Arab Spring (2011), resulting in governments falling across the Islamic Maghreb. In 2013, the cyber attack on Mossack Fonseca, a Panamanian legal firm, outed several Chinese and Russian officials' tax shelters. This was colloquially known as the Panama Papers. The Panama Papers also resulted in the abdication of the Sigmundur Gunnlaugsson, President of Iceland, in 2016.

Julian Assange's taking asylum in 2012 was uncanny timing, as this was also the same time frame that multiple political changes, and strategic cyber effects, became news. STUXNET was outed in 2010, Kim Jong Un was elevated to DPRK Supreme Leader in 2011, the Russian Federation experienced the Snow Revolution in 2012, Xi Jinpin became President of the People's Republic of China in 2013, Edward Snowden performed one of the largest leaks in U.S. intelligence history in 2013, and the Internet Research Agency (IRA) was formed in 2014, in time for elections in the Ukraine. As big hacktivism slowed down, nation-state cyber operations picked up.

I.1.3 2013–present[1]

In 2012, Russia experienced the Snow Revolution in Bolotnaya Square, a rally coordinated using Facebook that included tens of thousands of people protesting

---

1 It might be noted that these first two phases of cyber operations align with Healey's work on cyber operations, which spanned from 1986 to 2012 (Healey, 2013).

the lack of fair elections. This was a wakeup call that led to the formation of the Internet Research Agency (IRA) in 2014, with a goal of controlling the message as Russia annexed Crimea from the Ukraine (Chapter 5).

And in Iran, Dr Rouhani, assuming the presidency in 2013, expanded Iran's cyber program several fold in building out the National Information Network (NIN) during his term (Chapter 8).

By 2013, both the Russians (Operation Dragonfly) and the Chinese (Operation Night Dragon) were actively probing U.S. critical infrastructure networks. This included technically scanning critical infrastructure systems and using social engineering to get more information about the people, processes, and technologies supporting U.S. natural gas pipelines. These cyber operations included profiling the system administrators and computer support personnel responsible for keeping the systems available.

In totalitarian states, the evolution of cyber coincided with leadership transitions. Kim Jong Un, in the DPRK, ascended to Supreme Leader in 2011, followed by the DarkSeoul (2013) and Sony (2014) cyber attacks (Chapter 7). This was an unheard of DPRK cyber force that attacked Sony in 2014, outing private e-mails, destroying executive careers, and threatening terrorist attacks at theaters that played a film, "The Interview," parodying the new Supreme Leader, Kim Jong Un.

In 2013, Xi Jinpin became President of the Peoples Republic of China (PRC) (Chapter 6). This directly preceded a spate of cyber espionage attacks on the United States (e.g., OMB (2015), Anthem Insurance (2015), and Equifax (2017)).

As discussed in Chapter 3, around 2016 the U.S. intelligence community suffered one of the largest leaks in its history due to cyber at the NSA and CIA. These leaks, roughly corresponding in time with the Shadow Brokers advertising a new set of cyber tools for sale, directly preceded a rash of ransomware that continues to the time of this writing.

It was also during 2016 that the DPRK used an elaborate, multi-time zone, International, plan, in an attempted $1 billion heist from the Bank of Bangladesh. While the larger plan did not work, the DPRK still managed to steal $81 million in the effort (Chapter 7). 2016 was also a first for using social media to live broadcast a military offensive. In this case, it was ISIS, using a force of only 800 "soldiers," defeating a U.S. trained and equipped Iraqi Army in Mosul, on Twitter, for all to see.

With the large cache of Shadow Brokers tools coming on line in 2016, the DPRK used these tools in the WannaCry ransomware attack in 2017, causing $4–8 billion in damage. This was the beginning of the DPRK's presence on the cyber scene, beginning a rash of crypto theft operations that are believed to have produced over $1 billion in illicit gains by 2023, the same amount targeted in the 2016 Bangladesh Bank cyber attack, money that goes directly into nuclear weapons and delivery programs.

Current cyber operations are used to earn billions of dollars for criminals and pariah states, to extract nation-state secrets and to penetrate or to shut down strategic defense programs. It is hard to believe that these are mature cyber operations started as simple computer-based espionage or covert communications. As we will see in Chapter 1, both nation-states and guerillas started with the web as a necessary innovation in order to perform their collections, communications, financing, and coordination.

1

Cyber Operations

1.1 Cyber Operations Introduction

Cyber operations include the collection of data. This collecting of information is an enduring activity that existed long before cyber (Crumpton, 2012). However, with the advent of networked persistent memory devices (e.g., personal computers, and iPhones), using technology to access "end points" and exploit resident data became both a viable alternative to conventional spying and a new, usable tradecraft.

1.1.1 Cyber – A 21st-Century Collection Channel

One of the key issues inspiring the recent increase in the use of cyber, as a collection channel, is the volume of information that can be collected by cyber means. For example, a Cold War spy's ability to move information, even with the most advanced collection and data transfer techniques, likely peaked on the order of kilobytes, megabytes at best, of information transfer. With the current capacity of cyber storage and communication, however, terabyte downloads are common for commercial attacks (Warner, 2017).

Cyber provides a geometric increase in data transfer. In addition, the comprehensive collection provides the cyberattacker with the ability to distill the current situation, frame the desired effects, and perform cyber operations in order to produce the desired effects without traveling to the event location. The amount of data collected, and remediation cost due to a cyberattack, can be significant (Figure 1.1).

As shown in Figure 1.1, cyberattacks are increasing in both record count and subsequent remediation cost, and this is just in the commercial sector. Many private companies do not disclose that they have experienced a cyberattack due to the

Cyber Operations: A Case Study Approach, First Edition. Jerry M. Couretas.
© 2024 John Wiley & Sons, Inc. Published 2024 by John Wiley & Sons, Inc.

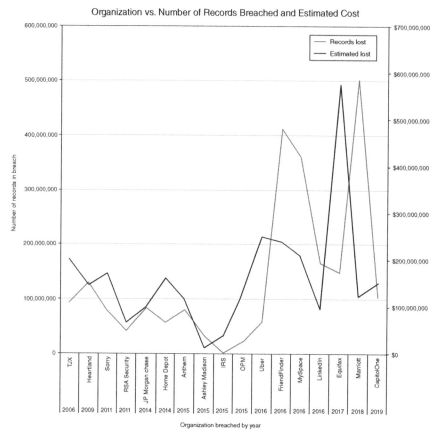

Figure 1.1   Example Commercial Cyberattacks and Cost (2006–2019).

feared loss of customers. Government-operated, or provoked, cyberattacks can be an order of magnitude higher than the commercial attacks as found in Figure 1.1.

Government attacks are not so clearly spelled out, in terms of the number of records compromised or the remediation cost. In addition, government-operated attacks can be much larger. For example, the estimated $10 billion NotPetya attack in 2017 (Greenberg, 2019) brought global shipping to a standstill after infecting the back office planning and scheduling computers of Maersk, one of the largest goods transporters in the world. Computing the cost of cyber is an active area of research (Swallow, 2022).

The development of network-based computers also included a broad set of actors coming online. From media organizations to political campaigns to banks – every direct marketing organization interested in accessing a specific demographic developed an Internet presence. Political campaigns went online to bond with

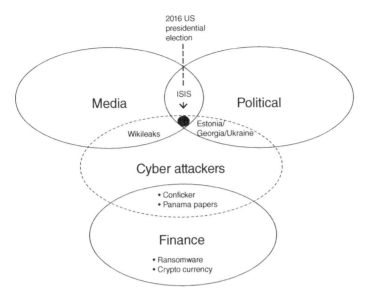

Figure 1.2 Cyberattackers Operate in Multiple Domains.

their potential voters, banks went online to do business with their customers in real time, and people who just wanted to connect went online via social media. In addition, sales and marketing players use the Internet in order to increase their mind share through well-connected, lightly secured data, with cyberattackers (i.e., hackers) not far behind (Figure 1.2).

Media, political, and finance organizations shown in Figure 1.2 came online in order to expand their market reach and subsequently became common locations for cyberattack. One thing that each online organization has in common is a similar data access, management, and storage technique. Similar means and technical understanding are used to access, extract, and exploit the data of a media company, a political campaign, or a bank's key data stores. For example, cyberattackers used similar tools to access data from the U.S. State Department (i.e., cables exposed by Wikileaks) (Domscheit-Berg, 2011) or divulge data about shady offshore investments by global leaders (Panama Papers) (Bernstein, 2017). Each of these operations included collecting data from an "end point," and using that data to embarrass or steal from a target.

1.1.2 Hackers – Pre-Cyber Operations

Cyber operators span from hackers to nation-state operators. Hackers are often characterized as genuinely curious, computer-savvy folks who exceed their boundaries in tapping into private computer systems. White Hat hackers are known to tell the vulnerable system owner about what they found. Other hackers might publicize private data, believing that "information wants to be free" (Levy, 2014).

Even before the rollout of personal computers, hacking was a game of wits between the hacker and the machine – a game of mental prowess. Early incarnations of the Internet (e.g., Arpanet) included hundreds, then thousands, of networked computers. It was only a matter of time before a determined hacker would test the limits of this new, networked, cyber world. The 1980s were therefore a time of early, but significant, activity in the cyber domain.

- The U.S. Government published the Computer Fraud and Abuse Act (Congress, 1986)
- The Morris Worm (1988), a rapidly replicating worm, was the first malware to shut down the ARPANET and cost hundreds of thousands of dollars to remediate
- "The Cuckoo's Egg," (Stoll, 2005), a book published in 1989, put a Soviet Russian KGB attack on U.S. government computers into story form – the goal of the KGB attack was to gain U.S. missile defense secrets

The popular movie "WarGames" (Badham, 1983) raised awareness about the dangers of computers and led to policymakers writing the Computer Fraud and Abuse Act (Congress, 1986). It was only a few years later, in 1988, that this law was used to prosecute Robert Tappan Morris for the damages that his "Morris Worm" perpetrated on the early Internet.

Due to the government's use of the pre-Internet to connect government and university computers, one of the first documented cyber operations included the KGB experimenting with the use of West German hackers to steal information on the U.S. Star Wars missile defense system in the 1980s. This occurred just before the breakup of the Soviet Union and subsequent government turmoil that delayed Russian use of cyber for espionage and information operations for approximately a decade.

In terms of technical development, Judge Greene broke up the AT&T telecommunications monopoly in 1984 (PINHEIRO, 1987). This ruling opened up the information technology market space in unforeseen ways, leading to the rich cyberspace landscape that we now have. The 1980s were also the years when Microsoft (1986) and Cisco (1990) went public, providing the computing and connectivity that dominates cyber terrain to this day.

At the same time that personal computers and networking were rapidly changing, the geopolitical order was put in flux due to the fall of the Soviet Union (1991) and the rapid changes in the military/political landscape. Russia started working its way toward a non-Soviet system and client states (e.g., Iraq) lost their superpower sponsorship.

Within a decade, during the late 1990s, Russian cyber operators were found hacking U.S. Air Force sites via Operation Moonlight Maze, pilfering approximately 5.5 GB of documents (Kaplan, 2017). It was also around the end of the 20th century that Patriotic Hackers made their debut, becoming famous for defacing the White House website to protest the crash of one of their fighters harassing a U.S. EP-3 spy plane in the South China Sea (2000).

It was a few years later, in 2006, that Wikileaks came on the scene, using the Internet to expose offshore money laundering capers by foreign dignitaries, even causing Sigmundur Davíð Gunnlaugsson, President of Iceland, to abdicate over revelations in the Panama Papers (Bernstein, 2017).

Al Qaeda in Iraq (AQI) also debuted in the 2004–2005 time frame, using cyberspace to recruit, move money, and perform command and control. AQI's use of the web continued as the organizations morphed into the Islamic State of Iraq and Syria (ISIS) only to emerge from cyberspace as a military organization in 2011 and acquire a physical capitol in Raqaa, Syria, by 2014.

At the same time that ISIS and other players were sharpening their operational web techniques, Russia developed its cyber playbook by using Ukraine as a cyber-test bed (Greenberg, 2019). Russia conducted technical cyberattacks on power systems, banks, and tax authorities (i.e., NotPetya resulted in $10 billion in damage (Greenberg, 2019)). In addition, Russia mixed these technical cyberattacks with kinetic force to challenge governments in Georgia (2008) and Ukraine ($\geq$2014). Russia also transitioned traditional active measures to the cyber domain in order to manipulate elections in the United States (2016 U.S. Presidential Election) (Mueller, 2019) and Europe (Cyware, 2021). Russia's use of cyber therefore goes above "the line" of non-kinetic conflict defined in Joint Doctrine Note 1–19, "Competition Continuum" (Joint Chiefs of Staff, 2019)(Figure 1.3).

As shown in Figure 1.3, cyber operations are generally "below the line." However, as cyber increasingly finds tactical applications, "above the line" actions have the potential to become more common for military/intelligence applications.

1.1.3 Cyber and Counter-Terror/Insurgency

Other examples of cyber operations include the ISIS using social media messaging to recruit, fund, and coordinate attacks. This included combining operations in ISIS' media and political domains in order to project a fundamentalist image and advertise battlefield successes during their development and operational stages, resulting in a 10 million person proto-state with a capitol in Raqaa, Syria, and a land mass that covered the size of Britain (Fox, 2019).

The development of Al Qaeda, AQI, and ISIS cyber operations coincided with the counter-terror (CT) and counter-insurgency (COIN) missions that spanned the first decades of the 21st century. As CT and COIN operations developed, the use of cyber to support tactical coalition operations rapidly expanded during counter-insurgency campaigns in Afghanistan and Iraq.

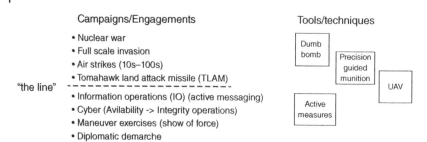

"the line"

Campaigns/Engagements

- Nuclear war
- Full scale invasion
- Air strikes (10s–100s)
- Tomahawk land attack missile (TLAM)
- Information operations (IO) (active messaging)
- Cyber (Avilability -> Integrity operations)
- Maneuver exercises (show of force)
- Diplomatic demarche

Tools/techniques

Dumb bomb

Precision guided munition

UAV

Active measures

Figure 1.3 Kinetic/Non-Kinetic Line of Hostility. *Source:* Adapted from Joint Chiefs of Staff, 2019.

While the use of the Internet by 9/11 attackers was a wake-up call, it was not until Coalition Operations in Afghanistan and Iraq, CT missions that morphed into COIN operations, that all source analysis started leveraging cyber in the form of social network analysis (SNA). For example, the overall theme of "Attack the Network" (AtN) (U.S. Joint Forces Command, 2011) required human targeting that included capturing leadership elements of adversary organizations on an unprecedented scale (Figure 1.4).

As shown in Figure 1.4, SNA is used to understand the composition and command structure of a given terror cell in order to identify cell members. Some of this membership/relationship information may be available via cyber, providing counter-IED/insurgency analysts with a tool for reducing the threat to coalition forces.

More specifically, counter-improvised explosive device (C-IED) operations used all source analysis in order to provide some of the beginnings of cyber analysis

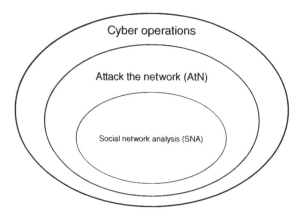

Figure 1.4 Tactical Cyber Operations – Social Network Analysis (SNA) and Attack the Network (AtN).

and targeting. The employment of AtN and SNA techniques and technologies, therefore, developed into a solution to find and target these key individuals via their e-mail, social media, and communications traffic.

1.2 Early Internet and Cyber Operations

The importance of command and control (C2) in military operations inspired the idea of providing a network that could withstand a nuclear war. This resilient network eventually became the Internet (RAND). The Internet, provided to the public at the end of the Cold War, gave the world the ability to communicate globally, post information on newly pioneered websites, and search this information, for free. This was an incredible gift to a pre-Internet world that paid high rates for long-distance telephone calls and information searches that required a trip to the library.

A decade or so later, in the early 2000s, Chinese patriotic hacktivists were defacing the White House website as a means to protest the crash of a People's Liberation Army (PLA) jet, in the South China Sea, that was harassing a U.S. Navy EP-3 surveillance aircraft (2001) (Elisabeth Rosenthal, 2001). These were early signs that the Internet was being used by foreign actors to perform cyber operations. Then, in the aftermath of the 9/11 attacks (2001), the revelation that al Qaeda was using the Internet to communicate and transfer funds ended the Internet's age of innocence, with terrorists using the Internet for command and control (9/11 Commission, 2004).

The use of the Internet by Al Qaeda for e-mail communications/coordination, and website postings to disseminate their message, initially surprised counter-terror analysts. While "Network Centric Warfare" was still seen as a next-generation technical capability in the West, the employment of social media for tactical effect was already a developing tactic on the part of terror and IED networks in Iraq and Afghanistan (Schachtman, 2007).

1.2.1 Maturing of Cyber Operations – ISIS and Russia

Growing terror organizations' use of the web to publicize their activities, to attract funding, and to mobilize recruits created a new, cyber, domain of terror operations. Al Qaeda, then AQI, ISIL, and finally ISIS, refined their web presence, broadcasting many of their attacks in real time on Twitter (e.g., Capture of Mosul (2014)) (Emerson T. Brooking and Singer, 2016). ISIS effectively expanded from proselytization and funding operations to live messaging of kinetic attacks. ISIS also developed an ability to manufacture crowds on social media (Diresta, 2018), providing an implied substance, via the number of observable followers, that made them seem much larger than they were actually.

Terrorist organizations increased their coordination and media skills in conjunction with the growth of social media. Social media was just beginning during the AQI period (2004–2006). Facebook, for example, the main social media application for connecting people to long-lost classmates, friends, and relatives, debuted in 2004. Similarly, Twitter, the social media app for sending quick messages, pictures, and videos dates back to 2006.

The year 2006 was also the year that AQI remnants were defeated in Western Iraq's Al Anbar province via the U.S. Marine counter-insurgency program (Russell, 2010). This success inspired the U.S. Army's 2007 Surge, including the infusion of thousands of U.S. and Coalition troops into Eastern Iraq. The goal of the 2007 Surge was to isolate and defeat AQI and other groups, causing many of the insurgents to now conduct their propaganda, finance, and recruiting exclusively in cyberspace. This resulted in the remnants of the AQI guerilla network retreating to cyberspace, only to emerge as ISIS.

1.2.2   ISIS Cyber Operations

In the 2010–2011 time frame, the same time that the post-AQI organization was regrouping on the Internet, Wikileaks released a batch of U.S. Government "cables" that provided an insider's view of what U.S. diplomats thought of their peers across the world. These documents included an unflattering picture of Tunisia's ruling family, resulting in civil unrest and an eventual overturning of the government (Dickinson, 2011).

Starting in Tunisia, these mass protests spread across North Africa, with the governments of Egypt and Libya soon being overturned, as well. Called the Arab Spring (Rodenbeck, 2013), much of the reporting and coordination was performed on social media (e.g., Facebook, Twitter), showing the value of these platforms to target niche populations and messages for effect. The Arab Spring therefore became a cyber means to channel protestor frustration and overturn a Government locally, with International participation via online supporters and Internet-based social media technology (i.e., Facebook and Twitter). The Arab Spring also used social media to provide an alternative means to enfranchise both resident and nonresident (e.g., diaspora) "voters," in order to select candidate leaders and provide the messaging required to fuel protests, rallies, and demonstrations. These movements used social media to coordinate rallies and remove the existing government structure, leaving a power vacuum to be filled by more organized, and less liberal, politico-religious factions.

While the Arab Spring was overturning governments in North Africa, protests broke out in Syria, with a similar intent of overturning the Syrian government. Syrian government forces, however, fought back violently, resulting in a civil war that left large areas of the country effectively ungoverned. One of these geographical security vacuums was filled by ISIS, emerging in January 2014, with a physical capitol in Raqaa, Syria, and near continuous social media operations. This was on the heels of Facebook's 2012 initial public offering (IPO) (Weidner, 2013) of their stock, and nearly coincided with Twitter's 2013 IPO (July 11, 2013) (Gabbatt, 2013).

1.2.3 Russian Cyber Operations

While social media was being used as a channel for antiregime protests and coordination in the North African Maghreb and Syria, Facebook was also being used to channel political angst in Russia. For example, the Snow Revolution (2011–2013) had up to 85,000 protestors showing up in Moscow's Bolotnaya Square to protest election results on December 10, 2011 (Ioffe, 2011). The power of social media was quickly recognized, with the Russian people starting to show their political Internet presence via Facebook accounts and tweets.

In reaction to the Snow Revolution, the Putin regime became aware of the power of social media. One action coming out of the Snow Revolution was for Putin's friend, Ilya Prigozhin[1], "Putin's Chef," to start the Internet Research Agency (IRA), in 2014. Among the IRA's tasks was to develop counter-messaging for adversaries to the Putin regime. As shown in Figure 1.5, the 2009–2018 time-line describes how the IRA provided a blitz of tweets against Ukraine during key events that include the Crimean invasion, the Internet response to the downing of Malaysian airliner MH-17, and the angry response to the 2014 Ukrainian elections.

The graph in Figure 1.5 shows the number of IRA-linked accounts created per day, overlaid with the number of tweets referencing Ukraine. The IRA was therefore developing additional accounts in conjunction with its message dissemination, adding an implied substance, via the size/scope of followers, in combination with the messaging. This is similar to what was observed in ISIS operations through the artificial construction of a movement via false accounts, manufactured personas, and super users "liking" content to provide implied validity.

Both Russia and ISIS showed a scaling up of followers, either from other countries/regions (ISIS) or completely virtual (Russia), in order to increase the online credibility of their messaging. And, while ISIS remained focused on political messaging and military exploits, Russia quickly shifted its cyber operations/propaganda between Ukrainian election results to counter-messaging on the reporting on Russian troops' shooting down of a civilian

---

1 Mr. Prigozhin is also famous for the June 23, 2023 "mutiny" against Russian Federation troops, resulting in him moving to Belarus with his Wagner Group private army. Mr. Prigozhin died in an airplane crash on August 23, 2023.

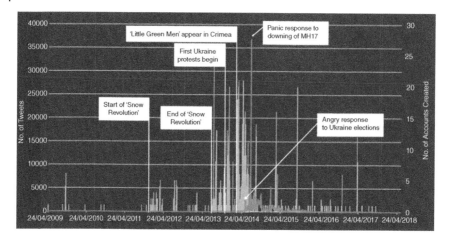

Figure 1.5 Graph of tweets regarding Ukraine over time. *Source:* Cardiff Crime and Security Research Institute, 2019/Cardiff Crime and Security Research Institute.

aircraft (Bellingcat, 2015), to whitewashing its 2014 invasion of the Crimea. In short order, Russia showed the agility of its cyber operations to expand both the scale and scope of Internet messaging over a broad range of issues in order to promote the regime's objectives.

The longer-term response to the Snow Revolution included the Russian Federation's scaling up of online political operations. For example, the IRA set up a large number of new accounts in 2014 in order to target elections in Ukraine (Figure 1.5). In addition, these new accounts contributed to a campaign of increased scale and intensity surrounding the annexation of Crimea and the shooting down of Malaysia Airlines flight MH-17. This was also when Russia first turned off Ukraine's power with Industroyer malware (Slowik, 2019), duplicating their physical shutdown of Ukrainian gas pipelines in the 1990s (Smolansky, 1995).

1.3   Cyber Operations' Stage Descriptions

Long before the Russian use of cyber to bring active measures into the 21st century, the Internet was used by Al Qaeda and AQI to manage media, communications, recruiting, and money (Economist, 2007). Initial Al Qaeda use of the Internet was primarily the action of hackers. These initial Al Qaeda cyber operations were the first actions in what will be shown to be a three-staged progression of cyber tactics that range from the late 1990s to the present, and scale from early ideological hacking to current nation-state operations.

1.3.1   Stage I (late 1990s – ~2010)(Community Development)

One of Al Qaeda's first reported webmasters, Younis Tsoulis (aka Irhabi007), managed money, recruiting, and website content from an apartment in London's West End during the early 2000s (Economist, 2007). Irhabi007 was followed by Anwar al-Awlaki, who provided direct inspiration for multiple attacks, several inside the United States, including Fort Dix (New Jersey) (2007), the Little Rock (Arkansas) military recruitment center (2009), and Fort Hood (Texas) (2009).

1.3.2   Stage II (~2010 – ~2015)(Tactical)

Following Anwar al Awlaki was Junaid Hussain (aka TriCk), who was already in trouble for hacking the phone of former British Prime Minister Tony Blair's chief aid, and publishing the downloaded information on the web, before joining ISIS. Hussain became the ISIS webmaster and was said to be in direct contact with the pro-ISIS players in the Garland, Texas, attack (2015). In addition, the ISIS that Hussain supported coordinated both the 2015 Paris nightclub attack (131 dead) and the 2016 Orlando nightclub attack (49 dead). Junaid Hussain, originally a simple hacker, proved to be more lethal by coordinating ISIS-inspired attacks. Stage II cyber operators therefore graduated from simple support to a command and control (C2) role.

1.3.3   Stage III (~2015 to present)(Tactical and Strategic)

The Stage II innovation of using cyber as a C2 method to guide operations was scaled up during Stage III. While terrorists were providing example Internet-based kinetic effects in the United States during Stage II, Russia used cyber to support military operations (from simple denial of service (DoS) operations to cyber-based active measures, e.g., 2007 Estonia, 2008 Georgia), shaping their campaigns through information operations. By 2014 Russia entered Stage III through the use of cyber operations to achieve strategic effects via election tampering, first documented in Ukraine (Figure 1.5), and then used in the 2016 U.S. Presidential election (Mueller, 2019).

The progressive development of cyber operations into what we are calling Stage III (Table 1.1), active election interference, looks a lot like traditional active measures, practiced extensively by the Soviet Union during the Cold War. An "active measure" is a term used for the political warfare actions conducted by the Soviet and Russian security services to influence the course of world events (Ewing, 2018). The goal of an active measure is to shape relationships to Soviet, now Russian, advantage, should an actual war break out. In addition, the term active measure is also used to describe the collecting of

Table 1.1 Example Stages of Internet Use for Coordination, C2, and Social Media Weaponization.

Cyber Operational Stage	Operator	Time Period	Description
Stage I	Younis Tsoulis (aka Irhabi007)	Early 2000s	Younis Tsoulis, a 22-year-old from London's West End, was the online webmaster for Al Qaeda (Economist, 2007)
	Anwar al-Awlaki	Late 2000s	Was in direct contact with perpetrators for • 2007 Fort Dix Shooting • 2009 Little Rock Recruiting Office Shooting • 2009 Nidal Hasan attack at Fort Hood (killed 12, wounded 32) • 2010 Times Square (New York City) bomber (failed)
Stage II	Junaid Hussain (aka TriCk)	Early 2010s	• 2011 Hacked British Prime Minister's (i.e., Tony Blair) personal assistant and published on the web • Principal of TeaMp0isoN, executing Guerilla Warfare via the web • Key ISIS cyberattacker • 2015 In contact with Garland, Texas, physical attackers
Stage III		Mid-2010s	• 2013 ISIS maintains a physical base in Raqaa, Syria • 2015 ISIS responsible for coordinating 7 perpetrators for the November 2015 Paris attacks, initiated by 3 suicide bombers and resulting in the death of 131 victims and 413 critically injured • 2016 ISIS-inspired Omar Mateen in the killing of 49 people in a mass shooting in Orlando, FL, USA
	Guccifer2.0		• Social media campaigns including over 10 million tweets in the 2016 U.S. Presidential Election (Cleary, 2019) • Organized dozens of violent rallies in the United States between violent factions (Mueller, 2019) • Used cyber to attack voting machines in several U.S. states with unclear objectives (e.g., disruption and influence outcome) (Pegues, 2018)
	Ransomware Groups (multiple)	Late 2010s	• Ransomware as a Service (RaaS) – 2021 Colonial Pipeline and JBS Foods

information and then the framing of that information to the information operator's advantage. While well known for almost 100 years (Popken, 2018), Russian active measures recently moved to the Internet in the form of information operations. The gradual maturing of cyber operations from hacking to providing strategic effects is provided in Table 1.1.

As shown in Table 1.1, while ISIS developed into a Stage III cyber operational actor out of its combined battlefield successes and persistent web presence, Russia's main intelligence agency, the GRU, built on ISIS' empirically proven web techniques and used similar social media tactics to participate in the 2016 U.S. presidential election. In addition, Russia's Internet Research Agency (IRA), formally a news organization, provided a steady stream of news and opinions (i.e., an estimated 10 million tweets (Cleary, 2019)), leading up to the 2016 U.S. Presidential Election. This includes the organization of dozens of issue-based rallies within the United States (Mueller, 2019), some of them turning violent (e.g., Garland Texas (2015), Charlottesville, Virginia (2017)).

The progression of cyber operations in Table 1.1 includes a timeline of the weaponization of social media from a simple tool for connecting friends and family, to a safe haven for terrorists, to a tool that is used to provide strategic economic and political effects. A quick look at this rapid progression of social media from hobby to weapon is provided in Figure 1.6.

As shown in Figure 1.6, Al Qaeda, AQI, and the ISIS were early users of social media for recruitment and C2. AQI was a Salafi Jihadist terrorist organization local to Iraq, loyal to the broader al Qaeda organization, led by Abu Musab Al Zarqawi. AQI was active from approximately 2004 to 2006, the time of Zarqawi's death (Burns, 2006). AQI also served as one of the initial anticoalition insurgent organizations in Iraq. For example, Abu Bakr al-Baghdadi, the ISIS leader from 2010 to 2019, served in AQI (The Wilson Center, 2019). ISIS therefore drew several lessons learned from AQI, including web-based communications.

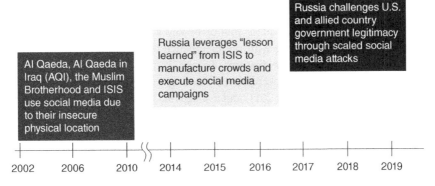

Figure 1.6 Weaponized Social Media Timeline.

Russian cyber operations generalized on ISIS' proven social media successes in order to restore their ability to provide political effects through cyber-based active measures. For example, Russian cyber operations started with denial (2007 Estonia), gradually incorporated active measures (2008 Georgia, 2014 Crimea), while at the same time dabbling with operational technology surveillance (HAVEX malware (2014) in the United States and destruction (Industroyer (Ukraine 2014)) in Ukraine. Russia continued developing its active measures in cyber, using (1) the IRA to participate in the 2016 U.S. Presidential Election and (2) the Ghostwriter campaign to tamper with Western European election results (Cimpanu, 2021). More recently, the IRA's sister organization, the Wagner Group, has been shown to use ISIS recruitment techniques to provide additional manpower to the Russian war in Ukraine (Temple-Raston, 2023).

1.4 Cyber Operations Wrap-up

As shown in Figure 1.6, initial cyber operations in the information domain graduated to a physical presence in the case of both ISIS and Russia. And, while strategic communications are a recognized element of any military campaign, cyber adds a speed and scale unprecedented by print media. Similarly, we reviewed the evolution of cyber operations in Table 1.1, from hackers to professional intelligence services, that provide the social media presence and messaging that have become modern-day cyber effects.

The use of cyber for traditional espionage and information operations occurred over three stages (Section 1.3). Stage I, hacking and early coordination, spanned from the first networking of computers until approximately 2010. Stage I accelerated its development with the introduction of social media and the rollout of smartphones, culminating in the protestor coordination that formed the Arab Spring.

With the Internet as a proven medium for community organizing, Stage II included the command and control (C2) of tactical operations, including the control of terrorist attacks. The mass rollout of key social media channels (e.g., Facebook and Twitter), along with the emergence of ISIS from the web into a physical presence, were the key features of Stage II.

The Islamic State's cyber "occultation," starting with the 2006 defeat of AQI, had them emerging as ISIL in 2011, and a state (ISIS) with the capture of Raqaa, Syria, by 2014. This was a novel development that used new social media techniques. Supporters could now help ISIS from afar by manufacturing crowds and "liking" ISIS content in order to get it to the top of social media feeds. ISIS's social media techniques paid off. ISIS challenged the Iraqi government with a potential march on Baghdad in August 2014 (Freeman Spogli Institute, 2021). In addition,

ISIS's social media techniques were keenly observed by Russia, with the IRA using personas and Facebook messaging to participate in multiple elections, including the 2016 U.S. Presidential Election.

Stage III was the nation-state assimilation (Russia) of proven ISIS tactics for strategic effect. Elections in the Ukraine and the United States are two examples of where Russia used cyber effects in an attempt to influence election outcomes. For example, starting around the run-up to the 2016 U.S. Presidential Election, Russia showed how a web-based actor (e.g., IRA, Guccifer 2.0) could induce political/kinetic effects in another country through the organization of rallies between extremists on opposing sides of a political spectrum. The IRA and Guccifer 2.0 were the perpetrators identified in the investigation of over 100 violent rallies in the days leading up to the 2016 U.S. Presidential Election (Mueller, 2019).

By 2015, a 20-year-old Internet had matured through three stages of operational development in becoming a mechanism for 21st-century political manipulation; a means to achieve strategic effects. Cyberspace had also become a breeding ground for radical operators to coordinate recruits and financing, with ISIS proving that an organization could take refuge, maneuver, and emerge from cyberspace as a political entity with a physical presence.

Bibliography

9/11 Commission. (2004). *The 9/11 Commission Report*. Retrieved 8 4, 2019, from https://www.9-11commission.gov/report/911Report.pdf.

Badham, J. (Director). (1983). *WarGames* [Motion Picture].

Bellingcat. (2015). *MH17 – The Open Source Evidence*. Retrieved from Bellingcat: https://www.bellingcat.com/app/uploads/2015/10/MH17-The-Open-Source-Evidence-EN.pdf.

Bernstein, J. (2017). *Secrecy World – Inside the Panama Papers Investigation of Illicit Money Networks and the Global Elite*. New York, NY, USA: Henry Holt and Company.

Burns, J. F. (2006). *U.S. Strike Hits Insurgent at Safehouse*. Retrieved 2 20, 2022, from New York Times: https://www.nytimes.com/2006/06/08/world/middleeast/08cnd-iraq.html.

Cardiff Crime and Security Research Institute. (2019). *THE Internet Research Agency in Europe 2014-2016*. Retrieved 2 26, 2022, from Cardiff Crime and Security Research Institute: https://www.cardiff.ac.uk/__data/assets/pdf_file/0004/1490548/CSRI-IRA-Report-Final.pdf.

Cimpanu, C. (2021). *EU Formally Blames Russia for GhostWriter Influence Operation*. Retrieved from The Record: https://therecord.media/eu-formally-blames-russia-for-ghostwriter-hack-and-influence-operation.

Cleary, G. (2019). *Twitterbots: Anatomy of a Propaganda Campaign*. Retrieved 7 6, 2019, from Symantec: https://www.symantec.com/blogs/threat-intelligence/twitterbots-propaganda-disinformation.

Congress. (1986). *H.R.4718 – Computer Fraud and Abuse Act of 1986*. Retrieved from 99th Congress: https://www.congress.gov/bill/99th-congress/house-bill/4718.

Crumpton, H.A. (2012). *The Art of Intelligence: Lessons from a Life in the CIA's Clandestine Service*. Penguin.

Cyware. (2021). *Ghostwriter: A Russia-Linked Influence Campaign*. Retrieved 9 1, 2021, from Cyware: https://cyware.com/news/ghostwriter-a-russia-linked-influence-campaign-51f90ed0.

Dickinson, E. (2011). *The First WikiLeaks Revolution?* Retrieved 5 15, 2023, from Foreign Policy: https://foreignpolicy.com/2011/01/13/the-first-wikileaks-revolution/.

Diresta, R. (2018). *How ISIS and Russia Won Friends and Manufactured Crowds*. Retrieved 7 7, 2019, from Wired: https://www.wired.com/story/isis-russia-manufacture-crowds/.

Domscheit-Berg, D. (2011). *Inside Wikileaks – My Time with Julian Assange at the World's Most Dangerous Website*. New York: Crown.

Economist. (2007). *A World Wide Web of Terror*. Retrieved 8 11, 2019, from Economist: https://www.economist.com/briefing/2007/07/12/a-world-wide-web-of-terror.

Elisabeth Rosenthal, D. E. (2001). *U.S. Plane in China After it Collides with Chinese Jet*. New York Times.

Emerson T. Brooking, Singer, P.W. (2016). *WAR GOES VIRAL – How Social Media is Being Weaponized Across the World*. Retrieved 2 27, 2022, from The Atlantic: https://www.theatlantic.com/magazine/archive/2016/11/war-goes-viral/501125/.

Ewing, P. (2018). *The Russia Investigations: What You Need To Know About Russian 'Active Measures'*. Retrieved from NPR: https://www.npr.org/2018/04/25/586099619/the-russia-investigations-what-you-need-to-know-about-russian-active-measures.

Fox, G. (2019). *ISIS Caliphate Defeated: A Timeline of the Terror Group's Brutal Project*. Retrieved 2 26, 2022, from Independent: https://www.independent.co.uk/news/world/middle-east/isis-timeline-caliphate-iraq-syria-territory-defeated-a8782351.html.

Freeman Spogli Institute. (2021). *The Islamic State*. Retrieved from Stanford Center for International Security and Cooperation: https://cisac.fsi.stanford.edu/mappingmilitants/profiles/islamic-state.

Gabbatt, A. (2013). *This Article is more than 8 Years Old Twitter IPO: Shares Begin Trading at $45.10 – Live Coverage*. Retrieved 2 20, 2022, from Guardian: https://www.theguardian.com/technology/2013/nov/07/twitter-ipo-public-stock-live-updates.

Greenberg, A. (2019). *Sandworm: A New Era of Cyberwar and the Hunt for the Kremlin's Most Dangerous Hackers*. Doubleday.

Ioffe, J. (2011). *Julia Ioffe*. Retrieved 2 27, 2022, from New Yorker: https://www.newyorker.com/news/news-desk/snow-revolution.

Joint Chiefs of Staff. (2019). *Joint Doctrine Note 1–19 – Competition Continuum*. Retrieved 5 10, 2020, from Joint Chiefs of Staff.

Joint Staff. (2018). *Joint Publication 3–12 Cyberspace Operations*. Retrieved 9 16, 2019, from Joint Publications: https://www.jcs.mil/Portals/36/Documents/Doctrine/pubs/jp3_12.pdf.

Kaplan, F. (2017). *Dark Territory: The Secret History of Cyber War*. New York: Simon & Schuster.

Levy, S. (2014). *Hackers at 30: "Hackers" and "Information Wants to Be Free"*. Retrieved 5 15, 2023, from Wired: https://www.wired.com/story/hackers-at-30-hackers-and-information-wants-to-be-free/.

Mandiant. (n.d.). *Advanced Persistent Threats (APTs)*. Retrieved 5 2, 2023, from Mandiant: https://www.mandiant.com/resources/insights/apt-groups.

Microsoft. (2022). *Ransomware as a Service: Understanding the Cybercrime Gig Economy and how to Protect Yourself*. Retrieved 11 15, 2022, from Microsoft Defender Threat Intelligence Microsoft Threat Intelligence Center (MSTIC): https://www.microsoft.com/en-us/security/blog/2022/05/09/ransomware-as-a-service-understanding-the-cybercrime-gig-economy-and-how-to-protect-yourself/#threat-actors-campaigns.

Mueller, R. (2019). *Report On The Investigation Into Russian Interference In The 2016 Presidential Election*. U.S. Department of Justice. Washington: U.S. Department of Justice.

Pegues, J. (2018). *Kompromat – How Russia Undermined American Democracy*. Amherst, NY: Prometheus.

Pinheiro, J. (1987). AT&T divestiture & the telecommunications market. *High Technology Law Journal 2* (2): 303–355.

Popken, B. (2018). *Factory of lies: Russia's disinformation playbook exposed*. Retrieved 3 22, 2020, from NBC News: https://www.nbcnews.com/business/consumer/factory-lies-russia-s-disinformation-playbook-exposed-n910316

RAND. (n.d.). *Paul Baran and the Origins of the Internet*. Retrieved 2 20, 2022, from RAND: https://www.rand.org/about/history/baran.html.

Rodenbeck, M. (2013). Special Report – The Arab Spring. *Economist*.

Russell, J. A. (2010). *Innovation in War: Counterinsurgency Operations in Anbar and Ninewa Provinces, Iraq, 2005–2007*. Retrieved 2 19, 2021, from Taylor and Francis: https://www.tandfonline.com/doi/full/10.1080/01402390.2010.489715.

Schachtman, N. (2007). *How Technology Almost Lost the War: In Iraq, the Critical Networks Are Social — Not Electronic*. Retrieved 5 13, 2023, from Wired: https://www.wired.com/2007/11/ff-futurewar/.

Slowik, J. (2019). *CRASHOVERRIDE: Reassessing the 2016 Ukraine Electric Power Event as a Protection-Focused Attack*. Retrieved 9 24, 2019, from DRAGOS: https://dragos.com/wp-content/uploads/CRASHOVERRIDE.pdf.

Smolansky, O. M. (1995). Ukraine's Quest for Independence: The Fuel Factor. *Europe-Asia Studies*, *47*(1), 67–90. Retrieved from https://www.jstor.org/stable/153194.

Stoll, C. (2005). *The Cuckoo's Egg: Tracking a Spy Through the Maze of Computer Espionage*. Pocket Books.

Swallow, C. (2022). *Considering the Cost of Cyber Warfare: Advancing Cyber Warfare Analytics to Better Assess Tradeoffs in System Destruction Warfare*. Retrieved 12 14, 2022, from Journal of Defense Modeling and Simulation: https://journals.sagepub.com/doi/abs/10.1177/15485129221114354?journalCode=dmsa.

Temple-Raston, D. (2023). *Russia's Wagner Group Uses Recruitment Efforts Honed by ISIS*. Retrieved from TheWorld: https://theworld.org/media/2023-06-07/russias-wagner-group-uses-recruitment-efforts-honed-isis.

The Wilson Center. (2019). *Timeline: The Life and Death of Abu Bakr al Baghdadi*. Retrieved 2 20, 2022, from https://www.wilsoncenter.org/article/timeline-the-life-and-death-abu-bakr-al-baghdadi.

U.S. Joint Forces Command. (2011). *Commander's Handbook for Attack the Network*. Retrieved 8 4, 2019, from https://www.jcs.mil/Portals/36/Documents/Doctrine/pams_hands/atn_hbk.pdf.

Warner, M. (2017). Intelligence in Cyber – and Cyber in Intelligence. In: *Understanding Cyber Conflict – 14 Analogies* (ed. A.L.G. Perkovich), 265–272. Washington DC: Georgetown.

Weidner, D. (2013). *Facebook IPO Facts, Fiction and Flops*. Retrieved from Wall Street Journal.

2

ISIS and Web-Based Insurgency

2.1 Introduction

In Chapter 1, we discussed the phased development of tactical and strategic operations on the Internet. These stages included

- Stage I (late-1990s to approximately 2010)(Communication)
  - Simple communication
  - Use of the Internet for proselytization and recruiting
- Stage II (~2010–~2015) (Tactical)
  - Use of the Internet to achieve tactical effects (e.g., denial, crowd mobilization ...)
- Stage III (~2015 to Present)(Strategic)
  - Use of the Internet to provide strategic effects (e.g., influence election results)

Operations on the Internet began with hackers experimenting with new technology. Shortly after, however, Patriotic hacktivists used Internet technologies to act out, usually protesting a perceived slight.

Online networking grew as more people joined social media applications. This included the use of Facebook and Twitter for political activities (e.g., campaigning) and coordinating rallies. Trolls, and other bad actors, picked up on the use of social media to coordinate these rallies, including the pitting of hostile groups against one another to result in violence. Along with trolls, AQI, and then ISIS, used the Internet to raise funds, to recruit, and to command and control operations. In fact, ISIS was the first example of the use of the Internet to recruit, mobilize, and build a state on the Internet.

Cyber Operations: A Case Study Approach, First Edition. Jerry M. Couretas.
© 2024 John Wiley & Sons, Inc. Published 2024 by John Wiley & Sons, Inc.

2.1.1 Terrorist Development of the Internet for Messaging

A recent "cyber" phenomenon is the non-nation state, terrorist, use of the Internet to disseminate its message and to provide a communications mechanism for members. Theohary (Theohary and Rollins, 2011) points out that in a July 2005 letter to Abu Musab al-Zarqawi, the late leader of Al Qaeda operations in Iraq, senior Al Qaeda leader Ayman al-Zawahiri wrote –

> We are in a battle, and more than half of this battle is taking place in the battlefield of the media. (Global Security, 2005)

Operating for over a decade, Al Qaeda Central's media arm, the As-Sahab Institute for Media Production, has distributed video, audio, and well-designed media products online through jihadist blogs, forums, and file-hosting websites (Theohary and Rollins, 2011). These fora provide instructional lectures, videos, and podcasts on how to develop physical munitions, to pass through border control points, to develop cyber denial of service (DoS) capabilities, and to network with like-minded operators.

2.1.2 ISIS Adaptation of the Internet for Coordination, Command and Control (C2)

ISIS uses the Internet as a key platform to disseminate irredentist sentiments. ISIS publishes its message via an online magazine (i.e., "Inspire") in order to report on current operations, attract followers, and obtain funding. ISIS is credited with multiple attacks whose tactical command and control (C2) occurred in cyberspace (i.e., Phase II insurgent). ISIS made the additional step to a Phase III insurgent with the capture of a physical capitol (Raqaa, Syria), the defeat of the Iraqi Army in Anbar Province, and the capture of Mosul in 2014.

The stages in Chapter 1 highlight the increasing use of the web as a domain to perform tactical and strategic operations. ISIS is featured as performing both C2 and information operations (IO) in support of their political–military development. ISIS' beginnings, as discussed in Chapter 1, included parts of Al Qaeda in Iraq (AQI), a Salafi Jihadist terrorist organization local to Iraq, loyal to the broader al Qaeda organization, and led by Abu Musab Al Zarqawi during the development of the Iraqi insurgency in the early 2000s. AQI was active from approximately 2004 to 2006, Zarqawi's death. AQI also served as one of the initial anti-coalition insurgent organizations in Iraq. For example, Abu Bakr al-Baghdadi, the ISIS leader from 2010 to 2019, served in AQI. ISIS therefore drew several lessons learned from AQI, including web-based communications.

Social media was just beginning during the AQI period (2004–2006) and quickly became a key means to inspire recruits, to move funds, and to coordinate operations as AQI was defeated on the battlefield and needed a safe place to operate from. For example, disenfranchised groups across the Maghreb continued to communicate, collaborate, and coordinate using the Internet during the first decade of the 21st century. Then, during the early part of 2010, these protestors, often using Facebook, overturned governments in Tunisia, Libya, and Egypt. This was formally called the Arab Spring. Similar protests in Syria resulted in large, ungoverned spaces, providing an opportunistic physical location for the online insurgents, formerly AQI, to emerge as ISIS.

2.1.3 ISIS "Emergence" from Cyberspace to form a State

ISIS emerged in 2013 with a physical capital in Raqaa, Syria, and near continuous social media operations. ISIS soon proved themselves to be as adept on the battlefield as they were at social media operations. Table 2.1 shows additional details for the ISIS social media development timeline.

As shown in Table 2.1, ISIS transitioned from an Internet presence (2008–2012), to a physical "state" (2012–2017), and back to an Internet presence (2017). ISIS is the first documented case of an organization using the Internet, as a principal means of messaging, to move from cyberspace into a physical "state." This was a state that governed over 10 million people in a space the size of the United Kingdom. ISIS is still online and increasingly credited with physical operations in the 2020s (ADL, 2022).

Table 2.1 Al Qaeda in Iraq (AQI), the Arab Spring, and ISIS Information Operations.

Period	Description
1999–present	Al Qaeda uses the Internet for coordination, C2, and media operations (e.g., 9/11)
2004–2006	Al Qaeda in Iraq (AQI) used social media for operations
2009–2010	Arab Spring – civil unrest, channeled through the Internet, eventually resulted in the overturning of governments in North Africa (i.e., Tunisia, Libya, and Egypt) and with the beginning of the Syrian civil war, where ISIS developed as a fighting force and established a base
2010–2011	AQI morphs into ISIS and uses social media for media distribution and C2
2012–2016	ISIS expands its reach to include over 10 million people in a land mass the size of the United Kingdom under its control
2017–present	With ISIS having lost all of its physical territory, it maintains its web presence for proselytization and C2

2.2 Cyber-Based Irregular Operations

ISIS developed each stage of its organization, guerilla movement, and capture of territory in parallel with Internet operations. This resulted in active counter-insurgency (COIN) operations on the web, as well, employed to target Internet-based messaging, recruitment, and command and control (C2). Task Force Ares, for example, was a coalition campaign supporting the government of Iraq and was used to negate ISIS' online capabilities (Sanger, 2016).

2.2.1 Three-Phase Insurgency Model with Cyber – ISIS Example

We will now review cyber approaches to counter ISIS, as implemented by the U.S. military, and investigate how the ISIS occultation in cyber fits in with the classic three-phase insurgency model (Strategy and Tactics of Guerilla Warfare, n.d.), where insurgents move from

1) organization, consolidation, and preservation of base areas,
2) guerrilla warfare – armed skirmishes with government forces to heighten political effect
3) conventional conflict with the aim of defeating the current government forces in battle.

The three phases of ISIS' Internet-based insurgency included

1) Communicate via the Internet for coordination, consolidating their ideological group and creating a cadre willing to fight for their cause
2) Publicize, via social media, acts of terror for political effect from the organizational cells (e.g., IED or car bomb cells), coordinated via the Internet (step 1)
3) Challenged conventional Syrian and Iraqi forces and formed a state, with a capitol in Raqaa, Syria (2013–2017).

Having completed phase three of its insurgency, ISIS continually fought to expand its footprint, with the goal of taking over the current states of Iraq and Syria. ISIS' activity maps to the episodic timeline of Mao's classic three-phase insurgency model (Tse-tung, 1989), with phases one and two occurring partially in cyberspace.

2.2.2 ISIS Insurgency Phases

ISIS' Internet use during all three phases of its insurgency provides the cyber analyst with an opportunity to compare the physical space associated with each insurgency phase to cyberspace. This includes the gradual development of a foothold, in cyberspace, and leveraging that firm base to conduct both physical and cyber operations; the final step being to shift popular sentiment long enough to achieve political victory (Table 2.2).

As shown in Table 2.2, cyber operations primarily facilitate shaping operations for insurgency phases one and two. Similarly, the steps in Table 2.2 operate in parallel with the phases provided by Table 2.1 to transition from cyber to conventional operations. Counter-insurgency is challenging enough in the physical domain. ISIS' use of cyberspace to maneuver into a physical entity is new territory. IO are usually an adjunct capability for kinetic tactics.

Cyber is a new domain that presents challenges absent from legacy IO. The first, and maybe most important, challenge is that cyberspace is persistent. Traditional IO was perishable. Cyber media is out there, indexed, and searchable. This persistence becomes an implied substance that the "one and done" nature of traditional IO (e.g., leaflets) did not provide.

2.2.3 Counter-ISIS Operations in Cyber

Counter-ISIS operations are an excellent example of cyberspace counter-insurgency (COIN). For example, the 2015 targeting of ISIS leader Abu Sayyaf resulted in the confiscation of a treasure trove of information (i.e., 7 TB of data). Subsequent exploitation included intelligence analysts scrutinizing ISIS documents and finding records of member communications – a first step in developing a roadmap to penetrate ISIS' command structure (Youssef and Harris, 2017). Leveraging this new intelligence source led to both the standup of Task Force ARES (Sanger, 2016) and the development of several key cyberspace operations (Table 2.3).

The cyber operations in Table 2.3 are new methods for employing counter-insurgency against a web-based adversary. As shown in Table 2.3, some of the results are mixed, in terms of meeting expectations. These successes provided military leadership with faith that cyber operations are useful to counter online insurgents.

2.3 ISIS and Web-Based Insurgency Wrap-up

Cyberspace is a well-known compliment to the physical domain for strategic communications and information access. This is true for both conventional and guerilla forces. ISIS, for example, went through their insurgency Phase I, or coordination phase, on the Internet, after sustaining a loss in the kinetic domain as AQI. ISIS continued to develop, in cyberspace, becoming a Phase II insurgent by conducting attacks, advertising their prowess on social media, and thereby increasing credibility. This continued until ISIS emerged as a Phase III insurgent with both a semi-conventional army and a physical location in Raqaa, Syria (Figure 2.1).

Table 2.2 Insurgency Phases – Comparison of Physical and Virtual Space Operators.

Insurgency Phase	Guerilla Operations (Physical Space)	Cyber Operations (Virtual Space)
1) Organization, consolidation, and preservation of base areas	This means establishing a core cadre as part of the movement. Insurgents generally arrive in remotely located areas and live with the locals. These are places where the government has little or no presence. Insurgents propagate their ideas and recruit followers. This is the conceptual stage for the rebels, since the numbers in these areas are small, making it easy for the insurgents to keep tabs on the population.	*Chat rooms and social media provide the initial forum for like-minded individuals to meet virtually, discuss issues of common interest, and develop relationships*
2) Guerilla warfare	Phase 2 involves using military means to heighten political effect. This includes planning isolated kinetic attacks to serve a political purpose and to spread their propaganda. The goal is to put a fear of safety in the otherwise comfortable officials as well as to gather attention.	*ISIS combined guerilla operations with media operations, leveraging online technologies that promoted and anchored their messaging, working toward a popular opinion in line with the group's objectives (e.g., 2014 ISIS capture of Mosul, Iraq; accompanied by real-time broadcast on Twitter). (Brooking and Singer, 2016)*
3) Conventional warfare	Phase 3 involves an all-out war against the government. It may begin with the militia taking up arms against a small government structure to gather resources. This includes killing informants, looting weapons caches, etc. This results in the emergence of military objectives as well as encouraging more people to take up arms, building up a massive military force, and eventually taking over the country.	*This is the feared possible endstate where cyber, along with kinetic operations, is used to effectively shift popular opinion to the side of the insurgents, facilitating a conventional victory. To complement this, the insurgents may use cyber to provide strategic effects via the destruction of critical infrastructure. In addition, cyberattacks on telecommunications, energy logistics, and utilities are performed to cripple a modern economy (e.g., 2014 Russian DOS attack on Ukraine with annexation of Crimea (Clayton, 2014)).* *This is the stage where destructive cyber effects are used to mimic kinetic military attacks, contributing to a process of political overthrow.*

Table 2.3 News Reporting on Counter-ISIS Cyber Operations.

Item	Description
Counter terror use of the internet (Sanger, 2016)	A stated goal at the beginning of counter-ISIS missions included – "We're (US Government) trying to both physically and virtually isolate ISIL (i.e., Islamic State of Iraq and Levant – later Islamic State of Iraq and Syria (ISIS)), limit their ability to conduct command and control, limit their ability to communicate with each other, limit their ability to conduct operations locally and tactically."
Special operations connection with U.S. cybercom (Lamothe, 2017)	"When combined with traditional military operations, Thomas (Army Gen. Raymond A. 'Tony' Thomas III) said, the cyber strikes culminated in the 'destruction of that adversary on an epic scale'. He argued that the military can 'only achieve exquisite effects like this' with a task force that combines a variety of capabilities, including cyber weapons." "We should be conducting operations like this continuously in a campaign," Thomas said. "We are not there yet, but we are trending positively in that direction, more every day." "In May, Adm. Michael S. Rogers, who oversees U.S. Cyber Command, told the House Armed Services Committee's subcommittee on emerging threats and capabilities that he created Task Force Ares to coordinate the efforts of Cyber Command with other U.S. forces in the fight against the Islamic State."
Operation glowing symphony (Sanger and Schmitt, 2017)	"The most sophisticated offensive cyber operation the United States has conducted against the Islamic State sought to sabotage the group's online videos and propaganda beginning in November (2017), according to American officials. In the endeavor, called Operation Glowing Symphony, the National Security Agency and its military cousin, United States Cyber Command, obtained the passwords of several Islamic State administrator accounts and used them to block out fighters and delete content. It was initially deemed a success because battlefield videos disappeared."

Task Force Ares addressed the ISIS web presence with a special group organized to combat media operations, complimented by ground forces in order to maintain a physical pressure on ISIS. While ISIS lost its territorial footprint in 2017, it continues to operate in the cyber domain (Miller, 2020). In the example insurgency progression shown in Table 2.2, ISIS has therefore moved back, from a Phase III to a Phase I insurgency.

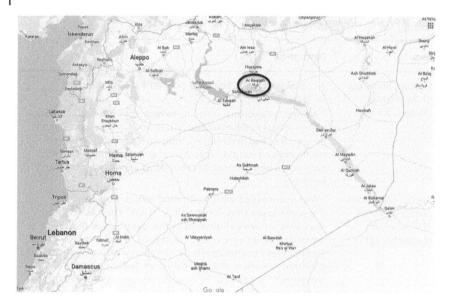

Figure 2.1 Raqaa, Syria (ISIS Headquarters (2014–2017)). *Source:* Google Maps.

Bibliography

ADL. (2022). *Islamists Launch Three New Magazines, Hoping One Will "Inspire"*. Retrieved 10 4, 2022, from Anti Defamation League (ADL): https://www.adl.org/resources/blog/islamists-launch-three-new-magazines-hoping-one-will-inspire.

Brooking, E. T., Singer, P. W. (2016). *WAR GOES VIRAL – How Social Media is Being Weaponized Across the World*. Retrieved 2 27, 2022, from The Atlantic: https://www.theatlantic.com/magazine/archive/2016/11/war-goes-viral/501125/.

Clayton, M. (2014). *Russia Hammers Ukraine with Massive Cyber-Attack*. Retrieved 5 15, 2023, from Business Insider: https://www.businessinsider.com/russia-cyberattack-ukraine-2014-3.

Global Security. (2005). *Global Security*. Retrieved from Letter from al-Zawahiri to al-Zarqawi: https://www.globalsecurity.org/security/library/report/2005/zawahiri-zarqawi-letter_9jul2005.htm.

Lamothe, D. (2017). *How the Pentagon's Cyber Offensive Against ISIS Could Shape the Future for Elite U.S. Forces*. Retrieved 8 27, 2018, from Washington Post: https://www.washingtonpost.com/news/checkpoint/wp/2017/12/16/how-the-pentagons-cyber-offensive-against-isis-could-shape-the-future-for-elite-u-s-forces/?utm_term=.8cce44e017f9.

Miller, C. (2020). *Inside the Secret Plan to Reboot ISIS from a huge Digital Backup*. Retrieved 9 22, 2022, from Wired: https://www.wired.co.uk/article/isis-digital-backup.

Sanger, D. E. (2016). *U.S. Cyberattacks Target ISIS in a New Line of Combat*. Retrieved 8 27, 2018, from New York Times: https://www.nytimes.com/2016/04/25/us/politics/us-directs-cyberweapons-at-isis-for-first-time.html.

Sanger, D. E., Schmitt, E. (2017). *U.S. Cyberweapons, Used Against Iran and North Korea, Are a Disappointment Against ISIS*. Retrieved 8 27, 2018, from New York Times: https://www.nytimes.com/2017/06/12/world/middleeast/isis-cyber.html.

Theohary, C. A., Rollins, J. (2011). *Terrorist Use of the Internet: Information Operations in Cyberspace*. Retrieved 8 22, 2018, from Congressional Research Service: https://digital.library.unt.edu/ark:/67531/metadc103142/m1/1/high_res_d/R41674_2011Mar08.pdf.

Tse-tung, M. (1989). *Mao Tse-tung on Guerrilla Warfare*. Retrieved from Internet Archive: https://archive.org/details/yuchichanenglish00unse/page/6/mode/2up.

Youssef, N. A., Harris, S. (2017). *Why Did Team Obama Try to Take Down Its NSA Chief?* Retrieved 8 27, 2018, from The Daily Beast: https://www.thedailybeast.com/why-did-team-obama-try-to-take-down-its-nsa-chief.

3

Cyber and Crime

3.1 Cyber and Crime

Cybercrime – criminal activities carried out by means of computers or the internet. Cybercrime groups are active both before and during military operations. In addition, cybercrime was reported to have overtaken drug trafficking as the key method for financing terrorist enterprises by 2011 (Theohary and Rollins, 2011).

Waiting in gas station lines during the spring of 2021 woke up many Americans to the devastation possible through cybercrime. The Colonial Pipeline ransomware attack produced socio-economic effects reminiscent of the 1973 Saudi oil embargo, resulting in delays and potential gasoline shortages unimagined by the current generation of Americans.

The Darkside cyber-criminal group shut down the U.S. East Coast for five days by performing a ransomware attack on Colonial Pipeline, a company that transports 2.5 million gallons of gas and oil per day, over 29,000 miles of pipeline, from the Gulf of Mexico to the U.S. East Coast.

The Colonial Pipeline ransomware attack debilitated the U.S. East Coast when the Darkside ransomware group encrypted 100 GB of front office financial data and was paid 75 bitcoin, worth approximately $5 million (Perlroth, 2021), after holding the data ransom for five days were from May 6, 2020 to May 12, 2020 (William Turton, 2021). Prior to this event, most Americans had never heard of ransomware, the Darkside or Colonial Pipeline, much less a gasoline shortage.

In attacking the Colonial Pipeline operations, DarkSide was a Russian cyber gang. This type of attack was unfortunately common in 2021, as it was reported that 74% of global ransomware revenue went to Russian hackers, to the tune of $400 million in cryptocurrencies, in 2021 alone (Tidy, 2022).

Cyber Operations: A Case Study Approach, First Edition. Jerry M. Couretas.
© 2024 John Wiley & Sons, Inc. Published 2024 by John Wiley & Sons, Inc.

While ransomware is one of the more famous types of cybercrime, it can be confusing to differentiate between cyber-enabled and straight cybercrime. One challenge in determining the type of crime performed via cyber means is to understand how cyber was used in the attack. We will therefore review cybercrime definitions before moving on to cybercrime examples.

3.1.1 Cybercrime Definitions

The Colonial ransomware cyberattack was just one of many cybercrimes in recent memory. Among the issues in prosecuting cyber criminals are unclear terms and definitions between similar cases, legal jurisdiction over the location of where the cybercriminal resides, and even an interpretation of the law during prosecution. Cybercrimes have different meanings, depending on whom you are talking to. For example, federal law enforcement is likely speaking from the context of the Computer Fraud and Abuse Act (CFAA) (DOJ). Local law enforcement, however, will have a different set of statutes, codes, local laws, and jurisdictions that are used when their Chief of Police or Sheriff is defining a cybercrime. From a technical standpoint, there is also the differentiation between cybercrime types –

> … cyber-enabled crime and cyber-native crime. Cyber-enabled crime is traditional crime abetted or facilitated by the use of cyber tools or means. Malicious and illegal activities under this category are often described as scams and frauds or involve the use of digital devices like phones or computers. Cyber-native crimes are those that cannot be committed outside the digital domain such as network intrusions, cryptocurrency mining, and malware. (Wright, 2021)

A simplified way to look at these crimes is in terms of a quadrant (Table 3.1).

Table 3.1 Cybercrime Quadrant.

Approaches to Cybercrime	Cyber-enabled Crime	Cyber-native (dependent) Crime
Malicious cyber activity	Doxing someone; Identifying targets for home robberies via social media; Using online street maps to plan a bank robbery	Writing malware code; scanning a network for vulnerabilities or open ports; failed credential stuffing attempts
Illegal cyber activity	Identity theft through misconfigured and exposed databases	Computer/network access and trespass (AKA intrusions); malware deployment

Source: Adapted from Wright (2021).

As shown in Table 3.1, cybercrime definitions span from the use of computers to facilitate traditional crime (cyber-enabled) to the development of computer-based techniques as the focus of the crime (cybernative). One reason to start with this simple set of definitions is that the current legal case history of crimes involving computers is not always so clear in differentiating cyber-enabled versus cyber-dependent crimes.

The lack of clear case histories is one issue causing ambiguity in classifying cybercrime in order to provide precedence in future legal decisions. With each cybercrime case individually determined, it is a challenge to compare future cases in an "apples to apples" type evaluation and judgment of the crime under inspection. Organizations often use their own terms for cyber activities, increasing the challenges of developing consistent legal precedents. For example, the U.S. Federal Trade Commission (FTC) currently tracks malicious cyber activity in terms of fraud, identity theft, and other complaints, similar to what companies and other Governments (e.g., Canadian Anti-Fraud Centre (Government of Canada), Australian Cyber Centre (Australian Signals Directorate), U.K. Action Fraud and Cyber Crime Reporting Centre (National Fraud & Cyber Crime Reporting)), provide. However, each organization has its own terms and definitions, making it a challenge to compare cybercrime statistics, forcing the analyst to understand both the nuances of the criminal allegation and the legal framework that it derives from.

3.1.2 Crimes Against Individuals

The challenges in terms and definitions associated with cybercrimes are being addressed in a U.S. National Academy of Sciences study with the goal of providing a taxonomy for categorizing different types of cybercrime faced by individuals and businesses (U.S. Congress, 2021). Clearly defining the terms associated with cybercrime is potentially more difficult than understanding the process that composes a cybercrime. For example, each cybercrime will follow a standard attack cycle (Director of National Intelligence). The elements involved in cybercriminal activities span both the vulnerabilities in the underlying computer-based technologies and the range of human weaknesses. Social engineering, either from a person or a bot, is therefore a first step in the technical and financial compromise of many of the individuals targeted by malicious actors.

3.1.2.1 Cyber-Fraud Reporting
Since 1997, the FTC has collected tens of millions of reports concerning fraud, identity theft, and other consumer protection topics (Federal Trade Commission, 2021). This included 4.7 million reports over the course of 2020,

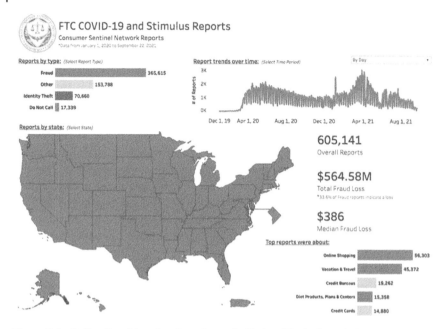

Figure 3.1 Online Fraud Landing Page Example (Federal Trade Commission).

sorted into 29 categories. In addition, the FTC provides a data science landing page for exploring the types of fraud experienced (Figure 3.1).

In populating their data sets, the FTC uses a call center along with an active data collection program from state, local, international law enforcement, and other organizations. Using this set of collections for 2020 resulted in the following breakdown of crimes (Table 3.2).

Table 3.2 Top 5 Cybercrime Types (2020).

Top Cybercrime Type	Percentage (%)
Identity theft	21
Impostor scams	17
Credit bureaus, information furnishers, and report users	13
Online shopping and negative reviews	9
Banks and lenders	4
Other	12

Source: Adapted from Federal Trade Commission (2021).

Categorizing cybercrime, as shown in Table 3.2, is a national priority in the United States. The U.S. Congress recently introduced a bill for providing cyber-crime metrics (U.S. Congress, 2021) –

- Department of Justice (DOJ) must enter into an agreement with the National Academy of Sciences to develop a taxonomy for categorizing different types of cybercrime faced by individuals and businesses
- DOJ must establish a category in the National Incident-Based Reporting System for collecting cybercrime reports from federal, state, and local officials
- DOJ's Bureau of Justice Statistics and the Bureau of the Census must include questions about cybercrime in the annual National Crime Victimization Survey
- The Government Accountability Office (GAO) must assess the effectiveness of reporting mechanisms for cybercrime and disparities in reporting cybercrime data and other types of crime data

The bullets provided above, used to scope the Better Cybercrimes Act (U.S. Congress, 2021), show the lawmakers' interest in developing a comprehensive reporting system that captures both the breadth and detail of current cybercrime. Improving metrics helps in understanding where to focus efforts. Estimates of cybercrime include

> ... the top-three categories (of cyber-crime) in the U.S. are identity theft, imposter scams and online shopping and negative reviews, representing $3.3 billion in losses in 2020, with an average median loss of $311. (Giovanna Garofalo, 2021)

It is believed that the numbers will keep going up due to the continually increasing consumption of online shopping and media, exposing unwary users to threats such as phishing.

3.1.2.2 Spam

Cybercrimes can start with spam, which comes unsolicited, and delivered in the same messaging formats (i.e., e-mail, social media, text messages) as interpersonal communications. And, while spam is generally considered a nuisance, there exists a group of people that positively respond to spam messaging in order to acquire medications and other products currently unavailable at a price point that the spam merchant is charging (Krebs, 2014).

A key reason for the burgeoning spam enterprise is due to the profits that ultimately accrue from the sales of counterfeit drugs and other paraphernalia that bombard our inboxes. These profits fuel the production of botnet-based malware, estimated to deploy 82,000 new malicious software variants every day (Krebs, 2014). A quick overview of the spam conversion rate (Kreibich, 2019) includes

- 1 in 12,500,000 pharmacy spam leads to a purchase
- 1 in 265,000 greeting card spam leads to an infected machine
- 1 in 178,000 April Fool's Day spam leads to an infected machine
- 1 in 10 people visiting an infection website downloaded the executable and ran it

A more general picture of the spam ecosystem was provided in a detailed evaluation of the spam value chain, profiling the key areas that each of the spam providers have in common (e.g., payment processing) (Levchenko, 2011). A simple spam-based Viagra purchase has an International trajectory that includes making the purchase from a spammer with an affiliate program located overseas (Russia), getting funds from the user's bank (USA), Visa, paying the seller's merchant bank (Azerbaijan) and shipping from the manufacturer (India) to the purchaser in the United States (Talbot, 2011)

Spam King Example   In Brian Krebs's book "Spam Nation," a key figure responsible for generating and benefiting from spam was Pavel Vrubelsky. Mr. Vrubelsky became famous for fraud and facilitating money laundering for Hydra, the largest Russian darknet market, operating from 2015 to 2022 (Krebs, 2022).

Spam often originates from botnets, scanning for new victims to compromise for personal, technical, or financial credentials. These spam botnets, and supporting servers, are constantly updated to improve the probability that their malware gets past the antivirus tools that are continuously updated to protect our machines. One method to capture positive responses to spam messages is through phishing, where the cyberattacker develops a "backdoor" in order to maintain persistent access to the target's machine.

3.1.2.3 Phishing

Crimes against individuals sometimes start with spam, and are often exploited via "phishing." Phishing is a key method for using a false persona to acquire the personal and financial credentials from a target for follow-on theft operations. Phishing, used for years, remains a key technique to compromise targets (Verizon, 2021) and includes six different approaches (Bisson, 2021) (Table 3.3).

As shown in Table 3.3, forms of phishing are used across the current communication technologies, including e-mail and SMS text messaging, tailored to targets of interest. Due to the human factor in each major cyber security failure, a culture of security, similar to the culture of quality introduced in manufacturing a generation ago, is increasingly seen as an answer to cybersecurity problems (Keman Huang, 2019).

Table 3.3 Phishing Types (6).

Phishing Type	Description
Deceptive phishing	• Most common type • Email from a recognized sender • Steals info by imitating a legitimate provider
Spear phishing	• Common on social media sites • Email from recognized sender • Uses personalized information
Whaling	• Targets executives • Used to transfer funds, find financial information on employees
Vishing	• Contacts targets by telephone • Compromises targets from known entities to steal data/funds
Smishing	• Contacts targets via SMS messaging • Compromises targets from known entities to steal data/funds
Pharming	• Uses cache poisoning • Redirects traffic to malicious site

3.1.3 Crimes Against Organizations

Cybercriminals often buy large batches of identification (IDs) and credit cards from the Internet and attack all of them, with small businesses often becoming victims. For example, an estimated 58% of financial losses in 2020 were from small businesses, with 80% of those businesses being reattacked (Hallo, 2021). In addition to the use of spam and phishing for individuals, these same techniques are used against organizations. Small businesses and healthcare organizations, especially their payment processors, are key targets for more advanced telephony phishing.

3.1.3.1 Telephony Phishing

A recent cyberattack type that is growing (i.e., responsible for 10% of 2022 first quarter cyberattacks (Pangilinan, 2022)) is to use telephony, where the victim does all the heavy lifting in executing the attack. This occurs when a potential small business victim is instructed to dial a phony call center and download malware onto their machines, helping the attacker get around the common cyber security control of "not clicking a potential malicious link." The attacker's goal is to carry out a ransomware attack without being detected.

Telephony phishing is a primary means of getting payment information in order to divert healthcare payments. For example, cybercriminals are compromising the user login credentials of healthcare payment processors and diverting the payments to accounts controlled by the cybercriminals. Recent reporting indicates cybercriminals will continue to target healthcare payment processors through a variety of techniques, such as phishing campaigns and social engineering, to spoof support centers and obtain user access (FBI, 2022). FBI examples include

- In April 2022, a healthcare company with more than 175 medical providers discovered an unauthorized cybercriminal posing as an employee had changed Automated Clearing House (ACH) instructions of one of their payment processing vendors to direct payments to the cyber-criminal rather than the intended provider. The cyber-criminal successfully diverted approximately $840,000 dollars over two transactions prior to the discovery.
- In February 2022, a cybercriminal obtained credentials from a major healthcare company and changed direct deposit banking information from a hospital to a consumer checking account belonging to the cybercriminal, resulting in a $3.1 million loss. In mid-February (2022), a separate incident included a different cybercriminal using the same method to steal approximately $700,000.
- From June 2018 to January 2019, cyber criminals targeted and accessed at least 65 healthcare payment processors throughout the United States to replace legitimate customer banking and contact information with accounts controlled by cybercriminals. One victim reported a loss of approximately $1.5 million. The cybercriminals used a combination of publicly available PII and phishing schemes to gain access to customer accounts. Entities involved in processing and distributing healthcare payments through processors remain vulnerable to exploitation via this method.

Losses due to telephony phishing are substantial and growing, especially in the healthcare industry. Telephony phishing has common traits with traditional e-mail spam messaging, both having the same goal of engaging unwary targets in order to extract funds.

While spam is something well understood by anyone using e-mail, ransomware is relatively new. Ransomware includes traditional phishing of unwary victims and then includes holding the victims' data hostage, usually by encrypting it, and only releasing the data after a ransom is paid.

3.1.3.2 Ransomware Introduction

Ransomware by itself is really just a model of monetizing an organization's (network) access. 2022 Verizon Data Breach Intrusion Report (DBIR) (Verizon, 2022)

Ransomware is a key form of malware that is used to extort a victim into paying for access to their own data, held hostage by the ransomware gang. Ransomware gangs encrypt a target's data and demand a ransom for the decryption key

> In recent years, ransomware has moved from a model where a single "gang" would both develop and distribute a ransomware payload to the ransomware as a service (RaaS) model. RaaS allows one group to manage the development of the ransomware payload and provide services for payment and extortion via data leakage to other cybercriminals—the ones who actually launch the ransomware attacks—referred to as "affiliates" for a cut of the profits. This franchising of the cybercrime economy has expanded the attacker pool. The industrialization of cyber-criminal tooling has made it easier for attackers to perform intrusions, exfiltrate data, and deploy ransomware. (Microsoft, 2022)

The scale-up of ransomware is sometimes described as America's new war on terror (Ambinder, 2021), with former counter-terror consultants now helping firms manage the messaging around cyberattacks. This correlation between cyber and terrorism may increase due to the loss of life with the targeting of hospitals (Wetsman, 2020) and fuel supplies (Perlroth, 2021).

Several players, sometimes called by their tool or team name, interchangeably, currently use ransomware to extort money from businesses, hospitals, and other organizations by threatening to publish their private information on the web (Table 3.4).

As shown in Table 3.4, there are overlaps (e.g., CONTI and HIVE) and even possible transitions (e.g., GandCrab/Sodinokibi to ReVIL, DarkSide to BlackMatter) over time that make identifying a cyber-criminal gang challenging. Target types and tool signatures help provide clues as to how a gang, or at least its members, have changed or realigned their affiliations.

Ransomware is used to encrypt an organization's information technology system, requiring a "ransom" payment for decryption. In the course of a ransomware attack, the organization losing its computer system can become nonfunctional. For example, it is said that the delays in providing care to a woman in Germany, during a ransomware attack, resulted in her death (Wetsman, 2020). Similarly, in a current lawsuit, a mother filed suit against a hospital undergoing a cyberattack during her difficult childbirth experience, with the baby dying afterward due to lack of proper care during the childbirth (Collier, 2021).

3.1.3.3 Ransomware Tools Background

In the 2015–2016 timeframe, an ambitious computer scientist, all but dissertation (ABD) at the University of Maryland, went down a path of finishing his doctoral

Table 3.4 Ransomware Groups.

Name	First Noticed	Operations Description
AlphV (Blackcat)	11/2021	AlphV has a novel business model in publishing target organizations' data on the web and leaving it there to be indexed by the major search engines. This pressures the data owners to pay up in order to get their sensitive data off of the web (Ilascu, ALPHV ransomware adds data leak API in new extortion strategy, 2023)
BlackByte	7/2021	The BlackByte group, a spinoff of CONTI, is a ransomware team that brought down the Albanian government's IT systems in July 2022, on Iran's behalf (Oghanna, How Albania Became a Target for Cyberattacks, 2023)
BlackMatter	7/2021	BlackMatter is a possible rebranding of the DarkSide, and is implicated in the 9/2021 attack on the NEW Cooperative, an Iowa-based farmer's cooperative. BlackMatter has also attacked numerous U.S.-based organizations and has demanded ransom payments ranging from $80,000 to $15,000,000 in Bitcoin and Monero (DHS CISA, 2018)
CLOP	2/2019	Usually associated with healthcare file compromise, used by the FIN11 group to exploit the Accellion File Transfer Appliance. Also associated with the MoveIT file transfer appliance compromise (Gatlan, 2023), estimated to have resulted in $75 million in ransom (Ilascu, ALPHV ransomware adds data leak API in new extortion strategy, 2023)
CONTI	2020	Thought to have been led by the cyber malicious operator Wizard Spider, CONTI accounted for 20% of the ransomware attacks in the first three months of 2022; performing a denial-of-service operation on the Costa Rican government before the group disbanded (Burt, 2022)
DopplePaymer	4/2019	DopplePaymer targets include healthcare, emergency services, and education and is known to make phone calls in order to ask for payment (Trend Micro, 2021)

Table 3.4 (Continued)

Name	First Noticed	Operations Description
Evil Corp		Maksim Yakubets began employing malware in 2009 using Zeus, a password capture and account number acquisition script for bank account theft. Yakubets continued to improve his malware, eventually developing Dridex. In the 2017 time frame, Evil Corp developed Bitpaymer ransomware, which could not be decrypted. 2017 was also the time frame where Yakubets began working with the Russian Federation's Federal Security Service (FSB), a successor to the KGB (Renee Dudley, 2022)
HIVE	7/2021	HIVE was a pioneer of the double ransomware approach, which included publishing sensitive data in order to pressure victims to pay. HIVE is mostly known for attacking medical organizations – Missouri Delta Medical Center, Memorial Health System in Ohio. However, in May 2022, HIVE attacked the Costa Rican Social Security Fund, showing a possible connection to CONTI. When Hive was apprehended in January 2023, the ransomware group had targeted more than 1500 victims in over 80 countries and received over $100 million in ransom payments. Law enforcement in the United States, Germany, and the Netherlands provided approximately 300 sets of decryption keys to victims, saving over $300 million in ransom demands (DoJ, 2023)
Lapsus$	12/2021	The Lapsus$ model differs in deploying a pure extortion and destruction model, communicating directly with the public through Telegram and conducting polls among their members on who to attack next (Roth, 2023)
LOCKBIT	2019	Lockbit was credited with 38% of the ransomware operations during the first quarter of 2022 with steal bit, their encoder, said to be the fastest file encryptor in the business (CISA, 2023)

(Continued)

Table 3.4 (Continued)

Name	First Noticed	Operations Description
ReVIL (Sodinokibi) ... 2018 GandCrab)	4/2019	ReVIL is believed to be responsible for 1/3 of the ransomware attacks (e.g., 2/3 of attacks on remote desktop protocol (RDP) sessions) over 2021, earning approximately $100 million. This includes attacks on accounting and law firms, which make up approximately 14% of US businesses but account for 25% of ransomware attacks (Constantin, 2021). When GandCrab's developers retired in May 2019, they claimed to have earned $2 billion in ransom payments (Renee Dudley, 2022)
Ryuk	2017	One of the top perpetrators in attacking banking software in 2021, Ryuk, is estimated to be responsible for over $61 million in losses and now has a "worm-like" capability for traversing a network (Arntz, 2021)

Source: Saraie (2022), Jeffs (2022).

work using real cyberattack tools. This included bringing home Government-developed capabilities from his employer, the U.S. National Security Agency (NSA). Experimenting with these high-end cyber exploit tools on his home network, Hal Martin (Kirk, 2016) was wary about the possibility of getting hacked, and thereby protected his system with a Kaspersky firewall. The Kaspersky firewall (Scott Shane, 2017), combined with taking a few too many tools home from his employer (e.g., approximately 50 TB worth (Farivar, 2017)) landed him 19 counts of espionage and a lengthy Federal prison sentence (Dilanian, 2016).

In 2017, at the same time that Hal Martin was in the process of being sentenced, a programmer for the U.S. Central Intelligence Agency (CIA), Joshua Schulte, who was "pissed off at his colleagues," also disclosed a large number of tools (Keefe, 2022). This CIA compromise was called Vault7, disclosed on Wikileaks (Lawler, 2022). Figure 3.2 provides a general timeline that covers the development of cyber tools, including their proliferation into the criminal domain.

As shown in Figure 3.2, hacking, spam, and computer-based annoyances started with the introduction of networked computers in the 1990s. By the early 2000s, select nation-state attacks were already under way. However, with the release of nation-state tools to the hacking community in the 2015–2017 time frame, we arrived at a whole new era of ransomware, with individuals, organizations, and governments under attack from sophisticated, well-developed tools. This transition

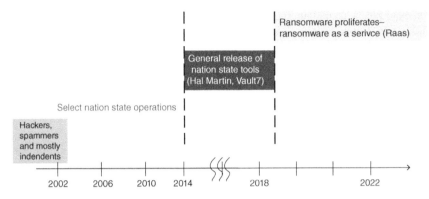

Figure 3.2 Cyber Tool Development Timeline.

of nation-state tools to criminals establishes a distinct period of cyber operations, extending Stage Three from Chapter 1 (Table 1.1).

Hal Martin was a prime suspect in the leak known as the Shadow Brokers (Vijayin, 2019), a mysterious group, believed to be of Russian origin, that became responsible for one of the biggest cyber-tool leaks to date (Goodin, 2017a). For example, the ransomware tool associated with NotPetya included exploits obtained from the Shadow Brokers (Goodin, 2017b). NotPetya used an encrypting tool on targeted systems and resulted in over $10 billion in damages in 2017. This was due to the ill-targeted malware on the Ukrainian tax authority, meDoc, getting out in the wild and shutting down Maersk shipping and multiple other systems across the globe (Greenberg, 2019).

3.1.3.4 Ransomware as a Service

Colonial Pipeline is a famous ransomware attack in the United States (Chapter 3 Introduction). Ransomware was also used to hold the government of Costa Rica hostage in 2022, with the CONTI ransomware gang, also a Russian cyber gang, recommending the overthrow of the Costa Rican government when officials did not pay up (Burgess, 2022).

Criminal cyber events are increasingly ransomware operations. This includes ransomware as a Service (RaaS). For example, in 2021 alone, RaaS was responsible for the Colonial Pipeline attack, the JBS Foods attack, and the New Cooperative attack. This targeting of energy (Perlroth, 2021) and food (FBI, 2021), key elements of society, takes cybercrime from a nuisance to a means of changing our way of life.

Ransomware as a Service (RaaS) Operational Example As shown in Figure 3.2, there was an exceptional increase in ransomware during the 2020 COVID-19 lockdown, resulting in tens of millions in losses due to cyberattacks on medical facilities.

For example, a Canadian member of the ransomware gang using Netwalker, Russia-based ransomware as a service affiliate, was convicted with a potential of 40 years in prison for stealing an estimated $40 million in cryptocurrency from victims around the world (Molloy, 2022). An example operations model is from the purchase of an exploit, to the deployment and cryptocurrency payment (Namisha, 2022). RaaS provides an end-to-end capability for affiliates to manage their infections

> Every affiliate has a control panel that allows them to track and monitor how many infections their strain of Ransomware had caused. They can also see the current price of their product and change some general settings (such as changing encryption keys). (Namisha, 2022)

Ransomware as a Service is entirely decentralized, so there is no central point of failure (i.e., no server to take down). The system backend serves the purpose of managing affiliates and their products. Since each affiliate uses their unique Bitcoin address to purchase a ransomware copy, there is no way for law enforcement officers to connect them.

The ransomware attack cycle parallels the standard cyber-attack cycle (MITRE), spanning from initial network access through target extortion (Table 3.5).

Prevention techniques are possible for ransomware attacks. For example, the cyber-security company FireEye estimates that at least three days passed between malicious detection and the deployment of ransomware (Vanderlee, 2020). This statistic, decreasing time for detection rates, was also noted in the 2022 Verizon DBIR (Verizon, 2021), and also called out as a mixed blessing, as the decrease in time is usually due to the attacker providing the detection as he is asking for ransom.

3.1.3.5 Cryptocurrency

Cryptocurrency is a key element in the RaaS value chain. This was discussed in the 2021 Colonial Pipeline attack (Section 3.3.4), where a payment of 75 bitcoin was required for Colonial to decrypt their business management systems and resume operations. In the Colonial Pipeline case, many of the bitcoin were tracked, through their ledger, and recovered (Perlroth, 2021).

In order to obfuscate the tracking of bitcoin through their blockchain ledger, operators sometimes use a "mixer." The mixer makes it a challenge to track transactions through a system and was used in the largest virtual currency heist to date, as described in recent sanctions posting by the U.S. Treasury against the Democratic People's Republic of Korea (DPRK) for their use of a mixer service called "Blender":

> On March 23, 2022, "Treasury says," Lazarus Group, a DPRK state-sponsored cyber hacking group, carried out the largest virtual currency heist to date,

Table 3.5   Ransomware Attack Stages.

Stage	Description	Example
Delivery	The network is compromised by a phishing email, exploit, or worm.	Social engineering is one way to get an unsuspecting user to click on a malicious e-mail. The CONTI group was also known to use Emotet to drop Trickbot malware in order to provide initial access for ransomware (e.g., Ryuk) (Abrams, Emotet malware is back and rebuilding its botnet via TrickBot, 2021)
Command and control (C2)	Once inside, the ransomware establishes a connection with the attacker's command and control server to receive instructions.	C2 methods are designed to extract information and update the malware, as needed. A C2 description that includes anonymization of commands is provided for Conficker (Bowden, 2011)
Credential access	Still undetected, the malware continues to set the stage for its attack by stealing credentials and gaining access to more accounts across the network.	This includes both initial access to the target system and access to associated systems. The EternalBlue (NVD, 2018) exploit was famous for taking advantage of vulnerable Microsoft systems.
Canvas	The virus searches for files to encrypt – both on the local workstation and on any networks it has gained access to through lateral movement.	Sometimes viruses are wormable (e.g., NotPetya (Greenberg, 2019)) and used EternalBlue (see "Credential Access") to spread to any connected device that is not protected against that strain of malware.
Extortion	Cybercriminals begin to exfiltrate and/or encrypt local and network files. The attacker demands payment to have them decrypted or released back to the business.	Colonial Oil (Perlroth, 2021) and the Costa Rican Government (Burgess, 2022) are a few of the top ransomware attacks that shut down the U.S. East Cost and Costa Rican Government systems, respectively.

Source: Adapted from JP Morgan Chase (2022).

worth almost $620 million, from a blockchain project linked to the online game Axie Infinity; Blender was used in processing over $20.5 million of the illicit proceeds. The sanctions are believed to be the first levied against a mixer service. (U.S. Treasury Department, 2022)

Cryptocurrencies play a role in many ransomware attacks, providing law enforcement with an additional challenge in tracking down an obfuscated money trail for these events.

3.1.4 Cyber Gangs – Membership Analogy to Organized Crime

The use of cryptocurrency is a key method that cyber gangs use to collect their ransom. Another question might be about the size of these ransomware gangs, and how they compare to traditional organized crime. Robb estimated the size of illegal organizations (i.e., Mafia) when they were responsible for a large part of the North American illicit economy; this included a footprint with global connections (Table 3.6).

As shown in Table 3.6, these globe-spanning criminal organizations had a relatively small core membership. For the CONTI group, the personnel estimate comes from a pay leaked ledger that shows 81 members on the payroll. Full-time gang membership for cyber gangs is approximately half the size of gang membership for the traditional mafia, with tenure on the order of months (Table 3.7).

Table 3.6 Organized Crime Membership Size Example.

Organized Crime Organization	No. Members ("made men")
Genovese (largest gang)	152
Gambino	130
Lucchese	113

Source: Kenney (2008).

Table 3.7 Cyber Gang Life Time (average).

Cyber Gang	Cyber Gang Lifetime (months)
BlackMatter (Page, BlackMatter ransomware gang says it's shutting down over law enforcement pressure, 2021)	9
CONTI (Robert McMillan, 2022) (Flashpoint, 2022)	24
DopplePaymer (Toulas, 2023)	6
GandCrab (Abrams, 2019)	50
HIVE (DoJ, 2023)	17
Ragarok (Montalbano, 2021)	20
ReVIL/Sodinokibi (Sayegh, The REvil Gang Story: The "Good Guys" Can Still Prevail, 2023)	32
Average	**22**

And cyber gangs are approximately half the size of classic mafia organizations "made men." There are likely other differences that contribute to the differences in organization size. Roles, responsibilities, and education level are different for traditional organized crime vs. current ransomware gangs. Ransomware gangs are also very different structures, with reduced gang tenure that are more in line with street gangs (e.g., one to two years) (National Gang Center) than the duration of an organized crime family (i.e., working lifetime of the founding "Don").

3.1.5 Cybercrime Wrap-Up

Ransomware is increasingly bringing cybercrime to headline news. This is especially true when we see lines at the gas station reminiscent of 1970s oil embargoes, caused by ransomware, or when a cybercrime group attempts to bring down a government, as in the case of Costa Rica (2021). The small size and tenure of ransomware gangs is surprising due to the havoc that they seek, not only in shutting down target systems, but in the seemingly complex paths that they take to acquire their funds. Crypto currencies, and their mixing, create roadblocks in the detecting, tracking, and apprehending of cybercriminals.

One legal challenge is to compare current cybercrime cases. While case law, and cybercrime attacks, may be similar between Australia, Canada, the United Kingdom, and the United States, the terms and definitions are different enough to make developing legal precedent a challenge. This will require a concerted effort among the nations, in developing a clear lexicon – currently a goal of the U.S. National Academy of Sciences.

Bibliography

Abrams, L. (2019). *GandCrab Ransomware Shutting Down After Claiming to Earn $2 Billion*. Retrieved from Bleeping Computer: https://www.bleepingcomputer.com/news/security/gandcrab-ransomware-shutting-down-after-claiming-to-earn-2-billion/.

Abrams, L. (2021). *Emotet Malware is Back and Rebuilding its Botnet via TrickBot*. Retrieved 5 18, 2023, from Bleeping Computer: https://www.bleepingcomputer.com/news/security/emotet-malware-is-back-and-rebuilding-its-botnet-via-trickbot/.

Ambinder, M. (2021). *America's New War on Terror has Gone Digital*. Retrieved 10 22, 2021, from MSNBC: https://www.msnbc.com/opinion/america-s-new-war-terror-has-gone-digital-n1282011.

Arghire, I. (2021). *BlackMatter Ransomware Gang Announces Shutdown*. Retrieved from SecurityWeek: https://www.securityweek.com/blackmatter-ransomware-gang-announces-shutdown/.

Arntz, P. (2021). *Ryuk Ransomware Develops Worm-like Capability*. Retrieved from Malwarebytes: https://www.malwarebytes.com/blog/news/2021/03/ryuk-ransomware-develops-worm-like-capability.

Australian Signals Directorate. (n.d.). *Australian Cyber Security Centre*. Retrieved 9 14, 2021, from Australian Signals Directorate: https://www.cyber.gov.au/acsc/view-all-content/reports-and-statistics.

Bisson, D. (2021). *6 Common Phishing Attacks and How to Protect Against Them*. Retrieved 10 20, 2021, from TripWire: https://www.tripwire.com/state-of-security/security-awareness/6-common-phishing-attacks-and-how-to-protect-against-them/?utm_source=The%20State%20of%20Security%20Newsletter&utm_medium=email&utm_campaign=FO-10-18-2021&utm_content=httpswwwtripwirecom stateofsecuritysecurityawareness6commonphishingattacksandhowtoprotectagainst them&mkt_tok=MzE0LUlBSc3ODUAAAGAOE6idBytVtQKcRD9fZkM_q9B5SZgs8lt3QSY-bA_BQ3hCjEY5GejSdHi1Qzv38MvBmbOptz1L_dmBbq1bFn cv9RgUUYg9j_h5_dBcPKz5bWtkAI.

Bowden, M. (2011). *Worm – The First Digital World War*. New York: Atlantic Monthly Press.

Browne, R. (2021). *Hackers Behind Colonial Pipeline Attack Reportedly Received $90 Million in Bitcoin Before Shutting Down*. Retrieved from CNN: https://www.cnbc.com/2021/05/18/colonial-pipeline-hackers-darkside-received-90-million-in-bitcoin.html#.

Burgess, M. (2022). *Conti's Attack Against Costa Rica Sparks a New Ransomware Era*. Retrieved 9 28, 2022, from Wired: https://www.wired.com/story/costa-rica-ransomware-conti/.

Burt, J. (2022). *Meet Wizard Spider, the Multimillion-dollar Gang Behind Conti, Ryuk Malware*. Retrieved from The Register: https://www.theregister.com/2022/05/18/wizard-spider-ransomware-conti/.

CISA. (2023). *#StopRansomware: LockBit 3.0*. Retrieved from CISA: https://www.cisa.gov/news-events/cybersecurity-advisories/aa23-075a.

Collier, K. (2021). *Baby Died Because of Ransomware Attack on Hospital, Suit Says*. Retrieved 7 10, 2022, from NBC News: https://www.nbcnews.com/news/baby-died-due-ransomware-attack-hospital-suit-claims-rcna2465.

Constantin, L. (2021). *REvil Ransomware Explained: A Widespread Extortion Operation*. Retrieved 7 10, 2022, from CSO Online: https://www.csoonline.com/article/3597298/revil-ransomware-explained-a-widespread-extortion-operation.html.

DHS CISA. (2018). *BlackMatter Ransomware*. Retrieved 7 10, 2022, from Alert (AA21-291A): https://www.cisa.gov/uscert/ncas/alerts/aa21-291a.

Dilanian, K. (2016). *NSA Leak Mystery Not Solved With Arrest of Hal Martin*. Retrieved 9 27, 2022, from NBC News: https://www.nbcnews.com/news/us-news/nsa-leak-mystery-not-solved-arrest-hal-martin-n662161.

Director of National Intelligence. (n.d.). *Cyber Threat Framework*. Retrieved 10 20, 2018, from https://www.dni.gov/index.php/cyber-threat-framework.

DoJ. (2022). *Justice Department Investigation Leads to Shutdown of Largest Online Darknet Marketplace*. Retrieved 5 18, 2023, from Department of Justice: https://www.justice.gov/opa/pr/justice-department-investigation-leads-shutdown-largest-online-darknet-marketplace.

DoJ. (2023). *U.S. Department of Justice Disrupt Hive Ransomware Variant*. Retrieved 1 27, 2023, from U.S. Department of Justice: htttps://www.justce.gov/opa/pr/us-department-justice-disrupts-hive-ransomware-variant.

DOJ. (n.d.). *Prosecuting Computer Crimes (Computer Fraud and Abuse Act)*. Retrieved 9 14, 2021, from Department of Justice: https://www.justice.gov/sites/default/files/criminal-ccips/legacy/2015/01/14/ccmanual.pdf.

Farivar, C. (2017). *New Charges for Ex-NSA Contractor for Allegedly Taking Elite Hacking Tools – Hal Martin Allegedly was Found with 50TB of Data when Arrested in August 2016*. Retrieved 10 4, 2022, from Ars Technica: https://arstechnica.netblogpro.com/tech-policy/2017/02/new-charges-for-ex-nsa-contractor-for-allegedly-taking-elite-hacking-tools/.

FBI. (2021). *Cyber Criminal Actors Targeting the Food and Agriculture Sector with Ransomware Attacks*. Retrieved 9 4, 2021, from FBI: https://www.documentcloud.org/documents/21053957-fbi-tlp-white-pin-cyber-criminal-actors-targeting-food-agriculture-sector-ansomware-attacks-9-1-21.

FBI. (2022). *Cyber Criminals Targeting Healthcare Payment Processors, Costing Victims Millions in Losses*. Retrieved 9 16, 2022, from FBI: https://www.ic3.gov/Media/News/2022/220914-2.pdf.

Federal Trade Commission. (2021). *Consumer Sentinel Network*. Retrieved 9 30, 2021, from Data Book 2020: https://www.ftc.gov/system/files/documents/reports/consumer-sentinel-network-data-book-2020/csn_annual_data_book_2020.pdf.

Federal Trade Commission. (n.d.). *Data and Visualizations*. Retrieved 9 30, 2021, from Consumer Sentinel Network Data Exploration: https://www.ftc.gov/enforcement/data-visualizations/explore-data.

Flashpoint. (2022). *Conti Ransomware: Inside One of the World's Most Aggressive Ransomware Groups*. Retrieved from Flashpoint: https://flashpoint.io/blog/history-of-conti-ransomware/.

Gatlan, S. (2023). *Clop Ransomware Likely Testing MOVEit Zero-day since 2021*. Retrieved from Bleeping Computer: https://www.bleepingcomputer.com/news/security/clop-ransomware-likely-testing-moveit-zero-day-since-2021/.

Giovanna Garofalo. (2021). *Cyber Fraud Costing Millions to Puerto Rico Residents, Businesses*. Retrieved 9 30, 2021, from The Weekly Journal: https://www.theweeklyjournal.com/business/cyber-fraud-costing-millions-to-puerto-rico-residents-businesses/article_d5662fb0-208f-11ec-be2b-6311c3932998.html.

Goodin, D. (2017a). *NotPetya Developers may have Obtained NSA Exploits Weeks Before their Public Leak*. Retrieved 9 27, 2022, from Ars Technica: https://arstechnica.com/information-technology/2017/06/notpetya-developers-obtained-nsa-exploits-weeks-before-their-public-leak/.

Goodin, D. (2017b). *NSA-leaking Shadow Brokers Lob Molotov Cocktail Before Exiting World Stage*. Retrieved 9 27, 2022, from Ars Technica: https://arstechnica.com/information-technology/2017/01/nsa-leaking-shadow-brokers-lob-molotov-cocktail-before-exiting-world-stage/.

Government of Canada. (n.d.). *Canadian Anti-Fraud Centre*. Retrieved 9 14, 2021, from Government of Canada: https://www.antifraudcentre-centreantifraude.ca/index-eng.htm.

Greenberg, A. (2019). *Sandworm: A New Era of Cyberwar and the Hunt for the Kremlin's Most Dangerous Hackers*. Doubleday.

Hallo, S. (2021). *How & Why Small Businesses are Targeted by Cybercriminals*. Retrieved 9 28, 2021, from PropertyCasualty360: https://www.propertycasualty360.com/2021/09/27/how-why-small-businesses-are-targeted-by-cybercriminals/?slreturn=20210828043340.

Ilascu, I. (2020). *REvil Ransomware Gang Claims over $100 Million Profit in a Year*. Retrieved from Bleeping Computer: https://www.bleepingcomputer.com/news/security/revil-ransomware-gang-claims-over-100-million-profit-in-a-year/#:~:text=REvil%20ransomware%20developers%20say%20that,in%20their%20pursuit%20of%20wealth.

Ilascu, I. (2023). *ALPHV Ransomware Adds Data Leak API in New Extortion Strategy*. Retrieved from Bleeping Computer: https://www.bleepingcomputer.com/news/security/alphv-ransomware-adds-data-leak-api-in-new-extortion-strategy/.

Jeffs, A. (2022). *Five Ransomware Gangs and their Tactics (part two)*. Retrieved 7 10, 2022, from CSHUM: https://www.cshub.com/attacks/articles/five-ransomware-gangs-and-their-tactics-part-two.

JP Morgan Chase. (2022). *The Anatomy of a Ransomware Attack*. Retrieved 5 18, 2023, from JP Morgan Chase: https://www.jpmorgan.com/commercial-banking/insights/the-anatomy-of-a-ransomware-attack.

Keefe, P. R. (2022). *The Surreal Case of a C.I.A. Hacker's Revenge*. Retrieved 10 21, 2022, from The New Yorker: https://www.newyorker.com/magazine/2022/06/13/the-surreal-case-of-a-cia-hackers-revenge.

Keman Huang, K. P. (2019). *For What Technology Can't Fix: Building a Model of Organizational Cybersecurity Culture*. Retrieved 5 2, 2022, from MIT Sloan School of Management: https://web.mit.edu/smadnick/www/wp/2019-02.pdf.

Kenny, M. (2008). *From Pablo to Osama: Trafficking and Terrorist Networks, Government Bureaucracies, and Competitive Adaptation*. Retrieved 15 11, 2008 from https://www.amazon.com/Pablo-Osama-Trafficking-Bureaucracies-Competitive/dp/0271029323/ref=sr_1_1?crid=3E8UHU1L7R8B&keywords=pablo+to+osama+2007&qid=1707314398&s=books&sprefix=.

Kirk, J. (2016). *NSA Contractor's Alleged Theft 'Breathtaking'*. Retrieved from Bank Info Security: https://www.bankinfosecurity.com/nsa-contractors-alleged-theft-breathtaking-a-9470.

Krebs, B. (2014). *Spam Nation – The Inside Story of Organized Cybercrime – from Global Epidemic to your Front Door*. Sourcebooks.

Krebs, B. (2022). *'Spam Nation' Villain Vrublevsky Charged With Fraud*. Retrieved 5 18, 2023, from KrebsOnSecurity: https://krebsonsecurity.com/2022/03/spam-nation-villain-vrublevsky-charged-with-fraud/.

Kreibich, C. (2019). *Spamalytics – An Empirical Analysis of Spam Marketing Conversion*. Retrieved 11 16, 2021, from ICIR: http://www.icir.org/christian/spamalytics/.

Lawler, R. (2022). *Ex-CIA Engineer Convicted for Sending Classified Hacking Tools and Info to WikiLeaks*. Retrieved from The Verge: https://www.theverge.com/2022/7/13/23208635/cia-wikileaks-vault-7-joshua-schulte-conviction.

Levchenko, K. (2011). *Click Trajectories: End-to-End Analysis of the Spam Value Chain*. Retrieved 11 18, 2021, from International Computer Science Institute (ICSI): https://www.icsi.berkeley.edu/icsi/node/4793.

Meegan-Vickers, J. (2022). *The Rise and Fall of the Conti Ransomware Group*. Retrieved from Global Initiative Against Transnational Organized Crime: https://globalinitiative.net/analysis/conti-ransomware-group-cybercrime/#:~:text=Over%20the%20previous%2018%20months,US%24180%20million%20in%20payouts.

Microsoft. (2022). *Microsoft Digital Defense Report 2022*. Retrieved 11 15, 2022, from Microsoft: https://query.prod.cms.rt.microsoft.com/cms/api/am/binary/RE5bUvv?culture=en-us&country=us.

Molloy, M. C. (2022). *Canadian Man Pleads Guilty in Tampa to Ransomware Scheme that Stole Millions*. Retrieved 7 16, 2022, from Tampa Bay Times: https://www.tampabay.com/news/tampa/2022/07/11/canadian-man-pleads-guilty-in-tampa-to-ransomware-scheme-that-stole-millions/.

Montalbano, E. (2021). *Ragnarok Ransomware Gang Bites the Dust, Releases Decryptor*. Retrieved from Threat Post: https://threatpost.com/ragnarok-releases-decryptor/168976/.

Namisha. (2022). *Ransomware as a Service – The Trending Business Model for Attacks*. Retrieved 3 22, 2022, from Security Boulevard: https://securityboulevard.com/2022/03/ransomware-as-a-service-the-trending-business-model-for-attacks/.

National Fraud & Cyber Crime Reporting. (n.d.). *ActionFraud*. Retrieved 9 14, 2021, from National Fraud & Cyber Crime Reporting: https://www.actionfraud.police.uk/a-z-of-fraud.

National Gang Center. (n.d.). *Frequently Asked Questions about Gangs*. Retrieved from National Gang Center: https://nationalgangcenter.ojp.gov/about/faq#faq-10-what-proportion-of-adolescents-join-gangs-and.

NVD. (2018). *CVE-2017-0144*. Retrieved 5 19, 2023, from National Vulnerability Database: https://nvd.nist.gov/vuln/detail/cve-2017-0144

Oghanna, A. (2023, 3 25). *How Albania Became a Target for Cyberattacks.* Retrieved from Foreign Policy: https://foreignpolicy.com/2023/03/25/albania-target-cyberattacks-russia-iran/

Page, C. (2021a). *BlackMatter Ransomware Gang Says it's Shutting Down over Law Enforcement Pressure.* Retrieved from TechCrunch: https://techcrunch.com/2021/11/03/blackmatter-ransomware-shut-down/.

Page, C. (2021b). *Ragnarok Ransomware Gang Shuts Down and Releases its Decryption Key.* Retrieved from TechCrunch: https://techcrunch.com/2021/08/30/ragnarok-ransomware-gang-shuts-down-and-releases-its-decryption-key/.

Page, C. (2023). *Police Arrest Suspected Members of Prolific DoppelPaymer Ransomware Gang.* Retrieved from TechCrunch: https://techcrunch.com/2023/03/06/police-arrest-suspected-members-of-prolific-doppelpaymer-ransomware-gang/.

Pangilinan, M. (2022). *MGA Sounds Alarm on "BazarCall" Ransomware Attack.* Retrieved 7 16, 2022, from Insurance Business America: https://www.insurancebusinessmag.com/us/news/cyber/mga-sounds-alarm-on-bazarcall-ransomware-attack-412935.aspx.

Perlroth, N. (2021). *Colonial Pipeline Paid 75 Bitcoin, or Roughly $5 million, to Hackers.* Retrieved 9 26, 2022, from New York Times: https://www.nytimes.com/2021/05/13/technology/colonial-pipeline-ransom.html.

Renee Dudley, D.G. (2022). *The Ransomware Hunting Team – A Band of Misfits' Improbable Crusade to Save the World from Cybercrime.* New York: Farrar, Straus and Giroux.

Robert McMillan, K. P. (2022). *Leak Reveals Secret World Of Pro-Russia Hacking Gang.* Retrieved from Wall Street Journal.

Roth, E. (2023). *Lapsus$ Cyberattacks: The Latest News on the Hacking Group.* Retrieved from The Verge: https://www.theverge.com/22998479/lapsus-hacking-group-cyberattacks-news-updates.

Saraie, C. (2022). *Five Active Ransomware Gangs and their Tactics.* Retrieved 7 10, 2022, from CSHUB: https://www.cshub.com/attacks/articles/five-active-ransomware-gangs-and-their-tactics-part-one?preview=1882a995f678930583a8722943f42babe42f1e92.

Sayegh, E. (2023). *The REvil Gang Story: The "Good Guys" Can Still Prevail.* Retrieved from Forbes: https://www.forbes.com/sites/emilsayegh/2023/03/22/the-revil-gang-story-the-good-guys-can-still-prevail/?sh=29103b27658a.

Scott Shane, D. E. (2017). *New N.S.A. Breach Linked to Popular Russian Antivirus Software.* Retrieved 9 28, 2022, from New York Times: https://www.nytimes.com/2017/10/05/us/politics/russia-nsa-hackers-kaspersky.html.

Sussman, B. (2023). *Hive Ransomware: $100 Million in Profits, Then the FBI Hid Inside their Network.* Retrieved from BlackBerry: https://blogs.blackberry.com/en/2023/01/hive-ransomware-100-million-in-profits-then-the-fbi-hid-inside-their-

network#:~:text=Inside%20Their%20Network-,Hive%20Ransomware%3A%20
%24100%20Million%20in%20Profits%2C%20Then%20the,FBI%20Hid%20Inside%20
Their%20Netw.

Talbot, D. (2011). *Anatomy of a Spam Viagra Purchase*. Retrieved 10 3, 2010, from
MIT Technology Review: https://www.technologyreview.com/2011/05/20/194575/
anatomy-of-a-spam-viagra-purchase/.

Theohary, C. A., Rollins, J. (2011). *Terrorist Use of the Internet: Information
Operations in Cyberspace*. Retrieved 8 22, 2018, from Congressional Research
Service: https://digital.library.unt.edu/ark:/67531/metadc103142/m1/1/high_
res_d/R41674_2011Mar08.pdf.

Tidy, J. (2022). *74% of Ransomware Revenue goes to Russia-linked Hackers*. Retrieved 9
21, 2022, from BBC: https://www.bbc.com/news/technology-60378009.

Toulas, B. (2023). *Core DoppelPaymer Ransomware Gang Members Targeted in Europol
Operation*. Retrieved from Bleeping Computer: https://www.bleepingcomputer.com/
news/security/core-doppelpaymer-ransomware-gang-members-targeted-
in-europol-operation/.

Trend Micro. (2021). *An Overview of the DoppelPaymer Ransomware*. Retrieved from
Trend Micro: https://www.trendmicro.com/es_es/research/21/a/an-overview-of-
the-doppelpaymer-ransomware.html.

U.S. Congress. (2021). *S. 2629 (IS) – Better Cybercrime Metrics Act*. Retrieved 10 10,
2021, from GovInfo: https://www.govinfo.gov/app/details/BILLS-117s2629is.

U.S. Treasury Department. (2022). *U.S. Treasury Issues First-Ever Sanctions on a
Virtual Currency Mixer, Targets DPRK Cyber Threats*. Retrieved 9 28, 2022, from
U.S. Treasury Department: https://home.treasury.gov/news/press-releases/jy0768.

Vanderlee, K. (2020). *They Come in the Night: Ransomware Deployment Trends*.
Retrieved 5 2, 2022, from Mandiant Threat Research: https://www.mandiant.com/
resources/they-come-in-the-night-ransomware-deployment-trends.

Verizon. (2021). *2022 Data Breach Investigations Report (DBIR)*. Retrieved 10 20, 2021,
from Verizon: https://enterprise.verizon.com/resources/reports/2021/2021-data-
breach-investigations-report.pdf?_ga=2.104515456.1203943201.1634719020-
1809100645.1633781925.

Verizon. (2022). *Data Breach Intrusion Report (DBIR)*. Retrieved 7 9, 2022, from
Verizon: https://www.verizon.com/business/resources/reports/dbir/2022-data-
breach-investigations-report-dbir.pdf?cmp=emc:emc:aw:smb:dbir:dbiremail2smbc
ta2&utm_medium=emc&utm_source=emc&utm_campaign=dbir&utm_content
=aw:smb:dbiremail2smbcta2&mkt_tok=MTU3LUlQVy04NDYAAAGEn6nMYUl
OU7HLj_oRV1RBmbVJbgeuNHxHCGEGrIYXfofDrMs5SGXJU0xyBCsEblLRrj3jq
FLRYp-4JIzYBvT43x0QG2TJoUPjj5JzGevnAU02q2o.

Vijayin, J. (2019). *Ex-NSA Contractor Was a Suspect In Shadow Brokers Leak*.
Retrieved 9 27, 2022, from Dark Reading: https://www.darkreading.com/attacks-
breaches/ex-nsa-contractor-was-a-suspect-in-shadow-brokers-leak.

Wetsman, N. (2020). *Woman dies During a Ransomware Attack on a German Hospital.* Retrieved 5 2, 2022, from The Verge: https://www.therverge.com/2020/9/17/21443851/death-ransomware-attack-hospital-germany-cybersecurity.

William Turton, K. M. (2021). *Hackers Breached Colonial Pipeline Using Compromised Password.* Retrieved 5 3, 2022, from Bloomberg: https://www.bloomberg.com/news/articles/2021-06-04/hackers-breached-colonial-pipeline-using-compromised-password.

Wright, S. A. (2021). *My "Cybercrime" Isn't Your "Cybercrime".* Retrieved 9 14, 2021, from Tripwire: https://www.tripwire.com/state-of-security/security-data-protection/my-cybercrime-isnt-your-cybercrime/.

4

Nation-State Cyber Operations

4.1 Nation State Cyber Operations

We will do a little review on how we arrived at this chapter. In Chapter 1, we looked at how some of the earliest known cyber operators attempted espionage through cyber collection. We also looked at terrorist operations over cyber. For example, Al Qaeda in Iraq (AQI) and its successor, ISIS, used terrorist media messaging that was developed and improved during the Iraqi Insurgency (2004–2008) and post Coalition operations. These media operations included crowd emulation techniques that were eventually adopted by Russia and later used to provide strategic effects in the 2016 U.S. Presidential Election.

In Chapter 2, we looked at the evolution of Al Qaeda, AQI, and ISIS in using the web. For example, AQI used cyber for covert communications and social media to post videos of their attacks and show results to their donors and potential recruits. ISIS then used social media to promote its interests while using the web as a means to communicate and transfer funds. This took us through the 2010s, when the ISIS proto-state emerged from the web, lived as a physical entity, and then later (2017) went back into the web to further regroup.

In Chapter 3, we differentiated cyber native versus cyber-enabled crime. This is a difference between a crime that is defined by cyber technical means versus a crime that is relatively well known (e.g., credit card theft) and is now being performed via web-based technologies. In Chapter 3, we also looked at nation-state-level tool theft. Popularized by the Shadow Brokers, this tool theft in the 2015–2017 time frame occurred at both the U.S. CIA and the U.S. NSA, unleashing tools with an amazing amount of potential mayhem if they fell into the wrong hands. And the Shadow Brokers, based in Russia, were in the wrong hands. By 2017, Shadow Brokers' tools were key topics in Russian and Chinese darknet forums (Muncaster, 2017).

Cyber Operations: A Case Study Approach, First Edition. Jerry M. Couretas.

The 2017 NotPetya attack on the Ukrainian tax authority included Russian criminal use of a ransomware tool and ended up causing approximately $10 billion worth of damage (Greenberg, 2019). This NotPetya "worm" made its way into the broader cyber environment, paralyzing Maersk shipping and shutting down computers across the globe. While the Russian GRU, also called SandWorm, is credited with the NotPetya attack, the malware used to execute NotPetya came into circulation on the heels of the Shadow Brokers attempt to sell nation-state-level cyber offensive tools.

The GRU (Sandworm) Nation-State cyber operators that performed the NotPetya attack were different from the web-based insurgents introduced in Chapter 2, or the cyber criminals discussed in Chapter 3. Nation-state cyber operators have the human and capital resources to access, to maneuver, and, to achieve both tactical and strategic effects. In addition, while hackers and cyber criminals necessarily focus on a specialty in order to survive, nation-state cyber operators have the broader remit to deny and manipulate their targets with effects that span from information operations to capital destruction.

Each cyber operation fits in the spectrum from denial to manipulation, with effects spanning from physical to information operations (IO). Denial and manipulation are the key effects found in U.S. joint publication 3–12 (Joint Staff, 2018). A simplified approach for looking at where the line is crossed between nonkinetic and kinetic operations is shown in Figure 1.3, with cyber "below the line" of formally defined conflict (Joint Chiefs of Staff, 2019). Along with staying "below the line," nation-state cyber operators sometimes masquerade as criminals to provide cover for their attacks (CFR, 2012). For example, the "cyber criminals" that participated in the 2016 U.S. Presidential Election (e.g., Guccifer 2.0) were found to be working out of the Internet Research Agency (IRA). And these "IRA cyber operators[1]" were traced back to one of Russia's key intelligence agencies, the GRU. The IRA benefited from nation-state-level human and technical resources through its GRU reach back.

4.1.1 Advanced Persistent Threats

An additional attribute of a nation-state actor is persistence. For example, some operations have found bad cyber actors to be persistent, or present on a target for years (Verizon, 2021). This persistence likely led Mandiant, a key organization for tracking cyber bad actors, to develop their catalog of Advanced Persistent Threats (APTs), where an APT is defined

---

1 The IRA is a "private" Russian Internet media company started by one of Vladimir Putin's best friends, Yevgeny Prigozhin, colloquially known as Putin's chef, famous for the Wagner Group's June 23, 2023, "mutiny" (Stanovaya, 2023) and deceased in an airplane crash on August 23, 2023.

Advanced Persistent Threat (APT): An advanced persistent threat (APT) is a stealthy threat actor, typically a nation-state or state-sponsored group, which gains unauthorized access to a computer network and remains undetected for an extended period (Cisco)

Mandiant provides tens of actors that fit this APT definition (Mandiant). APTs are also differentiated from one another by the tools employed, target types, and the threat actor's observed operational lifetime. As discussed in Chapter 1, Microsoft has an expanded naming system that attempts to move away from simply naming the team after the tool observed to be used. Microsoft's naming system includes at least three levels based on the estimated threat actor maturity (Chapter 1, Question 7).

The types of operations, or targets, that a nation-state chooses will depend on available team and tool maturity. Access and exploitation capability may also depend on the strength of local research institutions, along with the ability of supporting intelligence services to execute an operation. And, while APTs can exist on any type of system, they are especially threatening when found on systems that can access critical infrastructure. Critical infrastructure provides the power, water, and other supporting services that we use for our everyday lives.

4.1.2 Nation-State Cyber Operations against Critical Infrastructure

Critical infrastructure provides us with the water, electricity, and other supporting services that underpin many of the comforts and conveniences that we take for granted. The U.S. Cybersecurity and Infrastructure Security Agency (CISA) defines critical infrastructure:

> Critical infrastructure describes the physical and cyber systems and assets that are so vital to the United States that their incapacity or destruction would have a debilitating impact on our physical or economic security or public health or safety. The Nation's critical infrastructure provides the essential services that underpin American society. (Cybersecurity and Infrastructure Security Agency (CISA))

The sectors in Table 4.1 are currently viewed as mostly being threatened by nation-state operators. However, due to the insecurity of current control systems, we have examples of water systems being attacked by disgruntled employees (Smith, 2001). Similarly, we have critical infrastructure systems being probed by nation-state organizations (Table 4.2).

As shown in Table 4.2, nation-state cyber operations against critical infrastructure are already occurring and have been occurring for over a decade. Critical

Table 4.1 DHS Critical Infrastructure List (CISA).

The critical infrastructure consists of 16 sectors:

- Chemical sector
- Commercial facilities sector
- Communications sector
- Critical manufacturing sector
- Dams sector
- Defense industrial base sector
- Emergency services sector
- Energy sector
- Financial services sector
- Food and agriculture sector
- Government facilities sector
- Healthcare and public health sector
- Information technologies sector
- Nuclear reactors, materials and waste sector
- Transportation systems sector
- Water and wastewater systems sector

Table 4.2 Nation-State Critical Infrastructure Scan and Attack Examples.

Year	Operation	Description
2023	Volt typhoon	People's Republic of China (PRC) covert penetration of U.S. trans-pacific communications for shutdown in the case of a conflict over Taiwan (Cavanaugh, 2023)
2014	Operation dragonfly	Russian targeting of U.S. energy infrastructure via Microsoft-based supervisory control and data acquisition systems (SCADA) (DoJ, 2023)
2014	Ukraine grid shut down	Russia tailored malware for Ukrainian industrial control system destruction (e.g., Industroyer) and shut down the Ukrainian grid as part of the ongoing Ukraine cyberattack campaign (Greenberg, 2019)
2012	Operation night dragon	Chinese penetration of U.S. natural gas systems (CISA, 2021)

infrastructure attacks, "shutting off the lights," are the use of cyber to achieve the same effects as a traditional bombing and are the types of attacks that we fear a nation-state attacker will carry out. For example, a 2015 Lloyd's of London study, "Business Blackout," showed a potential 93 million Americans, across 10 states and the District of Columbia, being without power due to a cyberattack; costing an estimated $243 billion; $1 trillion in the most stressing scenario (Trevor Maynard, 2015).

Hackers attack critical infrastructure, including hospitals and utilities, to charge a ransom in order to restore operations. For example, in Chapter 3, we saw how the CONTI gang paralyzed the U.S. East Coast with a cyberattack on the Colonial Oil Company (Perlroth, 2021a). CONTI also shut down Costa Rican government systems with ransomware. These were strategic attacks carried out by criminal groups. And this threat to critical infrastructure, especially in the transport of fuel, is now a key element to a developing U.S. National Strategy on cyber (Ellen Nakashima, 2023).

4.1.3 Elements of a Nation-State Cyber Organization

With ransomware groups achieving strategic effects against critical infrastructure, it is sometimes a challenge to separate criminals from nation-state cyber operations (Uberti, 2022). A cybercriminal and nation-state cyber operation can look a lot alike due to the broad access to pilfered nation-state-level tools (Section 3.1.3.3).

And nation-states also use tools released on the darknet. For example, the Shadow Brokers' release of cyberattack tools led to the Russian GRU team Sandworm using NotPetya malware to attack the Ukrainian tax software meDoc in 2017. This resulted in approximately $10 billion in damages as the malware infected systems across the globe (Greenberg, Sandworm: A New Era of Cyberwar and the Hunt for the Kremlin's Most Dangerous Hackers, 2019).

In addition to the NotPetya attack in 2017, the DPRK launched WannaCry ransomware, taking the UK National Health Service (NHS) computers offline and causing over $100 million in damages (Field, 2018). The DPRK performed WannaCry (Newman, 2017) using EternalBlue (NVD, 2017) (MSIAC, 2019), a general access capability for Microsoft systems that was retrieved from the Shadow Brokers' tool set (Bing, 2017). The Shadow Brokers release of nation-state-level tools in the 2017 time frame preceded the early 2020s rash of Ransomware as a Service (RaaS) attacks that debilitated fuel supplies on the U.S. East Coast, locked the government of Costa Rica out of their own systems (Burgess, 2022), and shut down hospitals across the United States and Europe in 2021 alone (DoJ, 2023).

Looking a little closer at the early 2020s outbreak of ransomware, we find some key characteristics that are generally true for nation-state-level cyber tools. For example, seeing that at least some of the Shadow Brokers' stolen tools came from U.S. Government resources, the development of the ransomware tool set benefited from advanced technical infrastructure that included professional engineering, personnel management, and technical development processes. Due to the Shadow Brokers' tools' effectiveness, we have reason to believe that a fair amount of research was involved in making sure that these tools had general capability against a broad set of contemporary attack surfaces. For example, EternalBlue (NVD, 2017) (MSIAC, 2019) was so effective against Microsoft products (e.g., 70% of desktops are Microsoft Windows (StatCounter, 2023)) that a special advisory was provided to Microsoft upon the Shadow Brokers tools' release. These special access tools were employed by operators from clandestine services, rounding out the nation-state cyber capability triad (Figure 4.1).

As shown in Figure 4.1, we can start to think about nation-state-level cyber in terms of the types of resources used in the preparation and execution of a cyber operation. For example, an international clandestine service provides "boots on the ground" for any close access requirements that are not available on the net. Sometimes cyber and close action personnel are on the same team. For example, a member of the GRU Sandworm team, a Russian cyber intelligence agent, was spotted on the ground physically collecting chem-bio intelligence in the Netherlands (Greenberg, 2023a).

Along with having persistent clandestine operators, keeping a dedicated team of researchers and engineers to support the development of target understanding is also useful. Cyber research also provides an ability to use staff for both target system analysis (TSA), or vulnerability understanding, and to design exploits. Supporting engineering processes are then used to follow through on developing these exploits into usable tools.

4.1.3.1 Cyber Research Institutions

Research institutions are usually thought of in terms of universities, where a school is judged by its level of research funding, its number of published patents, and its industry relationships. Cyber, however, is currently more practical, or applied, than the traditional medical and physical sciences where theory development provides an anchor for future clinical trials or technical experimentation.

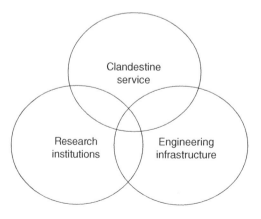

Figure 4.1 Research/Engineering/ Intelligence – Nation-State Cyber Organization Elements.

And, while math and computer science provide practical advances in security, the majority of known vulnerabilities are due to software developed without security in mind. Therefore, finding addressable vulnerabilities for zero-day development, or general means of system access, is sometimes more of a software development problem in converting a software vulnerability into zero-day access. Cyber, therefore, lends itself to more straightforward development than the traditional, theoretical, scientific development problems that require theory development and subsequent proofs of concept(s).

Cyber research institutions are communities of practice, real or virtual fora where knowledge can be exchanged for tool development. Traditional research institutions are just one place where research and development happen. The darknet also provides a market mechanism where buyers and sellers evaluate tools and develop methods for using them (Perlroth, 2021b), as described in the exploitation of the Shadow Brokers suite (Muncaster, 2017).

4.1.3.2 Cyber Engineering and Development

The darknet was a key forum for cyber criminals and nation-state operators to meet, discuss, and even develop tutorials for Shadow Brokers' tools in 2017 (Section 3.1.3.3) (Muncaster, 2017). These tool markets are global, as described by Nicole Perlroth (Perlroth, 2021b). In her book, she describes how markets provide some of the most advanced exploits in the form of reusable tools.

In terms of engineering and development, the current composition of cyberspace is primarily determined by commercial companies. For example, in 2021, Alphabet, Amazon, and Microsoft invested a combined $90 billion in research and development and were awarded 6,966 patents (Bajpai, 2021). In addition, these Internet-related companies work with the Department of Homeland Security (DHS), CISA, and NIST to track vulnerabilities and try to ensure that they are patched. While this system generally works to keep our cyber infrastructure up and running, some clandestine services are tempted by reported vulnerabilities to convert them into zero days to be used by their cyber spies (e.g., China (Microsoft, 2022)).

4.1.3.3 Cyber and Clandestine Services

While commercial software companies drive the development and maintenance of cyberspace, nation-state actors are right behind them in leveraging networked computers for espionage operations. For example, clandestine services, tasked with carrying out nation-state policies, stated or implied, have a long history of using cyber.

As shown in Table 4.3, cyber has been used since the inception of networked computers to collect information that will help nation-state policymakers better understand national and tactical military capabilities. For example, in the late 1980s,

Table 4.3 Cyber and Espionage from the Beginning of Networked Computers.

Year	Operation	Description
1980s	Cuckoo's egg	Former Soviet Union's KGB using hackers to collect on U.S. Star Wars program
1990s	Moonlight maze	Russian Federation collected U.S. military-related information
2000s	Titan rain	Chinese collection on U.S. military programs (e.g., F-35)
2010s	Night dragon	Chinese collection on U.S. natural gas infrastructure
2020s	SolarWinds	Russian Federation targets software supply chain

"The Cuckoo's Egg" provided an example of how a system administrator tracked a billing error on a Lawrence Livermore mainframe to Russian KGB cyber operators trying to collect data on the U.S. Star Wars missile defense system (Stoll, 2005). Similarly, in the early 1990s, Operation Moonlight Maze included a broad collection of U.S. military documents from open-source websites (Greenberg, 2023). And Operation Titan Rain was the first, of many, Chinese cyber collections that resulted in data on U.S. politicians and defense programs (Denning, 2017). In the early 2010s, China stepped up its collections to U.S. energy infrastructure in Operation Night Dragon. And the 2020s brought a more focused collection on software company infrastructure, resulting in cyber actors getting a back door into over 30,000 organizations due to a software supply chain attack (e.g., SolarWinds).

4.1.4 Structure of Nation-State Cyber Operations and Maneuver

Shadow organizations that are designated as criminals (e.g., CONTI, HIVE, ... [Chapter 3]) are often the main culprits in Ransomware as a Service (RaaS). However, connections back to nation-state clandestine services are often suspected, if not explicitly determined (Uberti, 2022). Criminal cyber operations are different from direct military applications of cyber in performing information operations. The two primary cyber effects are manipulation and denial (Joint Staff, 2018).

Denial is a common cyberattack. For example, one of the first famous cyber denial attacks was in Estonia (2007), where Russian cyber actors shut down Estonian networks due to the moving of a statue celebrating Soviet victory in World War II (Heli Tiirmaa-Klaar, 2014). This distributed denial of service (DDoS) attack might be looked at as tactical, in simply jamming Estonia's Internet. However, there was also a strategic element to the attack due to Russian angst at the Estonians' moving of a statue that commemorated the Russian liberation of

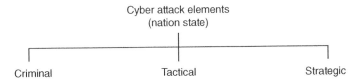

Figure 4.2 Cyber Attack Elements (Criminal, Tactical, Strategic).

Estonia from the Germans in World War II. Russia did not take responsibility for the attack, claiming it was the work of Patriotic Hackers, an uncontrolled group of cyber nationalists that Russia allows to operate on its soil. Therefore, we have three threads to the Estonian DDoS attack (Figure 4.2).

As shown in Figure 4.2, cyber operations can be viewed in terms of criminal, tactical, and strategic. These cyber operations' elements sometimes overlap. For example, Wikileaks' release of U.S. State Department cables was the work of a hacker, whose theft and publishing of the cables is a criminal offense. However, the effects of Wikileaks were strategic, challenging governments to respond.

4.1.4.1 Cryptocurrencies, Sanctions, and Subversion

Using cyber to achieve policy objectives extends to finance. For example, the same cyber actors that use cyber for espionage (i.e., Russia, DPRK, Iran) also use their cyber capabilities to avoid sanctions. Crypto mining converts sanctioned energy reserves into convertible cryptocurrencies.

While Bitcoin might have been released in 2009, with Satoshi Nakamoto's (Nakamoto, 2008) call to a non-state-backed peer-to-peer currency following the 2008 financial collapse, it was not until the mid to late-2010s that cryptocurrencies really took off. This was the period when technology gurus started investing their company capitalizations in Bitcoin. Elon Musk of Tesla and Michael Saylor of Microstrategy are a few big names that went heavily into Bitcoin (Beganski, 2022).

Along with these technology gurus converting their company assets into cryptocurrency, cryptocurrency is also used for sanctions avoidance (FinCEN, 2022). One example is Venezuela introducing the "Petro" as a cyber currency designed to tie their nationally controlled currency to the price of oil.

As described by Karsten (Jack Karsten, 2018), at the Petro's inception, it included a tie to the price of oil, but not exchangeability, along with Venezuelan Government control, reducing the decentralized promise of the other cryptocurrencies.

> The petro differs significantly from other popular cryptocurrencies like Bitcoin, Dashcoin, and Litecoin that circulate widely. The price of one petro is pegged to the price of one barrel of Venezuelan oil – claimed by Maduro to be about $60 as of this writing. In contrast, a cryptocurrency like Bitcoin's price fluctuates based on demand. Additionally, the petro/bolivar

exchange rate, as explained in the petro whitepaper, includes a discount factor determined by the Venezuelan government. Rather than avoid centralized control over the market, the petro is subject to arbitrary discount factor adjustment, fluctuating oil prices, and a corrupt government known for manipulating its currency. There exists a very real danger that the petro will not only fail to cure Venezuela's economic woes but will also weaken the integrity of cryptocurrencies writ-large. (Jack Karsten, 2018)

The Venezuelan regime attempted to use the Petro as a means to circumvent sanctions. This is more direct than the well-known Russian and Iranian use of their energy resources to mine Bitcoin. Cyber and cryptocurrency, however, are just one element of Iranian sanction evasion that has developed over the last 40-plus years. A current issue is the adoption of Iranian sanction evasion techniques, including crypto, by Russia due to its ongoing war against Ukraine (Keatinge, 2023).

4.1.5 Nation-State Cyber Operations Wrap-up

While cryptocurrency is often associated with ransomware, as discussed in Chapter 3, we see how nation-states use their research, engineering, and clandestine services to develop and execute cyber operations. The evolution of cryptocurrency as a means to circumvent sanctions is just one example of how nation-states use cyber to achieve strategic objectives.

Nation-states use cyber to accomplish policy objectives that are a challenge to meet using other means. This is a reason for cyber sometimes being called the "in between" option. Cyber is a possible tool in between policy prescription and kinetic options to be used for achieving nation-state-level objectives. For example, while cyber is used for espionage and denial operations, we also have examples of nations using cyber for sanctions evasion. For example, Russia maintains cryptomining operations in Siberia in order to convert the available energy resources into exchangeable currency.

Bibliography

Bajpai, P. (2021). *Which Companies Spend the Most in Research and Development (R&D)?* Retrieved from Nasdaq: https://www.nasdaq.com/articles/which-companies-spend-the-most-in-research-and-development-rd-2021-06-21.

Beganski, A. (2022). *Michael Saylor Takes Shot at Elon Musk on Twitter Over Tesla's $936M Bitcoin Sale.* Retrieved from decrypt.co: https://decrypt.co/105674/michael-saylor-takes-shot-at-elon-musk-on-twitter-over-teslas-936m-bitcoin-sale.

Bing, C. (2017). *Leaked NSA Hacking Tools are a Hit on the Dark Web*. Retrieved 4 10, 2023, from CyberScoop: https://cyberscoop.com/nsa-hacking-tools-shadow-brokers-dark-web-microsoft-smb/.

Burgess, M. (2022). *Conti's Attack Against Costa Rica Sparks a New Ransomware Era*. Retrieved 9 28, 2022, from Wired: https://www.wired.com/story/costa-rica-ransomware-conti/.

Cavanaugh, B. (2023). *China's Latest Cyberattack Is an Active Threat to Critical US Infrastructure*. Retrieved 5 2023, from Daily Signal: https://www.dailysignal.com/2023/05/26/chinas-latest-cyberattack-active-threat-critical-us-infrastructure/

CFR. (2012). *Denial of Service Attacks Against U.S. Banks in 2012–2013*. Retrieved from Council on Foreign Relations: https://www.cfr.org/cyber-operations/denial-service-attacks-against-us-banks-2012-2013.

CISA. (2021). *Critical Infrastructure Sectors*. Retrieved 3 19, 2022, from https://www.cisa.gov/critical-infrastructure-sectors.

Cisco. (n.d.). *What is an Advanced Persistent Threat*. Retrieved 11 15, 2022, from Cisco: https://www.cisco.com/c/en/us/products/security/advanced-persistent-threat.html.

Cybersecurity and Infrastructure Security Agency (CISA). (n.d.). *Cybersecurity and Infrastructure Security Agency (CISA)*. Retrieved 3 19, 2022, from DHS: https://www.cisa.gov/infrastructure-security.

Denning, D. (2017). *Cyberwar: How Chinese Hackers Became a Major Threat to The U.S.* Retrieved 6 26, 2020, from Newsweek: https://www.newsweek.com/chinese-hackers-cyberwar-us-cybersecurity-threat-678378.

DoJ. (2023). *U.S. Department of Justice Disrupt Hive Ransomware Variant*. Retrieved 1 27, 2023, from U.S. Department of Justice: htttps://www.justce.gov/opa/pr/us-department-justice-disrupts-hive-ransomware-variant.

Ellen Nakashima, T. S. (2023). *U.S. National Cyber Strategy to Stress Biden Push on Regulation*. Retrieved 2 10, 2023, from Washington Post: https://www.washingtonpost.com/national-security/2023/01/05/biden-cyber-strategy-hacking/.

Field, M. (2018). *WannaCry Cyber Attack Cost the NHS £92m as 19,000 Appointments Cancelled*. Retrieved 5 1, 2023, from The Telegraph: https://www.telegraph.co.uk/technology/2018/10/11/wannacry-cyber-attack-cost-nhs-92m-19000-appointments-cancelled/.

FinCEN. (2022). *FinCEN Advises Increased Vigilance for Potential Russian Sanctions Evasion Attempts*. Retrieved from FinCEN: https://www.fincen.gov/sites/default/files/2022-03/FinCEN%20Alert%20Russian%20Sanctions%20Evasion%20FINAL%20508.pdf.

Greenberg, A. (2019). *Sandworm: A New Era of Cyberwar and the Hunt for the Kremlin's Most Dangerous Hackers*. Doubleday.

Greenberg, A. (2023a). *The Underground History of Russia's Most Ingenious Hacker Group*. Retrieved 6 2023, from Wired: https://www.wired.com/story/turla-history-russia-fsb-hackers/.

Greenberg, A. (2023b). *This Is the New Leader of Russia's Infamous Sandworm Hacking Unit*. Retrieved 4 14, 2023, from Wired Magazine: https://www.wired.com/story/russia-gru-sandworm-serebriakov/.

Heli Tiirmaa-Klaar, J.G.-P. (2014). *Botnets*. New York: Springer.

Jack Karsten, D. W. (2018). *Venezuela's "petro" Undermines other Cryptocurrencies – and International Sanctions*. Retrieved from Brookings: https://www.brookings.edu/articles/venezuelas-petro-undermines-other-cryptocurrencies-and-international-sanctions/.

Joint Chiefs of Staff. (2019). *Joint Doctrine Note 1–19 – Competition Continuum*. Retrieved 5 10, 2020, from Joint Chiefs of Staff.

Joint Staff. (2018). *Joint Publication 3–12 Cyberspace Operations*. Retrieved 9 16, 2019, from Joint Publications: https://www.jcs.mil/Portals/36/Documents/Doctrine/pubs/jp3_12.pdf.

Keatinge, T. (2023). *Developing Bad Habits What Russia Might Learn from Iran's Sanctions Evasion*. Retrieved from RUSI.

Mandiant. (2013). *APT1: Exposing One of China's Cyber Espionage Units*. Retrieved from Mandiant: https://www.mandiant.com/resources/reports/apt1-exposing-one-chinas-cyber-espionage-units.

Mandiant. (n.d.). *Advanced Persistent Threats (APTs)*. Retrieved 5 2, 2023, from Mandiant: https://www.mandiant.com/resources/insights/apt-groups.

Microsoft. (2022). *Microsoft Digital Defense Report 2022*. Retrieved 11 15, 2022, from Microsoft: https://query.prod.cms.rt.microsoft.com/cms/api/am/binary/RE5bUvv?culture=en-us&country=us.

MSIAC. (2019). *EternalBlue*. Retrieved 2 10, 2023, from CISA: https://www.cisecurity.org/wp-content/uploads/2019/01/Security-Primer-EternalBlue.pdf.

Muncaster, P. (2017). *Shadow Brokers Attack Tools Light Up Chinese and Russian Darknet*. Retrieved 5 2, 2023, from Info Security: https://www.infosecurity-magazine.com/news/shadow-brokers-attack-tools-china/.

Nakamoto, S. (2008). *Bitcoin: A Peer-to-Peer Electronic Cash System*. Retrieved 1 9, 2023, from https://www.ussc.gov/sites/default/files/pdf/training/annual-national-training-seminar/2018/Emerging_Tech_Bitcoin_Crypto.pdf.

Newman, L. H. (2017). *How an Accidental 'Kill Switch' Slowed Friday's Massive Ransomware Attack*. Retrieved 4 12, 2023, from Wired Magazine: https://www.wired.com/2017/05/accidental-kill-switch-slowed-fridays-massive-ransomware-attack/.

NVD. (2017). *CVE-2017-0144*. Retrieved from NIST: https://nvd.nist.gov/vuln/detail/cve-2017-0144.

Perlroth, N. (2021a). *Colonial Pipeline Paid 75 Bitcoin, or Roughly $5 Million, to Hackers*. Retrieved 9 26, 2022, from New York Times: https://www.nytimes.com/2021/05/13/technology/colonial-pipeline-ransom.html.

Perlroth, N. (2021b). *This Is How They Tell Me the World Ends: The Cyberweapons Arms Race*.

Rombado, L. (2019). *Grant Cyber Letters of Marque to Manage "Hack Backs".* Retrieved from U.S. Naval Institute: https://www.usni.org/magazines/proceedings/2019/october/grant-cyber-letters-marque-manage-hack-backs#:~:text=Used%20extensively%20during%20the%20War,empower%20private%20sector%20hack%20backs.

Smith, T. (2001). *Hacker Jailed for Revenge Sewage Attacks.* Retrieved 4 27, 2023, from The Register: https://www.theregister.com/2001/10/31/hacker_jailed_for_revenge_sewage/.

Stanovaya, T. (2023). *Beneath the Surface, Prigozhin's Mutiny has Changed Everything in Russia.* Retrieved from Carnegie Endowment for International Peace: https://carnegieendowment.org/politika/90275.

StatCounter. (2023). *Desktop Operating System Market Share Worldwide.* Retrieved from StatCounter: https://gs.statcounter.com/os-market-share/desktop/worldwide/.

Stoll, C. (2005). *The Cuckoo's Egg: Tracking a Spy Through the Maze of Computer Espionage.* Pocket Books.

Trevor Maynard, N.B. (2015). *Business Blackout – The Insurance Implications of a Cyber attack on the US Power Grid.* London: Lloyd's.

Uberti, D. (2022). *Line Between Criminal Hackers and Nation-State Threats Blurs, U.S. Officials Say; Ransomware Groups and Foreign Intelligence Services Increasingly Overlap to Rake in Money and Cover their Tracks, Complicating U.S. Efforts to Stop them.* Retrieved from Wall Street Journal.

Verizon. (2021). *2022 Data Breach Investigations Report (DBIR).* Retrieved 10 20, 2021, from Verizon: https://enterprise.verizon.com/resources/reports/2021/2021-data-breach-investigations-report.pdf?_ga=2.104515456.1203943201.1634719020-1809100645.1633781925.

5

Russian Cyber Operations

5.1 Russian Cyber Operations

Russian cyber operations are a unique blend of modern technology and a creative use of information that dates back at least as far as the Okhrana, or the Czar's secret police (Warner, 2017). One of the first acts of a newly created Soviet Union was to start an office of disinformation in 1923 (Agursky, 1989), operations that continued throughout the lifespan of the Former Soviet Union (Pacepa and Rychlak, 2013).

Russian information operations continue to be performed over cyber. Russian cyber operations are a general information-related capability (IRC) that leverages a rich national legacy of deception, often using remnants of KGB intelligence organization constructs to perform cyber operations. Russia performs nation-state cyber campaigns that span from denial to manipulation.

In addition to a history of information operations, Russia has a sizable community of highly educated, underemployed, technically savvy computer programmers that play a large role in the criminal cyber community. This includes developing and selling unauthorized access to systems of interest, maintaining nefarious botnets for various operations, and providing ransomware as a service (RaaS). These cyber skills and services are not lost on the Russian state-sponsored cyber efforts (CISA, 2022).

5.1.1 Russian Policy, Tools, and Historical Use of Information Operations

While some postulate that the Russian clandestine use of cyber stems from the "Gerasimov Doctrine" (Kramer, 2019), the Russian military does not develop

Cyber Operations: A Case Study Approach, First Edition. Jerry M. Couretas.
© 2024 John Wiley & Sons, Inc. Published 2024 by John Wiley & Sons, Inc.

doctrine, but is responsible for implementing it. According to Nicole Ng, the real impetus for aggressive Russian actions, including cyber, is the Primakov Doctrine –

> The major shift in Russian foreign policy did not occur in 2013 with the publication of Gerasimov's article. Nor did it occur in 2014 with Russia's annexation of Crimea. It occurred in 1996, when Yevgeny Primakov, then the director of Russia's foreign intelligence service, was elevated to the post of foreign minister. Up to that point, post-Soviet Russia had largely sought accommodation and integration with the West. But Primakov put forward the argument that a unipolar world dominated by the United States was unacceptable to Russia. He envisioned a multipolar world managed by a concert of major powers, with Russia as an indispensable actor with a vote and veto on key issues. Securing Russia's primacy in the post-Soviet space and opposing NATO enlargement were also crucial to Primakov's vision. In this context, the so-called Gerasimov doctrine is better understood as just one manifestation of the Primakov doctrine in action. Rather than an over-arching philosophy, it is an operational concept adapted to the strategic environment in which Russia has found itself. (Nicole and Rumer, 2019)

The Primakov doctrine, and Gerasimov's implementation of an integrated vision for projecting Russian power, includes a need to control the information space. This idea stems from the traditional employment of active measures. The use of cyber to circumvent sanctions, and to create cryptocurrency, is a novel technical twist paralleling this hybrid war vision.

5.1.1.1 Policy, Statecraft Tools, and Cryptocurrency

The Russian Federation implements the Primakov Doctrine in unique ways. For example, Russia is a de facto petro-state hindered by geography, and now sanctions. This limits Russia from using its 10 million barrels of oil production per day to achieve the swing producer status of Saudi Arabia or the United States.

Implementing the spirit of the Primakov Doctrine via energy reserves is a challenge due to Russia's inability to get its oil to market. A creative solution to this issue is simply to convert the energy reserves into bitcoin in order to provide buying power for goods and services on the International market. Large bitcoin mining operations in Siberia are one method that Russia uses to avoid sanctions that came with invading Ukraine in 2022.

Bitcoin mining is popular enough in Siberia for local miners to erect a statue to their work –

> Cryptocurrencies make up a greater part of Russia's financial system than most other nations due to a distrust in its banking system, said Marlon Pinto,

director of investigations at London-based risk advisory firm AnotherDay. A Russian government report estimates that there are more than 12 million cryptocurrency wallets, where the digital assets are stored, opened by Russian citizens, and the amount of the funds is about 2 trillion rubles, equivalent to about $23.9 billion. (Caitlin Ostroff, 2022)

Cryptocurrency provides a key method for Russian citizens to convert their Rubles to Internationally exchangeable currency –

At Binance's main exchange business, trading volumes in Russia are down compared with a peak in early 2022, but have rebounded somewhat in recent months, according to data provider CCData. Binance handled $8 billion of ruble-to-crypto trades in July (2023), mostly for Tether, CCData said. (Berwick and Kowsmann, 2023)

Distrust in the national currency is just one element of the Russian people's suspicion of their government. During the early 20th century, an Office of Disinformation, dating back to 1923, or the beginning of the Former Soviet Union, soured the Russian citizenry with misinformation for generations, until the Former Soviet Union's collapse in 1991. In parallel with this internal disinformation program, the Former Soviet Union/Russia also developed overseas propaganda programs, widely called active measures.

5.1.1.2 Information Operations, Developing Doctrine, and Russian Cyber Teams

The Former Soviet Union conducted political warfare-style operations under an umbrella of "active measures" against foreign and domestic targets over the course of its history. Akin to contemporary political warfare, these actions ranged from assassinating *émigré* leaders who participated in anti-Soviet activities to manufacturing and spreading the lie that the Pentagon started the AIDS epidemic (Mark Kramer, n.d.; Sherman, 2022)

Russia's modern structure for information operations reportedly even mirrors the Soviet approach; after the collapse of the Soviet Union, the military transferred its propaganda directorate to the military intelligence agency (*Glavnoye Razvedyvatelnoye Upravlenie*, or GRU), rebranding it GRU Unit 54,777 in 1994. This unit still exists today and, per the US Department of the Treasury's 2021 sanctions, falls under Russia's Information Operations Troops. (Sherman, 2022)

In his book "Disinformation," Ion Pacepa (Pacepa and Rychlak, 2013) talked about the vast network of people supporting information operations in the former

Soviet Union. More recently, Justin Sherman provides a modern-day depiction of the Russian Federation's information operations –

> The extensive Russian network includes: internal government cyber and information units; front companies established and run by the government; private companies leveraged by the government to develop capabilities and recruit talent; criminals recruited by state officials; industry developers recruited by state officials; independently operating patriotic hackers (often with state encouragement or as cover for state-run action); hackers independently building their capabilities and pitching them to the state; and murky, mafia-style familial entanglements between hackers and Russian government officials. Experts have published excellent research on cyber proxies. (Sherman, 2022)

The use of proxies is a possible precursor to a more automated, more information-dominant, future battlefield that minimizes the use of nation-state soldiers, according to Russian military theorists S. G. Chekinov and S. A. Bogdanov, who together wrote several articles between 2013 and 2017 (Thomas, 2020). The Second Karabakh War, for example, provides a glimpse into this vision of automatons in battle (Kott, 2020).

Cyber is just one of the automated technologies that are featured in Chekinov and Bogdanov's visions of future battles. Maintaining information superiority is a key requirement in future battlefields populated by more automata than humans. These articles came after the more famous Gerasimov Doctrine (2013) and provided a guide to hybrid warfare until the 2022 Ukraine invasion challenged ideas in an actual campaign.

The theories of Chekinov, Bogdanov, and Gerasimov feature the use of technology as proxies in future warfare. As these technologies develop, they may be using foreign proxies, criminals, and other actors in order to provide plausible deniability in the gray zone between peace and war, and during military operations. For example, as discussed in Chapter 3, criminal cyber operations might be one of the "hybrid methods" that a nation-state operator uses to manipulate or deny a targeted adversary in cyberspace. And, while the Russian Federation is developing theory for the next stage of warfare, it is also conducting operations, possibly experiments, to verify and validate select hypotheses.

Russian cyber operations began with the pre-Internet exfiltration attempts of U.S. Star Wars data (the 1980s) (Stoll, 2005) and continued as either exfiltration (late-1990s to early 2000s Operation Moonlight Maze), denial (2007 Estonia, 2008 Georgia, 2014–present Ukraine), or information operations (2008 Georgia, 2014–present Ukraine).

There are multiple Russian cyber teams that span the criminal/tactical/strategic spectrum. Russian nation-state cyber operators are commonly described in terms of their intelligence agency designation of FSB, GRU, or SVR, each one a legacy element of the FSU's KGB (Table 5.1).

Each organization in Table 5.1 has had a hand in recent cyber operations. Examples of Russian APTs are provided in Table 5.2.

Looking at Table 5.2, both the GRU and the SVR have clear connections to APT 28 and APT 29. The GRU famous for attacks on the 2016 U.S. Presidential elections and inciting riots leading up to the election. In addition, the SVR is known for the SolarWinds attack and multiple other recent incursions (DHS CISA, 2021) (Figure 5.1).

Figure 5.1 breaks into APT28 and APT29, along with some perishable team names that go with specific operations. It has long been hypothesized that there is an explicit connection between criminals and nation-state teams (Uberti, 2022).

Table 5.1 Russian Federation Intelligence Agencies.

Organization	Description	Legacy
Federal security service (FSB) (FAS, 2000)	Counterintelligence directorate (i.e., Vladimir Putin was once a director)	Responsible for counterintelligence during the Soviet Union. Seems to have a broader remit under the Russian Federation.
		Implicated in Operation Moonlight Maze as Turla (Cimpanu, 2017) during the early years of cyber operations (1996–1998) (Greenberg, 2023a). In addition, Operation Dragonfly (2012–2017), the probing of technical and personnel of U.S. natural gas pipelines was an FSB operation.
GRU	Military intelligence agency – rebranded to GRU Unit 54,777 in 1994	Propaganda directorate during the Former Soviet Union. Responsible for several major cyber-attacks in Ukraine, the United States, and across the globe (e.g., Sandworm Group (Greenberg, 2019))
SVR (foreign intelligence service)	Political, military, and technical intelligence services outside of Russia (i.e., Yevgeny Primakov was once a director)	Official successor to the NKVD, which preceded the KGB (Murphy, 2022). The SVR is the primary organization for liaising with foreign intelligence services (e.g., Iran's Ministry of Intelligence and Security (MOIS), …)

Table 5.2 Russian Cyber Teams (APTs).

Team	Started	Targets	Description
APT 28	2008	Strategic	APT28 believed to be sponsored by the Russian Military Intelligence Service (GRU) and focuses on propaganda targeting.
APT 29	2014	Strategic	APT29 believed to be sponsored by both the Russian Foreign Intelligence Service (SVR) and the FSB. APT 29 focuses on diplomatic targets (e.g., European policy-making organizations). APT 29 is known as Nobelium by Microsoft (Bienstock, 2022).

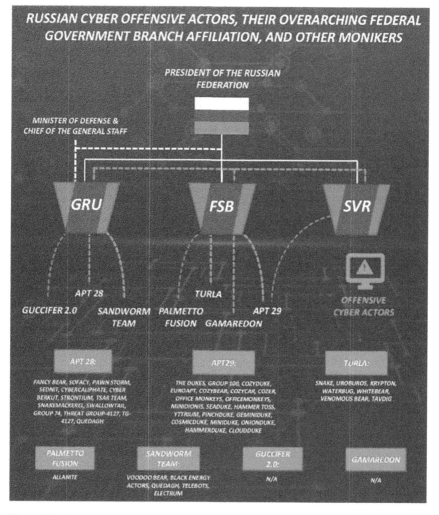

Figure 5.1 Russian Intelligence Organizations, APTs, and Operations. *Source:* Cunningham (2020)/University of Washington.

5.1.1.3 Estonia Denial of Service Attack (2007)

Along with legacy active measures, the Russian Federation first tried its hand at cyber denial operations against Estonia, where over 90% of the banking and government services are online. In 2007, the Estonian government moved a statue commemorating Russia's liberating Estonia from the Germans in World War II. Russia had already threatened Estonia not to move the statue. Once the statue was moved, Russians in Estonia performed mass demonstrations. In addition, a cyberattack was launched against –

- Banks
- Telecommunications
- Media outlets
- Government offices

The cyberattack against Estonia included –

- Denial of service
- Botnets
- Hacking

The three-week siege of Estonia's online services included hackers at varying levels of skill (Heli Tiirmaa-Klaar, 2014) (Table 5.3).

As shown in Table 5.3, the DoS attacks on Estonia were phased by operational skill level, increasing over the three weeks of the denial campaign. The DoS effects are a challenge to quantify. These cyberattacks, from April 26 to mid-May 2007, coincided with a major economic impact due to ongoing street protests that contracted the internal economy and decreased external trade due to Russia

Table 5.3 Estonia Cyber Campaign – Phases and Skill Levels.

Phase	Description
Initial (after 4/26–4/28 street riots)	Hactivists – people of limited skills following instructions on certain websites. Due to the monument relocation being a surprise, the first wave of attacks included a simple denial of service and website defacement attacks – this was meant more to disrupt Internet availability and disable websites.
Main attack (5/2–5/18) (5/9 – Russia's WWII Victory Day)	Large botnets, consisting of millions of hijacked computers, targeted Estonian servers. This included coordinated attacks, with increasingly precise timing, resulting in Estonian authorities limiting connectivity as a countermeasure

Source: Adapted from Ottis (2008).

imposing sanctions. In addition, it is believed that the one-month timeframe for the campaign was the duration of a botnet rental agreement on the dark web (Heli Tiirmaa-Klaar, 2014).

The 2007 Estonian DoS attack, while crippling civil infrastructure and challenging the government's legitimacy, seemed to be an experiment that included Russian patriotic hactivists with unclear involvement from the Russian Federation. In any case, Russian Federation officials saw the potential of using cyber from the Estonian case study, developing more formal cyber operations capability going forward.

5.1.2 Russian Information Operations

According to Romanian General Ion Pacepa (Pacepa and Rychlak, 2013; Joseph Farah et al., 2017), a key player in Soviet Bloc information operations during the Cold War, Russian disinformation dates back at least to Count Potemkin's false-front villages, which implied economic growth. "Potempkin Villages" were used to impress Catherine the Great during a late 18th-century tour of Crimea.

Modern-day disinformation is delivered by cyber means. Russian cyber operators develop messaging, work as criminals for profit, and perform reconnaissance and surveillance operations via the web. One assessment is that current Russian cyber operations trace directly to the remnants of the Former Soviet Union's KGB –

> There is a whole array of these hacker groups that all work for the Kremlin, but the simplest way to split them up is probably among the three major intelligence agencies in Russia: the FSB, a domestic law enforcement agency and a successor to the KGB. Another successor to the KGB is the SVR: the foreign intelligence agency, sort of their equivalent to the CIA. Then there is the agency that I am most focused on or obsessed with: the GRU, a military intelligence agency that can easily be said to be the most reckless and brazen and disruptive of the three in its hacking activities. (Greenberg, 2017)

During the 1990s, when the new Russian Federation was believed to be focused on building a new country, Turla, an FSB team, performed Operation Moonlight Maze, collecting over 5.5 GB of data from the U.S. Air Force (Greenberg, 2023b).

5.1.2.1 The Russian Federal Security Service (FSB)

> Russia is particularly focused on improving its ability to target critical infrastructure, including underwater cables and industrial control systems, in the United States as well as in allied and partner countries, because

compromising such infrastructure improves and demonstrates its ability to damage infrastructure during a crisis. (Office of the Director of National Intelligence (ODNI), 2023)

The FSB was created in 1995 from the KGB's Federal Counterintelligence Service with a remit that includes general surveillance, border security, and counter-terror. The elevation of Vladimir Putin to lead the FSB in 1999 resulted in a broad reorganization and the incorporation of the border guard service, with over 200,000 personnel, and the Federal Agency of Government Communication and Information (FAPSI). With Putin ascending to become prime minister, the FSB is a natural base of his support (FAS, 2000) (Figure 5.2).

The FSB is considered a domestic law enforcement agency along the lines of the U.S.' Federal Bureau of Investigation (FBI). However, the FSB is believed to maintain a connection to all the networked devices inside Russia (NATO, 2007). The FSB is therefore a cross between the pre-breakup AT&T, when it dominated U.S. telecommunications, and an intelligence agency with arrest authority[1]. There is nothing like this in the Western World, to the author's knowledge.

Figure 5.2 Moscow Headquarters of Russia's Federal Security Service, the Successor to the KGB. *Source:* Andrei Soldatov (2012)/Condé Nast.

---

1 When Mikhail Khodorkovsky was arrested for being a potential threat to Putin's regime, it was FSB officers who made the arrest (Coll, 2013)

The FSB's cyber operations' scope spans from political operations to critical infrastructure. This includes collecting on commercial U.S.-based companies and even trying to run their own candidate in a local St Petersburg, Florida, election with ideas about winning higher office (DoJ, 2023). In addition, Turla is a team associated with the FSB and is known for political and media targeting (e.g., German Bundestag, France TV Monde, ...) (Sayegh, 2023). In the early days of cyber, Turla was implicated in Operation Moonlight Maze (Cimpanu, 2017).

1996–1999 Operation Moonlight Maze As described by Chris Doman, Operation Moonlight Maze consisted of a probe on the Air Force Institute of Technology (AFIT) and the Air Force Research Labs (AFRL) through Internet accounts at multiple universities. Operation Moonlight Maze was traced back to the Russians due to operator's time and date signatures (Greenberg, 2023b) –

- 3 a.m. login time on a Sunday (i.e., time zone anomaly)
- conspicuous lack of activity during Russian Orthodox holidays

The goal of Operation Moonlight Maze was information collection and resulted in the exfiltration of approximately 5.5 GB of data before concluding. About a decade after Operation Moonlight Maze, the FSB was found probing U.S. critical infrastructure.

2012–2017 Operation Dragonfly (U.S. Energy Grid)(HAVEX) Some of the more famous grid surveillance operations by the FSB include the 2014 reconnaissance of U.S. and Ukrainian power systems (DoJ, 2022). In the United States, this operation was called HAVEX, named after the tool used to target the Microsoft OLE for Process Control (OPC) software that is used to manage Supervisory Control and Data Acquisition (SCADA) systems.

The effectiveness of Operation Dragonfly may have been due to the operators' ability to target the supply chain for operational technology, disseminating malware through the standard patching system in order to maintain system security (Table 5.4).

As shown in Table 5.4, FSB operators actively targeted SCADA manufacturers during Dragonfly I. This supply chain attack was the initial phase used to gain general access (i.e., area targeting) to both the SCADA suppliers and their customers. Follow on the exploitation of the energy networks during Dragonfly I, and then Dragonfly II, included targeting specific energy sectors. In addition, this targeting included key individuals and engineers working on the SCADA systems. The scale and scope of Dragonfly I and II, in preparing targets in the U.S. power and electrical grid, are likely unimaginable to the average American.

Table 5.4 Operation Dragonfly (2012–2017).

Operation	Description
Dragonfly (2012–2014)	"In the first phase, which took place between 2012 and 2014 and is commonly referred to by cyber security researchers as "Dragonfly" or "Havex," the conspirators engaged in a supply chain attack, compromising the computer networks of ICS/SCADA system manufacturers and software providers and then hiding malware – known publicly as "Havex" – inside legitimate software updates for such systems. After unsuspecting customers downloaded Havex-infected updates, the conspirators would use the malware to, among other things, create backdoors into infected systems and scan victims' networks for additional ICS/SCADA devices. Through these and other efforts, including spear phishing and "watering hole" attacks, the conspirators installed malware on more than 17,000 unique devices in the United States and abroad, including ICS/SCADA controllers used by power and energy companies." (DoJ, 2022)
Dragonfly 2 (2014–2017)	"In the second phase, which took place between 2014 and 2017 and is commonly referred to as 'Dragonfly 2.0', the conspirators transitioned to more targeted compromises that focused on specific energy sector entities and individuals and engineers who worked with ICS/SCADA systems. As alleged in the indictment, the conspirators' tactics included spear phishing attacks targeting more than 3300 users at more than 500 U.S. and international companies and entities, in addition to U.S. government agencies such as the Nuclear Regulatory Commission. In some cases, the spear phishing attacks were successful, including in the compromise of the business network (*i.e.*, involving computers not directly connected to ICS/SCADA equipment) of the Wolf Creek Nuclear Operating Corporation (Wolf Creek) in Burlington, Kansas, which operates a nuclear power plant. Moreover, after establishing an illegal foothold in a particular network, the conspirators typically used that foothold to penetrate further into the network by obtaining access to other computers and networks at the victim entity."

5.1.2.2 Russia and Ukrainian Power System Attacks

The Russian attack that stopped power for 225,000 Ukrainians in December of 2015 (i.e., BlackEnergy) included the use of spear-phishing emails to obtain access into the three energy distribution companies' computer systems and then using destructive malware against the computer systems (U.S. Department of Justice, 2020)-

a) The spearphishing campaign targeted the companies' information technology staff and system administrators using emails attaching malware-laced files.

b) Once they had obtained access to the victims' computer systems, the Conspirators used a particular variant of malware called "BlackEnergy" to steal user credentials. The Conspirators used the stolen credentials to access the Supervisory Control and Data Acquisition ("SCADA") networks at the Ukrainian energy distribution companies. The Conspirators also used destructive malware called "KillDisk" at the conclusion of the attacks to delete computer event logs and other files and reboot the infected computers. Once rebooted, the infected computers were inoperable.

Russia has attacked the Ukrainian electrical system multiple times (2014, 2016, 2022) and initially had success turning off their power system. In addition, Russian malware (e.g., Triton) was found in a middle-eastern power system (U.S. Treasury, 2020).

FSB, Cyber Gangs, and Commercial Compromise A novel Russian organizational construct, the FSB is implicated in the cyber scanning of U.S. critical infrastructure, –

> … FSB, the KGB's successor agency, has conducted malicious cyber operations targeting the Energy Sector, including UK and U.S. energy companies, U.S. aviation organizations, U.S. government and military personnel, private organizations, cybersecurity companies, and journalists. FSB has been known to task criminal hackers for espionage-focused cyber activity; these same hackers have separately been responsible for disruptive ransomware and phishing campaigns. (CISA, 2022)

As discussed in Chapter 3, the release of tools at the NSA and CIA directly preceded the WannaCry and NotPetya ransomware attacks. In the case of the NSA, Hal Martin, the hoarder who had taken home 50 TB worth of U.S. Government-developed tools, was using a Kaspersky firewall on his home network to prevent bad actors from accessing his files. This Kaspersky firewall was sending data back to corporate headquarters, employees of which work with the FSB (Nakashima, 2017).

In addition to working closely with the Kaspersky software security company, the FSB is believed to be connected to the former CONTI ransomware gang (Burgess, 2022). This is where the line between criminal hackers and nation-state sponsors is blurred (Uberti, 2022). For example, this FSB gang connection extends to Evil Corp's leader Maksim Yakubets (Renee Dudley, 2022) –

> In addition to his leadership role within Evil Corp, Yakubets has also provided direct assistance to the Russian government. As of 2017, Yakubets

was working for the Russian FSB, one of Russia's leading intelligence organizations that was previously sanctioned pursuant to E.O. 13,694, as amended, on December 28, 2016. As of April 2018, Yakubets was in the process of obtaining a license to work with Russian classified information from the FSB. As a result, Yakubets is also being designated pursuant to E.O. 13,694, as amended, for providing material assistance to the FSB. Additionally, as of 2017, Yakubets was tasked to work on projects for the Russian state, to include acquiring confidential documents through cyber-enabled means and conducting cyber-enabled operations on its behalf. (U.S. Treasury, 2019)

FSB operations' skills therefore span from global cyber security corporations to criminal cyber gangs in performing collection and manipulation operations. An example relationship between the FSB, CONTI, Kaspersky, and Evil Corp is provided in Figure 5.3.

The FSB is therefore resourceful in the use of ransomware gangs, their members, and commercial companies. CONTI successfully probed and encrypted the Colonial Pipeline business computing systems in the summer of 2021; a ransomware attack that resulted in the U.S. East Coast running out of fuel for five days (Perlroth, 2021).

It is not clear how much the FSB used either gangs or commercial companies in its development of the HAVEX supply chain attack that marked phase one of Operation Dragonfly. Using the supply chain as a means to access sensitive systems seems to be a consistent Russian approach. As far back as 2014 HAVEX malware was distributed via the supply chain. This is a similar threat vector to the SolarWinds attack of 2020, this time performed by the SVR.

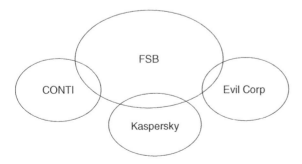

Figure 5.3 Corporations, Criminal Gangs, and the FSB. *Source:* Nakashima (2017), U.S. Treasury (2019).

5.1.2.3 Foreign Intelligence Directorate (SVR)(APT 29 – Nobelium)

The SVR, one of the children organizations of the Former Soviet Union's KGB, is a foreign intelligence agency and is often compared to the U.S. Central Intelligence Agency (CIA). In contrast to the FSB's domestic policing and telecommunications responsibilities, the SVR seems to primarily use cyber surveillance in order to extract information for intelligence development. For example, the SVR primarily targets government networks, think tanks, and policy analysis organizations. In addition, the SVR is also known to target information technology companies. One of the more famous attacks credited to the SVR is the 2020 SolarWinds compromise, which resulted in access to an estimated 30,000 machines (Zetter, 2023).

5.1.2.4 2020 SolarWinds (SVR)

SolarWinds was an unprecedented cyber-attack that resulted in the compromise of approximately 30,000 machines (Securities and Exchange Commission (SEC), 2020). One goal of the SolarWinds attack was to obtain U.S. legal information concerning the prosecution of current Russian operators (Temple-Raston, 2021). As General Keith Alexander pointed out, SolarWinds ended up becoming a much broader targeting campaign –

> Now, look at SolarWinds. I think their intent was (to determine) what the U.S. (was) doing with indictments against Russian actors, what's the U.S. position on these actors, what's the Commerce Department doing, what's Treasury doing, what's Justice doing, what's State doing. I think that was their target, and IT capabilities to get into there. I think they were focusing on their target set and saw SolarWinds as a way of getting in, so they were focused down, and when they put that in and let that go, I believe they didn't want 18,000 companies. "Oops. But oh, look at what we could do if we needed to." The oops was now you had to weed out the 17,800 to find the 200 that you need. That's a lot of work and (they) should have thought about it – and they will in the future. (Janofsky, 2021)

The SolarWinds attack, starting in late 2019 and not detected until the world was deep into the pandemic in 2020, impacted both government and commercial software systems (QUENTIN E. Hodgson and Shokh, 2022). Due to the widespread use of the SolarWinds Orion platform, multiple government agencies were compromised with the Trojan included in the SolarWinds software updates. In addition, Microsoft noted that a foreign intelligence service was viewing its code during this time period (GAO, 2021). The SVR therefore accessed a large supplier of desktop software via a supply chain attack on SolarWinds. This is a much broader attack than the HAVEX supply chain compromise discussed in the context of Operation Dragonfly (Section 2012–2017 Operation Dragonfly (U.S. Energy Grid)(HAVEX)).

5.1.2.5 Military Intelligence Directorate (GRU)

While the SVR and FSB provide sophisticated examples of software supply chain penetration, even using cyber gangs to access systems and to deliver cyber effects, the GRU takes off the gloves in delivering strategic effects by any cyber means available. For example, in one of the more famous cyber/kinetic campaigns, the GRU incited over 100 riots within the United States and mortally wounded the Democratic National Committee's internal organization cohesion leading up to the 2016 Presidential Election (Mueller, 2019).

GRU cyber operations use strategic cyber effects on targets that range from taking down the Ukrainian power grid (2014), via Industroyer malware (CISA, 2022), to attacking the 2016 U.S. Presidential Election. As described by Andy Greenberg of Wired magazine, the GRU has two active hacking units –

> ... The two most active hacking units I know of within the GRU are Unit 26,165, also known as Fancy Bear or APT28, who famously were the ones who led the breach of the Democratic National Committee and the Clinton campaign in 2016 and leaked those documents. Then, there is Unit 74,455 of the GRU, also known as Voodoo Bear or, most famously, Sandworm. They, you could say, are the most active cyberwarfare hacker group in the world. This is a group that specializes in just inflicting maximum chaos globally. (O'Leary, 2022)

As shown in Table 5.5, GRU units used cyber in the 2016 U.S. Presidential Election to stir up trouble (Dan Black, 2023). GRU units are both virtual, operating remotely from Russia, and known to be on the ground (e.g., 2018 physical collection on biochemical agency in the Netherlands (Greenberg, 2023b)).

Table 5.5 GRU Cyber Operations Units.

GRU Unit	Description
26,165 – also called Fancy Bear, APT 28	APT 28 was responsible for breaching the Democratic National Committee in 2016
74,455 – Sandworm (Greenberg, How an Entire Nation Became Russia's Test Lab for Cyberwar, 2017)	Specializes in inflicting chaos globally

This cyber/tradecraft combination was honed through operations ongoing in the Ukraine for almost a decade at the time of this writing.

2017 MeDoc – NotPetya Malware Attack on Ukrainian Tax System   Along with the GRU attempting to take down the Ukrainian grid, they also tried to take down the Ukrainian tax system. For example, one of the first uses of Shadow Brokers' malware (Chapter 3) was the GRU targeting of the Ukrainian tax software MeDoc through the NotPetya worm. The NotPetya malware/worm was used to deny not only Ukrainian tax services but also spread uncontrollably, leading to a shutdown in global shipping that resulted in an estimated $10 billion in damages worldwide (Greenberg, 2017).

2016 U.S. Presidential Election   Along with the Ukrainian grid and tax operations, the GRU also tried their hand at election interference. The 2016 U.S. presidential election saw heavy use of social media, especially Facebook, as a means to develop stories, with manufactured personas of "real people" posting news on both ends of the political spectrum (Mazetti, 2018) (Parham, 2017). In fact, the 2016 U.S. presidential election includes several manipulation examples (e.g., 10 million tweets, over a hundred rallies in the United States – dozens of the rallies turning violent), and it remains a challenge to determine what to do about it (Harris, 2018). It is also unclear whether the "trolls" (Andrei Soldatov, 2015) had a focused outcome, or just wanted to add uncertainty to the U.S. election process (Ben Collins, 2018).

The issue-based trolls that participated in the 2016 U.S. presidential election worked for the Internet Research Agency (IRA) with funding ultimately coming from a Russian intelligence service (the GRU) (Mueller, 2019). Trolls are paid antagonists, using social media to stir up issues that strike a nerve with the targeted demographic. This was targeted propaganda generated by a corporate source (i.e., the IRA).

Ukrainian Cyberattacks   Ukraine, in an actual shooting war with Russia in its eastern provinces at the time of this writing, has sustained multiple cyberattacks from Russia. This includes attacks on its electrical power system, with one attack leaving people without power for 96 hours in the middle of winter –

> On December 23, 2015, Ukrainian power companies experienced unscheduled power outages impacting a large number of customers (i.e., an estimated 225,000) in Ukraine. In addition, there have also been reports of malware found in Ukrainian companies in a variety of critical infrastructure sectors. Public reports indicate that the BlackEnergy (BE) malware was

discovered on the companies' computer networks, however it is important to note that the role of BE in this event remains unknown pending further technical analysis. (DHS CISA, 2021)

As shown in the writeup by DHS CISA, the electrical utility targeting was diagnosed by the tools used to prosecute the attack (Greenberg, 2019). This attack included intruders virtually grabbing the computer mouse and using it to take step-by-step actions to disable Ukrainian power systems (Zetter, 2023). The tool used to access Ukrainian systems in 2015, Industroyer, is reportedly much more advanced in its current upgrade to Industroyer 2.0 (Zafra and Leong, 2022), which was developed in preparation for the continued attacks on the Ukraine leading up to the 2022 invasion.

5.1.3   2022 Ukraine Invasion

One view of the 2022 Ukraine invasion by Russian forces is a resort to kinetic weapons after a multiyear campaign of using cyber that did not accomplish the goal of making the Ukrainian people lose faith in their government. For example, Andy Greenberg observed –

> The goal of these cyberattacks shifts over time based on what Russia needs to accomplish, what their tactical aims of the moment are. In 2014, 2015, 2016, and 2017, Russia had sort of sparked a war in the east of Ukraine, but that was a limited war, kind of a frozen conflict as people say, designed to weaken Ukraine but not to reach the capital. These cyberattacks were a way to send a message to the rest of Ukraine that you too are vulnerable. Even though you're hundreds of miles away from the fronts, *we can reach you, too*. You're all subject to our sphere of influence. (O'Leary, 2022)

Leading up to the 2022 invasion, Russia used Ukraine as a cyber operations test bed for over a decade (Greenberg, 2017). This included election influence to counter the 2004 Orange Revolution, critical infrastructure attacks starting in 2014, and finally mixed cyber/military operations in the 2022 invasion and continuing war. However, even though the Russian campaign against Ukraine continued, a resort to kinetic weapons was still required to attempt to minimize the Ukrainian government's authority.

Cyber Aspects of Russia's Ukraine Invasion

Russia's invasion of Ukraine included both kinetic (conventional munitions) and wiper (cyber) attacks on key government information technologies. Ukraine adeptly disbursed its government systems into the public cloud, distributing the targeted Ukrainian IT systems among several noncombatant countries, thereby challenging Russian efforts to effectively deny these government services to Ukrainian citizens.

Microsoft also notes that Russia's cyber actions have focused on point, versus area, targets. For example, in the past, Russia used "wormable" weapons that were prone to cross borders and cause indiscriminate damage (e.g., NotPetya). In Ukraine invasion, weapons have been focused on Ukraine-specific domains in an attempt to confine the damage.

In Ukraine, Russia has been observed coordinating attacks and using cyber to disable targets before striking them kinetically (Figure 5.4).

In addition to the coordinated cyber-kinetic attacks shown in Figure 5.4, Russia also attacked 10,000 Viasat modems, designed to eliminate satellite communications, in conjunction with a cruise missile attack on Ukraine's main TV tower, during the February 24, 2022, invasion (Szondy, 2022). This attack on Viasat modems was likely the most effective attack by cyber means that Russia prosecuted in the war at the time of this writing (O'Neill, 2022).

5.1.4 Russian Cyber Operations Wrap-up

As shown in Figure 5.4, Russia performed multiple cyber-kinetic operations over the course of the war. Current estimates, however, are that the effectiveness of Russian cyber operations has been limited (Szondy, 2022). One hypothesis as to why Russian cyber effects in Ukraine have been limited may be due to Russia keeping its best tools in reserve.

While power grids are the feared targets due to their potential to "turn off the lights," they are also strategic targets and by the Schmitt Criteria (M. N. Schmitt 2013) might result in a traditional, kinetic, response, similar to what the Hamas and ISIS cyber operators experienced in Chapters 1 and 2.

The key takeaways from this quick look at Russian cyber operations include –

1) The Russian Federation is a success in transitioning legacy KGB espionage and active measures to cyberspace. Cyber provides the stealth and non-attribution that helps Russia stay "below the radar" and exercise policy without the physical commitment that Ukraine is showing to be expensive in terms of physical and political capital.
2) Supply chain attacks provide disproportionate returns. Both Operation Dragonfly and SolarWinds provided unprecedented access to strategic targets.

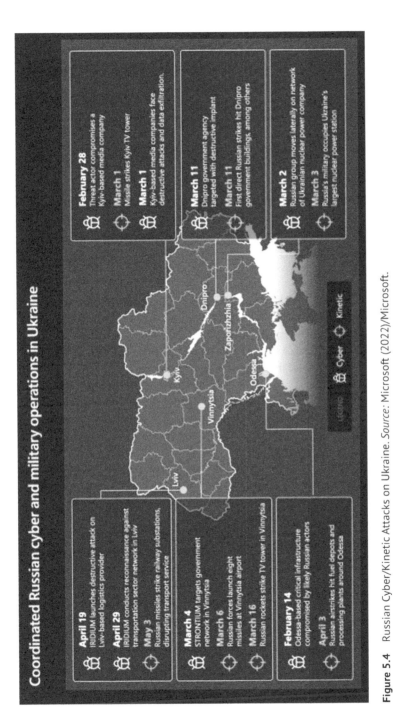

Figure 5.4 Russian Cyber/Kinetic Attacks on Ukraine. *Source:* Microsoft (2022)/Microsoft.

Bibliography

Agursky, M. (1989). *Soviet Disinformation and Forgeries*. Retrieved from JSTOR: https://www.jstor.org/stable/20751319.

Andrei Soldatov, I. B. (2012). *The Kremlin's New Internet Surveillance Plan Goes Live Today*. Retrieved from Wired: https://www.wired.com/2012/11/russia-surveillance/.

Andrei Soldatov, I.B. (2015). *The Red Web – The Struggle between Russia's Digital Dictators and the New Online Revolutionaries*. New York, NY, USA: Public Affairs.

Ben Collins, G. R. (2018). *Leaked: Secret Documents From Russia's Election Trolls*. Retrieved 9 9, 2018, from Daily Beast: https://www.thedailybeast.com/exclusive-secret-documents-from-russias-election-trolls-leak?ref=scroll.

Berwick, A., Kowsmann, P. (2023). *Binance is Helping Russians Move Money Abroad, Potentially Adding to Its Sprawling Legal Problems in the U.S.* Retrieved from Wall Street Journal.

Bienstock, D. (2022). *You Can't Audit Me: APT29 Continues Targeting Microsoft 365*. Retrieved 11 10, 2022, from Mandiant: https://www.mandiant.com/resources/blog/apt29-continues-targeting-microsoft.

Burgess, M. (2022). *Leaked Ransomware Docs Show Conti Helping Putin From the Shadows*. Retrieved from Wired: https://www.wired.com/story/conti-ransomware-russia/.

Caitlin Ostroff, V. S. (2022). *Russian Bitcoin and Other Cryptocurrencies Could Be Part of Future Sanctions*. Retrieved 1 31, 2023, from Wall Street Journal: https://www.wsj.com/articles/russian-bitcoin-and-other-cryptocurrencies-could-be-part-of-future-sanctions-11645902740.

Cimpanu, C. (2017). *21 Years Later, Experts Connect the Dots on One of the First Cyber-Espionage Groups*. Retrieved from Bleeping Computer: https://www.bleepingcomputer.com/news/security/21-years-later-experts-connect-the-dots-on-one-of-the-first-cyber-espionage-groups/.

CISA. (2022). *Russian State-Sponsored and Criminal Cyber Threats to Critical Infrastructure*. Retrieved 4 11, 2023, from CISA: https://www.cisa.gov/news-events/cybersecurity-advisories/aa22-110a.

Coll, S. (2013). *Private Empire – ExxonMobil and American Power*. New York: Penguin.

Cunningham, C. (2020). *A Russian Federation Information Warfare Primer*. Retrieved 1 1, 2023, from University of Washington: https://jsis.washington.edu/news/a-russian-federation-information-warfare-primer/.

Dan Black, G. R. (2023). *The GRU's Disruptive Playbook*. Retrieved from Mandiant: https://www.mandiant.com/resources/blog/gru-disruptive-playbook.

David Maynor, M. O. (2017). *The MeDoc Connection*. Retrieved from Cisco Talos: https://blog.talosintelligence.com/the-medoc-connection/#:~:text=M.E.Doc%20 is%20a%20widely,interact%20with%20Ukrainian%20tax%20systems.

DHS CISA. (2021). *Russian Foreign Intelligence Service (SVR) Cyber Operations: Trends and Best Practices for Network Defenders*. Retrieved 9 15, 2022, from Alert (AA21-116A): https://www.cisa.gov/uscert/ncas/alerts/aa21-116a.

DoJ. (2022). *Four Russian Government Employees Charged in Two Historical Hacking Campaigns Targeting Critical Infrastructure Worldwide*. Retrieved from U.S. Department of Justice: https://www.justice.gov/opa/pr/four-russian-government-employees-charged-two-historical-hacking-campaigns-targeting-critical.

DoJ. (2023). *U.S. Citizens and Russian Intelligence Officers Charged with Conspiring to Use U.S. Citizens as Illegal Agents of the Russian Government*. Retrieved 4 19, 2023, from DoJ: https://www.justice.gov/opa/pr/us-citizens-and-russian-intelligence-officers-charged-conspiring-use-us-citizens-illegal.

FAS. (2000). *FSB History*. Retrieved from Federation of American Scientists: https:// irp.fas.org/world/russia/fsb/history.htm.

GAO. (2021). *SolarWinds Cyberattack Demands Significant Federal and Private-Sector Response (infographic)*. Retrieved from GAO: https://www.gao.gov/blog/ solarwinds-cyberattack-demands-significant-federal-and-private-sector-response-infographic.

Greenberg, A. (2017). *How an Entire Nation Became Russia's Test Lab for Cyberwar*. Retrieved 1 27, 2023, from Wired: heeps://www.wired.com/story/russian-hackers-attack-ukraine/.

Greenberg, A. (2019). *Sandworm – A New Era of Cyberwar and the Hunt for the Kremlin's Most Dangerous Hackers*. NY, NY: Doubleday.

Greenberg, A. (2023a). *The Underground History of Russia's Most Ingenious Hacker Group*. Retrieved 6 2023, from Wired: https://www.wired.com/story/turla-history-russia-fsb-hackers/.

Greenberg, A. (2023b). *This Is the New Leader of Russia's Infamous Sandworm Hacking Unit*. Retrieved 4 14, 2023, from Wired Magazine: https://www.wired. com/story/russia-gru-sandworm-serebriakov/

Harris, G. (2018). *State Dept. Was Granted $120 Million to Fight Russian Meddling. It Has Spent $0. Image*. Retrieved 9 9, 2018, from New York Times: https://www. nytimes.com/2018/03/04/world/europe/state-department-russia-global-engagement-center.html.

Heli Tiirmaa-Klaar, J.G.-P. (2014). *Botnets*. New York: Springer.

Hodgson, Q. E., Shokh, Y. (2022). *Many Hands in the Cookie Jar – Case Studies in Response Options to Cyber Incidents Affecting U.S. Government Networks and Implications for Future Response*. Retrieved from RAND: https://www.rand.org/ content/dam/rand/pubs/research_reports/RRA1100/RRA1190-1/RAND_ RRA1190-1.pdf.

Janofsky, A. (2021). *Former NSA and Cyber Command Chief Keith Alexander on SolarWinds, Cyberwar, and China.* (R. Futures, Producer) Retrieved 9 14, 2022, from TheRecord: https://therecord.media/former-nsa-and-cyber-command-chief-keith-alexander-on-solarwinds-cyberwar-and-china/.

Joseph Farah, G. E. (Producer), Ion Pacepa, D. K. (Writer), & Moore, S. (Director). (2017). *Disinformation – The Secret Strategy to Destroy the West* [Motion Picture]. WND Films. Retrieved 2 7, 2019, from YouTube: https://www.youtube.com/watch?v=LF9-xdj_8oQ&t=692s.

Keatinge, T. (2023). *Developing Bad Habits What Russia Might Learn from Iran's Sanctions Evasion.* Retrieved from RUSI.

Kott, A. (2020). *Karabakh War of 2020: S&T Implications.* Retrieved from Dupuy Institute: http://www.dupuyinstitute.org/blog/wp-content/uploads/2023/02/Kott-HAAC-Karabakh-War.pdf.

Kramer, A. E. (2019). *Russian General Pitches 'Information' Operations as a Form of War.* Retrieved 4 14, 2023, from New York Times: https://www.nytimes.com/2019/03/02/world/europe/russia-hybrid-war-gerasimov.html.

Mark Kramer, D. S. (n.d.). *Lessons From Operation "Denver," the KGB's Massive AIDS Disinformation Campaign.* Retrieved 9 21, 2022, from The MIT Press Reader: https://thereader.mitpress.mit.edu/operation-denver-kgb-aids-disinformation-campaign/.

Mazetti, M. (2018). 12 Russian Agents Indicted in Mueller Investigation.

Microsoft. (2022). *Defending Ukraine: Early Lessons from the Cyber War.* Retrieved 8 30, 2022, from Microsoft: https://query.prod.cms.rt.microsoft.com/cms/api/am/binary/RE50KOK.

Mueller, R. (2019). *Report On The Investigation Into Russian Interference In The 2016 Presidential Election.* U.S. Department of Justice. Washington: U.S. Department of Justice.

Muncaster, P. (2017). *Shadow Brokers Attack Tools Light Up Chinese and Russian Darknet.* Retrieved 5 2, 2023, from Info Security: https://www.infosecurity-magazine.com/news/shadow-brokers-attack-tools-china/.

Murphy, A. (2022). *SVR Russia: Inside the Secret Intelligence Agency once Known as the Infamous KGB.* Retrieved from Independent: https://www.independent.co.uk/news/world/europe/svr-russia-meaning-putin-agency-b2252416.html.

Nakashima, E. (2017). *Court Document Points to Kaspersky Lab's Cooperation with Russian Security Service.* Retrieved 5 5, 2023, from Washington Post: https://www.washingtonpost.com/world/national-security/court-document-points-to-kaspersky-labs-cooperation-with-russian-security-service/2017/12/13/14ba9450-df42-11e7-bbd0-9dfb2e37492a_story.html.

NATO. (2007). *2007 Cyber Attacks on Estonia.* Retrieved 5 11, 2023, from STRATCOMCOE: https://stratcomcoe.org/cuploads/pfiles/cyber_attacks_estonia.pdf.

Nicole NG, Rumer, E. (2019). *The West Fears Russia's Hybrid Warfare. They're Missing the Bigger Picture*. Retrieved 9 21, 2022, from Carnegie Endowment for International Peace: https://carnegieendowment.org/2019/07/03/west-fears-russia-s-hybrid-warfare.-they-re-missing-bigger-picture-pub-79412.

Office of the Director of National Intelligence (ODNI). (2023). *Annual Threat Assessment of the U.S. Intelligence Community*. Retrieved 3 9, 2023, from ODNI.

O'Leary, L. (2022). *Russia's Invisible War on Ukraine*. Retrieved from Slate: https://slate.com/technology/2022/02/ukraine-russia-cyberwar-sandworm-gru.html.

O'Neill, P. H. (2022). *Russia Hacked an American Satellite Company One Hour Before the Ukraine Invasion*. Retrieved from MIT Technology Review: https://www.technologyreview.com/2022/05/10/1051973/russia-hack-viasat-satellite-ukraine-invasion/.

Ottis, R. (2008). *Analysis of the 2007 Cyber Attacks Against Estonia from the Information Warfare Perspective*. Retrieved from CCDCOE: https://www.ccdcoe.org/uploads/2018/10/Ottis2008_AnalysisOf2007FromTheInformationWarfarePerspective.pdf.

Pacepa, I.M. and Rychlak, R.J. (2013). *Disinformation – Former Spy Chief Reveals Secret Strategies for Undermining Freedom, Attacking Religion and Promoting Terrorism*. Washington, DC: WND.

Parham, J. (2017). *Russians Posing as Black Activists on Facebook is More Than Fake News*. Retrieved 8 22, 2018, from Wired: https://www.wired.com/story/russian-black-activist-facebook-accounts/.

Perlroth, N. (2020). *This is How they Tell me the World Ends*. New York: Bloomsbury.

Perlroth, N. (2021). *Colonial Pipeline paid 75 Bitcoin, or Roughly $5 Million, to Hackers*. Retrieved 9 26, 2022, from New York Times: https://www.nytimes.com/2021/05/13/technology/colonial-pipeline-ransom.html.

Renee Dudley, D.G. (2022). *The Ransomware Hunting Team – A Band of Misfits' Improbable Crusade to save the World from Cybercrime*. New York: Farrar, Straus and Giroux.

Sayegh, E. (2023). *Turla Hacking Group: A Persistent International Threat*. Retrieved from Forbes: https://www.forbes.com/sites/emilsayegh/2023/03/07/turla-hacking-group-a-persistent-international-threat/?sh=33dc4ec07498.

Securities and Exchange Commission (SEC). (2020). *SolarWinds Corporation FORM 8-K*. 8-K, Securities and Exchange Commission (SEC).

Sherman, J. (2022). *Untangling the Russian web: Spies, Proxies, and Spectrums of Russian Cyber Behavior*. Retrieved 9 21, 2022, from Atlantic Council: https://www.atlanticcouncil.org/in-depth-research-reports/issue-brief/untangling-the-russian-web/.

Stoll, C. (2005). *The Cuckoo's Egg: Tracking a Spy Through the Maze of Computer Espionage*. Pocket Books.

Szondy, D. (2022). *Why Russia's Cyber War in Ukraine hasn't Played Out as Predicted*. Retrieved 9 7, 2022, from New Atlas: https://newatlas.com/military/russia-cyber-war-ukraine/.

Temple-Raston, D. (2021). *A 'Worst Nightmare' Cyberattack: The Untold Story Of The SolarWinds Hack*. Retrieved from NPR: https://www.npr.org/2021/04/16/985439655/a-worst-nightmare-cyberattack-the-untold-story-of-the-solarwinds-hack.

Thomas, T. (2020). *THE Chekinov-Bogdanov Commentaries of 2010-2017: What did they Teach Us About Russia's New Way of War?* Retrieved 4 4, 2023, from MITRE: https://apps.dtic.mil/sti/citations/AD1141587.

U.S. Department of Justice. (2020). *United States of America vs Yuriy Sergeyevich Andrienko, Sergey Vladimirovich Detistov, Pavel Valeryevichfrolov, Anatoliy Sergeyevich Kovalev, Artem Valeryevich Ochichenko, and Petr Nikola Yevich Pliskin*. (U. S. PENNSYLVANIA, Producer) Retrieved 9 21, 2022, from https://www.justice.gov/opa/press-release/file/1328521/download.

U.S. Treasury. (2019). *Treasury Sanctions Evil Corp, the Russia-Based Cybercriminal Group Behind Dridex Malware*. Retrieved from U.S. Department of the Treasury: https://home.treasury.gov/news/press-releases/sm845.

U.S. Treasury. (2020). *Treasury Sanctions Russian Government Research Institution Connected to the Triton Malware*. Retrieved 9 21, 2022, from U.S. DEPARTMENT OF THE TREASURY: https://home.treasury.gov/news/press-releases/sm1162.

Uberti, D. (2022). *Line Between Criminal Hackers and Nation-State Threats Blurs, U.S. Officials Say; Ransomware Groups and Foreign Intelligence Services Increasingly Overlap to Rake in Money and Cover their Tracks, Complicating U.S. Efforts to Stop them*. Retrieved from Wall Street Journal.

Warner, M. (2017). Intelligence in Cyber – and Cyber in Intelligence. In: *Understanding Cyber Conflict – 14 Analogies* (ed. A.E.G. Perkovich), 265–272. Washington DC: Georgetown University Press.

Zafra, D. K., Leong, R. (2022). *INDUSTROYER.V2: Old Malware Learns New Tricks*. Retrieved from Mandiant: https://www.mandiant.com/resources/blog/industroyer-v2-old-malware-new-tricks.

Zetter, K. (2023). *The Untold Story of the Boldest Supply-Chain Hack Ever*. Retrieved 5 17, 2023, from Wired: https://www.wired.com/story/the-untold-story-of-solarwinds-the-boldest-supply-chain-hack-ever/?utm_source=substack&utm_medium=email

6

Chinese Cyber Operations

6.1 Chinese Cyber Operations

> China probably currently represents the broadest, most active, and persistent cyber espionage threat to U.S. Government and private-sector networks. China's cyber pursuits and its industry's export of related technologies increase the threats of aggressive cyber operations against the U.S. homeland, suppression of the free flow of information in cyberspace – such as U.S. web content – that Beijing views as threatening to the CCP's hold on power, and the expansion of technology-driven authoritarianism globally. (Office of the Director of National Intelligence (ODNI), 2023)

Similar to Russia, Chinese clandestine services have used cyber as a means of spying since the beginning of networked computers. For example, Operation Tiger Trap (Wise, 2011) and Operation Parlor Maid (Campbell, 2003) included Chinese intelligence penetrations at U.S. National Laboratories and the FBI, respectively. In addition, cyber was used as a means to complement these essentially human intelligence operations (Trulock, 2004).

Chinese cyberspace operations began with patriotic hacktivists during the late 1990s, performing online protests of the persecution of ethnic Chinese during riots in Indonesia (1998) (Henderson, 2007). This was followed a few years later by hacktivist operations that included defacing a U.S. White House web page in order to protest a Chinese fighter aircraft's crashing, after it ran into a U.S. surveillance airplane in the South China Sea (2001) (Elisabeth Rosenthal, 2001). Chinese cyber capabilities then grew quickly in the early 2000s.

Cyber Operations: A Case Study Approach, First Edition. Jerry M. Couretas.
© 2024 John Wiley & Sons, Inc. Published 2024 by John Wiley & Sons, Inc.

Chinese cyber power grew from patriotic hacktivists to a nation-state cyber operator capable of strategic-level espionage during the first decade of the 21st century. These strategic intelligence collections, including fifth-generation aircraft technology, were clear examples of cyber operations' effectiveness – examples that were not lost on Chinese leadership.

During the second decade of the 21st century, China successfully performed record collection on U.S. defense and intelligence personnel. This included downloading records on over 20 million people, many with a security clearance, from the Office of Personnel Management (OPM) in 2014 (KOERNER). Subsequently, China collected health records on approximately 80 million U.S. civilians by a breach of Anthem Insurance (2014) (Vaas, 2019) and credit records on 147 million people through the Equifax breach (2017) (Newman, 2017), potentially providing a cleared U.S. personnel database complete with medical records and credit ratings.

The development of China's cyber operations' capability coincides with the development of the Internet, and China's industrial growth. Similar to the rise of the United States and Germany, near the turn of the 20th century, due to the development of locomotive technology and the global lay down of railways, China's economic growth, 100 years later, seems to be a beneficiary of the Internet. Booz Allen Hamilton (BAH) provides an example timeline of China's cyber capability development that parallels the development of the Internet in Figure 6.1.

As shown in Figure 6.1, China's cyber operations' development started in the mid-1990s, at the same time that China was digesting strategic and tactical lessons observed from Operation Desert Storm (1991).

6.1.1 Chinese Cyber Doctrine Development

Chinese information warfare (IW) theorists started publishing their own version of net-centric warfare following Operation Desert Storm (1991). Chinese theorists foretold victory on this information battlefield to be different, resulting in a shift in the focus of operations. In the words of two People's Liberation Army (PLA) authors

> ... the key to gaining the upper hand on the battlefield is no longer mainly dependent on who has the stronger firepower, but instead depends on which side discovers the enemy first (observe – orient), responds faster than the latter (decide), and strikes more precisely than the latter (act). (The two sides) vie for the advantage in intelligence and command and control, i.e. to see which side holds a larger amount of and more accurate information and is faster in transmitting and processing the information.

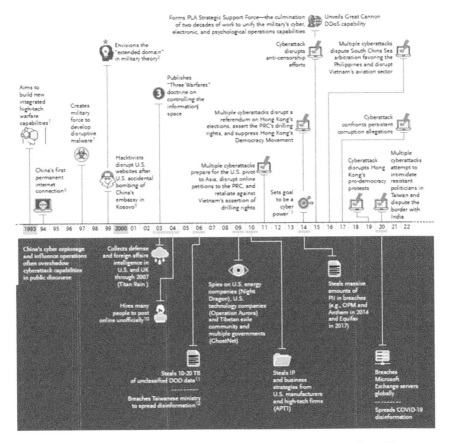

Figure 6.1 China's Timeline of Cyber Capabilities Development. *Source:* Booz Allen Hamilton (2022)/Booz Allen.

On the other hand, they have to vie for advantage in the precision of the strike, i.e., to see which side can hit the other at a longer distance and hit the other side first at the same distance. (Mulvenon, 1999)

The Chinese IW strategists seem to have adapted the classical Observe–Orient–Decide–Act (OODA) loop (Boyd) with a more modern "big data" element in the "orient" phase. Reducing information warfare to a big data search problem may have been the impetus for the espionage focus in the first decade of the 21st century, and the continuing collection on U.S. people, processes, and technologies during the second decade of the 21st century.

The turn of the century was dominated by an almost giddy conception that information dominance could trade for traditional military innovation. "Net Centric Warfare" (Schachtman, 2007) was a movement that seemed to extend Metcalf's law (Metcalfe, 2013) on the geometric returns of connectivity to possible military engagement efficiencies. The first two decades of the 21st century might also be looked at as a "big data" era (Gilder, 2018).

One version of Chinese lessons learned from Operation Desert Storm (1991) was released in the 1999 book "Unrestricted Warfare" (Qiao Liang, 2020), which lays out a whole-of-government approach for shaping the battlefield for success long before any military conflict (Spalding, 2022). "Unrestricted Warfare" does not propose any new warfighting technologies. Instead, it supports tactically side-stepping international law in order to accomplish strategic objectives.

Indeed, many writings suggest that IW will permit China to fight and win an information campaign, possibly precluding the need for military action. When this train of thought is combined with the notions of "overcoming the superior with the inferior," one can quickly see the argument's logical conclusion: IW as a preemption weapon (Linzhi, 1996). According to Lu Linzhi,

> In military affairs, launching a preemptive strike has always been an effective way in which the party at a disadvantage may overpower its stronger opponent ... For the weaker party, waiting for the enemy to deliver the first blow will have disastrous consequences and may even put it in a passive situation from which it will never be able to get out ...

As a concrete example, Lu Linzhi points to Operation Desert Storm (1991), where Iraq's failure to launch a preemptive attack resulted in defeat. The belief is that if the Iraqis had launched an attack on Coalition forces as they were being deployed to Saudi Arabia in the six months leading up to Operation Desert Storm (1991), it is possible that the Iraqis would have achieved a better outcome in the conflict. Chinese strategists may have digested their Desert Storm lesson in terms of using a cyber campaign as a low-risk way to assault the United States, attacking key data systems, and perform a non-attributable, long-term "first strike." The early hacktivist successes may have inspired further development of a cyber capability.

6.1.2 2002–2012 Chinese Cyber Development Phase

China's initial cyber operations included hackers with patriotic fervor. These were independent cyber operators who talked about China's "lost century" (i.e., the period between the mid-19th century opium wars and Mao's communist takeover in 1949) (Henderson, 2007). Chinese patriotic hacktivists operated in the mid- to late 1990s and had a number of named groups (e.g., the Honker Union), famous for their debut as ethno-nationalist hacktivists during the anti-Chinese riots in Indonesia during the late 1990s.

Patriotic hacktivists have a brief overlap with the development of formal cyber operations, as shown in Figure 6.1. And, while it is unclear how formal Chinese cyber doctrine developed, Chinese cyber operations seem rooted in the theory developed from Operation Desert Storm (1991). Within the first decade of the 21st century, Chinese cyber collections included F-35 designs (Operation Byzantine Hades) and some of Google's source code (Operation Aurora).

China's early cyber efforts quickly converged to extracting key data from targets of interest. In addition, by the summer of 2008, Chinese hackers had successfully penetrated the computer network of Democratic presidential nominee Barack Obama, exfiltrating policy documents to understand the campaign's internal debates (Carlin, 2018). The Chinese also penetrated Republican challenger John McCain's campaign network, extracting documents that included a sympathetic letter to the President of Taiwan – which later resulted in a diplomatic complaint to the McCain campaign (Isikoff, 2013).

The first years of the 21st century were marked by an unexpected number of Chinese cyber operations. Patriotic hacktivists were quietly superseded by professional cyber operators in an intrusion set titled Operation Titan Rain.

6.1.2.1 2002–2007 Operation Titan Rain

Operation Titan Rain is the first documented attack by China as a nation-state and is believed to have lasted from 2002 to 2007.

> By 2003, China's interest in cyberespionage was apparent: A series of cyber intrusions that U.S. investigators code-named "Titan Rain" was traced back to computers in southern China. The hackers, believed by some to be from the Chinese army, had invaded and stolen sensitive data from computers belonging to the U.S. Department of Defense, defense contractors and other government agencies ... Titan Rain was followed by a rash of espionage incidents that originated in China and were given code names like "Byzantine Hades," "GhostNet" and "Aurora." The thieves were after a wide range of data. (Denning, 2017)

Operation Titan Rain (2002–2007) included Chinese cyber-based intelligence collection against U.S. and United Kingdom diplomatic and military agency targets. This included technical collection on the U.S. F-35 military aircraft that was still in development, including exfiltrations from Australia, a key U.S. ally

Figure 6.2 China's J-31 Versus U.S. F-35. *Source:* NextBigFuture / https://www.
nextbigfuture.com/2015/01/confirmation-that-china-stole-f35-f22.html/ Last Accessed
November 08, 2023.

on the program (Security Week, 2017). In fact, the Chinese J-31 fighter, demonstrated to fly in 2012, has some uncanny flight surface similarities to the F-35 (Weisberger, 2015) (Figure 6.2).

The capture of design diagrams from the U.S. F-35 occurred pretty early in the use of cyber for China's cyber operators, so this prize was likely as much a shock to China as it was to the unwary defense contractors who lost their drawings. This sounds similar to Russia's unexpected bonanza with Operation Solar Winds (Section 5.2.2.1), where the goal was approximately 200 accesses and the supply chain attack resulted in an estimated 30,000.

China transformed into a nation-state cyber actor during the course of Operation Titan Rain. With cyber operations a proven success for collecting advanced aerospace designs, Chinese cyber planners then turned their attention to technical infrastructure. The massive amounts of data being collected likely led the cyber operators to target Google with Operation Aurora.

6.1.2.2 2009 Operation Aurora

Along with the collection of F-35 designs and the development of the J-31 program, Chinese cyber operators also penetrated Google and downloaded source code

(2009 Operation Aurora). Operation Aurora included Chinese cyber operators penetrating the networks of Google, Yahoo, Dow Chemical, JP Morgan, and others with the goal of stealing their trade secrets. Operation Aurora also led Google to cease its operations in China.

With the extraction of development code from Google and aerospace designs from the F-35, China had a proven cyber capability by 2011. And it was around this time that the United States announced a "pivot to Asia." Chinese cyber operators had already started Operation Night Dragon, a surveillance campaign on U.S. gas pipelines.

6.1.2.3 2007–2013 Operation Night Dragon – U.S. Gas Pipeline Intrusion Campaign

Starting around 2007, China began Operation Night Dragon, a probing of U.S. natural gas pipelines and their supporting companies, which was thought to be a possible preparation for a critical infrastructure attack against the United States.

During the gas pipeline intrusion campaign, Chinese operators attempted to exploit, sometimes successfully, the people, processes, and technologies of the targeted companies. For example, Operation Night Dragon employed spear phishing in order to compromise personnel at select natural gas pipeline operations. This activity appears to have started in late December 2011. From December 9, 2011, through at least February 29, 2012, oil and natural gas organizations received spear-phishing emails specifically targeting their employees. The emails were constructed with a high level of sophistication to convince employees to view malicious files. Chinese cyber operators were able to penetrate natural gas pipeline systems and probe internal networks and their connected control systems. For example,

> Based on incident data, CISA and FBI assessed that Chinese state-sponsored actors also compromised various authorized remote access channels, including systems designed to transfer data and/or allow access between corporate and ICS networks. Though designed for legitimate business purposes, these systems have the potential to be manipulated by malicious cyber actors if unmitigated. With this access, the Chinese state-sponsored actors could have impersonated legitimate system operators to conduct unauthorized operations. According to the evidence obtained by CISA and FBI, the Chinese state-sponsored actors made no attempts to modify the pipeline operations of systems they accessed. (CISA, 2021)

Along with Operation Night Dragon, the PRC more recently performed surveillance of U.S. and international communications infrastructure, believed to be preparing for an attack that eliminates transpacific communications in the event of a war over Taiwan (e.g., Operation Volt Typhoon) (Cavanaugh, 2023).

6.1.3 2012 to Present – Cyber Professionalization

Looking at the original diagram of Chinese cyber operations as evolving from simple retribution to espionage, the maiden flight of the J-31 in 2012 was likely a milestone for Chinese cyber espionage operations. Then, in 2013, Xi Jinping took power. With a proven cyber espionage capability and a goal of having a more muscular foreign policy, China used cyber operations to accelerate data collection and information operations.

6.1.3.1 Hacking/Cracking Training in China

Training cyber operators spans from "cracking academies" to cyber ironman competitions. For example, the Wuhan Kerui Cracking Academy provides focused training and networking opportunities for disciples who show exceptional promise.

Wuhan Kerui Cracking Academy Wuhan, famous for riverboat cruising along the Chongqing river and COVID, is also famous for (reverse) cyber training. Qian Linsong, an associate professor at the National Cyber Security College of Wuhan University also founded the Wuhan Kerui Cracking Academy.

Many of the professor's students are believed to find employment with the Chinese security services, as some of the testimonials on his site are marked "Keep Confidential" and "Mystery Unit." (Intrusiontruth, 2023)

The mass rollout of cyber operations provides demand for talented cyber operators throughout the government and underground network of Chinese hacking teams. With increasingly sophisticated defenses, however, there is a need to find top talent among China's best cyber operators, a cyber ironman.

6.1.3.2 Information Security Ironman

This expansion of cyber operations included a search for talent. For example, the "Information Security Ironman Competition," introduced in 2016, helped screen cyber talent and provide extensive training once a candidate was identified (Cary, 2022). One of the key winners of these early competitions is Tan Dailin, whose exploits are sometimes synonymous with APT 41 (RUFUS BROWN, 2023) (Figure 6.3).

Figure 6.3 Tan Dailin (APT 41). *Source:* FBI (n.d.)/Federal Bureau of Investigation.

Some of the training that goes into training future operators like Mr. Tan include Chinese cyber confrontation skills and development, which are summarized in the "4 + 3 Method." The "4" key competencies taught in this method for cybersecurity professionals include

- Actual confrontation
- Software vulnerability discovery
- "combat impact assessment" (believed to be some kind of security evaluation)
- engineering and development skills

The "3" represents the methods for demonstrating each of the four capabilities:

- Cybersecurity competitions (confrontation, defensive exercises, and vulnerability discovery)
- "confrontation practices" (cyber range practice and actual network confrontation)
- "crowd testing and incident response" (open security testing, software vulnerability awards, security competitions, and technology sharing

This extensive cyber operations' training started to bear fruit almost immediately. By the mid-2010s,

> Beijing's spies were ransacking Americans' data at an almost Olympian scale. In addition to masterminding the OPM breach, hackers linked to Chinese intelligence would filch private information from over 383 million individuals, including passport and credit card data, in a massive 2014 compromise of the hotel giant Marriott; pilfer personal information from over 78 million Americans in a 2014 breach of Anthem, the major health insurance provider; breach the networks of American Airlines, United Airlines, and Sabre, a top travel reservation provider (and key target for China's travel intelligence program); and burrow into computer systems belonging to the U.S. Department of the Navy, stealing sensitive data linked to over 100,000 naval personnel, among other penetrations of the U.S. private and public sectors. The Chinese "were always a Hoover, sucking up mountains of data beyond anything else in the world," recalled a former senior National Security Agency official. (Dorfman, 2020)

Chinese cyber operations include extensive exfiltration of U.S. personnel data from the 2014 OPM, 2014 Anthem Insurance, and 2017 Equifax credit rating service exploitations.

6.1.3.3 Cyber Collections on U.S. Personnel

The Xi Jinping administration came to power in 2013 with a clear understanding of the power of cyber intelligence and the need for operator development. Therefore, by 2014, China had expanded its collection efforts and was implicated in the U.S. Office of Personnel Management (OPM) breach, which was believed to include over 20 million personnel files for U.S. Government employees and contractors. In addition, a large medical record heist from Anthem Insurance took place in 2014. Having both the OPM and Anthem records provided the possibility of China now cross-referencing U.S. classified personnel with their medical records. In 2017, an additional Equifax breach provided Chinese analysts with a look at the creditworthiness of this target population (Figure 6.4).

As shown in Figure 6.4, China collected key data on the personnel who make up the military/intelligence component of one of its key adversaries. And this was at the same time as the U.S. "pivot to Asia" (Figure 6.1).

6.1.3.4 Espionage and Five-Year Plans

Five-year plans are important for understanding China's cyber espionage efforts due to the likely influence that some commercial and military planning goals have on choosing cyber collection targets. For example, when analyzing APT 1, China's English language targeting team, Mandiant, found the following:

> We believe that organizations in all industries related to China's strategic priorities are potential targets of APT1's comprehensive cyber espionage campaign. While we have certainly seen the group target some industries

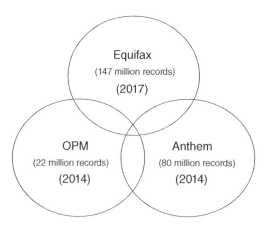

Figure 6.4 2010s Chinese Data Extractions – Identity, Health, and Credit Score of U.S. Classified Personnel.

more heavily than others, our observations confirm that APT1 has targeted at least four of the seven strategic emerging industries that China identified in its 12th Five Year Plan. (Mandiant, 2021)

China continues with the five-year plan construct and is currently on its 14th. Goals for the 14th five-year plan are outlined by eight key areas of vital economic interest for development and production that it views as essential to maintaining global competitiveness, under the following categories: energy, healthcare, railway transportation, telecommunications, national defense and stability, advanced manufacturing, network power, and sports and culture (Rogier Creemers, 2022).

6.1.3.5 Information Operations

China's cyber-based information operations include the 2017 campaign to disseminate the China Message, using Western Journalists, to cast China in a favorable light (Louisa Lim, 2018). Less positive use of information operations includes China's anti-Western messaging from Operation Dragonbridge (2022).

2022 Operation Dragonbridge The success of the Russian Internet Research Agency (IRA) in the use of IO leading up to the 2016 U.S. Presidential Election has China now experimenting with IO as a means to create dissent in the United States and to generally discredit the U.S. Government and businesses (Mandiant, 2022). This includes plagiarizing, altering, and mischaracterizing legitimate news reports in order to support their allegations.

Operation Dragonbridge includes both industrial (e.g., rare earth metals mining protest instigation) and anti-democracy messaging (e.g., discouraging Americans from voting in the 2022 midterm elections). China is using information operations in order to ease its interests forward (Daniel Kliman, 2020), resulting in four of its state media outlets being designated "state propaganda outlets" (Delaney, 2020).

Environmentalist Actions Against Non-Chinese Rare Earth Metal Mining Chinese IO campaigns are used to disparage non-Chinese rare earth metal mining companies in order to maintain their industrial hegemony in this critical market for batteries and other staple technologies for the electric car market. In one example, Operation Dragonbridge was used, as an IO campaign, to target Australian, Canadian, and U.S. rare earth mining companies with negative messaging designed for China's benefit. Companies, including Australia's Lynas Rare Earths Ltd., Canada's Appia Rare Earths and Uranium Corp., and an American company, USA Rare Earth, were targeted with environmental destruction narratives in order to support China's dominance of the rare earth metals market (Lakshmanan, 2022).

Discredit U.S. Election Process (2022 Midterms) Most Dragonbridge messaging in the 2020 U.S. midterms was to discourage people not to vote. Messaging ran along the lines of the ineffectiveness of the system, and how it needs to be removed. This advice was given without a replacement candidate for current government structures.

Mandiant's assessment is that Dragonbridge messaging is ineffective, largely due to poor execution. For example, Google reported disrupting over 50,000 instances of Dragonbridge activity during 2022. This includes deleting pro-China blog posts and over 100,000 Dragonbridge accounts over the known lifetime of the information operation.

6.1.3.6 2022 Booz Allen Hamilton (BAH) Cyber Analytic Framework for China

In describing the various threads of China's cyber operations, Booz Allen Hamilton (BAH) developed an analytic framework that structured China's cyber operations in terms of their key objectives, or "Core Interests." These Core Interests included security, sovereignty, and development. In addition, this analytic framework described the teams, spanning from the military, People's Liberation Army (PLA), to less well-known players such as the United Front Department (UFD) that included core interests, agencies/actors, and strategies/goals as shown in Figure 6.5.

Each of these objectives and cyber operations teams was then evaluated through the lens of 13 case studies. Evaluating China's behavior in terms of their core interests, and among the agencies/actors (Figure 6.5), BAH categorized the case

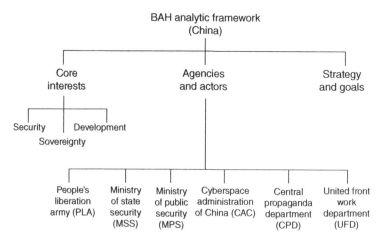

Figure 6.5 Booz Allen Hamilton China Analytic Framework. *Source:* Adapted from Booz Allen Hamilton (2022).

Table 6.1 BAH Themes and Supporting Case Studies.

Threats	Theme	Case Studies
Threats to domestic interests	Foreign information threats	4/2011 disrupting online petitions to the PRC
		3/2015 disrupting anti-censorship efforts
		2017–2018 confronting persistent corruption allegations
	Hong Kong democracy movement	6/2014 disrupting a referendum on Hong Kong's election
		Sep–Oct 2014 suppress Hong Kong's democracy movement
		2019–2020 disrupting Hong Kong's pro-democracy protests
Threats to foreign interests	Competing south China sea claims	2011 retaliating against Vietnam's assertion of drilling rights
		2014 asserting the PRC's drilling rights
		7/2016 disrupting south China sea arbitration favoring the Philippines
		7/2016 disrupting Vietnam's aviation sector
	Indo-Pacific Competition	2011–2013 preparing for the U.S. pivot to Asia
		5/2020 attempting to intimidate resistant politicians in Taiwan
		2020–2022 disputing the border with India

Source: Adapted from Booz Allen Hamilton (2022).

studies into threats, from a Chinese perspective (e.g., Domestic and Foreign), with specific themes for grouping the case studies, as shown in Table 6.1.

As shown in Table 6.1, the BAH study divided China's cyber operations into domestic and foreign threats, with supporting themes, backed by case studies, in order to provide a descriptive example for each of the threats.

6.1.4 Chinese Cyber Operations Wrap-up

The BAH framework provides a flexible structure to organize how cyber is used as a mechanism to provide denial effects in response to domestic and foreign threats. This framework is a great complement to the theft and exfiltration and operations that we covered in Section 6.1.2.

The current Chinese cyber capability, proven through both aggressive operations and clear results (e.g., J-31 fifth-generation fighter), directly descends from an aggressive group of hackers, guided by doctrine informed by Desert Storm (1991). And, while Chinese cyber actions are nation-state espionage, in any other context this would be theft. Theft is one way to describe Chinese cyber doctrine (Shakarian, 2013).

Bibliography

Bangladesh Defense News. (2017). *Chinese Official: J-31 Stealth Fighter Could 'Definitely Take Down' F-35 . . .* Retrieved 3 26, 2017, from Facebook: https://www.facebook.com/defensebdn/posts/-chinese-official-j-31-stealth-fighter-could-definitely-take-down-f-35-nationali/1007473432721914/

Booz Allen Hamilton. (2022). *Same Cloak, More Dagger: Decoding How the People's Republic of China Uses Cyberattacks.* Retrieved 11 8, 2022, from Booz Allen.

Campbell, D. (2003). *The Parlour Maid and Her Lovers Leave the FBI with a Chinese Puzzle.* Retrieved 3 1, 2023, from Guardian: https://www.theguardian.com/world/2003/apr/22/china.usa.

Carlin, J. P. (2018). *Dawn of the Code War – America's Battle Against Russia, China and the Rising Global Cyber Threat.* PublicAffairs.

Cary, D. (2022). *How Xi Jinping Leveled-up China's Hacking Teams.* Retrieved 11 24, 2022, from Cyberscoop: https://www.cyberscoop.com/china-hacking-talent-xi-jinping-education-policies/.

Cavanaugh, B. (2023). *China's Latest Cyberattack Is an Active Threat to Critical US Infrastructure.* Retrieved 5 2023, from Daily Signal: https://www.dailysignal.com/2023/05/26/chinas-latest-cyberattack-active-threat-critical-us-infrastructure/.

CISA. (2021). *Chinese Gas Pipeline Intrusion Campaign, 2011 to 2013.* Retrieved 11 10, 2022, from CISA: https://www.cisa.gov/uscert/ncas/alerts/aa21-201a.

Daniel Kliman, A. K.-T. (2020). *Dangerous Synergies – Countering Chinese and Russian Digital Influence Operations.* Retrieved 6 6, 2020, from Center for New American Security (CNAS): https://s3.amazonaws.com/files.cnas.org/documents/CNAS-Report-Dangerous-Synergies-May-2020-DoS-Proof.pdf?mtime=20200506164642.

Delaney, R. (2020). *US Designates 4 more Chinese Media Organisations as 'State Propaganda Outlets'.* Retrieved 6 23, 2020, from South China Morning Post: https://www.scmp.com/news/world/united-states-canada/article/3090161/us-designates-four-major-chinese-media-outlets?utm_source=dailybrief&utm_medium=email&utm_campaign=DailyBrief2020Jun23&utm_term=DailyNewsBrief.

Denning, D. (2017). *Cyberwar: How Chinese Hackers Became a Major Threat to The U.S.* Retrieved 6 26, 2020, from Newsweek: https://www.newsweek.com/chinese-hackers-cyberwar-us-cybersecurity-threat-678378.

Dorfman, Z. (2020). *Beijing Ransacked Data as U.S. Sources Went Dark in CHINA*. Retrieved 9 20, 2022, from Foreign Policy: https://foreignpolicy. com/2020/12/22/china-us-data-intelligence-cybersecurity-xi-jinping/.

Elisabeth Rosenthal, D. E. (2001). *U.S. Plane in China After it Collides with Chinese JET*. New York Times.

FBI. (n.d.). *Tan Dailin Wanted Poster*. Retrieved 11 28, 2022, from FBI: https://www. fbi.gov/wanted/cyber/tan-dailin/@@download.pdf.

Gilder, G. (2018). *Life After Google: The Fall of Big Data and the Rise of the Blockchain Economy*. Regnery Gateway.

Goldsmith, J. (2015). *Disconcerting U.S. Cyber Deterrence Troubles Continue*. Retrieved 12 9, 2022, from Lawfare: https://www.lawfareblog.com/disconcerting-us-cyber-deterrence-troubles-continue.

Henderson, S. (2007). *The Dark Visitor*. Scott Henderson.

Intrusiontruth. (2023). *What's Cracking at the Kerui Cracking Academy?* Retrieved 5 16, 2023, from Intrusiontruth: https://intrusiontruth.wordpress.com/2023/05/11/article-1-whats-cracking-at-the-kerui-cracking-academy/.

Isikoff, M. (2013). *Chinese Hacked Obama, McCain Campaigns, Took Internal Documents, Officials Say*.

Koerner, B. I. (2016). *Inside the Cyberattack That Shocked the US Government*. Retrieved September 7, 2018, from Wired: https://www.wired.com/2016/10/inside-cyberattack-shocked-us-government/.

Lakshmanan, R. (2022). *Pro-China Group Uses Dragonbridge Campaign to Target Rare Earth Mining Companies*. Retrieved 8 29, 2022, from The Hacker News: https://thehackernews.com/2022/07/pro-china-group-uses-dragonbridge.html.

Linzhi, L. (1996, 2 14). Preemptive Strikes Crucial in Limited High-Tech Wars. *Jiefangjun Bao*, p. 6.

Louisa Lim, J. B. (2018). *Inside China's Audacious Global Propaganda Campaign*. Retrieved 2 1, 2019, from The Guardian: https://www.theguardian.com/news/2018/dec/07/china-plan-for-global-media-dominance-propaganda-xi-jinping.

Mandiant. (2021). *APT 1 – Exposing One of China's Cyber Espionage Units*. Retrieved 11 11, 2022, from Mandiant: https://www.mandiant.com/sites/default/files/2021-09/mandiant-apt1-report.pdf.

Mandiant. (2022). *Pro-PRC DRAGONBRIDGE Influence Campaign Leverages New TTPs to Aggressively Target U.S. Interests, Including Midterm Elections*. Retrieved 12 6, 2022, from Mandiant: https://www.mandiant.com/resources/blog/prc-dragonbridge-influence-elections.

Metcalfe, B. (2013). Metcalfe's Law after 40 Years of Ethernet. *Computer 46* (12): 26–31. Retrieved from IEEE Computer.

Microsoft. (2022). *Microsoft Digital Defense Report 2022*. Retrieved 11 15, 2022, from Microsoft: https://query.prod.cms.rt.microsoft.com/cms/api/am/binary/RE5bUvv?culture=en-us&country=us.

Mulvenon, J. (1999). *THE PLA AND INFORMATION WARFARE. The People's Liberation Army in the Information Age.* Santa Monica: RAND Retrieved 11 14, 2022, from RAND.

Newman, L. H. 2017 *The Equifax Breach Exposes America's Identity Crisis.* Retrieved September 7, 2018, from Wired: https://www.wired.com/story/the-equifax-breach-exposes-americas-identity-crisis/.

Office of the Director of National Intelligence (ODNI). (2023). *Annual Threat Assessment of the U.S. Intelligence Community.* Retrieved 3 9, 2023, from ODNI.

Qiao Liang, W.X. (2020). *Unrestricted Warfare.* Albatross Books.

Rogier Creemers, H. D. (2022). *Translation: 14th Five-Year Plan for National Informatization – Dec. 2021.* Retrieved from DIGICHINA: https://digichina. stanford.edu/work/translation-14th-five-year-plan-for-national-informatization-dec-2021/#:~:text=The%20"14th%20Five%2DYear%20Plan"%20period%20is%20an%20important,of%20industry%20chains%2C%20promote%20the.

Rufus Brown, V. T. (2023). *Does This Look Infected? A Summary of APT41 Targeting U.S. State Governments.* Retrieved 8 9, 2023, from Mandiant: https://www. mandiant.com/resources/blog/apt41-us-state-governments?wpisrc=nl_cybersecurity202

Schachtman, N. (2007). *How Technology Almost Lost the War: In Iraq, the Critical Networks Are Social – Not Electronic.* Retrieved 5 13, 2023, from Wired: https://www.wired.com/2007/11/ff-futurewar/.

Security Week. (2017). *F-35 Stealth Fighter Data Stolen in Australia Defence Hack.* Retrieved from Security Week: https://www.securityweek.com/f-35-stealth-fighter-data-stolen-australia-defence-hack/.

Shakarian, P. (2013). *The Dragon and the Computer: Why Intellectual Property Theft is Compatible with Chinese Cyber-Warfare Doctrine.* Retrieved from arxiv: https://arxiv.org/pdf/1309.6450.pdf.

Spalding, R. (2022). *War Without Rules: China's Playbook for Global Domination.* Sentinel.

Trulock, N. (2004). *Code Name Kindred Spirit: Inside the Chinese Nuclear Espionage Scandal.* Encounter Books.

Vaas, L. (2019). *Two People Indicted for Massive Anthem Health Data Breach.* Retrieved 7 7, 2019, from Naked Security: https://nakedsecurity.sophos. com/2019/05/13/two-chinese-hackers-indicted-for-massive-anthem-breach/.

Weisberger, M. (2015). *China's Copycat Jet Raises Questions About F-35.* Retrieved 11 8, 2022, from Defense One: https://www.defenseone.com/threats/2015/09/more-questions-f-35-after-new-specs-chinas-copycat/121859/.

Wise, D. (2011). *Tiger Trap – America's Secret War with China.* New York, NY: Houghton Mifflin Harcourt.

"Intrusiontruth" is an unknown group that has been outing Chinese cyber operatives since 2017 (Zetter). (n.d.). https://www.amazon.com/Tiger-Trap-Americas-Secret-China/dp/0547553102.

21Wang Jianghuai and Lin Dong, "Viewing Our Army's Quality Building from the Perspective of What Information Warfare Demands," Jiefangjun bao, March 3, 1998, p. 6, in FBIS-CHI-98-072, March 13, 1998.

Cyber Operation. (n.d.) https://www.cfr.org/cyber-operations/operation-aurora.

Advisories. (n.d.). https://www.cisa.gov/uscert/ics/advisories/ICSA-11-041-01A.

Dragonbridge. (n.d.). https://blog.google/threat-analysis-group/over-50000-instances-of-dragonbridge-activity-disrupted-in-2022/.

7

DPRK Cyber Operations

7.1 DPRK Cyber Operations

The Democratic People's Republic of Korea (DPRK), or North Korea, is a malicious cyber actor that uses cyber means to generate revenue and perform retribution attacks (e.g., 2014 Sony pictures). DPRK cyber operations are famous for the financial theft (e.g., 2016 Bangladesh Bank, 2017 WannaCry Ransomware attack, ongoing digital wallet attacks) that is used to support a developing nuclear weapons program, a key element to maintain the Kim Dynasty –

> Kim almost certainly views nuclear weapons and ICBMs as the ultimate guarantor of his autocratic rule and has no intention of abandoning those programs, believing that over time he will gain international acceptance as a nuclear power. In 2022, Kim reinforced that position by testing multiple ICBMs intended to improve North Korea's ability to strike the United States and revising his country's nuclear law, underscoring the nuclear forces as the backbone of North Korea's national defense. (DNI, 2023)

The DPRK received technical and materiel support from other countries (i.e., China and Russia) since its inception in 1948, due to common politics and borders (Figure 7.1). These technical and training relationships, including cyber, continue to this day.

As shown in Figure 7.1, the DPRK borders on both China and Russia to the north, and South Korea on its southern border.

Cyber Operations: A Case Study Approach, First Edition. Jerry M. Couretas.
© 2024 John Wiley & Sons, Inc. Published 2024 by John Wiley & Sons, Inc.

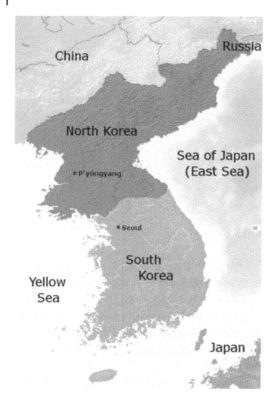

Figure 7.1 North Korea – Borders on South Korea, China and Russia. *Source:* Political Geography Now (2013)/Johannes Barre & Patrick Mannion.

7.1.1 DPRK Policy Development

The DPRK is the only remaining Stalinist command driven economy. In addition, the DPRK is resource poor and a challenge to farm due to mountainous terrain. The coal that the country does have is of limited value due to International sanctions on its sale (CFR, 2022). Therefore, the Kim regime is creative in its use of black markets and cyber to develop revenue streams for the government.

7.1.1.1 Kim Il Sung (1948–1994)

Born in 1912, Kim Il Sung, the father of the DPRK, was an active communist organizer during the Japanese occupation (1906–1946), and the leader of post-World War II North Korea. In addition, Kim Il Sung (Figure 7.2) was novel among communist leaders in that he grew up Presbyterian and taught Sunday School in his early years (2019). He is said to have later become an atheist, and descended into an autocrat, creating a small dynastic structure that persists to this day under his grandson.

Figure 7.2 Kim Il Sung. *Source:* Kim et al., 2019/Oxford University Press.

Supported by Russia and China, Kim Il Sung's DPRK adapted Stalinist government and political structures and implemented a centralized economic system that appeared to work for agricultural five-year plans, with the support of subsidies from the Former Soviet Union and China but missed industrial and technical development over the decades of his rule.

The map in Figure 7.1 does not highlight the mostly mountainous terrain that composes North Korea. The geography provides a challenge to develop agriculture, making it more expensive to feed the DPRK. In addition, maintaining a dynastic household is expensive for the Kim regime. Therefore, sometime in the mid-1970s, Kim Il Sung formed Room 39, a cell in the Worker's Party of Korea. Working with his son, Kim Jong Il, Room 39 produced revenue for the family. This revenue stream continues to this day and includes using several entities to bring in billions of dollars a year through schemes that range from producing and distributing counterfeit cigarettes and U.S. dollar bills to selling illegal drugs, minerals, arms, and even rare animal species (CHRISTIAN DAVIES, 2022) (Figure 7.3).

As China converted to "socialism with Chinese characteristics" (i.e., communist rule that includes some capitalism) in the late-1970s and the Soviet Union fell in the early 1990s, it was unclear what direction North Korea would go, both economically and in terms of succession upon Kim Il Sung's passing. The regime therefore enshrined and embellished Kim Il Sung's contributions to North Korea, his nationalism, his self-reliance (i.e., juche), and ability to stand up to the outside world, and deified Kim Il Sung as Supreme Leader for Eternity. Succession went to his son, Kim Jong Il, whose persona included being born at picturesque Mount Plaeku and the ability to win at any sport that he chose to participate in (Boren, 2011). Kim Jong Il was therefore a great person as well, and able to serve the governing institutions created by his father, the Supreme Leader for Eternity.

Figure 7.3 Kim Il Sung (left) with son and heir Kim Jong Il (right). *Source:* DIA (2021)/ Defense Intelligence Agency.

7.1.1.2 Kim Jong Il (1994–2011)

Being the son of a national hero/God-made earthly matters a challenge for Kim Jong Il during his first years as Supreme Leader. For example, the removal of subsidies with the fall of the Former Soviet Union in the early 1990s provided economic challenges that a less centralized economy might have used market forces to deal with. However, changing the command economy construct that Kim Il Sung founded would be admitting that the Supreme Leader was not perfect and imply insolence on the part of Kim Jong Il.

At the end of the Cold War (1991), the Soviet Union disbanded and Russia did not continue sending energy and other subsidies to the DPRK. Kim Il Sung died in 1994. Throughout the 1990s North Korea's economy continued to decline. Some of this was due to poor geography – when the Koreas were split, North Korea was mostly mountainous. Kim Il Sung ordered the mountainsides stripped for farming (White, 2022). This sort of worked to improve food production until heavy rains (1995) washed the hillsides into the rivers, causing them to silt up, resulting in floods. The floods destroyed much of the nation's rice crop. Food shortages produced a famine in the DPRK during the late 1990s that killed an estimated 2.5–3.5 million people, out of a population of 22–25 million, approximately 10% of the population (Natsios, 2002).

The 1990s were also when counterfeit U.S. currency, looking remarkably authentic, started showing up in different parts of the world and was ultimately found to have links back to the DPRK due to North Korean diplomats using these dollars. As a nation-state, the DPRK has access to specialized currency printing presses, paper, and inks. In addition, due to their impoverished economy, the DPRK had additional motivation to produce first-class "Superdollars" (BBC, 2021) in order to stave off bankruptcy (White, 2022).

Along with excellent counterfeit currency, Kim Jong Il started a nuclear weapons program. The DPRK detonated its first nuclear device in 2006 and continues to develop ballistic missile technology based on initial Russian Scud designs. As discussed, the nuclear program is seen as existential for the Kim regime and drives cyber collection/espionage and financial theft operations. In addition, the DPRK does an estimated $1.5 Billion/year business selling missile technology (Rossett, 2015).

Kim Jong Il, while ruling the DPRK for only 1/3 the time of his father, led the DPRK down technical paths that included counterfeit "super dollars," nuclear weapons and missile development. In addition, Kim Jong Il saw the benefit of networked computers, both for covert communications and, later, for theft. Developing cyber capabilities would be a key element for the next ruler of the DPRK.

7.1.1.3 Kim Jong Un (2011–present)

> Cyberwarfare is an all-purpose sword that guarantees the North Korean People's Armed Forces ruthless striking capability, along with nuclear weapons and missiles. (Ji Young Kong, 2019)
>
> —Kim Jong-un (2013)

Kim Jong Il's declining health left the DPRK with another succession challenge only 15 or so years after the Supreme Leader and President for Eternity, Kim Il Sung's death. Kim Jong Un, a favorite of Kim Jong Il, was portrayed as an energetic young leader who could provide North Korea with a leap forward in technology already experienced by the rest of the world.

Kim Jong Un, elevated in 2011 to Supreme Leader, is also the head of the Worker's Party of Korea (WPK). During this new reign, cell phones have proliferated, albeit tightly controlled (MARTYN WILLIAMS, 2022). In addition, so has the rollout of cyber operations, taking theft and ransomware operations to new heights. The evolution of DPRK cyber operations is unique in its singular focus on attempting to maintain the regime by creating revenue to be used to bolster a nascent nuclear weapons program.

Table 7.1 DPRK Cyber Teams (APTs).

Team	Started	Targets	Description
APT 37	2012	Strategic	APT37 (FireEye, 2018) believed to be sponsored by the DPRK Ministry of State Security (MSS) (Lakshmanan, 2023), mostly targeting South Korea (Mandiant, 2023)
APT 38	2016	Financial	APT38 is Lazarus, the team famous for financial and cryptocurrency heists
APT 43	2018	Strategic	APT43 is believed to be part of the reconnaissance general bureau (RGB), working on behalf of the DPRK's nuclear weapons program (Mandiant, 2023)

7.1.2 DPRK Intelligence Structure

While the Kim Jong Un regime receives a lot of attention for its cyber operations, there are only three DPRK Advanced Persistent Threat (APT) teams documented at the time of this writing (Table 7.1).

As shown in Table 7.1, APT 37 and APT 43 perform strategic intelligence operations, similar to traditional espionage. APT 38, however, is focused on financial targets in developing revenue for the DPRK.

While three APTs are the current number of teams designated, the DPRK is estimated to have over 6000 cyber personnel (Reuters, 2015) that span from information operations (i.e., propaganda) to penetration operations, generally lining up with major elements of the government. Mandiant provides an organization chart of the DPRK government, as it relates to cyber teams, in Figure 7.4.

The Reconnaissance General Bureau (RGB) includes cyber operations teams and is reported to have been formed in 2009, near the end of Kim Il Jong's reign (Bicker, 2021). As shown in Figure 7.4, DPRK cyber teams span the current government structure supporting the Workers Party of Korea, the RGB (APT 38, APT 43), and the MSS (APT 37).

7.1.2.1 Ministry of State Security

The MSS performs domestic counter espionage and overseas counter intelligence –

> The Ministry of State Security (MSS) is North Korea's primary counterintelligence service and is an autonomous agency of the North Korean government reporting directly to Kim Jong Un. The MSS is responsible for operating North Korean prison camps, investigating cases of domestic espionage, repatriating defectors, and conducting overseas counterespionage activities. (OSD, 2013)

The MSS cyber operator is believed to be APT 37 (Figure 7.4).

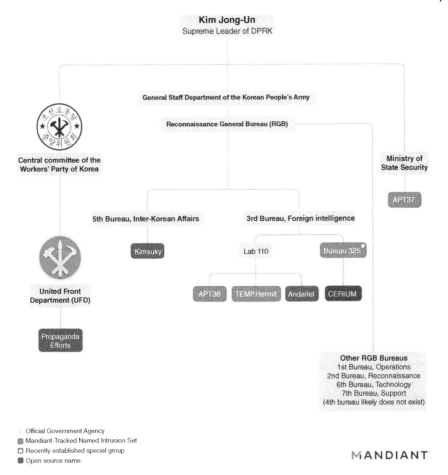

Figure 7.4 Mandiant Assessment of DPRK Cyber Programs. *Source:* MICHAEL BARNHART (2022)/Mandiant.

7.1.2.2 Worker's Party of Korea

Both the MSS and the Worker's Party of Korea are believed to report directly to the Kim regime. While the MSS has police functions, the Worker's Party of Korea includes propaganda (e.g., United Front Department) and revenue-generating operations (e.g., Room 39).

As discussed, Room 39 is a cell in the Worker's Party of Korea and develops revenue using cyber. For example, an estimated 1000 North Korean Information Technology (IT) personnel are used to generate revenue for the DPRK nuclear weapons program (U.S. Department of Treasury, 2022), in violation of sanctions. And, while the MSS and Worker's Party of Korea use cyber operations, the majority of the cyber teams are believed to be in the RGB (APT 38 and APT 43 in Table 7.1).

7.1.2.3 Reconnaissance General Bureau (APT 43)

> While cyber efforts are a portion of the organization's overall operations, the third Bureau (Foreign Intelligence) and fifth Bureau (Inter-Korean Affairs) appear to hold the 'meat and potatoes' of North Korea's cyber program. (MICHAEL BARNHART, 2022)

The RGB includes APT 38 and APT 43. Kimsuky (CISA, 2020), located in the fifth Bureau, is a cyber espionage operation that focuses on National Security and Foreign Policy issues (CISA, 2020). Kimsuky maintains a global intelligence mission against individuals and organizations in South Korea, Japan, and the United States. In addition, Kimsuky employs spearphishing, and watering hole attacks to exfiltrate foreign policy and national security issues related to the Korean peninsula, nuclear policy, and sanctions. This targeting includes Think Tanks and South Korean government entities.

The third Bureau, foreign intelligence, includes financial operations and is the home of APT 38, also known as Lazarus, famous for financial exploits. In addition, Lazarus divides into smaller subgroups.

Lazarus Group (APT 38) APT 38, shown in Figure 7.4's RGB, is also called "Lazarus." Lazarus is focused on financial gain and further decomposes into several names in the popular press including "Andariel" and "Bluenoroff."

Andariel The different names and operation specialties within the Lazarus group sometimes overlap. However, Lazarus specializes in financial theft, and Andariel has been observed attacking hospitals, small businesses, and foreign financial service firms (U.S. Treasury, 2019).

BeagleBoyz/Bluenoroff (>2014) Bluenoroff, within the Lazarus Group, was first noticed in the 2014 time frame and focuses on foreign financial institutions. Expertise includes international banking and a clear understanding of the SWIFT international funds transfer system, as exemplified by the $81 million (attempted $1 billion) theft from the Bank of Bangladesh in 2016 (BBC, 2021).

7.1.3 Example DPRK Cyber Operations

While the Bangladesh Bank theft caught law enforcement by surprise, it was one of the many DPRK cyber operations provided in Table 7.2.

The progression of attacks provided in Table 7.2, shows the relatively rapid development of DPRK cyber capabilities over the second decade of the 21st century. DPRK financial cyber operations combine traditional DPRK criminal capers

Table 7.2 DPRK Cyber Operations.

Year	Operation	Estimated Effects
2022	Axie Infinity	Took control of $600 million from digital wallets
2018–2021	CryptoCore	Hundreds of millions of U.S. dollars stolen by breaching cryptocurrency exchanges in the United States, Israel, Europe, and Japan (Ilascu, 2021)
2018	FastCash	Multiple ATM attacks (DoJ, 2021)
2017	WannaCry Ransomware	UK National Health Service – over $100 million in remediation costs; learned how to convert ill-gotten gains quickly through cryptocurrency
2016	Bank of Bangladesh	Extracted $81 million – stymied by SWIFT money transfer system and time to "wash" stolen money through Phillipino casinos
2014	Sony pictures	Delayed the release of a $44 million film parodying their leader. Denial of service and outing attack with additional terrorism threats for theaters who played the movie
2013	DarkSeoul	DPRK teams hacked South Korea's banks, TV stations, and government by overwriting the Master Boot Record (MBR) of infected machines and making them useless (White, 2022).

with cryptocurrency-specific theft and money laundering (Lyngaas, 2023). And it is estimated that the DPRK earns up to 1/3 of its weapons budget through these nefarious methods (Shull, 2022). Along with financial theft and ransom operations, the DPRK also performs denial operations (e.g., Sony), in retribution for perceived slights.

7.1.3.1 Sony Hack (2014)

With similar techniques to the DarkSeoul attack (2013), the DPRK hacked Sony in 2014 in order to stop the showing of "The Interview" (Evan Goldberg, 2014), a parody that included an assassination of Kim Jong Un, the current North Korean leader. This cost Sony Pictures the $44 million that it invested by halting the film's release. In addition, the Sony cyberattack included the outing of private e-mails in the 2014 Sony attack (Zetter, 2014) and was combined with terrorist-type threats at movie theaters should the film be shown, resulting in Sony possibly having blood on its hands if it released the film.

7.1.3.2 Bangladesh Bank Heist (2016)

The Bangladesh Bank heist in 2016 was carefully planned. For example, the Lazarus team clearly understood the SWIFT banking system and time zone differences that would result in a delayed response from authorities as the Lazarus group attempted to extract funds from the Bangladesh Bank.

A peculiarity that would have been a challenge to forecast was that the funds were to be sent from the Bangladesh bank, via the SWIFT money transfer system, to a bank on Jupiter Street in Manilla (Phillipines). Jupiter is also the name of an Iranian vessel on a watch list. Due to this unforeseeable detail, SWIFT banking officials were alarmed and stopped all pending funds transfers that the Lazarus group had sent through the SWIFT financial transfer system. This limited the $1 billion heist to approximately $81 million.

An additional issue that Lazarus experienced in the Bank of Bangladesh heist was laundering the transferred funds. While the Lazarus group had a clear plan for laundering the stolen funds through Phillippino casinos, it took weeks to "clean" the funds through Baccarat. Challenges in moving the money through SWIFT, and then the time-intensive process for laundering the cash, limited the financial damage to approximately one-tenth of the targeted theft (White, 2022).

7.1.3.3 Operation FashCash (2018)

Operation FastCash was a compromise of bank account confidentiality that used a number of paid participants at each ATM location in order to retrieve funds from compromised accounts. Developing this army of cash collectors required a relationship between DPRK intelligence, cyber team leadership, and organized crime. In the Operation FastCash example, Japanese gangsters, the Yakuza, colluded with DPRK operatives to produce hundreds of millions of dollars (Caesar, 2021).

7.1.3.4 WannaCry Ransomware Attack (2017)

WannaCry was one of the more famous attacks by the Lazarus Group. WannaCry may have also been the first ransomware operation to use the Shadow Broker's tools (Khandelwal, 2017a) (Chapter 3). WannaCry was propagated through EternalBlue and DoublePulsar, exceptionally capable access tools for exploiting the Microsoft Server Message Block (SMB) for remote code execution (Khandelwal, Turns Out Microsoft Has Already Patched Exploits Leaked By Shadow Brokers, 2017b). While Microsoft had already provided a patch, many users had not updated their systems. It is estimated that over 300,000 computers in 150 countries were affected by WannaCry (Newman, 2017), causing damage estimated between $4 and $8 billion (White, 2022).

The National Health Service in Britain was especially hard hit by WannaCry due to the widespread use of the Windows 7 operating system. For example, it is estimated that complications due to the WannaCry attack cost the NHS over $100 million (National Audit Office, 2017).

One of the saving graces of the WannaCry attack was the discovery of a "kill switch" that was used to turn off the attacking software (Newman, 2017). Marcus Hutchins discovered the "kill switch," an abstract URL name that the code would check in with once on a target, and shut down the malware.

7.1.3.5 Cryptocurrency

> North Korea has conducted cyber theft against financial institutions and cryptocurrency exchanges worldwide, potentially stealing hundreds of millions of dollars, probably to fund government priorities, such as its nuclear and missile programs. (Office of the Director of National Intelligence, 2021).

The DPRK has been mining cryptocurrency to generate cash for its nuclear and ballistic missile programs for years. For example, Priscilla Moriuchi, formerly of the U.S. National Security Agency (NSA), provides the following insight -

> Moriuchi, who is now at the digital intelligence firm Recorded Future, estimates that North Korea earns between $15 million and $200 million by creating and selling cryptocurrencies and then turning it into hard cash. (Their take fluctuates depending on the digital currency's worth when North Korea cashes out.) That's not enough money to fully fund North Korea's weapons programs, to be sure, but it ensures they don't completely shut down. (Ward, 2018)

Generating cryptocurrency is one example of how the DPRK converts its coal deposits, subject to sanctions, into convertible currency. Cryptocurrencies are also the means that online gamers and gamblers use to keep track of their winnings. These winnings, often stored in digital wallets, are accessible through standard social engineering means of compromising owners. The Crypto Core campaign is an example of digital wallet theft, while Axie Infinity is an online game that the DPRK exploited to extract player's accounts.

Crypto Core Campaign (2018–2021) One motivation for the DPRK to use cryptocurrencies is to circumvent sanctions and move money in less formal financial channels (DHS CISA, 2021). For example, CryptoCore was a campaign believed to have started around 2018 and continued for three years, targeting cryptocurrency wallets, with the Lazarus Group (DPRK) having pilfered hundreds of millions of dollars (ClearSky, 2021). In August 2019, the U.N. panel said North Korean cyber experts illegally obtained proceeds "estimated at up to $2 billion" to fund its weapons programs. (Lederer, 2021)

Axie Infinity (2022–2023) In one of the largest cryptocurrency heists, the DPRK was implicated in the theft of hundreds of millions of dollars of cryptocurrency tied to the online game Axie Infinity –

> Ronin, a blockchain network that lets users transfer crypto in and out of the game, said digital cash worth almost $615 million was stolen on March 23 (2022). (Reuters, 2022b)

The use of the crypto mixer for the Axie Infinity attack led to the U.S. Treasury sanctioning the address associated with the attack. While an estimated $615 million in "Axies," the game's famous nonfungible tokens (NFTs) were cordoned off by DPRK cyber operators through social engineering, although few of the funds have been converted into exchangeable currency (Reuters, 2022b). For example, each of the NFTs would need to use a crypto exchange (e.g., Huobi, Crypto.com, FTX …) in order to translate Axies into cash (e.g., U.S. dollars) that can be used for military programs and other Room 39 activities.

Bitcoin Theft Summary While cryptocurrency is a relatively "new" technology, almost all of the DPRK theft has been through traditional social engineering –

> North Korea's crypto-exchange hacks have a relatively straightforward methodology. Exchanges that trade bitcoin and other types of cryptocurrency typically hold escrow accounts full of their customers' coins. These storage facilities are known as "hot wallets," because they are connected to the Internet. (A more secure but laborious method of storing coins is in an offline "cold wallet" containing, say, QR-code printouts that contain the keys to blockchain accounts.) Hackers from North Korea often gain access to an exchange's internal systems using … Real-sounding people (that) propose real-sounding schemes, then persuade a network user at a targeted company to download an infected document. Typically, one or two admin-level members at a cryptocurrency exchange have access to a hot wallet's private keys. If hackers can compromise a sufficiently senior figure, they can reach the wallet and steal its coins. (Caesar, 2021)

Due to the social engineering proficiency required for bitcoin, cryptocurrency operations are similar to each of the other DPRK cyber operations – the need to compromise a person in order to gain system access.

7.1.4 DPRK Cyber Operations Wrap-up

With cyber operations estimated to be funding 1/3 of the DPRK weapons budget (Shull, 2022), North Korea may have one of the most nationally prized offensive cyber operations programs in the world. Having done damage to international banking (2016 Bank of Bangladesh), health care (2017 WannaCry), and cryptocurrency exchanges and gaming (2018 Crypto Core, 2022 Axie Infinity), DPRK cyber teams have earned well beyond a billion dollars.

Bibliography

BBC. (2021). *The Lazarus Heist: How North Korea Almost Pulled off a Billion-dollar Hack*. Retrieved 4 13, 2023, from BBC: https://www.bbc.com/news/stories-57520169.

Bicker, L. (2021). *Drugs, Arms, and Terror: A High-profile Defector on Kim's North Korea*. Retrieved from BBC: https://www.bbc.com/news/world-asia-58838834.

Boren, C. (2011). *Kim Jong-Il: A Sporting Life (with Golf, Bowling, Soccer and Basketball Interests)*. Retrieved from Washington Post: https://www.washingtonpost.com/blogs/early-lead/post/kim-jong-il-golf-bowling-and-basketball-interests-some-of-which-were-real/2011/12/19/gIQAmWSV4O_blog.html.

Caesar, E. (2021). *The Incredible Rise of North Korea's Hacking Army*. Retrieved 11 02, 2022, from New Yorker: https://www.newyorker.com/magazine/2021/04/26/the-incredible-rise-of-north-koreas-hacking-army.

CFR. (2022). *What to Know About Sanctions on North Korea*. Retrieved from Council on Foreign Relations: https://www.cfr.org/backgrounder/north-korea-sanctions-un-nuclear-weapons.

Christian Davies, S. C. (2022). *How North Korea Became a Mastermind of Crypto Cybercrime*. Retrieved 3 7, 2023, from Ars Technica: https://arstechnica.com/information-technology/2022/11/how-north-korea-became-a-mastermind-of-crypto-cyber-crime/.

CISA. (2020). *North Korean Advanced Persistent Threat Focus: Kimsuky*. Retrieved 9 20, 2022, from AA20-301A: https://www.cisa.gov/uscert/ncas/alerts/aa20-301a.

ClearSky. (2021). *Attributing Attacks Against Crypto Exchanges to LAZARUS – North Korea*. Retrieved 9 14, 2022, from ClearSky: https://www.clearskysec.com/wp-content/uploads/2021/05/CryptoCore-Lazarus-Clearsky.pdf.

DHS CISA. (2021). *Alert (AA21-048A) AppleJeus: Analysis of North Korea's Cryptocurrency Malware*. Retrieved 7 16, 2022, from CISA: https://www.cisa.gov/uscert/ncas/alerts/aa21-048a.

DIA. (2021). *North Korea Military Power – A Growing Regional and Global Threat*. Retrieved from DIA: https://www.dia.mil/Portals/110/Documents/News/North_Korea_Military_Power.pdf.

DNI. (2023). *Annual Threat Assessment of the U.S. Intelligence Community*. Retrieved from Office of the Director of National Intelligence: https://www.odni.gov/files/ODNI/documents/assessments/ATA-2023-Unclassified-Report.pdf.

DoJ. (2021). *Three North Korean Military Hackers Indicted in Wide-Ranging Scheme to Commit Cyberattacks and Financial Crimes Across the Globe*. Retrieved 2 17, 2021, fromDoJ:https://www.justice.gov/opa/pr/three-north-korean-military-hackers-indicted-wide-ranging-scheme-commit-cyberattacks-and

Evan Goldberg, S. R. (Director). (2014). *The Interview* [Motion Picture].

FireEye. (2018). *APT 37 (Reaper)*. Retrieved from FireEye: https://www2.fireeye.com/rs/848-DID-242/images/rpt_APT37.pdf.

Heeu Millie Kim, J. L. (2022). *North Korean Cryptocurrency Operations: An Alternative Revenue Stream*. Retrieved from Belfer Center: https://www.belfercenter.org/sites/default/files/files/publication/North%20Korean%20Cryptocurrency%20Operations%20-%20An%20Alternative%20Revenue%20Stream.pdf.

Ilascu, I. (2021). *North Korean Hackers Behind CryptoCore Multi-million Dollar Heists*. Retrieved from Bleeping Computer: https://www.bleepingcomputer.com/news/security/north-korean-hackers-behind-cryptocore-multi-million-dollar-heists/.

Ji Young Kong, J. I. (2019). The All-Purpose Sword: North Korea's Cyber Operations and Strategies. *2019 11th International Conference on Cyber Conflict: Silent Battle*. Tallinn: CCDOE.

Khandelwal, S. (2017a). *Shadow Brokers, Who Leaked WannaCry SMB Exploit, Are Back With More 0-Days*. Retrieved from The Hacker News: https://thehackernews.com/2017/05/shodow-brokers-wannacry-hacking.html.

Khandelwal, S. (2017b). *Turns Out Microsoft has Already Patched Exploits Leaked By Shadow Brokers*. Retrieved from The Hacker News: https://thehackernews.com/2017/04/window-zero-day-patch.html.

Lederer, E. (2021). *UN experts: North Korea using cyber attacks to update nukes*. Retrieved 9 19, 2022, from AP News: https://apnews.com/article/technology-global-trade-nuclear-weapons-north-korea-coronavirus-pandemic-19f536cac4a84780f54a3279ef707b33.

Lakshmanan, R. (2023). *North Korea's APT37 Targeting Southern Counterpart with New M2RAT Malware*. Retrieved 2 15, 2023, from The Hacker News: https://thehackernews.com/2023/02/north-koreas-apt37-targeting-southern.html.

Lyngaas, S. (2023). *Inside the International Sting Operation to Catch North Korean Crypto Hackers*. Retrieved 4 19, 2023, from CNN: https://www.cnn.com/2023/04/09/politics/north-korean-crypto-hackers-crackdown/index.html.

Mandiant. (2023). *APT43: North Korean Group Uses Cybercrime to Fund Espionage Operations*. Retrieved from Mandiant: https://mandiant.widen.net/s/zvmfw5fnjs/apt43-report.

Martyn Williams, N. S. (2022). *Twenty Years of Mobile Communications in North Korea*. Retrieved from 38North: https://www.38north.org/2022/11/twenty-years-of-mobile-communications-in-north-korea/.

Michael Barnhart, M. C. (2022). *Not So Lazarus: Mapping DPRK Cyber Threat Groups to Government Organizations*. Retrieved 4 12, 2022, from Mandiant: https://www.mandiant.com/resources/mapping-dprk-groups-to-government.

National Audit Office. (2017). *Investigation: WannaCry Cyber Attack and the NHS*. Retrieved from National Audit Office: https://www.nao.org.uk/reports/investigation-wannacry-cyber-attack-and-the-nhs/.

Natsios, A. S. (2002). *How Did the North Korean Famine Happen?* Retrieved 3 6, 2023, from Wilson Center: https://www.wilsoncenter.org/article/how-did-the-north-korean-famine-happen.

Newman, L. H. (2017). *How an Accidental 'Kill Switch' Slowed Friday's Massive Ransomware Attack*. Retrieved 4 12, 2023, from Wired Magazine: https://www.wired.com/2017/05/accidental-kill-switch-slowed-fridays-massive-ransomware-attack/.

Office of the Director of National Intelligence. (2021). *Annual Threat Assessment of the US Intelligence Community*. Retrieved 7 16, 2022, from DNI.gov: https://www.dni.gov/files/ODNI/documents/assessments/ATA-2021-Unclassified-Report.pdf.

OSD. (2013). *Military and Security Developments Involving the Democratic People's Republic of Korea*. Retrieved from OSD: https://irp.fas.org/world/dprk/dod-2013.pdf.

Political Geography Now. (2013). *What is North Korea*. Retrieved from Political Geography Now: https://www.polgeonow.com/2013/04/what-is-north-korea.html.

Reuters. (2015). *North Korea Boosted "Cyber-forces" to 6,000 Troops, South Says*. Retrieved from Reuters.

Reuters. (2022a). *Axie Infinity's $615 Million Crypto Hack: What to Know About the Heist*. Retrieved 4 13, 2023, from Reuters: Reuters.

Reuters. (2022b). *U.S. Ties North Korean Hacker Group Lazarus to Huge Cryptocurrency Theft*. Retrieved 10 27, 2022, from Reuters: https://www.reuters.com/technology/us-ties-north-korean-hacker-group-lazarus-huge-cryptocurrency-theft-2022-04-14/.

Rossett, C. (2015). *How Iran and North Korea Became Cyber-Terror Buddies*. Retrieved from The Tower: http://www.thetower.org/article/how-iran-and-north-korea-became-cyber-terror-buddies/.

Ryu, D.aY. (2019). Kim Il-Sung and Christianity in North Korea. *Journal of Church and State 61* (3): 403–430. Retrieved from https://academic.oup.com/jcs/article-abstract/61/3/403/5127077.

Shull, A. (2022). *Stolen Money from Cyberattacks Makes Up a Third of the Funds for North Korea's Missile Program, US Official Says*. Retrieved from Business Insider: https://www.businessinsider.com/north-korea-missile-program-funded-by-cyberattacks-us-official-2022-7.

Smith, J. (2022). *Kim Jong Un Says North Korea Aims to have the World's Strongest Nuclear Force*. Retrieved from Reuters: https://www.reuters.com/world/asia-pacific/kim-jong-un-says-north-koreas-goal-is-worlds-strongest-nuclear-force-2022-11-26/.

Time. (2004). *Kim Jong Il Looking at Things*. Retrieved from Time: https://time.com/3795807/kim-jong-il-looking-at-things/.

U.S. Department of Treasury. (2022). Guidance on the Democratic People's Republic of Korea Information Technology Workers. Retrieved 10 27, 2022, from U.S. Department of Treasury: https://home.treasury.gov/system/files/126/20220516_dprk_it_worker_advisory.pdf.

U.S. Treasury. (2019). *Treasury Sanctions North Korean State-Sponsored Malicious Cyber Groups*. Retrieved from U.S. Treasury: https://home.treasury.gov/news/press-releases/sm774.

Ward, A. (2018). *How North Korea Uses Bitcoin to get Around US Sanctions*. Retrieved 1 3, 2023, from VOX: https://www.vox.com/world/2018/2/28/17055762/north-korea-sanctions-bitcoin-nuclear-weapons.

White, G. (2022). *The Lazarus Heist – From Hollywood to High Finance: Inside North Korea's Global Cyber War*. New York: Penguin.

Zetter, K. (2014). *Sony got Hacked Hard: What We Know and Don't Know so Far*. Retrieved 9 9, 2018, from Wired: https://www.wired.com/2014/12/sony-hack-what-we-know/.

8

Iranian Cyber Operations

8.1 Iranian Cyber Operations

> Iran's growing expertise and willingness to conduct aggressive cyber operations make it a major threat to the security of U.S. and allied networks and data. Iran's opportunistic approach to cyber attacks makes critical infrastructure owners in the United States susceptible to being targeted by Tehran, particularly when Tehran believes that it must demonstrate it can push back against the United States in other domains. Recent attacks against Israeli targets show that Iran is more willing than before to target countries with stronger capabilities. (Office of the Director of National Intelligence (ODNI), 2023)

From the birth of the Islamic Republic in 1979, Iran has been concerned about threats to its revolutionary government. The Ministry of Intelligence and Security (MOIS) is therefore responsible for intelligence and counterintelligence, conducting operations both internal and external to Iran. MOIS operations also use cyber. For international operations, the MOIS uses the Quds Force to conduct covert operations outside of Iran, including cyber. The Quds Force reports to the Islamic Revolutionary Guards Corps (IRGC) (Figure 8.1).

As shown in Figure 8.1, the MOIS is in charge of all covert operations, using the Quds Force to perform missions outside of Iran. Many of these operations are counterintelligence, ensuring the security of the Islamic Republic and key programs that support the regime, including a developing nuclear program. It is believed that the development and management of external cyber operations are performed by the Islamic Revolutionary Guard Corps (IRGC).

> Iran's offensive cyber activities are almost exclusively overseen by the IRGC – likely without the oversight of the country's publicly "elected"

Cyber Operations: A Case Study Approach, First Edition. Jerry M. Couretas.
© 2024 John Wiley & Sons, Inc. Published 2024 by John Wiley & Sons, Inc.

Figure 8.1 MOIS and Quds Force – Internal and External Cyber Operations.

officials – and composed of a scattered set of independent contractors who mix security work, criminal fraud, and more banal software development. While the relationships between proxies and governments can range from passive support to complete control, Iran's indigenous threat actors maintain an arm's-length relationship to the state, with certain operations orchestrated to meet the needs of the government. (Colin Anderson, 2018)

The network of players that make up Iranian cyber operations were relatively unknown until the discovery of STUXNET malware in 2010. Centrifuges (Figure 8.2) are used to refine uranium for Iran's nuclear program. STUXNET was designed to take control of the centrifuges and make them self-destruct (Langner, 2011; Zetter, 2014).

The STUXNET cyberattack on the Iranian nuclear program was a counterintelligence failure by the Islamic Republic. This was a failure in both human and technical intelligence. Humans were believed to have moved malware, wittingly or not, into the centrifuge operations center, likely by thumb drive (Zetter, 2014). An understanding of the underlying centrifuge technology was also necessary to develop the virus that caused the centrifuges to spin out of control (Langner, 2011).

8.1.1 Iranian Cyber Operations Background

Iran started experimenting with offensive cyber operations in 2007. By 2009, Iran was performing a denial attack on the Twitter accounts of the Green Movement, an opposition group contesting the re-election results of the then-sitting President, Mahmoud Ahmadinejad (Colin Anderson, 2018).

In the wake of the STUXNET revelation in 2010 that Iran's nuclear program had been delayed by malware, Iran performed a number of cyberattacks. One of

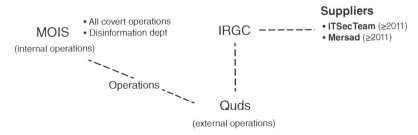

Figure 8.2 MOIS and Quds Force with Suppliers who Support Cyber Operations.

the largest Iranian cyber operations was the compromise of the Dutch certificate authority DigiNotar (2011) (Colin Anderson, 2018) in order to access approximately 300,000 Iranian citizens' Gmail inboxes (Hoffman, 2011). Accessing Gmail helped the MOIS understand how the Iranian population was communicating, via e-mail, with both each other and with the outside world. Domestic surveillance has been a pillar of the Iranian cyber program since its early beginning.

Following DigiNotar were the 2012 denial attacks against foreign adversaries – Operation Al Ababil (U.S. banks) and Operation Al Shamoon I (Saudi Aramco). These attacks were a surprise to both Western financial institutions and Saudi Arabia. Operation Al Shamoon I wiped out over 30,000 hard drives on Saudi Aramco systems (Perlroth, 2012) in the summer of 2012, depleting the global hard drive inventory. With Saudi Arabia being the swing supplier for the global oil market, and the U.S. being a financial center, Operation Al Shamoon I and Operation Ababil had the potential of creating a global energy and financial crisis. The year 2012 was also the beginning of a series of Iranian cyberattacks that included the U.S. Navy–Marine Corps Intranet (NMCI) (2012–2014), the Rye Dam (2013), and the Sands Corp (2014) (Table 8.1).

As shown in Table 8.1, attributed Iranian cyber operations include multiple physical effects operations, pseudo-kinetic operations that debilitate an organization's ability to use its computer-based systems. In addition to physical effects, the latter part of the 2010s saw Iran moving toward more information operations. For example, Iranian contractors ITSecTeam and Mersad contributed to the 2012 denial attacks on U.S. financial institutions (DoJ, 2016) (Figure 8.3).

Iranian cyber forces continued to develop over the late 2010s, including an expansion in the number of internal suppliers in order to increase the control of communications within the Islamic Republic.

Table 8.1 Example Iranian Cyber Operations.

Year	Operation	Description
2022–present	Counter protest	Iran uses cyber to penetrate communications and develop narratives that discredit the opposition in the ongoing protests against the regime (Khameneh, 2023)
2022	Albania	Iran performed a cyber campaign against Albanian systems due to their harboring MEK operatives. This included support from the BlackByte group, a spinoff of CONTI (i.e., Chapter 3 team that brought down the Costa Rican government's IT systems in May 2022 (Ilascu, 2022)), with FSB connections (Oghanna, 2023; Vijayan, 2022)
2022	U.S.–Iran nuclear agreement talks	Muddy Water (i.e., MOIS) Group attacked an Israeli company SysAid, through the Log4J vulnerability, in reaction to Israel's work to block a U.S.–Iran diplomatic deal (Kogosowski, 2022)
2020	U.S. presidential election	The Iranian government hired a contractor, Emmenet Pasargad, to intimidate voters and reduce election credibility (US Department of the Treasury, 2021)
2016–2017	Al Shamoon II	Operations against Saudi Arabia that included the employment of the disstrack wiper malware (CFR, 2012)
2014	Operation cleaver	Iranian cyber reconnaissance campaign that is credited with accessing multiple sensitive sites, including the U.S. Navy–Marine Corps Internet (NMCI). The word "cleaver" was said to be found in the source code of one of the tools (Vijayan, 2014)
2014	Sands corp	Wiper operation against a casino whose owner, Sheldon Adelson, made anti-Iran comments. Damages were estimated to be over $40 million (Brandom, 2014)
2013	Rye dam	Iranian cyber operators penetrated defenses at Rye dam, in Westchester, New York, gaining access to sluice gate controls. Damages estimated to be $30,000 (DoJ, 2016)
2012–2014	Navy–Marine corps internet	Compromise of NMCI network (800,000 users at 2500 sites) through public-facing web servers (Gallagher, 2014)

Table 8.1 (Continued)

Year	Operation	Description
2012	Al Ababil	DDoS attack on U.S. banks. Hundreds of thousands of customers were locked out of their accounts for long periods and estimated to have cost tens of millions of dollars to remediate the damage (Colin Anderson, 2018). Team attacking financial institutions included IRGC with support from Mersad and ITSecTeam (DoJ, 2016)
	Al Shamoon I	Wiper attack against Saudi Aramco that resulted in the destruction of over 30,000 computers (New York Times, 2012)
2011	Operation newscaster	Iranian operatives constructed a false front news operation, through a set of websites, that included posting real news (Finkle, 2014)
2011	DigiNotar	Iranian hacker breaches Dutch security firm DigiNotar, allowing the Iranian government to spy on Gmail users in Iran. This remains one of the largest security breaches in the history of the Internet (ENISA)
2009	Twitter attack	Iranian Cyber Army defaces Twitter – taking it offline for several hours – in response to the Green Movement (New York Times, 2009)
2007	Offensive cyber Experiments	Iran begins experimenting with offensive cyber operations
2002	First Initiative to censor the Internet	The first initiative to limit Internet access was issued by Iran's supreme leader in January 2002 in an order called the "Comprehensive Proclamation of Computer Information Network Policies" (Simurgh Aryan, 2013).
2001		Iran connects to internet

Source: Adapted from Collin Anderson (2018).

8.1.2 Iranian Cyber Support – Contractors, Proxies, and International Partners

Iranian cyber contractors develop technical solutions, install telecommunications systems, and support operations. In each case, Iran operates from a secure national Intranet that helps with monitoring external and internal communications within Iran.

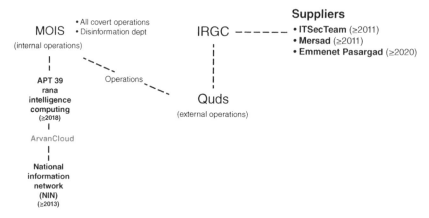

Figure 8.3 MOIS, the National Information Network (NIN) and Contractors.

8.1.2.1 Iranian Cyber Contractors (Internal to Iran)

Iran contracts with several private companies to develop tools and carry out cyberattacks (Table 8.2).

We see in Table 8.2 the multiple companies, projects/operations, and their respective contributions to Iranian cyber operations. Iran uses contractors to develop information operation narratives, to operate botnets for distributed denial of service (DDoS), and to monitor Iranian citizen's activities in cyberspace.

Iran also uses technical suppliers to build the National Information Network (NIN), the infrastructure that underpins the country-wide Intranet. Internet service for Iranian citizens, along with connecting to the Iranian Intranet, is usually provided via cell phone connection (Michel Martin, 2022).

The centralized nature of the Iranian Internet connection results in a lack of privacy. Many Iranians have started using virtual private networks (VPNs) in order to have some level of privacy in their Internet communications. The centralized nature of the national intranet results in authorities' ability to turn off the network at will (Article 19, 2016). In fact, ArvanCloud, the National Information Network (NIN) developer, has strong ties to the MOIS and was recently sanctioned by the U.S. Treasury for facilitating censorship (Reddick, 2023)(Figure 8.3).

As shown in Figure 8.3, both the MOIS and the IRGC use contractors for their cyber operations. Along with using internal suppliers and contractors to build infrastructure and run operations, Iran also has proxy relationships with multiple entities to perform cyber operations.

8.1.2.2 Iranian Cyber Proxies (External to Iran)

There is a body of theory developing from counter-terrorism and policy studies that provides a framework for the definition of cyber proxies (Maurer, 2016). For

Table 8.2 Iranian Companies Supporting Cyber Operations.

Company Name	Project/Operation	Contribution to Iranian Cyber Operations
ArvanCloud	National intranet development	Supplier of the national information network (NIN) (US Treasury, 2023)
Emmenet pasargad	2020 U.S. presidential election	Attempted to develop narratives and disseminate messaging to decrease election credibility (U.S. Treasury, 2021)
ITSecTeam	2012 operation ababil	Botnet for DDoS (DoJ, 2016)
Mersad	2012 operation ababil	Botnet for DDoS (DoJ, 2016)
Rana intelligence computing	Ongoing surveillance of iranian citizens	Front company for APT 39 (U.S. Department of the Treasury, 2020)

our purposes, we will consider cyber proxies to be cutouts, actors that limit sponsor-state attribution in order to provide plausible deniability upon the discovery of a cyber action.

> A mode of governance widely used by intergovernmental organizations (IGOs) and other governance actors. ... IGOs engage in orchestration when they enlist intermediary actors on a voluntary basis, by providing them with ideational and material support, to address target actors in pursuit of ... governance goals. Orchestration is thus both indirect (because the IGO acts through intermediaries) and soft (because the IGO lacks control over intermediaries). (Kenneth and Genschel, 2015)

One of Iran's first major cyber operations included masquerading as a cyber proxy. For example, Operation Ababil (2012) was conducted using a false flag of "Arab Terrorists," complete with faux Arabic conversations with the goal of deflecting blame to the Izz ad-Din al Qassem Brigade (Recorded Future, 2013). Iran also has cyber connections to Hezbollah (Lebanon), Kata'ib Hezbollah (Iraq), the Syrian Electronic Army (SEA), and the Yemen Cyber Army, all having conducted cyber-attacks that are in Tehran's interests.

Yemen Cyber Army   The Yemen Cyber Army, coming out of nowhere for an attack on the Saudi Foreign Ministry in May 2015, is believed to be Iran due to team and tool signatures (Frenkel, 2015). Some researchers believe that Iranian hackers are using the Yemen Cyber Army as another false flag operation (Franceschi-Bicchierai, 2015).

Conducting offensive cyber operations through covert organizations provides Tehran plausible deniability for any attacks thereby protecting its claim to victimhood while also allowing the state to signal its intentions to its opponents. These tactics are effective, there is still no definitive public agreement on who was behind the Yemen Cyber Army's attacks that led to stolen Saudi Arabian Ministry of Foreign Affairs documents being published by WikiLeaks, with the consensus split between Iran and Russia (Frenkel, 2015)

While the Yemen Cyber Army may be a front for Iranian cyber operations, Hezbollah stands out in terms of its cyber operations, tool sophistication, and impacts.

Lebanon (Hezbollah)   Hezbollah is the poster child of Iranian proxy success. Started during the Israeli invasion of Lebanon in 1982, Hezbollah was originally a gathering of several Shia militias, mostly in South Lebanon. An estimated 800 IRGC (Quds force) trainers infiltrated Lebanon through Syria and used the Bekaa Valley to train and organize members of the then Amal Militia and other groups that developed into Hezbollah, now both a participant in the Lebanese Government and an operator of multiple illicit enterprises that span the globe (Levitt, 2021).

Iran's use of cyber, via proxies, is effectively an implementation of policy orchestration, where orchestration is defined.

The Islamic State in Iraq and Syria's relentless use of social media has caused it to be widely regarded as the most innovative of the modern terrorist groups. But long before ISIS began significantly investing in propaganda, the Lebanese Shi'ite terrorist group Hezbollah had laid the groundwork for the effective use of information warfare, which is the ability to gain an advantage over an adversary through the management of information. (Clarke, 2017)

Hezbollah's foray into cyber, while hard to pin a date on, was mature by 2015 when Israel sustained a cyberattack that targeted Israeli military suppliers and persons of interest (Moskowitz, 2015). Titled Operation Volatile Cedar, this attack came as a surprise due to Hezbollah being thought of more as a militia than a cyber operator (Yaniv Balmas, 2015).

The Hezbollah cyber team performs proxy operations and conducts offensive cyber training courses (Wagenheim, 2020). While Hezbollah maintains its own offensive cyber operations, it is believed to use the same tools as Iran's Magic Kitten cyber operations team (Carnegie Endowment for International Peace, 2018;

Collin Anderson, 2018). This is the most direct link between Iran and Hezbollah's cyber activities.

Iraq (Kata'ib Hizballah)   While Hezbollah is a political force in Lebanon with proven ties to Iran for both traditional military and cyber equipment, Kata'ib Hizballah is an established Iranian proxy with much less, in terms of proven cyber capabilities. One description of Kata'ib Hizballah includes the following:

> Kata'ib Hizballah has arguably become the most dangerous Iranian proxy in Iraq. It has engaged in myriad activities to protect and expand Iran's influence in Iraq and the wider region. It has helped suppress an anti-Iran nationalist Iraqi protest movement. It has used Iraqi territory to conduct attacks on a neighboring country and has openly intimidated and threatened the Iraqi prime minister, the commander in chief. The group's influence has expanded enormously in recent years, and the militia has become the most reliable proxy for Iran to further its ambitions in Iraq. In Lebanon, Hizballah plays this role. In Yemen, it is the Houthi Ansar Allah that helps Iran expand its influence. In Iraq, Kata'ib Hizballah is emerging as the main group that implements Iran's plans. (Malik, 2020)

There is a connection between Hezbollah and Kata'ib Hizballah. For example, Imad Mughniyeh, Lebanese Hezbollah's former chief of staff, was an instrumental figure in establishing Kata'ib Hizballah in its early stages. And, while estimated to number at least 10,000 in the early 2020s, Kata'ib Hizballah's cyber capability was deemed strong enough to make it a U.S. cyberattack target in retribution for Iran's 2019 shooting down of a drone in the Persian Gulf (Melendez, 2019).

While Kata'ib Hizballah is relatively new, being formed by Iran's strongest proxy, Hezbollah, in Lebanon, the SEA is older, has less team or tool attribution, and has the least connection to Iran among the proxies discussed so far.

Syria (Syrian Electronic Army)   The SEA is believed to have developed from a set of universities, originally using the same computers and networks as the Syrian Computer Society, headed by current President Bashar Assad in his early days (Fowler, 2013). More recently, the SEA was implicated in attacks using Twitter and Facebook since 2011, often with an anti-Israel theme (Gerry Shih, 2013).

From a seemingly innocuous University base, the SEA develops its own tools to attack high-profile media organizations.

In terms of cyber tools and malicious code, SEA has invested over time in malware called SilverHawk. SilverHawk is being built into fake updates for various security and privacy-focused communications apps, including WhatsApp and Telegram. The SEA also created Microsoft Word, and YouTube fakes filled with the SilverHawk spyware in their attempts to hack into Google Android devices. (Brewster, 2018)

The connection between the SEA and Iran, however, is tenuous. Syria seems to have its own set of spyware tools, and the ability to employ them, without the need for Iran.

Hamas Cyber Operations   Hamas, the governing entity in the Gaza Strip, uses cyber mostly for information operations that promote the Palestinian cause with fellow Palestinians in the West Bank and abroad. Active since approximately 2012, Hamas cyber operations include defacement and app development (Table 8.3).

Hamas cyber operators have garnered enough Israeli attention to become the target of aerial bombardment in 2019, as discussed in Table 8.3.

Iran uses cyber proxies to accomplish its policy objectives. This set of partners spans from the Yemen Cyber Army, as a direct cut out of Iranian teams and tools, to the independently operating Hezbollah (Figure 8.4).

Table 8.3 Hamas Cyber Operations.

Year	Hamas Effects/Objectives
2012	Defaced Israeli websites in response to Operation Cast Lead
2013–2015	Hamas luring in Israelis with pornographic videos that were actually malware apps
2014	Gained control of an Israeli broadcasting satellite. Also, Hamas claimed credit for hacking the Israeli Defense Force's (IDF) classified network and posting multiple videos taken earlier in the year of Israel's Operation Protective Edge in the Gaza Strip
2018	Masked spyware in the app called "Red Alert" – a rocket siren app
2018	IDF found Hamas cyber operators posing as women to lure them into downloading apps that could collect contact information
2018	Operation Broken Heart was an awareness campaign to make Israelis aware of Hamas' social engineering activities (IDF, 2018)
2019	Hamas cyber building destroyed by IDF bombing

Source: Adapted from Handler (2022).

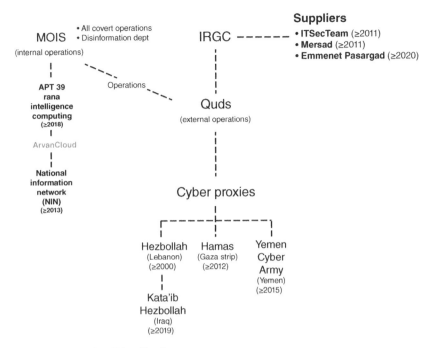

Figure 8.4 Iranian Cyber Proxies.

As shown in Figure 8.4, Iran mentors multiple proxies, each with varying cyber capabilities. In addition to coordinating with proxies and contractors, Iran partners with multiple countries for both general intelligence operations and cyber-specific coordination.

8.1.2.3 Iranian Cyber Partners (External to Iran)

The MOIS is believed to receive support from Russia's SVR (CTTSO IWSP, 2012), or Russia's foreign intelligence service, previously described in Table 5.1. Similarly, Iranian cyber operators have received training on industrial control systems through China's 863 program (Perlroth, 2012). In Table 8.1, we pointed out that the 2022 Iranian attack on the Albanian government included support from BlackByte, a CONTI (Chapter 3) spinout with ties to the Russian Federation's FSB (Chapter 5) (Oghanna, 2023; Vijayan, 2022). A diagram outlining these relationships is provided in Figure 8.5.

As described in Figure 8.5, Iranian cyber operations have multiple players. These players include Iranian cyber contractors who develop technical solutions and support operations. Proxies are also used for operational support, from being cutouts for plausible deniability (e.g., Yemen Cyber Army) to running full

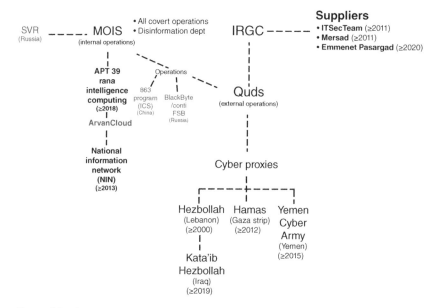

Figure 8.5 Iranian Cyber Operations Include Russian and Chinese Support.

operations and training (e.g., Hezbollah). Iran's network of cyber operators include the Advanced Persistent Threats (APTs) associated with well-publicized Iranian cyber operations (Table 8.1).

8.1.3 Iranian Cyber Teams and Targets

Iranian cyber operations are characterized by teams and tools often found to persist on certain target types. The five APTs currently identified blend the government requirements with contractor-supplied infrastructure and operational support, leveraging proxies and partnerships to perform cyber operations.

8.1.3.1 Iranian Cyber Teams (APTs)

Similar to other nation-states, Iran deploys teams with specific targets that span from collecting strategic intelligence to espionage. Strategic intelligence targeting is designed to help with policy decisions. Espionage includes industrial collections that help military and civilian industries develop better products and processes. There are five primary Iranian cyber teams identified at the time of this writing (Table 8.4).

Looking at Table 8.4, we see that Iranian APT tracking started around 2014, after the Twitter (2009), DigiNotar (2011), and the NMCI (2013) attacks.

Table 8.4 Iranian Cyber Teams.

Team	Started	Targets	Description
APT 33	2014	Aerospace, energy	APT 33 targets organizations that span multiple industries. This includes organizations headquartered in the United States, Saudi Arabia, and South Korea. APT33 is particularly interested in the aviation sector that supports both military and commercial capabilities. APT33 also targets organizations in the energy sector with ties to petrochemical production.
APT 34	2014	Middle east industry	APT 34 targets a variety of industries, including financial, government, energy, chemical, and telecommunications, and has largely focused its operations within the Middle East
APT 35	2014	Strategic intelligence	ATP 35 conducts long-term, resource-intensive operations to collect strategic intelligence that helps with policy-level decision-making.
APT 39	2014	Telecommunications, travel, and information technology (IT)	APT 39 is believed to be the Iranian Ministry of Intelligence and Security (MOIS), operating through the front company Rana Intelligence Computing.
APT 42	2015	Anti-Regime targets	APT 42 engages in spear phishing of targets that are believed to be enemies of the current Iranian regime. This includes women aligned with the Mahsa Amini protests that started in 2022 (Montalbano, 2023).

Source: Adapted from Mandiant.

As described in Table 8.4, Iranian cyber teams are used mostly for intelligence gathering. This collection spans from strategic intelligence to industrial secrets (Figure 8.6).

In Figure 8.6, we placed APTs where we believe they are operating. For example, APT 34, 35, and 42 are under the MOIS, along with Muddy Water, as the MOIS develops the requirements for strategic intelligence, technical espionage, and monitoring regime opponents. Similarly, for external operations, APT 33 and 39 are under the Al-Quds force, as this is most likely where aerospace and telecommunication intelligence operations will be operated from due to these being external operations.

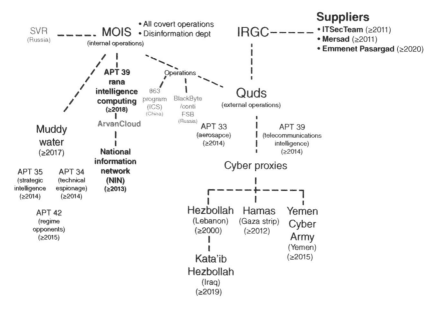

Figure 8.6 Iranian Cyber Advanced Persistent Threats (APTs).

Iran uses cyber for both espionage and as a punitive weapon to strike "below the line" (Figure 1.3) against perceived adversaries. Cyber espionage is used to collect both strategic information that helps with policy decisions and for data that help Iran collect intelligence on perceived adversaries. In one example, Iran was able to penetrate the U.S. Navy–Marine Corps Internet (NMCI).

8.1.3.2 2012–2014 Navy–Marine Corps Internet (NMCI) Attack
During the period 2012–2014, Iran was able to compromise the NMCI, a network of approximately 800,000 users at 2500 sites. This attack occurred through public-facing web servers (Julian Barnes, 2013). The NMCI was the biggest target in the Navy, and the cyberattack became a scaled headache across Navy commands and supporting organizations. While Iranian cyber operators likely stumbled into the NMCI as a target, they appear to have stumbled well, in finding an Achilles' heel (Gallagher, 2014).

8.1.3.3 2020 U.S. Elections
Iran attempted to influence the 2020 U.S. Presidential Election through a contractor, Emmenet Pasargad, disseminating fake videos on social media with illicitly gathered media content that was modified to appear realistic (U.S. Treasury, 2021). Emmenet Pasargad is believed to be responsible for an increase in cyber influence operations starting in 2022 (Watts, 2023).

U.S. election officials were threatened throughout the 2020 U.S. Presidential election. For example, the "Enemies of the People" website, including photographs of a number of U.S. officials and individuals from private sector entities involved with the 2020 election, was attributed to Iran (DoJ, 2021; FBI, 2020).

> Iran is increasingly active in using cyberspace to enable influence operations – including aggressive influence operations targeting the US 2020 presidential election – and we expect Tehran to focus on online covert influence, such as spreading disinformation about fake threats or compromised election infrastructure and recirculating anti-US content. Iran attempted to influence dynamics around the 2020 US presidential election by sending threatening messages to US voters, and Iranian cyber actors in December 2020 disseminated information about US election officials to try to undermine confidence in the US election. (DNI)

Using a cyber operations contractor (Emmenet Pasargad) to attack the 2020 U.S. Presidential Election process is an example of Iran's increasingly widespread use of influence operations. In addition, the use of a contractor is another example of Iran delegating operations to external organizations.

8.1.3.4   2022 Albanian Cyber Attack by Iran

The CONTI ransomware attack on Costa Rica was a surprise due to the boldness of shutting a government out of its systems. As the CONTI team broke up, members migrated to other teams, making their skills available for hire. Iran managed to find a team with these skills.

Due to Albania providing refuge to the Mujahideen e Khalq (MEK), an enemy of the current regime in Tehran, Iran launched a significant cyberattack on Albanian government systems in the early summer of 2022 that included the use of wipers. This cyberattack effectively denied the Albanian government systems' operability and resulted in the expulsion of Iranian diplomats from Albania (Microsoft Security Threat Intelligence, 2022).

> Between May and June 2022, Iranian state cyber actors conducted lateral movements, network reconnaissance, and credential harvesting from Albanian government networks. In July 2022, the actors launched ransomware on the networks, leaving an anti-Mujahideen E-Khalq (MEK) message on desktops. When network defenders identified and began to respond to the ransomware activity, the cyber actors deployed a version of ZeroCleare destructive malware. (CISA, 2022)

While denial operations are not new to Iran, teaming with BlackByte, a Russian ransomware expert, to shut down an entire government's network, was the first time that any cyber operator other than CONTI (e.g., in Chapter 3, we covered CONTI using cyber to shut down the Costa Rican IT government system) performed an attack at this kind of scale (Oghanna, 2023). This makes more sense when we factor in that BlackByte is a CONTI spinoff, with some team members likely having had experience with the Costa Rican operation.

8.1.4 Iranian Cyber Operations Wrap-up

The merging of Iranian cyber with seasoned Russian ransomware operators is an issue, as now both Iran and Russia provide safe havens for these destructive cyber operations. Current Iranian cyber operations have expanded over proxy networks, previously used for terror operations, to provide plausible deniability for cyberattacks on Iran's enemies. These proxy operations span from false flag operations (i.e., Yemen Cyber Army) to Hezbollah developing its own malware and training courses for export (Section 8.2.2.2). Hezbollah has already spawned its own proxy, Kata'ib Hizballah, which now operates through networks in Iraq. These first- and second-order proxies position Iran to extend its decades-old militia operations to include cyber (Figure 8.7).

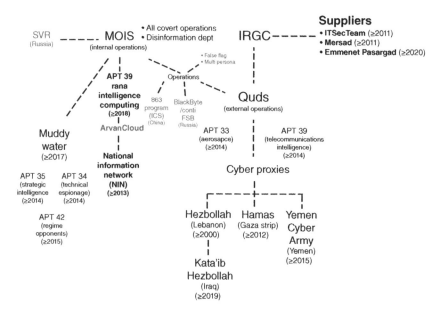

Figure 8.7 Iranian Cyber Operators, Suppliers, and Proxies.

Iranian cyber operators, barely known before the STUXNET delay of their nuclear program, have performed cyberattacks on international finance (i.e., Al Ababil), global energy (i.e., Al Shamoon), critical infrastructure (i.e., Rye Dam and Israeli water), and military networks (i.e., NMCI). Iranian cyber operations expanded on their internal and external information operations in order to counter domestic protests (i.e., 2009 Twitter and 2022 Mahsa Amini) and to manipulate foreign elections (i.e., 2020 U.S. Presidential Election).

8.A Cost of Iranian Cyber Attacks

Table A.1 Iranian Cyber Operations and Reconstitution Costs.

Year	Target	Cost	Source
2012–2014	NMCI	$10 million	(Gallagher, 2014)
2013	Bowman Dam	$30,000	(DoJ, 2016)
2014	Sands Casino	$40 million	(Brandom, 2014)

Bibliography

Article19. (2016). *Tightening the Net: Internet Security and Censorship in Iran (Part 1 – The National Internet Project)*. Retrieved from Article19: https://www.article19. org/data/files/The_National_Internet_AR_KA_final.pdf.

Associated Press. (2021). *Iran Calls Natanz Atomic Site Blackout 'Nuclear Terrorism'*. Retrieved from NBC: https://www.nbcnews.com/news/world/ electrical-problem-strikes-iran-s-natanz-nuclear-facility-n1263747.

Brandom, R. (2014). *Iran Hacked the Sands Hotel Earlier this Year, Causing over $40 Million in Damage*. Retrieved from The Verge: https://www.theverge.com/2014/12/11/7376249/ iran-hacked-sands-hotel-in-february-cyberwar-adelson-israel.

Brewster, T. (2018). *Syrian Electronic Army Hackers Are Targeting Android Phones With Fake WhatsApp Attacks*. Retrieved from Forbes: https://www.forbes.com/ sites/thomasbrewster/2018/12/05/syrian-electronic-army-hackers-are-targeting-android- phones-with-fake-whatsapp-attacks/?sh=6c2e200a6ce4.

Carnegie Endowment for International Peace. (2018). *Iran's Cyber Ecosystem: Who Are the Threat Actors?* Retrieved 8 20, 2022, from Carnegie Endowment for International Peace: https://carnegieendowment.org/2018/01/04/iran-s-cyber- ecosystem-who-are-threat-actors-pub-75140.

CFR. (2012a). *Compromise of Saudi Aramco and RasGas*. Retrieved from Council on Foreign Relations:https://www.cfr.org/cyber-operations/compromise-saudi-aramco-and-rasgas.

CFR. (2012b). *Denial of Service Attacks Against U.S. Banks in 2012–2013*. Retrieved from Council on Foreign Relations: https://www.cfr.org/cyber-operations/denial-service-attacks-against-us-banks-2012-2013.

CISA. (2022). *Iranian State Actors Conduct Cyber Operations Against the Government of Albania*. Retrieved 9 22, 2022, from Alert (AA22-264A): https://www.cisa.gov/uscert/ncas/alerts/aa22-264a.

Clarke, C. P. (2017). *How Hezbollah Came to Dominate Information Warfare*. Retrieved from RAND: https://www.rand.org/blog/2017/09/how-hezbollah-came-to-dominate-information-warfare.html.

Colin Anderson, K. S. (2018a). *Iran's Cyber Threat*. Retrieved 11 3, 2022, from Carnegie Endowment for International Peace: https://carnegieendowment.org/files/Iran_Cyber_Final_Full_v2.pdf.

Collin Anderson, K.S. (2018b). *Iran's Cyber Threat: Espionage, Sabotage, and Revenge*. Washington, DC: Carnegie Endowment.

CTTSO IWSP. (2012). *Iran's Ministry of Intelligence and Security: A Profile*. Retrieved 11 2023, 3, from https://irp.fas.org/world/iran/mois-loc.pdf.

DNI. (n.d.). *Annual Threat Assessment of the U.S. Intelligence Community*. Retrieved from DNI: 2021.

DoJ. (2016a). *Seven Iranians Working for Islamic Revolutionary Guard Corps-Affiliated Entities Charged for Conducting Coordinated Campaign of Cyber Attacks Against U.S. Financial Sector*. Retrieved from DoJ: https://www.justice.gov/opa/pr/seven-iranians-working-islamic-revolutionary-guard-corps-affiliated-entities-charged.

DoJ. (2016b). *USA vs Hamid Firoozi et al*. Retrieved from DoJ: https://www.justice.gov/media/824691/dl?inline.

DoJ. (2021) *Two Iranian Nationals Charged for Cyber-Enabled Disinformation and Threat Campaign Designed to Influence the 2020 U.S. Presidential Election*. Retrieved from U.S. Department of Justice: https://www.justice.gov/opa/pr/two-iranian-nationals-charged-cyber-enabled-disinformation-and-threat-campaign-designed.

DoJ. 2021 *Two Iranian Nationals Charged for Cyber-Enabled Disinformation and Threat Campaign Designed to Influence the 2020 U.S. Presidential Election*. Retrieved from U.S. Department of Justice: https://www.justice.gov/opa/pr/two-iranian-nationals-charged-cyber-enabled-disinformation-and-threat-campaign-designed.

Dov Lieber, B. F. (2023). *Russia Supplies Iran With Cyber Weapons as Military Cooperation Grows; Tehran is Receiving Advanced Surveillance Software After Providing Drones for Ukraine Battlefield*. Retrieved from Wall Street Journal:

https://news.yahoo.com/russia-supplies-cyber-weapons-iran-153015291. html?guccounter=1.

ENISA. (n.d.). *Operation Black Tulip: Certificate Authorities Lose Authority*. Retrieved from European Network and Information Security Agency: https://www.enisa. europa.eu/media/news-items/operation-black-tulip/.

FBI. (2020). *Iranian Cyber Actors Responsible for Website Threatening U.S. Election Officials*. Retrieved 9 20, 2022, from FBI: https://www.fbi.gov/news/press-releases/ press-releases/iranian-cyber-actors-responsible-for-website-threatening-us-election-officials.

Finkle, J. (2014). *Iranian Hackers Use Fake Facebook Accounts to Spy on U.S., Others*. Retrieved from Reuters: https://www.reuters.com/article/iran-hackers/ iranian-hackers-use-fake-facebook-accounts-to-spy-on-u-s-others-idUSL1N0O E2CU20140529.

Fowler, S. (2013). *Who is the Syrian Electronic Army?* Retrieved from BBC: https:// www.bbc.com/news/world-middle-east-22287326.

Franceschi-Bicchierai, L. (2015). *There's Evidence the 'Yemen Cyber Army' Is Actually Iranian*. Retrieved from Vice: https://www.vice.com/en/article/wnj9gq/ theres-evidence-the-yemen-cyber-army-is-actually-iranian.

Frenkel, S. (2015). *Meet the Mysterious New Hacker Army Freaking Out the Middle East*. Retrieved 3 16, 2023, from BuzzFeed: https://www.buzzfeednews.com/ article/sheerafrenkel/who-is-the-yemen-cyber-army.

Gallagher, S. (2014). *Iranians Hacked Navy Network for Four Months? Not a Surprise*. Retrieved from Ars Technica: https://arstechnica.com/information-technology/2014/02/iranians-hacked-navy-network-for-4-months-not-a-surprise/.

Gerry Shih, J. M. (2013). *New York Times, Twitter Hacked by Syrian Group*. Retrieved from Reuters: https://www.reuters.com/article/uk-newyorktimes-hacked/ new-york-times-twitter-hacked-by-syrian-group-idUKBRE97Q11K20130828.

Handler, S. (2022). *The Cyber Strategy and Operations of Hamas: Green Flags and Green Hats*. Retrieved from Atlantic Council: https://www.atlanticcouncil.org/ in-depth-research-reports/report/ the-cyber-strategy-and-operations-of-hamas-green-flags-and-green-hats/.

Hardcastle, J. (2022). *Iranian Cyberspies Exploited Log4j to Break into a US Govt Network*. Retrieved from The Register: https://www.theregister.com/2022/11/16/ iranian_cyberspies_log4j/.

Hoffman, S. (2011). *300,000 Iranian IP Addresses Compromised In DigiNotar SSL Hack*. Retrieved from CRN: https://www.crn.com/news/security/231600847/ 300-000-iranian-ip-addresses-compromised-in-diginotar-ssl-hack.htm.

IDF. (2018). *Hamas' Online Terrorism*. Retrieved from IDF: https://www.idf.il/en/ mini-sites/hamas/hamas-online-terrorism/.

Ilascu, I. (2022). *How Conti Ransomware Hacked and Encrypted the Costa Rican Government*. Retrieved from Bleeping Computer: https://www.bleepingcomputer.

com/news/security/how-conti-ransomware-hacked-and-encrypted-the-costa-rican-government/.

Jones, R. (2019). *What We Know About the Saudi Oil Attacks; U.S., Saudis say Direction of Projectiles and Type of Cruise Missiles and Drones Involved in Attacks Point to Iran; Vulnerabilities Exposed in Kingdom's Air Defense.* Retrieved from Wall Street Journal.

Julian Barnes, S. G. (2013). *U.S. Says Iran Hacked Navy Computers.* Retrieved 3 18, 2023, from Wall Street Journal: https://www.wsj.com/articles/us-says-iran-hacked-navy-computers-1380314771.

Kenneth, W. A., Genschel, P. G. (2015). *International Organizations as Orchestrators.* Retrieved from Cambridge University Press: https://www.cambridge.org/core/books/abs/international-organizations-as-orchestrators/orchestration/C6675B2E52836D5C6FACD5A5AB10C3DB.

Khameneh, A. (2023). *The Scorched-Earth Tactics of Iran's Cyber Army.* Retrieved from Wired: https://www.wired.com/story/iran-cyber-army-protests-disinformation/.

Kogosowski, M. (2022). *Ran Exploiting Log4j 2 Weakness to Attack Israel, Says Microsoft.* Retrieved 8 28, 2022, from Israel Defense: https://www.israeldefense.co.il/en/node/55602.

Langner, R. (2011). *Cracking Stuxnet, a 21st-century cyber weapon.* TED2011.

Levitt, M. (2021). *Hezbollah's Regional Activities in Support of Iran's Proxy Networks.* Retrieved from MEI: https://www.mei.edu/publications/hezbollahs-regional-activities-support-irans-proxy-networks.

Malik, H. (2020) *The Still-growing Threat of Iran's Chosen Proxy in Iraq.* Retrieved from War on the Rocks: https://warontherocks.com/2020/10/the-still-growing-threat-of-irans-chosen-proxy-in-iraq/.

Mandiant. (n.d.). *Advanced Persistent Threats (APTs).* Retrieved from Mandiant: https://www.mandiant.com/resources/insights/apt-groups.

Maurer, T. (2016). *'Proxies' and Cyberspace.* Retrieved 3 14, 2023, from Carnegie Endowment: https://carnegieendowment.org/files/JConflictSecurityLaw-2016-Maurer-383-403.pdf.

Melendez, P. (2019). *U.S. Carried Out Cyberattack on Kata'ib Hezbollah, an Iranian Proxy Militia: CNN.* Retrieved from The Daily Beast: https://www.thedailybeast.com/us-carried-out-cyberattack-on-kataib-hezbollah-an-iranian-proxy-militia-cnn.

Michel Martin, D. T.-R. (2022). *Iran tries to Crack Down on Protests, Even Online. Here's how Activists are Evading those Efforts.* Retrieved 11 4, 2022, from NPR: https://www.npr.org/2022/10/15/1129319097/iran-tries-to-crack-down-on-protests-even-online-heres-how-activists-are-evading.

Microsoft Security Threat Intelligence. (2022). *Microsoft Investigates Iranian Attacks Against the Albanian Government.* Retrieved 9 22, 2022, from Microsoft Security

Threat Information Center: https://www.microsoft.com/security/blog/2022/09/08/microsoft-investigates-iranian-attacks-against-the-albanian-government/.

Montalbano, E. (2023). *Iranian APT Targets Female Activists With Mahsa Amini Protest Lures*. Retrieved from DARKReading: https://www.darkreading.com/threat-intelligence/iranian-apt-uses-mahsa-amini-protests-to-target-female-activists.

Moskowitz, J. (2015). *Cyberattack Tied to Hezbollah Ups the Ante for Israel's Digital Defenses*. Retrieved from Christian Science Monitor: https://www.csmonitor.com/layout/set/print/World/Passcode/2015/0601/Cyberattack-tied-to-Hezbollah-ups-the-ante-for-Israel-s-digital-defenses.

New York Times. (2009). *Twitter Attacked by 'Iranian Cyber Army'*. Retrieved from New York Times.

New York Times. (2012). *In Cyberattack on Saudi Firm, U.S. Sees Iran Firing Back*. Retrieved from New York Times.

Office of the Director of National Intelligence (ODNI). (2023). *Annual Threat Assessment of the U.S. Intelligence Community*. Retrieved 3 9, 2023, from ODNI.

Oghanna, A. (2023). *How Albania Became a Target for Cyberattacks*. Retrieved from Foreign Policy: https://foreignpolicy.com/2023/03/25/albania-target-cyberattacks-russia-iran/.

Pamuk, H. (2019). *U.S. Probe of Saudi Oil Attack Shows it Came from North*. Retrieved from Reuters: https://www.reuters.com/article/us-saudi-aramco-attacks-iran-exclusive/exclusive-u-s-probe-of-saudi-oil-attack-shows-it-came-from-north-report-idUSKBN1YN299.

Perlroth, N. (2012. *In Cyberattack on Saudi Firm, U.S. Sees Iran Firing Back*. Retrieved 3 18, 2023, from New York Times: https://www.nytimes.com/2012/10/24/business/global/cyberattack-on-saudi-oil-firm-disquiets-us.html.

Recorded Future. (2013). *Deconstructing the Al-Qassam Cyber Fighters Assault on US Banks*. Retrieved from Recorded Future: https://www.recordedfuture.com/deconstructing-the-al-qassam-cyber-fighters-assault-on-us-banks.

Reddick, J. (2023). *US Treasury Sanctions Iranian Cloud Provider 'Facilitating' Tehran Censorship*. Retrieved from The Record: https://therecord.media/arvancloud-sanctions-iran-internet-us-treasury-department.

Simurgh Aryan, H. A. (2013). *Internet Censorship in Iran: A First Look*. Retrieved from Usenix: https://www.usenix.org/system/files/conference/foci13/foci13-aryan.pdf.

Toulas, B. (2022). *Microsoft: Iranian Hackers Still Exploiting Log4j Bugs Against Israel*. Retrieved from Bleeping Computer: https://www.bleepingcomputer.com/news/security/microsoft-iranian-hackers-still-exploiting-log4j-bugs-against-israel/.

U.S. Treasury. (2021). *Treasury Sanction Iran Cyber Actors for Attempting to Influence the 2020 U.S. Presidential Election*. Retrieved 5 3, 2023, from U.S. Treasury: https://home.treasury.gov/news/press-releases/jy0494.

US Department of the Treasury. (2020). *Treasury Sanctions Cyber Actors Backed by Iranian Intelligence Ministry*. Retrieved 9 17, 2020, from US Department of the Treasury: https://home.treasury.gov/news/press-releases/sm1127.

US Department of the Treasury. (2021). *Treasury Sanctions Iran Cyber Actors for Attempting to Influence the 2020 U.S. Presidential Election*. Retrieved from US Department of the Treasury: https://home.treasury.gov/news/press-releases/jy0494.

US Treasury. (2023). *Treasury Sanctions Iranian Company Aiding in Internet Censorship*. Retrieved from U.S. Department of the Treasury: https://home. treasury.gov/news/press-releases/jy1518.

Vijayan, J. (2014). *With Operation Cleaver, Iran Emerges As A Cyberthreat*. Retrieved from DARKReading: https://www.darkreading.com/attacks-breaches/ with-operation-cleaver-iran-emerges-as-a-cyberthreat.

Vijayan, J. (2022). *Post-Breakup, Conti Ransomware Members Remain Dangerous*. Retrieved from Dark Reading: https://www.darkreading.com/attacks-breaches/ breakup-conti-ransomware-members-dangerous.

VOA. (2022). *Iran Expands Advanced Centrifuge Work Underground, IAEA Finds*. Retrieved 6 8, 2022, from Voice of America: https://www.voanews.com/a/ iran-expands-advanced-centrifuge-work-underground-iaea-finds-/6609017.html.

Wagenheim, M. (2020). *Hezbollah Hones Expertise in Training Cyber-warfare Agents*. Retrieved from Jerusalem Post: https://www.jpost.com/middle-east/ hezbollah-hones-expertise-in-training-cyber-warfare-agents-638800.

Watts, C. (2023). *Rinse and Repeat: Iran Accelerates its Cyber Influence Operations Worldwide*. Retrieved 5 3, 2023, from Digital Threat Analysis Center: https://blogs. microsoft.com/on-the-issues/2023/05/02/dtac-iran-cyber-influence-operations-digital-threat/.

Yaniv Balmas, I. D. (2015. *Volatile Cedar – Analysis of a Global Cyber Espionage Campaign*. Retrieved from Checkpoint: https://blog.checkpoint.com/security/ volatilecedar/.

Zetter, K. (2014). *Countdown to Zero Day – Stuxnet and the Launch of the World's First Digital Weapon*. New York: Crown.

9

Independent Cyber Operators

9.1   Independent Cyber Operations

> Independent cyber operations are the original form of cyber hacking, with individual operators testing their skills in order to test both their personal capabilities and the limits of the available technology. The first widely documented hack, pre dating the Internet, was the Morris Worm (1988), taking down the entire University affiliated network. (Microsoft, 2022)

Nation-state cyber operations include the research, the development, and the clandestine service components introduced in Figure 4.1. A mainstay of nation-state cyber operations is that they are working toward a policy-driven purpose, even if it is theft for a nascent weapons program (i.e., DPRK and China) or surveillance of its own citizens (i.e., Russia and Iran). As potentially dangerous as these nation-state capabilities have proven to be, they are still within a disciplined governance structure and can be subject to sanctions and public outrage. A lone hacker is potentially far more dangerous with the same sets of tools.

Julian Assange, for example, created the news with the release of his "Collateral Murder" video, the Afghan War Logs (2010) (Leigh, 2010), and the release of State Department cables, which influenced the 2011 Arab Spring (DoJ, 2019). Wikileaks provided tangible examples of political and personal cyber effects. And, while Mr. Assange's cyber career effectively ended with his taking refuge in the Ecuadoran Embassy, in London (2012), this cyber genie did not go back in the bottle. Independent cyber operations span from pure theft (i.e., Conficker and RaaS) to harassing governments and leaders of state. The Mossack Fonseca (2012) outing, for example, provided information on leadership figures in China and

Cyber Operations: A Case Study Approach, First Edition. Jerry M. Couretas.
© 2024 John Wiley & Sons, Inc. Published 2024 by John Wiley & Sons, Inc.

Russia and is said to be responsible for Sigmundur Gunnlaugsson, the Prime Minister of Iceland, resigning in 2016 (Bernstein, 2017).

9.1.1 Hackers

While hacking was bringing down governments by the second decade of the 21st century, this was not the goal of the pioneering tech afficionados of the early 1980s. The original motivation was technical curiosity. For example, the Chaos Computer Club, founded in 1981, has provided hackers with a support community for over 40 years.

> The Chaos Computer Club (CCC) is Europe's largest association of hackers. For more than 30 years we are providing information about technical and societal issues, such as surveillance, privacy, freedom of information, hacktivism, data security and many other interesting things around technology and hacking issues. As the most influential hacker collective in Europe we organize campaigns, events, lobbying and publications as well as anonymizing services and communication infrastructure. There are many hackerspaces in and around Germany which belong to or share a common bond to the CCC as stated in our hacker ethics. (Chaos Computer Club)

This hacking community was not isolated to Germany or even Europe. For example, a decade before the Internet, Steven Levy published "Hackers: Heroes of the Computer Revolution" (Levy, 1984) to describe the people, machines, and culture developing around computers that folks were building in their garages and basements.

It was not long before nation-state intelligence services began to experiment with computer-based espionage. For example, in the mid-1980s, the KGB was found to be using West German hackers, members of the Chaos Computing Club, to access U.S. Government computers in order to get secrets on the Star Wars Missile Defense System (Stoll, 2005).

9.1.1.1 Star Wars, Computer Networks, and the Former Soviet Union's KGB (mid-1980s)

Cold War nation-state espionage usually took the form of human spies, along with secret communications and dead drop locations for a spy to leave satchels of purloined documents for a handler to pick up. The developing computer revolution, however, led the KGB to experiment with what a few smart hackers might be able to collect via computer, from a safe location back in Europe.

The story is best conveyed through "The Cuckoo's Egg" (Stoll, 2005), which provides an action novel narrative of how a postdoctoral student, initially looking to understand a computer time billing discrepancy at a U.S. national laboratory, ends up tracking down hackers paid by Russian intelligence to penetrate U.S. government networks in order to extract military secrets. In the mid-1980s, German hackers, working on behalf of the KGB, penetrated the Lawrence Berkeley Lab's computer network in an attempt to get information on the U.S. Star Wars missile defense program portfolio (Stoll, 2005). Each of the "Hanover Gang" perpetrators that Dr. Stoll's investigation eventually implicated was a Chaos Computer Club member, an organization that currently has over 7700 registered members who share hacking information and hold an annual conference (Chaos Computer Club).

The KGB was ahead of its time in using computer networks for espionage. This early network, connecting several thousand U.S. government laboratories and universities, was usually used for an early version of e-mail communication, or experimentation. This included testing rapidly replicating network "worm" programs.

9.1.1.2   Morris Worm (1988)

While the KGB was using hackers to perform traditional espionage activity, Robert Tappan Morris, a Cornell student, had an academic interest in the limits of the early Internet. During his research, Morris found vulnerabilities in a key early Internet operating system, Unix, and wrote a program to exploit these vulnerabilities, replicate itself, and propagate to other machines. The Morris Worm occurred when the "Internet" consisted of less than 100,000 connected computers and the Morris Worm is estimated to have shut down about 10% of that version of the Internet (Figure 9.1).

Robert Morris was sentenced under the Computer Fraud and Abuse Act of 1986 (United States Court of Appeals, Second Circuit, 1991). Morris Worm cleanup cost estimates started at $100,000 and went into the millions, without a clear number being arrived at (FBI, 2018).

9.1.1.3   Jester – Air Traffic Control and Telephone Service (1997)

Nearly 10 years after the Morris Worm, in March 1997, one of the first telephony denial of service attacks was performed by a teenage hacker in Massachusetts (a.k.a., "Jester") who dialed into the Bell Atlantic computer system, via modem, and knocked out systems that managed phone and radio communications for the

Figure 9.1 Robert Tappan Morris – author of the Morris Worm. *Source:* FBI (2018)/Federal Bureau of Investigation.

air traffic control tower at Worcester Airport, as well as phone service for 600 homes in the area. Communications for the airport's security and fire departments were down for 6 hours, as were the system pilots used to activate the runway lights. Air traffic controllers had to use cell phones and battery-powered radios to direct planes during the outage (Boston, 1998).

Jester showed how the increasing use of network technologies with telephony could become a life-threatening emergency if executed at the right time (e.g., planes needing to land and fires blazing out of control). While cell phones were used as a backup, one could imagine a scenario where cell phone jamming accompanied the attack (DHS Science and Technology (S&T) Directorate).

9.1.1.4 Chinese Hacktivists (1998)

While Jester was still in the realm of lone hackers, cyber also opened up the possibility for politically motivated actors. The FBI defines Hacktivism.

Hacktivism: A collective of cyber criminals who conduct cyber activities to advance an ideological, social, or political cause. Historically, hacktivist collectives conducted and advocated for cyber crime activity following high-profile political, socioeconomic, or world events (FBI, 2022).

In contrast to Russia's initial espionage-focused hacking, China's hackers developed over time with a patriotic fervor (Winnona DeSombre, 2018). China's hacker discussions included the "lost century" (i.e., the period between the mid-19th century opium wars and Mao's communist takeover in 1949) (Carr, 2012a, b). Chinese hackers debuted as ethno-nationalists during the 1990s anti-Chinese riots in Indonesia. Lin Yong, "The Lion," was an early leader of the Honker Union of China.

China's hacktivist community, inspired by nationalistic sentiment, is focused on the turn of the 21st century (Henderson, 2007) (Table 9.1).

Table 9.1 Chinese Hacker Group Development.

Time Period	Trigger	Activities	Groups
1998	Anti-Chinese riots in Indonesia	DoS, Website defacement	Green Army, China Eagle Union, Honker Union
1999	Kosovo embassy bombing by NATO	U.S. Government websites	
2001	PRC fighter collision with U.S. plane	Website defacement (e.g., U.S. White House)	

PRC Government connection developed due to the Hackers patriotic statements, such as the 100 years of humiliation narrative (i.e., China was great until the 1840s opium wars, fell in power, and is now on the ascendant)
Source: Adapted from Henderson (2007).

As shown in Table 9.1, many of the Chinese hacker incidents stem from International events surrounding either Chinese people or the interests of mainland China. This is why many people suspect a link between the Chinese government and hacking activities.

9.1.1.5 Maroochy Shire (2000)

While Chinese hacktivists act out against perceived oppressors, an Australian engineer made his protest local after being laid off from a local sewage plant in the year 2000. In Australia's Queensland, Maroochy Water Services had recently installed a wireless, automated controls system, for their sewage plant. Following the layoff of an engineer who installed the system, the controls started to malfunction, ultimately discharging over 265,000 gallons of raw sewage into public waterways. The former engineer was ultimately apprehended for remotely controlling the plant and discharging the raw sewage (Smith, 2001).

Maroochy Shire is the only documented misuse of a water treatment facility via cyber. More recent hacking includes an attempt to change the level of sodium hydroxide (i.e., lye) at the Oldsmar, Florida, water treatment plant in 2021 (CISA, 2020).

9.1.1.6 Slammer and Sobig – Business Systems, Nuclear Power Plants, and Train Signaling (2003)

While Maroochy Shire provided a wakeup call concerning how new, networked, technologies can pose a danger, the Slammer worm incapacitated the safety monitoring system and process control network of the Davis Besse nuclear power plant in Ohio for about five hours (RISI Data, 2003).

Similarly, in 2003, the train signaling systems on the U.S. East Coast went dark after computers belonging to CSX Corporation in Florida got infected with the

Sobig virus (CBS News, 2003; Symantec, 2003). Sobig was an automated e-mailer that sent messages to all the contacts in the compromised computer's recently sent addresses in order to get around spam-blocking software. Sobig infected CSX, which operates rail systems for passenger and freight trains in 23 states, and, as a result of the infection, stopped signals going out, causing trains running between Pennsylvania and South Carolina and in the DC Beltway to stop (Hancock, 2003). Cost estimates for the Sobig virus run into the billions of dollars (Vigderman, 2022).

9.1.1.7 Conficker (2008–2011)

Similar to Slammer, Conficker was a mysterious worm that spread quickly and infected an estimated 7–12 million computers worldwide at its peak around 2008 (Heli Tiirmaa-Klaar, 2014). Conficker's botnet spanned from the military to commercial banking. In terms of operations, once Conficker was on a machine

> ... it would perform a Ukrainian keyboard check; the worm would not activate Ukrainian machines. In addition, the Worm kept track of time – an internal timer gave it 6 days to spread before activation. When the worm came to life, it would try calling home, to a C2 server, by generating a list of seemingly random Internet domain names, 250 of them, every three hours. The next day it would create an entirely new list of 250 domain names. If the host computer was off line, it would check back every minute until it could resume the exercise. The worm generated domains appeared random, just meaningless strings of numbers and letters flowed by on the five Top Level Domain (TLD) indicators – .com, .org, .net, .info, or .biz – but they were, in fact, entirely predictable if you knew the algorithm that produced them. Whoever was controlling the worm needed only to be behind one of those 250 doors to issue a command. (Bowden, 2011)

As a technical solution, Conficker provided unprecedented scale and scope. Detecting a bot, or other backdoors, being used to exfiltrate data, is a challenge to detect. In addition, the complexity of Conficker communications made it a challenge to track down the team behind the worm. Detailed analysis (Phillip Porras, 2009), and persistent effort, therefore led to the June 2011 arrest of sixteen hackers in Kiev, highly educated young men. Authorities in the Ukraine, in cooperation with the FBI, arrested the young men for collecting $72 million online (Bowden, 2011). While the attack on banking due to the Conficker worm is quantifiable, at $72 million, the damages due to Wikileaks include reputations and political careers. These effects are more challenging to assess.

9.1.1.8 Wikileaks (2006 to present)

In terms of famous acts of hacktivism, Wikileaks was one of the first, and likely one of the most powerful independent venues on the Internet to "out" information marked secret, causing headaches for Government officials across the world. As exercises in "scientific journalism," each outing furthered Julian Assange's goal of "no secrets" (Khatchadourian, 2010). For example, the release of U.S. State Department cables embarrassed both U.S. and foreign diplomats from the frank comments that were meant to remain private. The cables and other associated information were transmitted from Chelsea (then Bradley) Manning to Julian Assange and then posted on the web.

Julian Assange was given information from Chelsea Manning for the 2010 "Collateral Murder" video. This same trove of data included State Department cables that likely influenced the 2011 Arab Spring. In addition, the Russian GRU, through the Guccifer 2.0 persona, provided information on the Democratic National Committee (DNC) with the intent to influence the 2016 U.S. Presidential Election. And, as discussed in Chapter 3, the Vault7 leak (2017), one of the largest in CIA history, directly preceded the rash of ransomware that continues to this day.

9.1.2 Hackers in the Russo-Ukraine War (2022+)

An unexpected result of Russia's February 2022 invasion of Ukraine included Anonymous, the famous network of hackers, attacking Russia, thereby opening up an additional "cyber front" (Table 9.2).

As shown in Table 9.2, Anonymous was able to penetrate and release data from multiple Russian civilian and security sites. For example, one action of the Ukrainian hacktivists during the 2022 Russo-Ukraine conflict included hacking into Russia's central bank and extracting approximately 28 GB of data, including confidential client information (Hope, 2022).

9.1.2.1 Independent Operations and the Russo-Ukraine War (2022+)

In the first months of the Russian attack on Ukraine, the hacking group NB65 used leaked CONTI ransomware to attack Russian organizations that include

> The Russian entities claimed to have been attacked by the hacking group include document management operator Tensor, Russian space agency Roscosmos, and VGTRK, the state-owned Russian Television and Radio broadcaster. The attack on VGTRK was particularly significant as it led to the alleged theft of 786.2 GB of data, including 900,000 emails and 4000 files, which were published on the DDoS Secrets website. (Abrams, 2022)

Table 9.2 Anonymous Attacks on Russia.

Date	Event
February 28, 2022	Anonymous hacks EV charging station + TV channels
March 4, 2022	Anonymous hacks the Russian Space Research Institute website
March 7, 2022	Anonymous hacks Russian TV and streaming sites with war footage
March 10, 2022	Anonymous hacks 90% of misconfigured Russian cloud databases
March 12, 2022	Anonymous sent 7M texts and hacked 400 Russian security cams
March 15, 2022	Anonymous DDoS'd Russian Fed Security Service and other sites
March 19, 2022	Anonymous hacked and leaked 79 GB of Russian pipeline giant data
March 23, 2022	Anonymous hacks printers in Russia to send anti-war messages

Source: Adapted from Waqas (2022).

In addition, Russian rail operator RZD was reported to go offline due to a massive cyberattack in the summer of 2023

> The Belarusian hacktivist collective Cyber Partisans, which claimed responsibility for the attack, said that some trains stopped running after hackers compromised the railway system's routing and switching devices and rendered them inoperable by encrypting data stored on them. (Antoniuk, 2023)

And, while the Russian Federation is sustaining attacks from NB65, the Ukrainian Cyber Army (Tidy, 2023), and the Cyber Partisans, alleged Russian hacktivists, "Killnet," are performing attacks against perceived enemies of Russia.

9.1.2.2 Killnet – Pro-Russian Operations

Killnet attacks both Ukrainian targets and any other entity with an opinion differing from Russia's. For example, Killnet attempted cyberattacks on the U.S. Treasury (Stahie, 2022), U.S. airports (Toulas, 2022), and several Eastern European government systems for supplying weapons to Ukraine in the Fall of 2022 (Martin, 2022). Killnet's primary weapon is to use Distributed Denial of Service (DDoS).

Killnet's independence is a little suspicious, as the Russian Federation's FSB monitors all telecommunications (e.g., SORM-3 (Lewis, 2014)). In addition, there are questions as to the effectiveness of independent cyber operations in the Russo-Ukraine war (2022–present) (Anh and Vu, 2022).

9.1.3 Independent Cyber Operations Wrap-up

While the contribution of independent cyber operators during wartime is still undetermined, it is clear that determined hackers can produce plenty of mayhem. Wikileaks, for example, may have been partly responsible for starting the Arab Spring (Coles, 2011) and multiple other events related to the disclosure of previously secret, or private, information. In Table 9.3, we see a chronology of hacker-related events from the late 1990s through the early 2020s.

Table 9.3 Independent Cyber Operations.

Event	Description
1980s to early 2000s (Hackers)	Hackers worked through a desire to better understand technology, sometimes with a potentially destructive outcome (e.g., 1988 Morris Worm)
1990s to early 2000s (Hacktivists)	Hacktivists used computers to express political protest. This could be in the form of maligning a perceived adversary's website and/or using cyber means to get a message out (1998 Chinese Hacktivists)
2010 Wikileaks	Initially publishing U.S. Diplomatic Cables, the Arab Spring was said to be one of the effects of releasing this information (David Leigh, 2011; Domscheit-Berg, 2011)
2012 Panama Papers	A group of journalists, some involved with Wikileaks, published offshore companies' legal filings from the Panamanian law firm Mossack Fonseca. This information included personal business records of high-level officials in Russia and China who participate in offshore money-hiding schemes (Bernstein, 2017).
2016 U.S. Presidential Election	Wikileaks published Democratic National Committee (DNC) e-mails provided by Russian intelligence. The effect was organizational changes in the Democratic candidates' campaign composition.
2017 Vault7 Cyber Tool Release	Wikileaks was used to release a treasure trove of cyber tools from the CIA in 2017. As discussed in Chapter 3, some of these tools were almost immediately found to be used in the WannaCry ransomware attack (Chapter 7).
2022+ Russo-Ukraine War	In support of Ukraine, Network Battalion 65 (NB65) attacked Russian communications and space agency assets with compromised CONTI ransomware, denying over 760 GB of data (Abrams, 2022)
	Alleged independent Russian cyber actor (Killnet) credited with denial of service attacks on U.S. Treasury and U.S. airports

As shown in Table 9.3, independent cyber operators likely had their peak effects around the time of Julian Assange's exit from the international stage. His site, Wikileaks, continued to be a venue for disclosures that included one of the largest releases of cyber tools in CIA history by Joshua Shulte in 2017. Independent cyber operations can therefore have strategic effects as shown by the Arab Spring, the Panama Papers, and the Vault7 cyber tool release.

Bibliography

Abrams, L. (2022). *Hackers Use Conti's Leaked Ransomware to Attack Russian Companies*. Retrieved 4 12, 2022, from Bleeping Computer: https://www.bleepingcomputer.com/news/security/hackers-use-contis-leaked-ransomware-to-attack-russian-companies/.

Anh, V., Vu, D. R. (2022). *Getting Bored of Cyberwar: Exploring the Role of the Cybercrime Underground in the Russia-Ukraine Conflict*. Retrieved 9 7, 2022, from arXiv: https://arxiv.org/pdf/2208.10629.pdf.

Antoniuk, D. (2023). *Russian Railway Site Allegedly Taken Down by Ukrainian Hackers*. Retrieved from The Record: https://therecord.media/russian-railway-site-taken-down-by-ukrainian-hackers#.

Bernstein, J. (2017). *Secrecy World – Inside the Panama Papers Investigation of Illicit Money Networks and the Global Elite*. New York, NY, USA: Henry Holt and Company.

Boston, G. (1998). Teen Hacker Pleads Guilty to Crippling Massachussetts Airport. Boston Globe.

Bowden, M. (2011). *Worm – The First Digital World War*. New York: Atlantic Monthly Press.

Carr, J. (2012a). *Inside Cyber Warfare*. Sebastopol, CA: O'Reilly Media.

Carr, J. (2012b). *Inside Cyber Warfare: Mapping the Cyber Underworld*. (https://www.amazon.com/Inside-Cyber-Warfare-Mapping-Underworld/dp/0596802153, Ed.) O'Reilly.

CBS News. (2003). *SoBig Virus May Be Spam Scam*. Retrieved 6 27, 2020, from CBS News: https://www.cbsnews.com/news/sobig-virus-may-be-spam-scam/.

Chaos Computer Club. (n.d.). *Chaos Computer Club*. Retrieved from Chaos Computer Club: https://www.ccc.de/en/?language=en.

CISA. (2020). *NSA and CISA Recommend Immediate Actions to Reduce Exposure Across Operational Technologies and Control Systems*. Retrieved 9 21, 2022, from Alert (AA20-205A): https://www.cisa.gov/uscert/ncas/alerts/aa20-205a.

Coles, I. (2011). *Assange: Wikileaks' Cables Spurred Arab Uprisings*. Retrieved from
   Reuters: https://www.reuters.com/article/us-britain-assange/assange-wikileaks-
   cables-spurred-arab-uprisings-idUSTRE72E9LO20110315.

Condon, B. (Director). (2013). *The Fifth Estate* [Motion Picture].

David Leigh, L.H. (2011). *WikiLeaks – Inside Julian Assange's War on Secrecy*.
   New York: Public Affairs.

DHS Science and Technology (S&T) Directorate. (n.d.). *Telephony Denial of Service*.
   Retrieved 6 27, 2020, from DHS Science and Technology (S&T) Directorate: https://
   www.dhs.gov/sites/default/files/publications/508_FactSheet_DDoSD_TDoS%20
   One%20Pager-Final_June%202016_0.pdf.

DoJ. (2019). *WikiLeaks Founder Julian Assange Charged in 18-Count Superseding
   Indictment*. Retrieved from U.S. Department of Justice: https://www.justice.gov/
   opa/pr/wikileaks-founder-julian-assange-charged-18-count-superseding-
   indictment.

Domscheit. (2011). *Inside WikiLeaks MY TIME WITH JULIAN ASSANGE AT THE
   WORLD'S MOST DANGEROUS WEBSITE*. (https://www.penguinrandomhouse.
   com/books/213295/inside-wikileaks-by-daniel-domscheit-berg/, Ed.) Penguin.

Domscheit-Berg, D. (2011). *Inside Wikileaks – My Time with Julian Assange at the
   World's Most Dangerous Website*. New York: Crown.

FBI. (2018). *The Morris Worm – 30 Years Since First Major Attack on the Internet*.
   Retrieved from FBI: https://www.fbi.gov/news/stories/
   morris-worm-30-years-since-first-major-attack-on-internet-110218.

FBI. (2022). *Hacktivists Use of DDoS Activity Causes Minor Impacts*. Retrieved 11 8,
   2022, from FBI: https://www.ic3.gov/Media/News/2022/221104.pdf.

Hancock, D. (2003). *Virus Disrupts Train Signals*. Retrieved 7 7, 2019, from CBS
   News: https://www.cbsnews.com/news/virus-disrupts-train-signals/.

Heli Tiirmaa-Klaar, J.G.-P. (2014). *Botnets*. New York: Springer.

Henderson, S. (2007). *The Dark Visitor*. Scott Henderson.

Hope, A. (2022). *Anonymous Publish 28 GB Data Dump Stolen From Russia Central
   Bank Detailing Secret Agreements and High Profile Client Information*. Retrieved
   from CPO: https://www.cpomagazine.com/cyber-security/
   anonymous-publish-28-gb-data-dump-stolen-from-russia-central-bank-detailing-
   secret-agreements-and-high-profile-client-information/.

Khatchadourian, R. (2010). *No Secrets – Julian Assange's mission for total
   transparency*. Retrieved from New Yorker: https://www.newyorker.com/
   magazine/2010/06/07/no-secrets.

Leigh, D. (2010). *WikiLeaks 'has Blood on its Hands' over Afghan War Logs, Claim US
   Officials*. Retrieved from Guardian: https://www.theguardian.com/world/2010/
   jul/30/us-military-wikileaks-afghanistan-war-logs.

Levy, S. (1984). *Hackers: Heroes of the Computer Revolution*. New York: Doubleday.

Lewis, J. A. (2014). *Reference Note on Russian Communications Surveillance*. Retrieved from CSIS: https://www.csis.org/analysis/reference-note-russian-communications-surveillance.

Martin, A. (2022). *Killnet Targets Eastern Bloc Government Sites, but Fails to Keep them Offline*. Retrieved 11 8, 2022, from The Record: https://therecord.media/killnet-targets-eastern-bloc-government-sites-but-fails-to-keep-them-offline/.

Microsoft. (2022). *Microsoft Digital Defense Report 2022*. Retrieved 11 15, 2022, from Microsoft: https://query.prod.cms.rt.microsoft.com/cms/api/am/binary/RE5bUvv?culture=en-us&country=us.

Phillip Porras, H. S. (2009). *An Analysis of Conficker's Logic and Rendezvous Points*. Retrieved 6 29, 2020, from USENIX: https://www.usenix.org/legacy/events/leet09/tech/full_papers/porras/porras_html/index2.html.

RISI Data. (2003). *Slammer Impact on Ohio Nuclear Plant*. Retrieved 7 7, 2019, from RISI Data: https://www.risidata.com/Database/Detail/slammer-impact-on-ohio-nuclear-plant.

Smith, T. (2001). *Hacker Jailed for Revenge Sewage Attacks – Job Rejection Caused a Bit of a Stink*. Retrieved 7 7, 2019, from The Register: https://www.theregister.co.uk/2001/10/31/hacker_jailed_for_revenge_sewage/.

Stahie, S. (2022). *KillNet Targeted US Treasury with DDoS Attack and Failed*. Retrieved from Bitdefender: https://www.bitdefender.com/blog/hotforsecurity/killnet-targeted-us-treasury-with-ddos-attack-and-failed/.

Stoll, C. (2005). *The Cuckoo's Egg: Tracking a Spy Through the Maze of Computer Espionage*. Pocket Books.

Symantec. (2003). *W32.Sobig.F@mm*. Retrieved 7 7, 2019, from Symantec: https://www.symantec.com/security-center/writeup/2003-081909-2118-99.

Tidy, J. (2023). *Meet the Hacker Armies on Ukraine's Cyber Front Line*. Retrieved from BBC: https://www.bbc.com/news/technology-65250356.

Toulas, B. (2022). *US Airports' Sites Taken Down in DDoS Attacks by Pro-Russian Hackers*. Retrieved from Bleeping Computer: https://www.bleepingcomputer.com/news/security/us-airports-sites-taken-down-in-ddos-attacks-by-pro-russian-hackers/.

United States Court of Appeals, Second Circuit. (1991). *UNITED STATES of America v. Robert Tappan MORRIS*. Retrieved from Google Scholar: https://scholar.google.com/scholar_case?case=551386241451639668.

Vigderman, A. (2022). *The Most Devastating Computer Viruses in History*. Retrieved from Security.org: https://www.security.org/antivirus/worst-viruses/#:~:text=Estimated%20cost%20of%20damage%3A%20%2430,it%20all%20the%20more%20destructive.

Waqas. (2022). *Confirmed: Anonymous Hacks Central Bank of Russia; Leaks 28GB of Data*. Retrieved 3 27, 2022, from Hackgread: https://www.hackread.com/anonymous-hacks-central-bank-russia-leaks-28gb-data/.

Winnona DeSombre, D. B. (2018). *Thieves and Geeks: Russian and Chinese Hacking Communities*. Retrieved 6 26, 2020, from Recorded Future: https://go.recordedfuture.com/hubfs/reports/cta-2018-1010.pdf.

Section I

Cyber Operations Summary

I.1 Introduction

Section I provides examples that span the current history and development of cyber operations. This progression spans from early hactivism to current political uses of social media platforms. Section I also includes examples from simple, experimental hacks, to nation-state operators performing cyberspace espionage and information operations (IO) (Table I.1).

As shown in Table I.1, cyber operations have often included a nation-state interest, starting with "The Cuckoo's Egg" (Stoll, 2005) documenting the Former Soviet Union (FSU) use of hackers to attempt to steal U.S. military secrets near the end of the Cold War (Chapter 4). The near success described in "The Cuckoo's Egg," in the late 1980s, likely inspired Russian operators to continue their cyber collection pursuits, eventually succeeding with Operation Moonlight Maze in the mid- to late 1990s.

During this hacking and experimentation period of networked computers, we also looked at potentially damaging hacks (Chapter 9). For example, the Jester Worm (1997), the Slammer Worm (2003), and the Sobig Worm (2003) were examples of critical infrastructure denial capabilities. These hacks produced effects that included shutting down telephony systems, nuclear reactors, trains, telephones, and air traffic control systems.

While hackers have provided worst-case scenarios by literally shutting off critical parts of our infrastructure, nation-states have also leveraged their hackers to develop cyber capabilities. For example, while Russia (Chapter 5) started with the use of cyber for espionage, China (Chapter 6) developed a little differently.

Starting in the late 1990s, China's hackers self-organized to deface Indonesian Government web sites (in 1998) in order to protest attacks on ethnic Chinese (Nuttall, 1998). Similarly, in 1999, Chinese hackers attacked U.S. Government web sites in order to protest the bombing of the Chinese embassy in Serbia

Cyber Operations: A Case Study Approach, First Edition. Jerry M. Couretas.
© 2024 John Wiley & Sons, Inc. Published 2024 by John Wiley & Sons, Inc.

Table I.1 Cyber Operations Development – 1980s to Present Day.

Time Period	Stage	Examples
1980s to late 1990s	Hacking and Experimentation	• 1988 Morris Worm • 1989 Cuckoo's Egg – example of Russian KGB collecting on U.S. Star Wars program (Former Soviet Union) • 1998 Moonlight Maze (Russian Federation) • 1998 Honker Union Hackers (1998 Indonesia, 2001 U.S. White House web page) (China)
Early 2000s to mid-2010s	Development	• 2002 Titan Rain (China) • 2007 Estonia Denial of Service (DoS) (Russia) • 2008 Georgia Multi-Domain (Russia) • 2010 Stuxnet attack on Iran's nuclear program • 2010 Wikileaks (State Department Cables) • 2011 DigiNotar (Iran) • 2011–2016 ISIS emergence from the Internet • 2014 Ukraine Denial of Service (DoS) (Russia)
≥mid-2010s	Implementation	• 2014–present Ukraine cyber kinetic attack (Russia) • 2014 Mosul Offensive broadcast live on Twitter (ISIS) • 2014–2018 "Big Data" exfiltrations (China) • 2016 U.S. Presidential election attack (Russia) • 2016 Bangladesh Bank (DPRK) • 2017 NotPetya (Russian Federation) • 2017 WannaCry (DPRK) • 2019 Great Cannon (China)
≥2020	Proliferation	• 2021 Colonial Pipeline Attack, JBS Foods … • 2022 Counter Protest (Iran)

(Messmer, 1999). Chinese hackers also attacked U.S. Government web sites in 2001 to protest a PRC plane colliding with a U.S. spy plane (Tang, 2001). China then matured this capability for wide-scale collection a few years later, in the form of Operation Titan Rain from 2003 to 2007.

While China was conducting its first widespread cyber collection campaign (i.e., Operation Titan Rain), Russia incorporated cyber into all-domain operations, initially using Denial of Service (DoS) in Estonia (2007), and expanding the use of cyber to include information operations in Georgia (2008). Russia subsequently developed the Gerasimov doctrine (2013) and then integrated cyber kinetic operations in their 2014 annexation of Crimea (Greenberg, 2019).

As introduced in Chapter 4, and elaborated on in Chapters 5 through 8, there are approximately 50 nation-state-level advanced persistent threat (APT) teams that are currently accounted for (Mandiant). Within this number are crypto currency operators, ransomware group members, tool suppliers, and other support folks working for foreign intelligence services who contribute to the cause. Independent cyber operators, discussed in Chapter 9, can also provide strategic effects. For example, we reviewed Wikileaks' publishing classified U.S. military documents, State Department cables, Panamanian corporate charters, and Democratic National Committee e-mails – each of which led to geopolitical change.

I.2   Phases of Cyber Operations

As discussed in the preceding chapters, cyber operations to date have transitioned in roughly three phases over the development from hackers to nation-state and professional ransomware cyber operations. Recent cyber operations, from publicized espionage operations to ongoing ransomware attacks, date back to approximately the 2012 time frame.

Prior to 2012, nation-states were experimenting with cyber, with Russia performing Denial of Service and information operations in Estonia (2007) and Georgia (2008). Iran (Chapter 8) used cyber to suppress Twitter in order to quash dissent to the re-election of political hard liner Mahmoud Ahmadinejad. The first decade of the twenty-first century was also the debut of China's cyber operations, including the collection of a surprising amount of data on U.S. defense programs during Operations Titan Rain and Byzantine Hades (Chesaux, 2019).

In 2010, STUXNET was outed as a first in the use of cyber to deny a nation-state nuclear development program. This unexpectedly effective use of cyber occurred just before new leaders ascended in China, DPRK, and Iran, with each of these countries having an already proven cyber capability. The early 2010s were also when Russia stepped up its cyber game with the formation of the Internet Research Agency (IRA). Looking back at the exponential increase and professionalization of cyber operations over the first two decades of the twenty-first century, it is hard to fathom that the movement started with a handful of hackers.

I.2.1   1980s–2002

Even before the roll out of personal computers, hacking was a game of wits between the hacker and machine. Early incarnations of the Internet (e.g., Arpanet) included thousands of networked computers. It was only a matter of time before a determined hacker would test the limits of this new, networked, cyber world. The popular movie "WarGames," (Badham, 1983), raised awareness about the dangers of computers and led to policy makers writing the Computer Fraud and Abuse Act (Congress, 1986). It was only a few years later, in 1988, that this law was used to prosecute Robert Tappan Morris for the damages that his "Morris Worm" perpetrated on the early Internet.

Due to the government's use of the pre-Internet to connect government and university computers, one of the first documented cyber operations included the KGB experimenting with the use of West German hackers to steal information on the U.S. Star Wars missile defense system in the 1980s.

The late 1980s were also the years when Microsoft went public (1986). In addition, Cisco, one of the first big Internet routing companies, went public in 1990. These are the companies that provide the building blocks for the current Internet.

At the same time that personal computers and networking were rapidly developing, the geopolitical order was put in flux due to the fall of the Soviet Union (1991) and the rapid changes in the military/political landscape. Russia started working its way toward a non-Soviet system and client states (e.g., Iraq, DPRK) lost their super power sponsorship.

1991 was also the year that the United States, along with a coalition, expelled Saddam Hussein's Iraq from Kuwait after a surprise invasion. This war included the use of "smart bombs" and cruise missiles, computer-based weapons fielded for the first time. The United States suffered few casualties, while winning decisively against Iraq's Soviet trained and equipped army in each engagement. This was at least partially due to the employment of new information related capabilities.

As discussed in Chapter 6, China watched the Gulf War closely and processed their lessons learned as the need to strike first, before an adversary builds a decisive position that predetermines a victorious engagement. China's offensive cyber ops tempo for the last two decades may very well be their longer term, slow motion, "first strike." The late 1980s were also the time period when China began to open up to foreign business and send scholars overseas for education, including post-doctoral appointments to U.S. national laboratories as discussed in Chapter 6.

The 1990s and early 2000s were characterized by hactivists, cyber operators using the web with a political axe to grind. One of the more famous hactivist groups was from mainland China (Chapter 9), protesting the treatment of ethnic Chinese during riots in Indonesia (1998) and the crashing of a Chinese fighter that was harassing a U.S. intelligence aircraft in the South China Sea (2001). One form of protest for these Chinese hactivists web site defacement, including the U.S. White House.

I.2.2   2003–2012

The latter 1990s included the disintegration of Soviet Russian institutions, minimizing Russia as a threat in the minds of Western policy makers. This was until U.S. government cyber operators discovered the Russian Federation's Operation

Moonlight Maze in 1999 (Chapter 5), a cyber exfiltration that resulted in the loss of 5 GB of data, an extraordinary amount at that time. As a newly organized Russian Federation, and intelligence service, Turla (i.e., FSB) performed Operation Moonlight Maze (1996–1999) against U.S. military targets (Chapter 5).

Shortly after the discovery of Operation Moonlight Maze was Operation Titan Rain, a Chinese cyber operation that, combined with Operation Byzantine Hades, resulted in the exfiltration of 24,000 diagrams related to the U.S. F-35 program (Chapter 6). And on the heels of Operation Titan Rain was the Russian Federation's use of cyber for tactical denial operations in Estonia (2007), and for joint cyber/ kinetic operations in Georgia (2008) (Chapter 5).

Nation-state operations developed in accordance with the structures provided in Chapter 4. Between 2004 and 2011, a novel development was found in al Qaeda and al Qaeda in Iraq (AQI) using cyber operations to support their recruiting, financing and communications. A plethora of videos and documents that spanned from recruitment sermons, weapons manuals, and executing infidels developed into a rich cyber footprint that characterized AQI. This included using cyber to coordinate and participate in physical attacks (Chapter 1). The web also provided a maneuver space for AQI's gestation into ISIS just after Coalition Forces left Iraq's Anbar province. This was also the same time frame that the Arab Spring occurred, which included Syria's partial disintegration. ISIS emerged from the web as a physical entity with a capital in Raqqa, Syria (2013). Uncannily, ISIS' development followed classic insurgency phases, using cyberspace for the initial phases (Chapter 2).

While ISIS used the web as a maneuver space, nation-states continued to experiment with espionage via cyber. By 2009, cyber had proven itself for both strategic/ espionage and tactical effects. Operation Aurora (2009), for example, included China exfiltrating key Google technologies. 2009 was also the year that China was found to be probing U.S. energy infrastructure via Operation Night Dragon. As discussed in Chapter 8, Iran debuted as a cyber actor in 2009 to perform its first denial attack against the Green Movement on Twitter. The Green Movement was protesting election results that favored political hardliner Mahmoud Ahmadinejad being re-elected.

In 2010, STUXNET was outed as being a cyber attack that was used to delay Iran's nuclear program. This resulted in a spate of Iranian cyber attacks. For example, DigiNotar (2011) was the compromise of a Dutch certificate authority so that the MOIS could access 300,000 gmail accounts in order to provide information on the internal and external communications of Iranian citizens. Operation Newscaster (2011) was a set of fake Facebook personas that imitated journalists and was used by Iran to get access to policy makers that could influence thinking on Iran. Operation Cleaver (2012) was an Iranian cyber penetration operation that directly preceded Operation Al Shamoon I (2012), a cyber denial attack that destroyed 30,000 disk drives at Saudi Aramco. Iran also used Operation Cleaver to develop access in order to penetrate the U.S. Navy's e-mail system (NMCI) (2012). 2012 was also the year that Iran executed a denial attack on the U.S. financial system (Operation Ababil).

These early stages of cyber operations also saw major outing attacks. For example, Wikileaks (Chapter 9) released secret U.S. military and State Department data that potentially influenced the Arab Spring (2011), resulting in governments falling across the Islamic Maghreb. In 2013, the cyber attack on Mossack Fonseca, a Panamanian legal firm, outed several Chinese and Russian officials' tax shelters. This was colloquially known as the Panama Papers. The Panama Papers also resulted in the abdication of the Sigmundur Gunnlaugsson, President of Iceland, in 2016.

Julian Assange's taking asylum in 2012 was uncanny timing, as this was also the same time frame that multiple political changes, and strategic cyber effects, became news. STUXNET was outed in 2010, Kim Jong Un was elevated to DPRK Supreme Leader in 2011, the Russian Federation experienced the Snow Revolution in 2012, Xi Jinpin became President of the People's Republic of China in 2013, Edward Snowden performed one of the largest leaks in U.S. intelligence history in 2013, and the Internet Research Agency (IRA) was formed in 2014, in time for elections in the Ukraine. As big hacktivism slowed down, nation-state cyber operations picked up.

I.2.3 2013–present[1]

In 2012, Russia experienced the Snow Revolution in Bolotnaya Square, a rally coordinated using Facebook that included tens of thousands of people protesting the lack of fair elections. This was a wakeup call that led to the formation of the Internet Research Agency (IRA) in 2014, with a goal of controlling the message as Russia annexed Crimea from the Ukraine (Chapter 5).

And in Iran, Dr Rouhani, assuming the presidency in 2013, expanded Iran's cyber program several fold in building out the National Information Network (NIN) during his term (Chapter 8).

By 2013, both the Russians (Operation Dragonfly) and the Chinese (Operation Night Dragon) were actively probing U.S. critical infrastructure networks. This included technically scanning critical infrastructure systems and using social engineering to get more information about the people, processes, and technologies supporting U.S. natural gas pipelines. These cyber operations included

---

1 It might be noted that these first two phases of cyber operations align with Healey's work on cyber operations, which spanned from 1986 to 2012 (Healey, 2013).

profiling the system administrators and computer support personnel responsible for keeping the systems available.

In totalitarian states, the evolution of cyber coincided with leadership transitions. Kim Jong Un, in the DPRK, ascended to Supreme Leader in 2011, followed by the DarkSeoul (2013) and Sony (2014) cyber attacks (Chapter 7). This was an unheard of DPRK cyber force that attacked Sony in 2014, outing private e-mails, destroying executive careers, and threatening terrorist attacks at theaters that played a film, "The Interview," parodying the new Supreme Leader, Kim Jong Un.

In 2013, Xi Jinpin became President of the Peoples Republic of China (PRC) (Chapter 6). This directly preceded a spate of cyber espionage attacks on the United States (e.g., OMB (2015), Anthem Insurance (2015), and Equifax (2017)).

As discussed in Chapter 3, around 2016 the U.S. intelligence community suffered one of the largest leaks in its history due to cyber at the NSA and CIA. These leaks, roughly corresponding in time with the Shadow Brokers advertising a new set of cyber tools for sale, directly preceded a rash of ransomware that continues to the time of this writing.

It was also during 2016 that the DPRK used an elaborate, multi-time zone, international, plan, in an attempted $1 billion heist from the Bank of Bangladesh. While the larger plan did not work, the DPRK still managed to steal $81 million in the effort (Chapter 7). 2016 was also a first for using social media to live broadcast a military offensive. In this case, it was ISIS, using a force of only 800 "soldiers," defeating a U.S. trained and equipped Iraqi Army in Mosul, on Twitter, for all to see.

With the large cache of Shadow Brokers tools coming on line in 2016, the DPRK used these tools in the WannaCry ransomware attack in 2017, causing $4–8 billion in damage. This was the beginning of the DPRK's presence on the cyber scene, beginning a rash of crypto theft operations that are believed to have produced over $1 billion in illicit gains by 2023, the same amount targeted in the 2016 Bangladesh Bank cyber attack, money that goes directly into nuclear weapons and delivery programs.

And, while the DPRK wreaks havoc on digital wallets, ransomware operators continue to attack small- and medium-sized businesses, hospitals, healthcare services, and any target of opportunity whose credentials show up for a ransomware affiliate to tap into and extract a ransom. This is the world that the leakers played a role in creating by disseminating tools for future criminal operations. In Chapter 3, we saw how intentional and unintentional leaks resulted in some of the largest breaches in U.S. intelligence community history in the 2016 time frame. Leaks that directly preceded the rash of ransomware that characterized the cyber landscape in the early 2020s.

Bibliography

Badham, J. (Director). (1983). *WarGames* [Motion Picture].

Chesaux, J. (2019). *Cyber Attacks: The Biggest Threat for Future Weapons.* Retrieved from Cyber Defense Magazine: https://www.cyberdefensemagazine.com/cyber-attacks-the-biggest-threat-for-future-weapons/.

Congress. (1986). *H.R.4718 – Computer Fraud and Abuse Act of 1986.* Retrieved from 99th Congress: https://www.congress.gov/bill/99th-congress/house-bill/4718.

Healey, J. (2013). *A Fierce Domain: Conflict in Cyberspace, 1986 to 2012.* (https://www.amazon.com/Fierce-Domain-Conflict-Cyberspace-1986/dp/098932740X, Ed.) Cyber Conflict Studies Association.

Mandiant. (n.d.). *Advanced Persistent Threats (APTs).* Retrieved from Mandiant: https://www.mandiant.com/resources/insights/apt-groups.

Section II

Introduction to Cyber Effects

II.1 Cyber Effects Introduction

As discussed in Section I, the rapid migration of organizations to the web included all aspects of society, including political, financial, and media, as shown in Figure II.1. This mass migration to the web was performed with limited accounting for security, thereby resulting in strategic, tactical, and criminal costs via cyber.

In Section 1, we looked at multiple cyber operations and their possible effects. These strategic, tactical, and criminal effects occur through the media, political, and finance domains (Figure II.1).

II.1.1 Example of Cyber Strategic, Tactical, and Criminal Effects

Cyber effects are denominated in terms of both decision complexity and time. For example, a criminal cyber effect (e.g., ransom) might be the simplest in having a fixed cost and time duration. Cyber is also used tactically, as a stepping stone for follow-on kinetic effects (Chapter 5). Strategic cyber effects are more challenging to estimate due to the technology, and skills employed, that compose the target.

II.1.1.1 Strategic Cyber Effects

A strategic effect causes an adversary to change plans. These are the types of plans that require specialized labor and complex coordination. It is a challenge to quantify the cost of a strategic plan even if the number of labor hours used to develop the plan is known.

II.1.1.2 Tactical Cyber Effects

Tactical effects are steps used to reach an overall objective. One example of a tactical effect is an air strike. And this is what both the United States and Israel have

Cyber Operations: A Case Study Approach, First Edition. Jerry M. Couretas.
© 2024 John Wiley & Sons, Inc. Published 2024 by John Wiley & Sons, Inc.

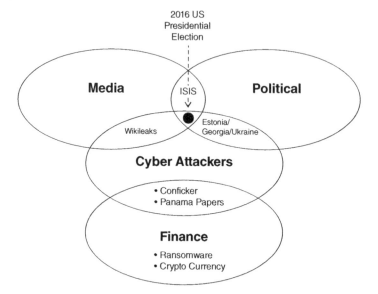

Figure II.1 Cyber Attackers Operate in Multiple Domains.

done to eliminate a few cyber threats. However, there are more nuanced ways to handle a cyber threat. For example, in 2016 the U.S. launched Operation Glowing Symphony from its Task Force ARES as a means to degrade ISIS' media operations. This was at the same time that Coalition Forces also used conventional intelligence, surveillance, and reconnaissance (ISR) and strike capabilities to reduce ISIS' military effectiveness in its area of operations.

II.1.1.3 Criminal Cyber Effects
Criminal cyber effects are quantifiable in terms of a cost. Criminal cyber operations, originally due to hackers and petty thieves stealing records and exploiting them, are a billion dollar business with the advent of ransomware. And, while multiple gangs are called out in the collection of ransom, some of the largest cyber criminal attacks are due to the DPRK stealing funds for its developing nuclear program as discussed in Chapter 7.

II.1.2 Wrap-up

The overlap between criminal, tactical, and strategic cyber effects can be a little murky. For example, the DPRK performing criminal acts to fund, and possibly speed up, a strategic nuclear program has elements that fit in two different effects categories – strategic and criminal cyber effects. Criminal cyber effects are usually thought of as being the most simple, due to their representation as a financial cost (e.g., ransom, remediation). Tactical cyber effects, as stepping stones to an overall goal, are a bit more abstract. For example, we might quantify a tactical cyber effect in terms of the time delay required to successfully complete the operation. And strategic cyber effects are even more challenging to describe due to target complexity, associated time, and cost implications.

Bibliography

Schechner, S. (2020). *Google, Amazon Fined $163 Million as France Takes Hard Line on Privacy*. Retrieved 9 20, 2022, from Wall Street Journal: https://www.wsj.com/articles/google-amazon-fined-163-million-as-france-takes-hard-line-on-privacy-11607601278.

10

Strategic Cyber Effects

10.1 Strategic Cyber Effects

> A strategic effect occurs if and only if an action disrupts an adversary's strategy.
>
> *(Thomas Tighe)*

Strategic effects include actions that change national-level decision making. In Figure 1.3, "The Line" is a demarcation of actions that span from diplomatic to kinetic options that might be used to change an adversary's mind. Cyber is sometimes called the "in-between" option that lives in a gray space between policy pronouncements and military action. STUXNET was one of the more famous strategic cyber effects, delaying Iran's nuclear program and providing a significant cost saving over the use of conventional air strikes to accomplish the same goal.

10.1.1 STUXNET (2010) – Delaying a Nation-State's Nuclear Program

The STUXNET campaign sought to slow Iran's nuclear enrichment program in order to delay Iran's acquisition of a nuclear weapon. General Hayden estimated that STUXNET did delay Iran's nuclear program by two to three years (Hayden, 2016). Using a variety of intelligence, surveillance, and reconnaissance (ISR) (e.g., Duqu, Flame, and Gauss) and code modification tools, the STUXNET campaign was a botnet focused specifically on destroying the Siemens industrial controllers powering the Uranium separation centrifuges at Iran's Natanz nuclear enrichment facility (Zetter, 2015).

Cyber Operations: A Case Study Approach, First Edition. Jerry M. Couretas.
© 2024 John Wiley & Sons, Inc. Published 2024 by John Wiley & Sons, Inc.

The international community wanted to delay Iraq's nuclear enrichment program in the 1990s. Policymakers chose to use air strikes in order to dissuade Saddam Hussein's Iraq from pursuing a nuclear weapon. Operation Desert Fox (U.S. Air Force, 1998) was an air campaign that used 325 TLAMs to disable Iraqi weapons research and development installations, costing an approximate $455 million for munitions.

If we use a very rough figure of 100 man-years of effort, at $250,000 per man-year to perform analysis, targeting, and weapon development for STUXNET, we estimate a $25 million dollar cost for the whole program. Comparing the approximate $455 million for a conventional campaign to cyber's $25 million, we get an 18:1 ratio of kinetic to cyber cost (Table 10.1).

The compelling cost advantage in Table 10.1 is an example of how a cyber effect provides a promising complement, if not a tradeable alternative, to the use of conventional munitions for select engagements. One hypothesis for the 18:1 resource multiplier is that this is the benefit of surprise. A surprise attack has the potential for the prepared offender to quickly overcome an unwary defender. For example, in Chapter 6, we discussed a surprise attack as one of China's lessons learned from the 1991 Gulf War (Section 6.1), as a low cost means that Iraq might have used to change the course of the war.

As a strategic capability, cyber necessarily requires stealth, and possibly deception, in order to reduce a cyber campaign's chance of being discovered. And deception is believed to be the cause of high loss exchange ratios (LERs) in Barton Whaley's long-term study of military engagements (Whaley and Aykroyd, 2007). Whaley discovered a 15:1 LER advantage for the combatant successfully using deception. With stealth being a requirement for successful cyber operations, this 15:1 resource ratio provides an analogous metric for cyber deception.

10.1.2 STUXNET Versus Operation Desert Fox Wrap-up

The potential cost savings of using cyber to provide strategic effects are provocative. For example, if we compare Operation Desert Fox with the STUXNET campaign, we find an approximate 18:1 cost advantage in using cyber over conventional weapons. As noted, however, TLAMs are off-the-shelf capabilities, usable at a moment's notice. Cyber weapons may take years to develop and deploy.

A key element of a cyber operation is that it relies on deception for success. Barton Whaley estimated a 15:1 LER advantage to be due to deception in conventional engagements over the last few hundred years. This provides one possible analogy for the estimated resource exchange ratio advantage found in Table 10.1.

In Chapter 5, we saw how Russia focuses on supply chain attacks (e.g., 2014 HAVEX, 2019 SolarWinds) that provide a geometric return on access based on the successful targeting of a single organization. Supply chain attacks, with

Table 10.1 STUXNET Versus Operation Desert Fox – Strategic Cyber Operations with Cost/Benefit Estimates.

Description	Cyber Effect	Military Effect	Cost Approach	Estimated Cyber Operation	Comparable Conventional Operation	Cost Approach for Comparable Operation	Estimated Conventional Operation Cost	Conventional/ Cyber Cost Ratio
2010 – STUXNET – malware attacking Siemens' controlled centrifuges delayed Iranian nuclear program for three to five years	Integrity of industrial control systems	Delayed Iranian Nuclear Program three to five years	Engineering project (estimated 100 man-years)	$25,000,000	1998 Operation Desert Fox (four-day campaign to degrade Iraqi CBRN programs)	Number of munitions (325) at $1.4 M/copy	$455,000,000	18

30,000 accesses provided by SolarWinds, likely far supersede the return on resources that we estimate for STUXNET.

Bibliography

Hayden, M.V. (2016). *Playing to the Edge: American Intelligence in the Age of Terror*. Peguin.

Swallow, R.C. (2022). Considering the cost of cyber warfare: advancing cyber warfare analytics to better assess tradeoffs in system destruction warfare. *Journal of Defense Modeling and Simulation 20* (1): 3–7.

Thomas Tighe, R. H. (n.d.). *A Decision for Strategic Effects: A Conceptual Approach to Effects Based Targeting*. Retrieved from Air University: https://www.airuniversity. af.edu/Portals/10/ASPJ/journals/Chronicles/Hill.pdf.

U.S. Air Force. (1998). *Operation Desert Fox*. Retrieved 6 24, 2020, from https://www. afhistory.af.mil/FAQs/Fact-Sheets/Article/458976/1998-operation-desert-fox/.

Whaley, B. and Aykroyd, S. (2007). *Textbook of Political-Military Counterdeception: Basic Principles and Methods*. Washington, D.C.: National Defense Intelligence College.

Zurasky, M. (2017). *Methodology to Perform Cyber Lethality Assessment (Dissertation)*. Old Dominion University.

Zetter, K. (2015). *Countdown to Zero Day - Stuxnet and the Launch of the World's First Digital Weapon*. New York: Crown.

11

Strategic Cyber Effects (2)

11.1 Critical Infrastructure Strategic Cyber Effects

Cyber attacks on critical infrastructure can produce nightmare scenarios. For example, a 2015 Lloyd's of London study, "Business Blackout," showed a possible 93 million Americans, across 11 states and the District of Columbia, being without power due to a cyber attack, costing an estimated $243 Billion, $1 Trillion in the most stressing scenario (Trevor Maynard, 2015).

In addition to catastrophic scenarios, we now have ransomware gangs, criminals, attacking critical infrastructure targets, and holding them hostage. For example, Russian ransomware gangs (e.g., CONTI) became famous for attacking critical infrastructure in Brazil (JBS Foods), Costa Rica (Government IT), and the United States (Colonial Oil, NEW Cooperative) in 2021. These critical infrastructure targets are considered strategic due to the life-sustaining necessity of keeping these services available.

11.1.1 Critical Infrastructure

The 16 critical infrastructure sectors (Chapter 4) are designated by the U.S. Department of Homeland Security (DHS) to provide an overview of how policymakers view the importance of certain public services. The denial or manipulation of any of the 16 critical infrastructure sectors therefore constitutes a strategic effect, meriting at least a law enforcement response.

11.1.1.1 Energy Sector
Energy, especially electricity, is used to support almost every other service. The possible harm due to an electrical grid attack is therefore extreme. For example, as discussed, the 2015 Lloyd's of London study, "Business Blackout," (Trevor

Cyber Operations: A Case Study Approach, First Edition. Jerry M. Couretas.
© 2024 John Wiley & Sons, Inc. Published 2024 by John Wiley & Sons, Inc.

Table 11.1   Energy System Attacks.

Year	Location	Event	Damages
2021	Colonial Pipeline	Darkside ransomware operators disabled Colonial oil's business systems, shutting off oil flow to the U.S. East Coast (Chapter 3)	$5 million ransom; U.S. East Coast without fuel for five days causing panic
2012	Saudi Arabia	Operation Al Shamoon – Iran launched wiper attacks on Saudi Aramco IT systems	Targeted 10% of the world's oil productions systems lost 30,000–50,000 hard drives

Maynard, 2015) showed an attack on the U.S. East Coast costing approximately $250 Billion. This is at least a 25× multiple on the NotPetya attack that propagated out of control, destroying multiple corporate computer systems and halting international shipping due to the disabling of Maersk IT systems, with an estimated $10 Billion in damages (Table 11.1) (Greenberg, 2017).

In 2014, Russia started attacking electric power grids in the Ukraine. This was a continuation of Russian critical infrastructure attacks on the Ukraine. For example, Russia physically turned off the Ukraine's natural gas in 1995 (Slowik). It was over a decade later that Iran performed the first cyber attack on Saudi Arabia's oil production via Al Shamoon I in 2012. Al Shamoon I was a wiper attack that had the potential of shutting down Saudi Aramco's production, a global swing supplier for oil. Table 11.1 provides example cyber effects against energy providers.

As shown in Table 11.1, shutting down Colonial Oil (2021), or Saudi Arabian oil production (2012), had the potential for producing a major impact on the economy. Just as fuel provides the transportation of goods throughout a modern economy, communications provide the flow of information.

11.1.1.2   Telecommunications

One of the most effective cyber attacks in the 2022 Russo-Ukrainian war was the Russian cyber attack on the Ukraine's Viasat satellites one hour before the onset of kinetic operations (O'Neill, 2022). This wiper, dubbed "AcidRain," ended up infecting other systems across Europe, including Internet-connected wind farms and other systems. AcidRain was deployed just before Russia launched another attack on Ukrainian government machines with a virus called hermetic wiper. While communications are a key target in any military campaign, possibly even more critical is an attack on an adversary's water supply.

11.1.1.3   Water

There are a few examples of cyber attacks on water supply systems. These include both a sewage release (e.g., Maroochy Shire (2009)) and an attempt to increase the lye level (e.g., Oldsmar Florida (2021)) (Table 11.2).

Table 11.2 Water System Attacks.

Year	Location	Event	Damages
2001	Maroochy Shire Tofino (2009)	Release 265,000 gallons of sewage	>$1 million
2021	Oldsmar, FL Frances Robles (2021)	Increase lye in water by 10×	Issue caught before causing damages

As shown in Table 11.2, the Maroochy Shire attack was criminal, with an estimated $1 million cleanup cost. However, Iran has been observed probing Israeli water suppliers, with minimal effect so far. And the 2021 attack on the Oldsmar water treatment facility was likely intended to produce death and illness through the community.

11.1.1.4 Agriculture

Similar to water supply attacks, most reported agriculture attacks have been criminal, so far. For example, in 2021 alone, both JBS Foods (Abrams, 2021a) and the NEW Cooperative (Abrams, 2021a) paid $11 million and $9 million in ransom, respectively, to get their data back from ransomware operators (Table 11.3).

The attacks shown in Table 11.3, perpetrated by ransomware gangs, had the ability to shut down critical food producers. Almost 20 years before these attacks, hackers showed their ability to compromise train system signaling via the Sobig virus.

11.1.1.5 Rail

In Chapter 9, we reviewed the train signaling systems on the U.S. East Coast going dark after computers belonging to CSX Corporation in Florida got infected with the Sobig virus (CBS News, 2003; Symantec, 2003). Hackers used Sobig to infect CSX, which operates rail systems for passenger and freight trains in 23 states, and

Table 11.3 Agriculture Company Attacks.

Year	Location	Event	Damages	Ransomware Team
2021	JBS Foods (Brazil)	Ransomware attack that shuts down JBS' slaughterhouses	$11 million Abrams (2021a)	REvil
2021	NEW Cooperative (Iowa, USA)	Locked systems and threatened to release data unless paid	$5.9 million Abrams (2021b)	Darkside

as a result of the infection stopped signals going out, causing trains running between Pennsylvania and South Carolina and in the DC Beltway to stop (Hancock, 2003). Cost estimates for the Sobig virus run into the billions of dollars (Vigderman, 2022).

In the 2022 Russo-Ukraine war, cyber partisan attacks have been used to take Russian rail services offline. For example, Russian rail operator Rossiyskie Zeleznye Dorogi (RZD) was reported to go offline due to a massive cyber attack in the summer of 2023 (Sergey, 2023).

11.1.1.6 Election Attacks (IO) (2011s)

As discussed in Chapter 4, the 2016 U.S. Presidential election attack, via cyber, provided insights into how cyber systems can be compromised to affect a political party. This was a strategic effect. We also discussed how denial-of-service attacks are used to lower confidence in the Government's ability to do its job (e.g., 2007 Estonia, 2008 Georgia, and 2014 Ukraine). These attacks provided initial lessons, at least qualitatively, on how cyber might be used for strategic effects, and were followed by cyber attacks within the European Union (EU)

> Denial-of-service attacks targeted two high-traffic electoral websites in the Netherlands in 2017. Similar incidents have struck Bulgaria's elections oversight body and election websites in the Czech Republic. E-mails stolen from (now) French President Emmanuel Macron's computer systems were published online before France's 2017 election, while employees of German Chancellor Angela Merkel's Christian Democratic Union received targeted spear-phishing e-mails in 2016.
>
> *(Borland, 2019)*

While these Denial of Service (DoS) attacks occurred at about the same time as U.S. attacks, they also helped the Europeans implement cyber security measures to ensure valid elections in 2018 and 2019, as no major issues were found under a heavily scrutinized election cycle.

Fortunately, EU members learned from the 2016 U.S. Presidential Election and took precautions to secure their elections. Strategic effects are performed by using a machine in an unintended way, from a water treatment plant to an election system. And, through the use of computer-based controls, cyber provides the means to do this.

Cyber also takes information operations (IO) to a whole new level due to the speed and scale of information that can be shared. While the Cold War was replete with active measures, WikiLeaks likely had more impact than all of the previous active measures combined due to the speed and global coverage provided by the Internet.

11.1.2   Media-Based Cyber Operations

Many of the actual media effects are "outing" attacks, simply embarrassing their respective targets (Table 11.4).

As shown in Table 11.4, one effect from media operations has been to release presumably secure information. A number of "effects" are hypothesized to have occurred from these media operations (e.g., 2011 Arab Spring), with cyber-based political operations often using media to do messaging.

While WikiLeaks and the Panama Papers coordinated with main stream media outlets to get their message out (Bernstein, 2017), the 2016 U.S. presidential election included a heavy use of social media, especially Facebook, as a means to develop stories. This included manufacturing personas of "real people" who posted news on both ends of the political spectrum (Mazetti, 2018; Parham, 2017). In fact, the 2016 U.S. presidential election included several examples of evidence for manipulation (e.g., 11 million tweets, dozens of violent rallies in the United States) and it remains a challenge to determine what to do about it (Harris, 2018). It is also unclear whether the "trolls" (Andrei Soldatov, 2015) had a focused outcome, or just wanted to add uncertainty to the U.S. election process (Ben Collins, 2018).

Table 11.4   Cyber Media Operations – The Panama Papers, the 2016 Presidential Elections and WikiLeaks.

Event	Description
2011 WikiLeaks	Initially publishing U.S. Diplomatic Cables, the Arab Spring was said to be one of the effects of releasing this information (BBC, 2016). Ongoing use of the WikiLeaks outlet included the Panama Papers (2012) (Bernstein, 2017), the Democratic Party private e-mails from the 2016 U.S. presidential election, and any available sensitive information that might not get through main stream media outlets (David Leigh, 2011) (Domscheit-Berg, 2011)
2012 Panama Papers	A group of journalists, some involved with WikiLeaks, published offshore companies' legal filings from the Panamanian law firm Mossack Fonseca. This information included personal business records of high-level officials in Russia and China that participate in offshore money-hiding schemes (Bernstein, 2017).
2016 – U.S. Presidential Elections	Democratic Party private e-mails were posted on WikiLeaks. Implications of foreign involvement cast a shadow on election process credibility. Russian actors were implicated in divulging personal e-mails on key figures in the Democratic Party (Katelyn Polantz, 2018; Mazetti, 2018; U.S. Justice Department, 2019)

Issue-based trolls that participated in the 2016 U.S. presidential election worked for the Internet Research Agency (IRA), with funding ultimately coming from the Russian intelligence services (GRU) (Mueller, 2019). Trolls are paid antagonists that use social media to stir up issues that strike a nerve with the targeted demographic. This is different from the standard net-based thieves, with computer hacking skills, that make headlines daily; responsible for acquiring our personally identifiable information (PII) from banks, credit agencies, and even from the government agencies.

11.1.3 Cyber Espionage Effects

The use of cyber to extract information, without paying (i.e., theft), is a cyber criminal effect. In Chapter 5, we saw China's successful exfiltration of F-35 designs.

11.1.3.1   Using Cyber to Speed Up the Development of a Fifth-Generation Fighter (e.g., J-31 from F-35 Drawings)

The Chinese J-31 was flying in 2012, approximately three years after the theft of F-35 design drawings was made public in 2009 (Gorman, 2009). The exfiltration of F-35 drawings was estimated to include several terabytes of data and was formally titled the Byzantine Hades intrusion set. Byzantine Hades is reported to date back to approximately 2006 (Fuhrman, 2021).

As a back of the envelope calculation, we can assume that the Chinese were already trying to create their own fifth-generation stealth fighter. However, we can usually expect a 10- to 15-year time line to produce a game changing technology. Therefore, the cyber collection of F-35 data likely accelerated Chinese production of the J-31/J-20 by something on the order of twice as fast (six years from 2006 to 2012).

11.1.4 Cyber Strategic Effects' Wrap-up

The cyber espionage the resulted in the exfiltration of F-35 design drawings provided a strategic effect that likely included a drastic decrease in the J-31/J-20 development timeline. Extracting information via cyber espionage complements the critical infrastructure denial operations (e.g., electricity, water, rail, etc.) that are more commonly discussed at cyber strategic effects.

11.A   Strategic Effect Examples

The asymmetric advantage of cyber is being realized by nation-states, their proxies and independent hackers, often armed with nation-state-level tools (Chapter 3). These teams are responsible for strategic-level cyber effects across civilian and military supply chains. Strategic cyber effects are deployed by teams that span from criminals to nation-states, for motives that range from profiteering to nuclear deterrence. Some of the more famous Russian strategic attacks include

1999 Moonlight Maze – Russian Federation intelligence collection on the U.S. Air Force, resulting in over 5 GB of data extracted – the largest cyber theft at that time.

2014 HAVEX – The Russian Federal Security Service (FSB) used a supply chain attack to access U.S. critical infrastructure via HAVEX malware. Called Operation Dragonfly, the HAVEX campaign spanned from approximately 2012–2017.

2016 U.S. Presidential Elections – leveraging WikiLeaks to publish e-mail traffic from the Democratic National Committee (DNC) and using online personas to voice political views, Russian GRU operatives participated in the election, with the goal of degrading the democratic process' legitimacy

2017 Blactivist Movement – Russian operatives sowed discord by injecting false messages, coordinating rallies, and posting false images of race-based police incidents in the United States (Parham, 2017)

2020 SolarWinds – as discussed in Chapter 5, the Russian Foreign Intelligence Service (SVR) Sluzhba Vneshney Razvedki managed to penetrate the software supply chain, via a commercial company, and gain access to approximately 30,000 systems

The Darkside ransomware group, operating from Russia, brought the U.S. East Coast to a standstill in the spring of 2021 through a ransomware operation against Colonial Oil. Similarly, the Conti ransomware group held the Costa Rican government hostage in the spring of 2022 through a sequestering of their data systems. Many strategic effects have their costs publicized, due to ransom requirements (Table 11.A.1).

Table 11.A.1 Estimated Costs of Strategic Effects.

Year	Operation	Effect	Cost Estimate
2021	Colonial oil	Denial	$5 million (ransom) (downtime – six days)
2021	JBS foods	Denial	$11 million (ransom)
2021	NEW Cooperative	Denial	$5 million (ransom)
2017	NotPetya	Denial	$11 Billion (remediation cost)
2017	WannaCry	Denial	$4–8 Billion (remediation cost)
2012	STUXNET	Manipulation	Two to three years of Uranium enrichment
2000	Maroochy Shire	Manipulation	$1 million

As shown in Table 11.A.1, the costs of cyber attacks on designated critical infrastructure vary from single-digit millions (e.g., Colonial Oil ransom) to over 10 billion dollars to clean up the NotPetya attack. Many strategic effects are not accounted for due to their not being reported. Simple ransomware has reported numbers due to the ransom extracted. Strategic project numbers are not so clear when both the attacker and the target are sensitive projects that only a handful of participants know about in detail.

While criminal cyber operators have simplified the cost of a cyber attack to a fixed ransom, along with internal remediation costs, damage to strategic military programs is not so easy to quantify. For example, the STUXNET attack on the Iranian nuclear program was likely humiliating, and caused at least a delay to account for computer system remediation and replanning, having had impacts across people, policy, process, and technologies involved.

Bibliography

Abrams, L. (2021a). *JBS Paid $11 Million to REvil Ransomware, $22.5M First Demanded*. Retrieved from Bleeping Computer: https://www.bleepingcomputer.com/news/security/jbs-paid-11-million-to-revil-ransomware-225m-first-demanded/.

Abrams, L. (2021b). *US Farmer Cooperative Hit by $5.9M BlackMatter Ransomware Attack*. Retrieved from Bleeping Computer: https://www.bleepingcomputer.com/news/security/us-farmer-cooperative-hit-by-59m-blackmatter-ransomware-attack/.

Andrei Soldatov, I.B. (2015). *The Red Web – the Struggle between Russia's Digital Dictators and the New Online Revolutionaries*. New York, NY, USA: Public Affairs.

BBC. (2016). *18 Revelations from Wikileaks' Hacked Clinton Emails*. Retrieved August 21, 2018, from BBC: https://www.bbc.com/news/world-us-canada-37639370.

Ben Collins, G. R. (2018). *Leaked: Secret Documents from Russia's Election Trolls*. Retrieved 9 9, 2018, from Daily Beast: https://www.thedailybeast.com/exclusive-secret-documents-from-russias-election-trolls-leak?ref=scroll.

Bernstein, J. (2017). *Secrecy World – Inside the Panama Papers Investigation of Illicit Money Networks and the Global Elite*. New York, NY, USA: Henry Holt and Company.

CBS News. (2003). *SoBig Virus may be Spam Scam*. Retrieved 6 27, 2020, from CBS News: https://www.cbsnews.com/news/sobig-virus-may-be-spam-scam/.

David Leigh, L.H. (2011). *WikiLeaks – Inside Julian Assange's War on Secrecy*. New York: Public Affairs.

Domscheit-Berg, D. (2011). *Inside Wikileaks – My Time with Julian Assange at the World's Most Dangerous Website*. New York: Crown.

Frances Robles, N. P. (2021). *'Dangerous Stuff': Hackers Tried to Poison Water Supply of Florida Town*. Retrieved from New York Times: https://www.nytimes.com/2021/02/08/us/oldsmar-florida-water-supply-hack.html.

Fuhrman, E. (2021). *How China Stole the Designs for the F-35 Stealth Fighter*. Retrieved 11 21, 2022, from 1945: https://www.19fortyfive.com/2021/07/how-china-stole-the-designs-for-the-f-35-stealth-fighter/.

Gorman, S. (2009). *Computer Spies Breach Fighter-Jet Project*. Retrieved 2 20, 2022, from Wall Street Journal: https://www.wsj.com/articles/SB124027491029837401.

Greenberg, A. (2017). *How an Entire Nation Became Russia's Test Lab for Cyberwar*. Retrieved 1 27, 2023, from Wired: heeps://www.wired.com/story/russian-hackers-attack-ukraine/.

Hancock, D. (2003). *Virus Disrupts Train Signals*. Retrieved 7 7, 2019, from CBS News: https://www.cbsnews.com/news/virus-disrupts-train-signals/.

Harris, G. (2018). *State Dept. was Granted $120 Million to Fight Russian Meddling. It has Spent $0. Image*. Retrieved 9 9, 2018, from New York Times: https://www.nytimes.com/2018/03/04/world/europe/state-department-russia-global-engagement-center.html.

Katelyn Polantz, S. C. (2018). *12 Russians Indicted in Mueller Investigation*. Retrieved 9 9, 2018, from CNN: https://www.cnn.com/2018/07/13/politics/russia-investigation-indictments/index.html.

Maroochy Shire - Tofino. (2009). *Maroochy Shire*. Retrieved from Tofino: https://www.tofinosecurity.com/sites/default/files/CP-102-Case_Profile-Maroochy_Shire-rev1.pdf.

Mazetti, M. (2018). 12 Russian Agents Indicted in Mueller Investigation.

Mueller, R. (2019). *Report on the Investigation into Russian Interference in the 2016 Presidential Election*. Washington: U.S. Department of Justice.

Oldsmar - Frances Robles, N. P. (2021). *Dangerous Stuff: Hackers Tried to Poison Water Supply of Florida Town*. Retrieved 2 8, 2021, from New York Times: https://www.nytimes.com/2021/02/08/us/oldsmar-florida-water-supply-hack.html.

O'Neill, P. H. (2022). *Russia Hacked an American Satellite Company One Hour Before the Ukraine Invasion*. Retrieved from MIT Technology Review: https://www.technologyreview.com/2022/05/10/1051973/russia-hack-viasat-satellite-ukraine-invasion/.

Parham, J. (2017). *Russians Posing as Black Activists on Facebook is more than Fake News*. Retrieved 8 22, 2018, from Wired: https://www.wired.com/story/russian-black-activist-facebook-accounts/.

Sergey, B. (2023). *Russian Railways Tested Remote Control of Two Lastochka EMUs Operation on MCC*. Retrieved from Rolling Stock: https://rollingstockworld.com/passenger-cars/russian-railways-tested-remote-control-of-two-lastochka-emus-operation-on-mcc/.

Slowik, J. (2019). *CRASHOVERRIDE: Reassessing the 2016 Ukraine Electric Power Event as a Protection-Focused Attack*. Retrieved 9 24, 2019, from DRAGOS: https://dragos.com/wp-content/uploads/CRASHOVERRIDE.pdf.

Symantec. (2003). *W32.Sobig.F@mm*. Retrieved 7 7, 2019, from Symantec: https://www.symantec.com/security-center/writeup/2003-081909-2118-99.

Tofino. (2009). *Maroochy Shire*. Retrieved from Tofino: https://www.tofinosecurity.com/sites/default/files/CP-102-Case_Profile-Maroochy_Shire-rev1.pdf.

Trevor Maynard, N.B. (2015). *Business Blackout – The Insurance Implications of a Cyber Attack on the US Power Grid*. London: Lloyd's.

U.S. Justice Department. (2019). *Report on the Investigation into Russian Interference in the 2016 Presidential Election*. Retrieved May 9, 2019, from U.S. Justice Department: https://www.justice.gov/storage/report.pdf.

Vigderman, A. (2022). *The Most Devastating Computer Viruses in History*. Retrieved from Security.org: https://www.security.org/antivirus/worst-viruses/#:~:text=Estimated%20cost%20of%20damage%3A%20%2430,it%20all%20the%20more%20destructive.

12

Tactical Cyber Effects

12.1 Cyber Tactical Effects

> Tactical – relating to or constituting actions carefully planned to gain a specific military end.
>
> *(Oxford English Dictionary)*

In Figure 1.3, we looked at cyber operations and where they fit on the spectrum of policy options. Strategic cyber operations, especially information operations, pick up where traditional Cold War era active measures leave off. However, tactical use of cyber is "above the line" and is used during operations that include military forces.

Even when used as part of a conventional military operation, cyber is similar to the use of stealth to cloak aircraft, with an ability to access enemy terrain at will without being detected by adversary sensor systems. While cyber has been used in information operations (e.g., 2008 Georgia and 2014 Ukraine/Crimea), the majority of cyber operations have been denial, often in advance of a conventional attack. Russia's evolution from denial of service (DOS) to cyber/kinetic military operations provides examples in the development of a 21st century tactical cyber actor. For example, multiple military and civil operations have included cyber –

Cyber Operations: A Case Study Approach, First Edition. Jerry M. Couretas.
© 2024 John Wiley & Sons, Inc. Published 2024 by John Wiley & Sons, Inc.

2007 Estonia/2008 Georgia – Distributed Denial of Service (DDoS) used by Russian "Patriotic Hackers" to attack banks, telecommunications, and critical infrastructure (Chapter 5)

2009 Twitter – Iran suppressed Twitter due to its use in protesting the re-election of the then sitting President, Mahmoud Ahmadinejad, being re-elected with perceived election malfeasance (Chapter 8)

2012 DigiNotar – a widespread compromise of a certificate authority in order to access approximately 300,000 Iranian citizen's Gmail inboxes (HOFFMAN, 2011) (Chapter 8)

2014 Sony – DPRK used cyber means to attack Sony Pictures for the debut of a film parodying their leader, Kim Jong Un (Chapter 7)

2014 Ukraine – similar to Georgia in 2008, denial of service (DoS) was performed. In addition, incitement of crowds led to Russia intervening in Crimea and Eastern Ukraine, taking permanent positions (Chapter 5)

2016 Counter Islamic State of Iraq and the Levant (ISIS) – U.S. and Coalition used Operation Glowing Symphony as a cyber means to suppress ISIS social media presence and production (Chapter 2)

2019 China and Hong Kong – China used its Great Cannon denial of service tool on pro-democracy protestors in 2019 (Chapter 6)

2022 Ukraine Invasion – the Russian Federation began its February 2022 invasion of the Ukraine with multiple cyber attacks (Chapter 5)

Tactical use of cyber spans from managing civil disorder to counter insurgency, usually framed in terms of being a denial operation. For example, the U.S. and Coalition operators used Operation Glowing Symphony (Cyberlaw, 2016) to deny ISIS' media operations. These denial operations, however, are not the hard-hitting, airstrike-like tactical effects that warfighters would like to see in a new weapon. Removing an enemy anti-aircraft system from the battlefield, traditionally done with a bomb, was performed by the Israeli Air Force in Operation Orchard (2007).

12.1.1 Conventional Example – Denying the Syrian Air Force's Ability to Operate

As a conventional example, we look at Operation Orchard (2007) (Richard Clarke, 2011), where the Israeli Air Force used cyber to blind Syrian anti-aircraft radars prior to bombing a potential nuclear development site. It is a challenge to determine the cost to develop the application that enabled the cyber attack, much less its delivery mechanism. Therefore, we will use a very gross, and I believe high, estimate of 50 man-years, at $250,000 per man year, to arrive at a $12.5 million total cost for a cyber weapon that can achieve tactical military effects. This is a weapon capable of prosecuting an operation to remove Syrian anti-aircraft radar from the battlefield for the duration of an Israeli Air Force air strike on the Syrian nuclear development facility.

Similarly, we can look at what it costs to achieve the same effect kinetically. In 2017, U.S. forces expended 59 Tomahawk Land Attack Missiles (TLAM), at $1.4 million per copy, to disable the Al Sharyat airfield, suspending the Syrian Air Force's ability to defend its area of operations (Michael and Gordon, 2017). Multiplying the 59 Tomahawk missiles by the cost of $1.4 million per missile adds up to approximately $82.6 million for the TLAMs used to disable the Al Sharyat airfield. Therefore, it costs an estimated $82.6 million to effectively prevent the Syrian Air Force from responding to a threat in a given area of operations using conventional air strikes.

Dividing our kinetic deployment option ($82.6 million) by our cyber development option ($12.5 million) comes out roughly to a multiplier of 7 for using cyber over kinetics in taking an anti-aircraft system off the battlefield for a desired time period. Of course, the lead time for analyzing a target and developing a cyber targeting solution is likely much longer than putting together a plan to use off-the-shelf TLAMs to achieve this denial effect. However, with advance planning, the cost savings can be compelling (Table 12.1).

The cost ratios provided by Table 12.1 show cyber's potential to be a promising complement, if not a tradeable alternative, to using conventional munitions when circumstances permit. Conventional employment of cyber is challenged, however, by the short timelines and the readily available bombs and munitions to produce effects. The increased use of cyber in military operations is usually to complement conventional forces (Heli Tiirmaa-Klaar, 2014).

12.1.2 Russian Uses of Cyber (From 2007)

Russia's first documented use of offensive cyber operations dates back to the 2007 denial of service attack against Estonia for the removal of a Soviet monument (NATO, 2007). Since that time, Russia has continued to develop cyber as a complement to conventional operations (Chapter 5). While it is a challenge to quantify the cost of Russian operations, we can see their use and development in Figure 5.5 (Microsoft, 2022). Russia's evolution from denial of service (DOS) to cyber/kinetic military operations is examples of the development of a 21st century tactical cyber actor.

Table 12.1 Operation Orchard – Conventional Cyber Operations with Cost/Benefit Estimates.

Description	Cyber Effect	Military Effect	Cost Approach	Estimated Cyber Operation Cost	Comparable Conventional Operation	Cost Approach for Comparable Operation	Estimated Conventional Operation Cost	Conventional/ Cyber Cost Ratio
2007 Operation Orchard – Stealth Aerial Entry whose "cyber" goal was binary, mission success; spoof the Syrian radars to provide Israeli aircraft target access	Integrity of integrated air defense system (IADS)	Denial of Syrian Air Force's ability to project force in an area of operations (AO)	Analyze system for cyber effects (estimated 50 man-years)	$12,500,000	2017–2020 Syrian aircraft destroyed at Al Sharyat Airfield Strike (Syria) – US reprisal on Syrian Government for Sarin Gas attack on Khan Shaykhun civilian population	Number of Munitions (59) at $1.4 M/copy	$82,600,000	7

> 2007 Estonia – Distributed Denial of Service (DDoS) used by Russian "Patriotic Hackers" to attack Estonian banks, telecommunications, and critical infrastructure in protest for the movement of a Soviet-era statue
>
> 2008 Georgia – Russian "Patriotic Hackers" blinded critical infrastructure, denied telecommunications, defaced websites, and rerouted web traffic before commencing with conventional military operations. Close coordination between cyber and conventional operations implied extensive preparation (FireEye, 2014). Georgia exemplified Russia's conception of cyber as an element of information warfare, rather than as an independent domain. This included the use of third parties (e.g., patriotic hackers) for the offense and for the defense; Atlanta-based Tulip systems came to Georgia's aid after the initial cyber attacks debilitated Georgia's Internet capability (White, 2018).
>
> 2014 Ukraine – similar to Georgia in 2008, denial of service (DoS) was performed. In addition, information operations accompanied Russia intervening in Crimea and Eastern Ukraine, taking permanent positions.
>
> 2022 Ukraine Invasion – the Russian Federation began its February 2022 invasion of the Ukraine with an attack on the Ukraine's Viasat communications network (i.e., AcidRain), and Ukrainian Government and civil systems (i.e., Hermetic wiper and Foxblade).

As shown in Chapter 5 (Figure 5.7), Russia uses cyber as an initial phase of conventional operations, taking advantage of modern, computerized systems, to produce confusion, and a potential blinding of the adversary. Russian cyber operations also include traditional active measures, via cyber, to provide divisive messaging. These cyber-enhanced operations, sometimes extending to military annexation, highlight the use of cyber capabilities in an engagement against an unprepared opponent.

Russia was therefore an "early adopter" of cyber for tactical uses, likely leveraging traditional Soviet active measures combined with legacy electronic warfare capabilities. While expert opinion expected a more pronounced effect during the invasion and occupation of the Ukraine, there are several examples of conventional use of cyber by Russia over the course of 2022.

As discussed in Chapter 1, Al Qaeda in Iraq (AQI) developed tactical cyber capabilities due to an insecure physical location. These cyber capabilities continued to develop as AQI morphed into ISIS. And cyber worked as a force multiplier for ISIS operations, making them appear much larger than they actually were.

12.1.3 ISIS and the Cost of Suppressing a Cyber Entity

A direct tactical use of cyber includes the fight against ISIS, whose debut as a state with a capitol in Raqqa coincided with terror attacks inspired and commanded by ISIS across the globe (Chapters 1 and 2).

Table 12.2 ISIS and Tactical Effects.

Year	Effect	Location	Description
2009	12 dead, 32 wounded	Fort Hood, Texas	MAJ Nidal Hassan attacked fellow U.S. Army soldiers
2015	Security officer wounded	Garland, Texas	2 perpetrators killed as soon as they attacked due to their being surveilled leading up to their attempting to attack a crowd
2015	131 dead	Paris, France	Multiple ISIS-inspired attackers bombed and shot nightclub patrons
2016	49 dead	Orlando, Florida	One ISIS-inspired attacker shot nightclub patrons

12.1.3.1 ISIS and Cyber-Based Attacks

While ISIS was successful in its use of media on the battlefield, it also performed expeditionary operations via the net. Providing a remote command and control element for attacks across the globe was unprecedented for a non-nation-state threat (Table 12.2).

Looking at Table 12.2, we see that most of the effects occurred, while ISIS was a Phase III insurgent (Chapter 2), with a firm base (i.e., capitol) in Raqqa, Syria. As discussed in Chapter 2, ISIS has a proven ability to maneuver within cyberspace. This transition across the levels of insurgency has already shown an ability to go full circle from a Phase I insurgent to a nation-state and back. We will now take a look at the cost of suppressing ISIS in the physical domain.

12.1.3.2 Monitoring ISIS

ISIS maintained both a physical capitol and a defining Internet presence. From both locales, ISIS could launch attacks. Traditional tactical intelligence assets and operations were used to defeat the physical component of ISIS.

ISIS and the Use of Conventional Intelligence, Surveillance, and Reconnaissance (ISR) During the campaign against ISIS, Todd Harrison from the Center for Strategic and Budgetary Assessments (CSBA) put together the following estimate of conducting a campaign at various levels of intensity in order to suppress ISIS.

The idea behind using Table 12.3 is to estimate the cost to prevent the types of attacks in Table 12.2. These two tables therefore give us references to reflect on the cost of potentially preventive security measures. For example, the most comprehensive solution, boots on the ground, could cost $1–2 billion/month with a goal of preventing global terror attacks. Of course the lower-intensity air campaign options look a lot better on paper, when effective.

Table 12.3 Estimated Steady State Costs to Suppress ISIS in the Physical Domain.

Scenario	Monthly Cost	Annualized Cost
Lower-Intensity air campaign	$200M–$320M	$2.4B–$3.8B
Higher-Intensity air campaign	$350M–$570M	$4.2B–$6.8B
Boots on the ground	$1.1B–$1.8B	$13B–$22B

Source: Harrison (2014)/Center for Strategic and Budgetary Assessments (CSBA).

Monitoring a Phase III insurgency with persistent ISR assets, especially with the ability to strike (e.g., use of hellfire missiles from unmanned aerial vehicles (UAVs)), is a financially more attractive option than maintaining boots on the ground, as shown in Table 12.3. In addition, maintaining a visible UAV presence may have other effects on the monitored population – including an increase in red force exposure. However, there is limited evidence that the full military solution will preclude the types of international terrorist attacks found in Table 12.2, even though each cyber attack did occur while ISIS was an independent "state" with a capitol in Raqqa.

Task Force ARES and Operation Glowing Symphony Along with conventional ISR monitoring, there is another option, discussed in Chapter 2, in using a dedicated cyber force along the lines of U.S. Cybercom's Task Force ARES' Operation Glowing Symphony. While a challenge to quantify in terms of resourcing, it is likely that Task Force ARES was less costly than any of the other options in Table 12.3.

The U.S. maintained a "boots on the ground" presence in Iraq from 2003 to 2012 in fighting the multiple factions that composed the insurgency. This approach is expensive. Therefore, the United States took a different approach with Task Force ARES (Chapter 2) combining cyber with extant in-theater special operations. Task Force ARES reduced ISIS' online capabilities. This included removing the Amaq News Agency from the battlefield (Temple-Raston, 2019). However, another option, exercised by both the United States and Israel, is to eliminate cyber operators with conventional munitions.

12.1.3.3 Israeli Bombing of Hamas Cyber Operators

While Junaid Hussain (i.e., ISIS cyber operator) may have been one of the first cyber operators to be removed from the battlefield by a kinetic weapon (2015), the Israelis have performed at least two similar missions to remove cyber operators in the Gaza Strip (Cimpanu, 2021).

Using a conventional strike implies that it was worth the cost to target a cyber operator through a nation-state intelligence service, to plan an air mission to prosecute the target, and to assess if the cyber operator was removed from the battlefield.

12.1.4 Tactical Cyber Effects' Wrap-up

There are likely many factors that go through a commander's calculus in determining the correct approach for managing a cyber adversary. An airstrike, one of the more expensive options, is likely influenced by the time criticality in removing a cyber operation from the battlefield. Cyber can also be used to simply degrade media operations, as was the charter of Task Force ARES in its conducting of Operation Glowing Symphony against ISIS in 2016.

While cyber compliments traditional ISR, we also saw the use of cyber independently in Operation Orchard (Section 12.1.1). It is a challenge to reduce military effects, including preventive ISR or cyber, to cost numbers. Platforms and munitions lend themselves to cost, due to the engineering efforts and associated cost analyses that are used in design, development, and manufacturing. Assessing operations based on possible preventive effects is even more of a challenge.

Along with hypothesizing about preventive measures, we can use remediation costs to describe known cyber attacks. For example, the NMCI attack in 2013 (Chapter 8) was estimated to cost the U.S. Navy $10 million to remediate (Chabrow, 2014). NotPetya (2017) was estimated to cost $10 billion.

And, when planning offensive cyber operations, the potential cost differences between cyber and conventional munitions are provocative, especially in terms of price per military effect. In the Operation Orchard (2007) versus Al Shariat (2017) example, we compared cyber effects with known cruise missile strike operations and arrived at a 7:1 cost advantage. As noted, however, TLAMs are off-the-shelf capabilities, usable at a moment's notice, while cyber weapons require tailoring that may take years to develop and deploy.

12.A Cost of Example Tactical Cyber Attacks (Iran)

Table A.1 Iranian Cyber Operations and Reconstitution Costs.

Year	Target	Cost	Source
2012–2014	NMCI	$10 million	(Gallagher, 2014)
2013	Bowman Dam	$30,000	(DoJ, 2016)
2014	Sands Casino	$40 million	(Brandom, 2014)

Bibliography

Brandom, R. (2014). *Iran Hacked the Sands Hotel Earlier this Year, Causing over $40 Million in Damage.* Retrieved from The Verge: https://www.theverge.com/2014/12/11/7376249/iran-hacked-sands-hotel-in-february-cyberwar-adelson-israel.

Chabrow, E. (2014). *Navy Intranet Breach Cost: $10 Million.* Retrieved from infoRisk Today: https://www.inforisktoday.com/navy-intranet-breach-cost-10-million-a-6517.

Cimpanu, C. (2021). *Israel Bombed Two Hamas Cyber Targets.* (RecordedFuture, Producer). Retrieved 9 15, 2022, from The Record: https://therecord.media/israel-bombed-two-hamas-cyber-targets/.

Cyberlaw. (2016). *Operation Glowing Symphony.* Retrieved from Cyberlaw: https://cyberlaw.ccdcoe.org/wiki/Operation_Glowing_Symphony_(2016)#:~:text=The%20operation%20was%20authorized%20on%208%20November%202016.&text=Joint%20Task%20Force%20Ares%20(JTF,operate%20against%20the%20Islamic%20State.

Director of National Intelligence. (n.d.). *Cyber Threat Framework.* Retrieved 2 15, 2019, from Cyber Threat Framework: https://www.dni.gov/index.php/cyber-threat-framework.

DoJ. (2016). *Seven Iranians Working for Islamic Revolutionary Guard Corps-Affiliated Entities Charged for Conducting Coordinated Campaign of Cyber Attacks Against U.S. Financial Sector.* Retrieved from DoJ: https://www.justice.gov/opa/pr/seven-iranians-working-islamic-revolutionary-guard-corps-affiliated-entities-charged.

FireEye. (2014). *APT28: A Window into Russia's Cyber Espionage Operations?* Retrieved 9 9, 2018, from FireEye: https://www.fireeye.com/content/dam/fireeye-www/global/en/current-threats/pdfs/rpt-apt28.pdf.

Gallagher, S. (2014). *Iranians Hacked Navy Network for Four months? Not a Surprise.* Retrieved from Ars Technica: https://arstechnica.com/information-technology/2014/02/iranians-hacked-navy-network-for-4-months-not-a-surprise/.

Handler, S. (2022). *The Cyber Strategy and Operations of Hamas: Green Flags and Green Hats.* Retrieved from Atlantic Council: https://www.atlanticcouncil.org/in-depth-research-reports/report/the-cyber-strategy-and-operations-of-hamas-green-flags-and-green-hats/.

Harrison, T. (2014). *Estimating the Costs of Operations Against ISIL.* Retrieved 2 2, 2023, from CSBA: https://csbaonline.org/research/publications/estimating-the-cost-of-operations-against-isil.

Heli Tiirmaa-Klaar, J.G.-P. (2014). *Botnets.* New York: Springer.

Hoffman, S. (2011). *300,000 Iranian IP Addresses Compromised In DigiNotar SSL Hack.* Retrieved from CRN: https://www.crn.com/news/security/231600847/300-000-iranian-ip-addresses-compromised-in-diginotar-ssl-hack.htm.

Michael, R. and Gordon, H. C. (2017). *Dozens of U.S. Missiles Hit Air Base in Syria.* Retrieved 8 21, 2019, from New York Times: https://www.nytimes.com/

2017/04/06/world/middleeast/us-said-to-weigh-military-responses-to-syrian-chemical-attack.html.

Microsoft. (2022). *Defending Ukraine: Early Lessons from the Cyber War*. Retrieved 8 30, 2022, from Microsoft: https://query.prod.cms.rt.microsoft.com/cms/api/am/binary/RE50KOK.

NATO. (2007). *2007 Cyber Attacks on Estonia*. Retrieved 5 11, 2023, from STRATCOMCOE: https://stratcomcoe.org/cuploads/pfiles/cyber_attacks_estonia.pdf.

Richard Clarke, R.K. (2011). *Cyber War: The Next Threat to National Security and What to Do about it*. Ecco.

Temple-Raston, D. (2019). *How The U.S. Hacked ISIS*. Retrieved from NPR: https://www.npr.org/2019/09/26/763545811/how-the-u-s-hacked-isis.

White, S. P. (2018). *Understanding Cyberwarfare – Lessons from the Russia-Georgia War*. Retrieved 9 25, 2021, from Modern War Institute at West Point: https://mwi.usma.edu/wp-content/uploads/2018/03/Understanding-Cyberwarfare.pdf.

13

Cyber Crime Effects

13.1 Criminal Cyber Effects

In Chapter 3, we differentiated between the use of cyber to perform conventional crime and the tailoring of cyber methods to perform cyber-specific crime. In addition, in Chapter 9, we discussed how computer viruses used new technologies to produce unforeseen mayhem. For example, the Jester worm dialed into the Bell Atlantic computer system, via modem, and knocked out systems that managed phone and radio communications for the air traffic control tower at Worcester Airport, as well as phone service for 600 homes in the area in 1997. Similarly, a rogue engineer used the controls in a water treatment facility to dump 265,000 gallons of waste into Maroochy Shire, Australia, to protest being laid off from his job in 2000. And the Sobig virus infected CSX, which operates rail systems for passenger and freight trains in 23 U.S. states, and as a result of the infection stopped signals going out, caused trains running between Pennsylvania and South Carolina, and in the DC Beltway, to stop (Hancock, 2003). Cost estimates for the Sobig virus run into the billions of dollars (Vigderman, 2022).

Each of these early attacks, while criminal, was the work of hackers with limited organizational support. Criminal effects both grew and became more organized over the second decade of the 21st century. For example, records theft was originally performed for the value of the data. However, data exfiltration caused the data thief extra work in the storing and selling of records. With the advent of ransomware, and the ability to monetize an organization's attack surface, a ransomware operator could get an upfront, lump sum, payment, reducing all the extra work involved in pre-ransomware cyber thievery.

Cyber Operations: A Case Study Approach, First Edition. Jerry M. Couretas.
© 2024 John Wiley & Sons, Inc. Published 2024 by John Wiley & Sons, Inc.

13.1.1 Records Theft

Healthcare centers are one of the most targeted data centers. This is primarily due to patient data being one of the most valuable assets for criminals today. Protected health information (PHI) is worth a fortune to cyber criminals and is one of the hottest commodities on the dark web. Experian tags stolen patient records as going for $1000 each, while credit card numbers are selling for around $5 each, a hacked Instagram account is $7, and Social Security numbers are worth a paltry $1 (Dickerson, 2022).

> ... criminals experienced in drug trafficking and money laundering eagerly buy medical records to obtain prescription medications, file bogus medical claims, or steal the information to open credit cards and take out fraudulent loans. Medical records are a rich resource of valuable and permanent data points, while accounts and credit cards are quickly canceled. Cyber attacks on healthcare also yield exorbitant ransoms. For example, the ransomware known as Ryuk has purportedly been used to extort millions from U.S. healthcare facilities since 2018. In addition, the average price tag of a healthcare data breach just climbed to $10 million, according to IBM Security's annual Cost of a Data Breach Report.
>
> *(Dickerson, 2022)*

Cyber crime includes the theft of records in order to monetize the user data. This does not include the remediation cost, which is the traditional cost of a data breach.

13.1.1.1 Cost of a Data Breach

In IBM's "Cost of a Data Breach" report (IBM, 2022), the following statistics were developed from 3600 interviews across 550 organizations in 17 countries and 17 industries.

Looking at Table 13.1, we see an over $1 million dollars and approximately one month savings in response time for organizations that employ extended detection and response. In addition to the growing costs associated with a data breach (Table 13.1), there is an increasing number of business records attacks.

13.1.1.2 Business Records Attacks (2006–2019)

As originally discussed in Figure 1.5, multiple organizations have been attacked and had their data stolen over last two decades (Table 13.2).

As shown in Table 13.2, there are challenges in limiting the exfiltration of data from commercial sites. In addition, there are developing policy costs due to identity information being compromised. For example, the General Data Protection

Table 13.1 Data Breach Statistics.

- $10.1 million USD – average cost of a healthcare data breach
- $9.44 million USD – average cost of a breach in the United States, the highest of any country
- $4.82 million USD – average cost of a critical infrastructure data breach
- $4.54 million USD – average cost of a ransomware attack, not including the cost of the ransom itself
- $4.5 million USD – average total cost of a data breach
- $3.1 million USD – average cost savings associated with fully deployed security AI and automation
- $2.7 million USD – average cost savings associated with an incident response (IR) team and regularly tested IR plan
- $1.0 million USD – average difference in cost where remote work was a factor in causing the breach versus when it was not a factor
- 13 years – consecutive years the healthcare industry had the highest average cost of a breach
- 83% of organizations studied have had more than one data breach
- 79% of critical infrastructure organizations did not deploy a zero trust architecture
- 45% of breaches occurred in the cloud
- 45% of the breaches were cloud-based
- 19% of breaches occurred because of a compromise at a business partner
- 19% of breaches caused by stolen or compromised credentials
- 60% of organizations' breaches led to increases in prices passed on to customers
- 59% of organizations that do not deploy zero trust
- 277 days – average time to identify and contain a data breach
- 29 days – savings in response time for those with extended detection and response (XDR) technologies

Source: Adapted from IBM (2022).

Regulation (GDPR), enacted by the EU in 2018, will fine an organization for irresponsible loss of private data. Costs included in these large data exfiltrations therefore include

- **People**: Both the organizations and the individuals who lose their data have an imposed cost, which includes reputation and remediation
- **Policy**: External policy organizations, with GDPR being the first example, are now a source of potential fines, should private information be lost
- **Process**: The organization will need to go through a remediation process to restore its internal business systems. In addition, the company will need to review its security processes for potential improvement

Table 13.2 Year versus Confidentiality Impact (2006–2019).

Year	Company	Records Lost Estimate
2006	TJX	94,000,000
2009	Heartland	130,000,000
2011	Sony	77,000,000
2011	RSA Security	40,000,000
2014	JP Morgan Chase	83,000,000
2014	Home Depot	56,000,000
2015	Anthem	80,000,000
2015	Ashley Madison	32,000,000
2015	IRS	724,000
2015	OPM	21,500,000
2016	Uber	57,000,000
2016	FriendFinder	413,000,000
2016	MySpace	360,000,000
2016	LinkedIn	165,000,000
2017	Equifax	147,000,000
2018	Marriott	500,000,000
2019	CapitolOne	106,000,000

- **Technology:** The compromised technology will need to be updated to ensure that the same compromise does on reoccur

Due to the challenges in enumerating the costs of a cyber breach, Romanosky estimated that the aggregated cyber security costs at approximately 0.4% of annual revenue. When looking at the tens, or hundreds, of millions of records compromised in Table 13.2, a natural question is "how long does a cyber extraction take?"

13.1.1.3 2017 Large Exfiltration Attack Example (Equifax (2017) – 143 Million Records)

The Equifax cyber attack was profiled by Popular Mechanics (Popular Mechanics, 2018), where they "… asked three experts to guess how large the files might be, and how long it would take for Boris J. Hackervich to siphon off 143 million records …"

- **1 day:** Herb Lin, senior research scholar at the Center for International Security and Cooperation at Stanford University, went with a more modest individual file size of 1 kb, which would wrap everything up in about a day.

- **2.5 days:** Vyas Sekar, an associate professor of electrical and computer engineering at Carnegie Mellon University, suggested a file size of 20 kb per record, which he considered generous. Collectively, he said, the stolen data would equate to about 800 Netflix movies, which could slip out the back door in about two and a half days.
- **38 days:** On the other end of the spectrum is Thomas Kilbride, a security consultant at IOActive, a cyber security firm that recently made headlines by hacking a personal-assistant robot and turning it into a stabbing machine. Kilbride used a worst-case estimate of 250 kb per record, coming up with a download time of 38 days.

Therefore, the persistent attacker time ranges from 1 to 38 days, all within the Mandiant estimate for the mean 2016 time to detect of 99 days.

Due to the current immaturity of Internet-connected devices, some of the more dangerous strategic cyber effects have been realized by cyber criminals. For example, shutting down the fuel supply to the U.S. East Coast in 2021, definitely a strategic effect, was performed by the CONTI ransomware gang, who also shut the government of Costa Rica out of their systems the same year. Therefore, it is sometimes a challenge to determine what is criminal vs strategic in looking at operations and their perpetrators. We will therefore focus on clearly defined crimes, mostly ransomware operations, in reviewing criminal effects in this chapter.

13.1.2 Cyber Crime Examples

The vast majority of day-to-day cyber crime operations are theft, which includes the exfiltration of data. However, the advent of crypto currency around 2010 provided a new venue for moving illicit goods on the Internet. For example, the Silk Road (2013) was one of the first uses of Bitcoin to buy and sell drugs on the Internet. Russia's Hydra market (2015–2022) expanded on the Silk Road idea. And ransomware (2017 to present) largely uses crypto currency to pay off the perpetrators.

Each of the crypto currency enabled cyber crimes paralleled the use of the Internet to perform bank theft. For example, as discussed in Chapter 7, the Democratic People's Republic of Korea (DPRK or North Korea) attempted a $1 billion heist on the Bank of Bangladesh in 2016. And this was several years after the use of Conficker for bank robbery in 2011.

13.1.2.1 Conficker (2011)

One common denominator among nefarious cyber actors is a high level of technical education combined with few job prospects. Russian trolls are a good example of underemployed, young, highly educated cyber operators. As shown in

Table 13.2's examples, theft is an ongoing theme in cyber attacks. For example, banks are constantly under cyber attack (Middleton, 2018) and they have some of the best defensive cyber operators available.

Conficker, the famous worm that was used to drain $72 million from banks in 2011 (Bowden, 2011), is a good example of the type of advanced threat that banks and financial institutions face. The 16 technically trained Ukrainian programmers convicted for the Conficker worm were all less than 30 years old.

13.1.2.2   Silk Road (2013)

The Silk Road used The Onion Router (ToR) as a means of covert communication to provide a marketplace for the sale of drugs on the Internet. While selling illicit drugs for profit was not a new idea, the use of cyber means to settle the transactions, and the use of crypto currency to complete the sales was a first (Russell, 2021). The Silk Road drug transactions had a total value of approximately $213 million (DoJ, 2023).

13.1.2.3   Bangladesh Bank (2016)

The Bangladesh Bank attack, resulting in the DPRK receiving $81 million of the attempted $1 billion heist, was discussed in Chapter 7 and is covered in detail by White (White, 2022). This was clearly a crime, committed by a nation-state.

13.1.2.4   Hydra (2015–2022)

For Russian speakers, Hydra provided a set of black-market products and services over the Internet from 2015 to 2022 (DoJ, 2022). In Chapter 3, we introduced Pavel Vrubelsky, a key figure in operating Hydra, which was responsible for clearing approximately 80% of the global crypto currency transactions, or approximately $5.2 billion over Hydra's operational lifetime (2015–2022).

13.1.2.5   Ransomware (>2017)

Ransomware is used to encrypt an organization's information technology system, requiring a "ransom" payment for the organization to get their data back. In the course of a ransomware attack, the targeted organization can lose its computer system and become non-functional.

As discussed in Chapter 3, the distribution of nation-state tools seems to have resulted in a bow wave of ransomware attacks. And, while we see news reporting of many large-scale attacks, it is estimated that only 5% of ransomware attacks are fully disclosed (Palmer, 2022). More recently, ransomware as a service (RaaS) operators have targeted hospitals and other public service organizations. For example,

> The ransomware families associated with or deployed by cracked copies of Cobalt Strike have been linked to more than 68 ransomware attacks

impacting healthcare organizations in more than 19 countries around the world. These attacks have cost hospital systems millions of dollars in recovery and repair costs, plus interruptions to critical patient care services including delayed diagnostic, imaging and laboratory results, canceled medical procedures and delays in delivery of chemotherapy treatments, just to name a few.

(Hogan-Burney, 2023)

Ransomware can lead to loss of life if the organization targeted is a healthcare provider. For example, it is said that the delays in providing care to a woman in Germany, during a ransomware attack, resulted in her death (Wetsman, 2020). Similarly, in a recent case, a mother filed suit against a hospital that was undergoing a cyber attack during her difficult child birth experience, with the baby dying afterward due to lack of proper care during the child's birth (Collier, 2021).

Ransomware Costs The FBI estimated that Americans lost $7 billion in 2022, mostly to ransomware (CBS Miami, 2022). An estimated 46% of organizations attacked in 2022 paid the ransom, with an average payout of $813,360. In addition, the cost of ransomware is expected to grow from $20 billion in 2021 to over $260 billion by 2031 (Braue, 2021) (Table 13.3).

As shown in Table 13.3, ransomware costs grew disproportionately, from $325 million in 2015 to approximately $5 billion in 2017. This is likely due to the Shadow Brokers release of nation-state-level tools over this time period, as discussed in Section 3.3. There also seems to be a level of specialization associated with ransomware tactics, tools, and techniques due to CONTI and ReVIL being responsible for 1/3 of the attacks in the 2021–2022 time period (Table 13.4).

As shown in Table 13.4, only 8 or so ransomware actors are responsible for 1/2 of the worldwide ransomware attacks in the 2021–2022 time period. With an

Table 13.3 Geometric Growth of Ransomware Costs.

Year	Estimated Cost
2015	$325 million
2017	$5 billion
Approximate time of Shadow Brokers tool release	
2021	$20 billion
2026	$72 billion
2028	$157 billion
2031	$265 billion

Source: Adapted from Braue (2021).

Table 13.4 2021 Ransomware Group Activity.

Ransomware Group	Percentage of Attacks (%)
CONTI	16
ReVIL	15
Ryuk	9
LockBit	4
Ragnarok	4
Black Kingdom	3
DarkSide	3
Maze	3
Other	43

Source: Adapted from https://techmonitor.ai/technology/
cybersecurity/conti-breached-panasonic.

estimated $20 billion in ransomware costs, that puts the top 2 ransomware groups, CONTI and ReVIL, responsible for approximately $6 billion per year in ransomware costs. These are not small businesses.

13.1.3   Cyber Criminal Organizations – Gangs and Nation-States

In Section 3.3.2, we reviewed ransomware gangs (Table 3.7) and found the lifetime of a gang to be relatively short term at approximately 22 months, with members migrating to new gangs as older gangs disbanded.

13.1.3.1 Cyber Gangs

While we discussed the evolution of cyber operations from hackers to nation-state teams, we will now talk about ransomware gangs. As discussed in Chapter 3, ransomware really made its debut after the intentional and unintentional release of nation-state tools from the U.S. NSA and CIA. In fact, several of the gangs we will look at existed from 2018 to 2022, just after the Shadow Brokers released these tools.

Average Life Span and Earnings of a Cyber Gang   As discussed in Chapter 3, cyber criminals are divided along the lines of using cyber to commit age-old crimes and technically savvy folks who tailor their methods with computer-based means. In addition, we have criminal gangs that work together temporarily, disband, and seem to reconnect based on the available opportunities. This is different from the identified nation-state operators who seem to persist for years (Table 13.5).

Table 13.5 Cyber Gangs, Lifetimes, and Earnings.

Cyber Gang Name	Cyber Gang Lifetime	Estimated Cyber Gang Earnings
BlackMatter (CISA, 2021)	9 months	>$50 Million (Arghire, 2021)
BlackByte	>7/2021	
CONTI (Flashpoint, 2022)	24 months	$180 million (Meegan-Vickers, 2022)
DarkSide (Schwirtz and Perlroth, 2021)	6 months	>$90 Million (Browne, 2021)
DopplePaymer	22 months (5/2019–3/2021)	>$90 Million (Page, 2023)
GandCrab	17 months (1/2018–6/2019)	>$2 Billion (Abrams, 2019)
HIVE	17 months (6/2021–13/2022)	>$100 Million (Sussman, 2023)
Ragnarok	20 months (~1/2020–9/2021)	>$4.5 Million (Page, 2021)
ReVIL/Sodinokibi	32 months (4/2019–1/2022)	>$100 Million (Ilascu, 2020; Sayegh, 2023)
DPRK Crypto Operators	>2017 (started with WannaCry)	>$1 Billion (White, 2022)
Average	~22 months	~$80 million

Looking at Table 13.5, the average ransomware gang/affiliate lasts approximately 22 months, same as what we discussed in Table 3.8, and earn approximately $80 million over their organizational lifetime. Also, note that the sum of the estimated per gang earnings is less than the estimated crypto currency amount cleared through the Hydra Exchange (~ $5 billion) (Section 13.1.2.4). This is due to variations in the news sources for the cited numbers, which are likely anecdotal.

And, for the documented cyber gangs, the life spans provided in Table 13.5 are from 2018 to 2022, the aftermath of the 2016–2017 tool releases discussed in Chapter 3. However, it is unclear whether the 2018–2022 ransomware gangs were a fleeting phenomenon, or they are simply a new generation of professional cyber operators starting the next era of cyber. For example, with nation-state actors getting involved (e.g., DPRK) cyber crimes are ongoing operations that have already gone into the billions of dollars of damages.

13.1.3.2 CONTI Ransomware Group

With an estimated $1 billion in imposed costs due to CONTI's ransomware efforts, CONTI is also famous for some of the larger ransomware attacks. For example,

CONTI shut down the government of Costa Rica in 2021–2022, which led to the CONTI group's demise. Similarly, in 2023 BlackByte supported Iran in performing a denial operation on Albania's government (Oghanna, 2023) (Chapter 8), very similar to what CONTI performed on Cost Rica.

Costa Rican Government Shutdown Due to Ransomware While the spring of 2021 ransomware attack on the Colonial Pipeline had a strong effect on travel and short-term fuel prices on the East Coast of the United States, the summer of 2021 saw the CONTI ransomware group shutting down the entire country of Costa Rica (Ilascu, 2022). This resulted in Cost Rica declaring a national emergency on May 8, 2022, and the eventual destruction of the CONTI ransomware group, with members making their way to other groups (e.g., BlackByte, HIVE). Criminal cyber effects, usually designed to extract money, often have physical implications. There are a wide variety of criminal actions using cyber. Ransomware as a service (RaaS) is one of the more famous, ongoing, threats. Similarly, the Silk Road took advantage of privacy technology designed to help the politically oppressed (i.e., The Onion Router (ToR)) to sell drugs on the web.

13.1.3.3 Nation-State Use of Cyber Crime

As discussed in Chapter 9, Iran uses cyber for suppression operations. In 2014, Iran used cyber to destroy the Sands Casino IT systems, whose owner, Sheldon Adelson, made negative comments about the Iranian regime (Chapter 8). This was a general wiper attack that destroyed three quarters of the company's Las Vegas servers, resulting in a cost of over $40 million (Alyza Sebenius, 2020).

Iran is known to work with criminal operators, as discussed in the use of ransomware on the Albanian government IT systems in 2022. This attack included help from the Russian BlackByte gang (Oghanna, 2023).

While Iran uses cyber for suppression operations, the DPRK has a rich history in criminal operations (i.e., Room 39) and has moved these operations to cyberspace. And North Korea's techniques have advanced substantially from their 2016 Sony attack, where they effectively shut down Sony's distribution of "The Interview," due to its unapproved portrayal of their leader, Kim Jong Un. This was the DPRK's version of a sanction, effectively a gag order or denial operation, issued via cyber, to censor an American company.

North Korea also uses cyber theft. For example, the DPRK is reported to have stolen over $2 Billion from digital wallets related to online gambling and gaming to fund their nuclear program (Nichols, 2019). One means that the DPRK uses to extract these funds is the theft of crypto currencies.

On March 23, 2022, Treasury says, "Lazarus Group, a DPRK state-sponsored cyber hacking group, carried out the largest virtual currency heist to date, worth almost $620 million, from a blockchain project linked to the online game Axie Infinity; Blender was used in processing over $20.5 million of the illicit proceeds." The sanctions are believed to be the first levied against a mixer service.

(U.S. Treasury Department, 2022)

In addition, North Korea's use of cyber theft, stealing $2 Billion to fund its nuclear program (Chapter 7), includes "cryptojacking" computers by infecting them with malware to use its resources to generate crypto currency (England, 2019).

13.1.4   Cyber Crime Effects' Wrap-up

Cyber crime was challenging even before nation-states came on the scene and started using the research, engineering, and espionage capabilities (Figure 4.1) of a nation-state against individuals and businesses. For example, ransomware is estimated to have cost businesses billions of dollars, mostly through cyber gangs. And while Conficker reportedly stole $72 million by 2011, the DPRK netted $81 million five years later, with a goal of collecting $1 billion in 2016.

Conficker was being prosecuted around the same time that the Silk Road, a cyber drug dealing operation, was in its heyday. Using The Onion Router (ToR) and Bitcoin to clear transactions, the Silk Road set the stage for Russia's Hydra market, a few years later, that is estimated to have been responsible for over $5 billion in crypto currency transactions. Among the players using Hydra were cyber gangs, washing their ransomware transactions, which only increased in the late 2010s. The criminal effects of ransomware and digital theft are in the billions of dollars and growing.

Bibliography

Abrams, L. (2019). *GandCrab Ransomware Shutting Down After Claiming to Earn $2 Billion*. Retrieved from BleepingComputer: https://www.bleepingcomputer.com/news/security/gandcrab-ransomware-shutting-down-after-claiming-to-earn-2-billion/.

Alyza Sebenius, K. M. (2020). *Iran's Cyber Attack on Billionaire Adelson Provides Lesson on Strategy*. Retrieved from Claims Journal: https://www.claimsjournal.com/news/national/2020/01/06/294849.htm.

Arghire, I. (2021). *BlackMatter Ransomware Gang Announces Shutdown*. Retrieved from SecurityWeek: https://www.securityweek.com/blackmatter-ransomware-gang-announces-shutdown/.

Bing, C. (2017). *Leaked NSA Hacking Tools are a Hit on the Dark Web*. Retrieved 4 10, 2023, from CyberScoop: https://cyberscoop.com/nsa-hacking-tools-shadow-brokers-dark-web-microsoft-smb/.

Bowden, M. (2011). *Worm – The First Digital World War.* New York: Atlantic Monthly Press.

Braue, D. (2021). *Global Ransomware Damage Costs Predicted To Exceed $265 Billion By 2031.* Retrieved 4 20, 2022, from Cybercrime Magazine: https://cybersecurity ventures.com/global-ransomware-damage-costs-predicted-to-reach-250-billion-usd-by-2031/.

Browne, R. (2021). *Hackers Behind Colonial Pipeline Attack Reportedly Received $90 Million in Bitcoin Before Shutting Down.* Retrieved from CNN: https://www.cnbc.com/2021/05/18/colonial-pipeline-hackers-darkside-received-90-million-in-bitcoin.html#.

CBS Miami. (2022). *FBI: Americans Lost Nearly $7 Billion to Cybercrime Last Year.* Retrieved 9 12, 2022, from CBS Miami: https://www.cbsnews.com/miami/news/fbi-americans-lost-nearly-7-billion-to-cybercrime-last-year/.

CISA. (2021). *BlackMatter Ransomware.* Retrieved from CISA: https://www.cisa.gov/news-events/cybersecurity-advisories/aa21-291a.

Collier, K. (2021). *Baby Died Because of Ransomware Attack on Hospital, Suit Says.* Retrieved 7 10, 2022, from NBC News: https://www.nbcnews.com/news/baby-died-due-ransomware-attack-hospital-suit-claims-rcna2465.

Dickerson, S. (2022). *Why is Healthcare a Top Target for Cybersecurity Threats?* Retrieved 9 16, 2022, from Security: https://www.securitymagazine.com/articles/98324-why-is-healthcare-a-top-target-for-cybersecurity-threats.

DoJ. (2022). *Justice Department Investigation Leads to Shutdown of Largest Online Darknet Marketplace.* Retrieved 5 18, 2023, from Department of Justice: https://www.justice.gov/opa/pr/justice-department-investigation-leads-shutdown-largest-online-darknet-marketplace.

DoJ. (2023). *Senior Adviser To The Operator Of The Silk Road Online Black Market Sentenced To 20 Years In Prison.* Retrieved from DoJ: https://www.justice.gov/usao-sdny/pr/senior-adviser-operator-silk-road-online-black-market-sentenced-20-years-prison#:~:text=Silk%20Road%20was%20massive%20in,%24183%20million%20in%20drug%20sales.

England, R. (2019). *UN Claims North Korea Hacks Stole $2 Billion to Fund Its Nuclear Program.* Retrieved 8 18, 2019, from Engadget: https://www.engadget.com/2019/08/13/un-claims-north-korea-hacks-stole-2-billion-to-fund-its-nuclear/.

Flashpoint. (2022). *Conti Ransomware: Inside One of the World's Most Aggressive Ransomware Groups.* Retrieved from Flashpoint: https://flashpoint.io/blog/history-of-conti-ransomware/.

Glover, C. (2022). *Panasonic Confirms Cyberattack After Conti Leaks Data.* Retrieved 4 20, 2022, from Techmonitor: https://techmonitor.ai/technology/cybersecurity/conti-breached-panasonic.

Hancock, D. (2003). *Virus Disrupts Train Signals.* Retrieved 7 7, 2019, from CBS News: https://www.cbsnews.com/news/virus-disrupts-train-signals/.

Hogan-Burney, A. (2023). *Stopping Cybercriminals from Abusing Security Tools.* Retrieved 4 10, 2023, from Microsoft: https://blogs.microsoft.com/on-the-issues/2023/04/06/stopping-cybercriminals-from-abusing-security -tools/.

IBM. (2022). *Cost of a Data Breach.* Retrieved 8 3, 2022, from IBM: https://www.ibm. com/downloads/cas/3R8N1DZJ.

Ilascu, I. (2020). *REvil Ransomware Gang Claims over $100 Million Profit in a Year.* Retrieved from Bleeping Computer: https://www.bleepingcomputer.com/news/ security/revil-ransomware-gang-claims-over-100-million-profit-in-a-year/ #:~:text=REvil%20ransomware%20developers%20say%20that,in%20their%20 pursuit%20of%20wealth.

Ilascu, I. (2022). *How Conti Ransomware Hacked and Encrypted the Costa Rican Government.* Retrieved 9 28, 2022, from Bleeping Computer: https://www. bleepingcomputer.com/news/security/how-conti-ransomware-hacked-and-encrypted-the-costa-rican-government/.

Meegan-Vickers, J. (2022). *The Rise and Fall of the Conti Ransomware Group.* Retrieved from Global Initiative Against Transnational Organized Crime: https:// globalinitiative.net/analysis/conti-ransomware-group-cybercrime/#:~:text= Over%20the%20previous%2018%20months,US%24180%20million%20in%20 payouts.

Middleton, C. (2018). *Cyber Attack Could Cost Bank Half of Its Profits, Warns IMF.* Retrieved 8 22, 2018, from Internet of Business: https://internetofbusiness. com/fintech-cyber-attack-could-cost-bank-half-of-its-profits-warns-imf/.

Nichols, M. (2019). *North Korea took $2 Billion in Cyberattacks to Fund Weapons Program: U.N. Report.* Retrieved 8 17, 2019, from Reuters: https://www.reuters. com/article/us-northkorea-cyber-un/north-korea-took-2-billion-in-cyber-attacks-to-fund-weapons-program-u-n-report-idUSKCN1UV1ZX.

Oghanna, A. (2023). *How Albania Became a Target for Cyberattacks.* Retrieved from Foreign Policy: https://foreignpolicy.com/2023/03/25/albania-target-cyberattacks-russia-iran/.

Page, C. (2021). *Ragnarok Ransomware Gang Shuts Down and Releases Its Decryption Key.* Retrieved from TechCrunch: https://techcrunch.com/2021/08/30/ ragnarok-ransomware-gang-shuts-down-and-releases-its-decryption-key/.

Page, C. (2023). *Police Arrest Suspected Members of Prolific DoppelPaymer Ransomware Gang.* Retrieved from TechCrunch: https://techcrunch. com/2023/03/06/police-arrest-suspected-members-of-prolific-doppelpaymer-ransomware-gang/.

Palmer, D. (2022). *Reported Ransomware Attacks are Just the Tip of the Iceberg. That's a Problem for Everyone.* Retrieved 11 8, 2022, from ZD Net: https://www.zdnet. com/article/reported-ransomware-attacks-are-just-the-tip-of-the-iceberg-thats-a-problem-for-everyone/.

Popular Mechanics. (2018). *How Long Does It Take Hackers To Pull Off a Massive Job Like Equifax?* Retrieved 3 13, 2018, from Popular Mechanics: https://www.popularmechanics.com/technology/security/a18930168/equifax-hack-time/

Russell, T. (Director). (2021). *Silk Road* [Motion Picture].

Sayegh, E. (2023). *The REvil Gang Story: The "Good Guys" Can Still Prevail*. Retrieved from Forbes: https://www.forbes.com/sites/emilsayegh/2023/03/22/the-revil-gang-story-the-good-guys-can-still-prevail/?sh=73209edf658a.

Schwirtz, M., Perlroth, N. (2021). *DarkSide, Blamed for Gas Pipeline Attack, Says It is Shutting Down*. Retrieved from New York Times.

Sussman, B. (2023). *Hive Ransomware: $100 Million in Profits, then the FBI Hid Inside their Network*. Retrieved from BlackBerry: https://blogs.blackberry.com/en/2023/01/hive-ransomware-100-million-in-profits-then-the-fbi-hid-inside-their-network#:~:text=Inside%20Their%20Network-,Hive%20Ransomware%3A%20%24100%20Million%20in%20Profits%2C%20Then%20the,FBI%20Hid%20Inside%20Their%20Netw.

U.S. Treasury Department. (2022). *U.S. Treasury Issues First-Ever Sanctions on a Virtual Currency Mixer, Targets DPRK Cyber Threats*. Retrieved 9 28, 2022, from U.S. Treasury Department: https://home.treasury.gov/news/press-releases/jy0768.

Vigderman, A. (2022). *The Most Devastating Computer Viruses in History*. Retrieved from Security.org: https://www.security.org/antivirus/worst-viruses/#:~:text=Estimated%20cost%20of%20damage%3A%20%2430,it%20all%20the%20more%20destructive.

Wetsman, N. (2020). *Woman Dies During a Ransomware Attack on a German Hospital*. Retrieved 5 2, 2022, from The Verge: https://www.theverge.com/2020/9/17/21443851/death-ransomware-attack-hospital-germany-cybersecurity.

White, G. (2022). *The Lazarus Heist – from Hollywood to High Finance: Inside North Korea's Global Cyber War*. New York: Penguin.

Section II

Cyber Effects Conclusions

II.1   Cyber Effects Overview

As reviewed in this section, operations in cyberspace produce effects that span the strategic, tactical, and criminal domains. Categorization is sometimes a challenge due to the team, target, tool, and effect having linkages stemming from more than one domain (Figure II.1).

As shown in Figure II.1, multiple operations over the last few decades have provided example operations in the strategic, tactical, and criminal areas. In addition, for STUXNET (2010) and Operation Orchard (2007), we have analogs from the kinetic warfighting domain that help us with estimating rough resource ratios. And rough estimates in the strategic and tactical realms provide multipliers in terms resource investments. Resource multipliers are assumed as a given in the criminal domain with the DPRK and ransomware gangs netting billions of dollars from companies and individuals.

Providing campaign level analysis, a challenge to even the most data centric of organizations, is even more challenging when making a comparison that crosses traditional warfighting and intelligence boundaries. We were therefore aided, here, in Whaley's analogous loss exchange rate (LER) advantages estimated to be due to the single factor of deception. Whaley's study of kinetic military campaigns for the last few centuries provided us with a 15:1 LER advantage, attributed to the winning opponent's use of deception. We also found similar financial cost ratios for the use of cyber in strategic operations. For example, Chapter 10's STUXNET example provides an 18:1 cost advantage, over the estimated of cost of the 1998 Operation Desert Fox air campaign, to delay a nation-state nuclear program. Similarly, Operation Orchard (2007) provided a 7:1 cost advantage over the kinetic 2017 Al Sharyat airfield attack – both designed to disable Syrian Aircraft response capabilities.

Cyber Operations: A Case Study Approach, First Edition. Jerry M. Couretas.
© 2024 John Wiley & Sons, Inc. Published 2024 by John Wiley & Sons, Inc.

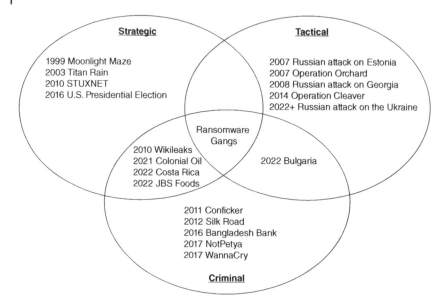

Figure II.1 Strategic, Tactical, and Criminal Domains and Operations.

II.2 Cyber Effects' Wrap-up

We completed the cyber effects section with cybercrime, including both traditional crime facilitated over cyber and cyber-specific crimes. Bank theft, for example, a traditional crime, moved to cyberspace with the increasing use of computers in financial transactions. Conficker (2011) and the Bank of Bangladesh (2016) are examples of the use of cyber to perform traditional bank robbery. In addition to traditional finance, cyber criminals also use crypto currency to both take payment for nefarious transactions, including ransomware operations, and to help their state sponsors avoid sanctions.

Similar to criminal use of cyber to provide clandestine communication, cyber is also used to improve tactical outcomes. Denial, for example, has a precedent in jamming communications. Similarly, deception is as old as spying. Managing a cyber adversary, however, is new. This includes financial, personnel, and technical players that we covered in Chapter 2 and described in Table 11.3 (counter ISIS air campaign).

We also observed tactical effects with the deployment of Task Force ARES as a complement to ground forces in the pursuit of ISIS between 2016 and 2017. While it is unclear how much it cost to perform Operation Glowing Symphony, the effects likely offset the $2 billion/month that it would have cost to deploy ground forces (Table 12.3). Operation Glowing Symphony provided some cyber unique effects in the destruction of the Amaq News Agency and the removal of ISIS videos from key web sites (Temple-Raston, 2019).

   While an air campaign is a traditional method for maintaining persistent surveillance, it is not a direct 1:1 relation for coupling an adversary to a defender on a next-generation battlefield. Traditional methods of modeling warfare will need updating when it comes to describing cyber contributions. Strategic cyber effects are the most hard hitting due to their analog of covert access. For example, the cost ratio of STUXNET to Operation Desert Fox, at 18:1, is an amazing cost savings provided via cyber. Unfortunately, this is same kind of advantage that we give away when critical technologies and designs go unprotected (e.g., F-35 (Section 11.3)).

   As discussed in Section II, we have criminal, tactical, and strategic cyber effects that include both ransom and remediation costs (Table II.1).

   As shown in Table II.1, the costs due to criminal attacks are much higher when perpetrated by a nation-state. For example, the DPRK executed WannaCry in 2017, costing an estimated $4–8 billion in remediation costs. The Russian GRU performed the NotPetya attack the same year costing approximately $10 billion. While cost approximations may be a bit crude to wrap all of the complexities of

Table II.1   Estimated Costs of Criminal Operations.

Year	Operation	Effect	Cost Estimate
2022	Ukrainian Space Communications Denial (Viasat)	Tactical	$80 million – cost for Starlink replacement
2017 – Present	DPRK kleptocratic operations	Criminal	>$1 billion – the DPRK is believed to have extracted over $1 billion through digital wallet theft and ransomware (White, 2022)
2020–2022	CONTI ransomware gang	Criminal	$150 million during CONTI's two years in existence
2015—2022	Hydra	Criminal	$5.2 billion in underground payments cleared via Hydra darknet operations
2021	Colonial Oil	Criminal	$5 million (ransom)
2021	JBS Foods	Criminal	$11 million (ransom)
2021	NEW Cooperative	Criminal	$5 million (ransom)
2017	NotPetya	Criminal	$10 Billion (remediation cost)
2017	WannaCry	Criminal	$100 million (remediation cost)
2016	Bank of Bangladesh	Criminal	$81 million – the DPRK stole $81 million in attempted $1 billion heist from the Bank of Bangladesh
2012	STUXNET	Strategic	two to three years delay in a strategic weapons program

(Continued)

Table II.1   (Continued)

Year	Operation	Effect	Cost Estimate
2011–2013	Silk Road	Criminal	$183 million – The Silk Road was one of the original Darknet markets that sold drugs by taking orders through anonymous network connections (e.g., ToR) and taking payment in Bitcoin. While a challenge to measure due to the covert nature of the Silk Road's operations, it is estimated that billions of dollars were transacted during the Silk Road's brief tenure (Department of Justice, 2022; Mullin, 2015)
2011	CONFICKER	Criminal	$72 million – Ukrainian authorities, cooperating with the FBI, arrested 16 hackers in Kiev, who had allegedly used the Conficker botnet to extract more than $72 million from unwary customers (Bowden, 2011).
2000	Maroochy Shire	Criminal	$1 million

each operation into a single number, we can use these cost assessments as a starting point for more detailed analysis.

Bibliography

Bowden, M. (2011). *Worm – The First Digital World War*. New York: Atlantic Monthly Press.

Department of Justice. (2022). *U.S. Attorney Announces Historic $3.36 Billion Cryptocurrency Seizure And Conviction In Connection With Silk Road Dark Web Fraud*. Retrieved 11 8, 2022, from U.S. Attorney Announces Historic $3.36 Billion Cryptocurrency Seizure And Conviction In Connection With Silk Road Dark Web Fraud: https://www.justice.gov/usao-sdny/pr/us-attorney-announces-historic-336-billion-cryptocurrency-seizure-and-conviction.

Mullin, J. (2015). *Silk Road Prosecutors Complete the Bizarre DPR Murder-for-hire story*. Retrieved from ArsTechnica: https://arstechnica.com/tech-policy/2015/02/silk-road-prosecutors-complete-their-bizarre-murder-for-hire-story/.

Temple-Raston, D. (2019). *How The U.S. Hacked ISIS*. Retrieved from NPR: https://www.npr.org/2019/09/26/763545811/how-the-u-s-hacked-isis.

White, G. (2022). *The Lazarus Heist – From Hollywood to High Finance: Inside North Korea's Global Cyber War*. New York: Penguin.

Section III

Cyberspace Environment and Tools Introduction

> "There were 5 exabytes of information created between the dawn of civilization through 2003, but that much information is now created every two days." (Carlson, 2010)

In an environment with an already rapidly expanding number of users, connections, and data production, we experienced a global pandemic starting in March 2020. This included taking the entire U.S. Government from their offices to work from home. A few excerpts on this transition include (CyberWire, 2021)

"Lieutenant General Stephen Fogarty, Commanding General, US Army Cyber Command, emphasized that DISA and the Joint Force Headquarters-Department of Defense Information Network (JFHQ-DODIN) played a central role in enabling the shift to remote work with the Defense Department's Commercial Virtual Remote (CVR) telework platform". Lieutenant General Charles Moore, Deputy Commander, US Cyber Command, stated that their use of the CVR

> ... was actually stood up and put into use within just a few short weeks – from beginning to end, we ended up with about 1.4 million people that were using that capability, and then of course have since burned that down and transitioned over to Microsoft 365.

"Likewise, Lieutenant General Timothy Haugh, Commander, Sixteenth Air Force; Commander, Air Forces Cyber, and Commander, Joint Force Headquarters-Cyber, noted that the Air Force

> increased from 7000 to 300,000 remote workers in a couple of weeks."

Cyber Operations: A Case Study Approach, First Edition. Jerry M. Couretas.
© 2024 John Wiley & Sons, Inc. Published 2024 by John Wiley & Sons, Inc.

The U.S. government therefore moved hundreds of thousands of its work force to home offices in a matter of weeks. This was an unprecedented transition to virtual work. On the front line of providing tools to make this workforce transition happen was Microsoft

> The last several years have seen unprecedented change in the digital world. Organizations are evolving to harness advances in computing capability from both the intelligent cloud and the intelligent edge. As a result of the pandemic forcing entities to digitize to survive and the rate at which industries worldwide are adopting internet-facing devices, the attack surface of the digital world is increasing exponentially. This rapid migration has outpaced the security community's ability to keep up. Over the past year, we have observed threats exploiting devices in every part of the organization, from traditional IT equipment to operational technology (OT) controllers or simple Internet of Things (IoT) sensors. Although security of IT equipment has strengthened in recent years, IoT and OT device security has not kept pace. Threat actors are exploiting these devices to establish access on networks and enable lateral movement or disrupt the organization's OT operations. We have seen attacks on power grids, ransomware attacks disrupting OT operations, IoT routers being leveraged for increased persistency, and attacks targeting vulnerabilities in firmware. (Microsoft, 2022)

Each cyber operation discussed in Sections I and II used component technologies from commercial companies. For example, the current cyber environment is continually developed and maintained by just a handful of companies. In 2021, Amazon, Alphabet, and Microsoft invested about $90 Billion in research and development and were awarded 6966 patents (Bajpai, 2021). Due to the uniformity of the current information technology terrain, this environment is prowled by cyber operators using pilfered tools, sometimes even stolen from governments (e.g., Chapter 3), and repurposed for denial and espionage operations. For example, the (mis) use of Cobalt Strike, a commercial penetration testing tool, made up approximately 2/3 of cyber attacks in 2022 (Rech, 2022).

In developing this cyber terrain, a handful of companies deliver the lion's share of operating systems and routers. For example, 70% of the operating systems are Microsoft Windows (StatCounter, 2023). Similarly, the global router market consists largely of Cisco and Huawei, with their combined 50% of the worldwide market (Statistica, 2023).

Along with common operating systems and connection software, software engineering relies on common libraries and development techniques in order to build and maintain cyberspace. For example, software engineers tend to use the same libraries over long periods of time (Veracode, 2022). One reason for mentioning code development is that it is a mirror image of where malware authors spend their time. In a recent review of nearly 60 million pieces of malware, AV-TEST Gmbh determined that 96.7% of the code was targeting Windows (Rashid, 2022).

In addition to targeting commercial software development, open-source software is also a means to penetrate the software supply chain, and, ultimately, targeted enterprises (HelpNet, 2022). For example, from 2019 to 2020, the Russian Federation's SVR performed a software supply chain attack on SolarWinds, garnering an estimated 30,000 accesses (Section 5.2.2.1). In an earlier example, the Russian Federation's FSB performed a supply chain attack against U.S. industrial control system (ICS) manufacturers from 2012 to 2017 (Operation Dragonfly [Section 5.2.1.2]). Similarly, the DPRK was found to be targeting developers on GitHub in order to get access to accounts associated with blockchain, cryptocurrency, and online gambling (Wales, 2023). This developer targeting complements the DPRK stealing online currencies at record levels (Chapter 7).

Along with being a key target for DPRK cyber operations, Bitcoin is also the principal currency for ransomware (Chapter 3). For example, the Silk Road and Hydra used Bitcoin to clear transactions for drugs and ransomware, respectively. Russia (Chapter 5) and Iran (Chapter 8) mine Bitcoin with their energy reserves in order to circumvent sanctions.

While mining Bitcoin to evade sanctions is a policy implementation of cyber, the majority of Section III will review the processes and technologies reported for the Section I operators. This includes exploitation tools and attack paths reported for operations that span from probing critical infrastructure to influencing elections.

Bibliography

Bajpai, P. (2021). *Which Companies Spend the Most in Research and Development (R&D)?* Retrieved from Nasdaq: https://www.nasdaq.com/articles/which-companies-spend-the-most-in-research-and-development-rd-2021-06-21.

Carlson, B. (2010). *Quote of the Day: Google CEO Compares Data Across Millennia.* Retrieved from The Atlantic: https://www.theatlantic.com/technology/archive/2010/07/quote-of-the-day-google-ceo-compares-data-across-millennia/344989/.

CyberWire. (2021). *Cyber Commanders Reflect on Lessons Learned from the Pandemic.* Retrieved 10 11, 2021, from CyberWire: https://thecyberwire.com/stories/de08014f8c914ec4a4924b17246d4a7d/cyber-commanders-reflect-on-lessons-learned-from-the-pandemic.

HelpNet. (2022). *Open Source Projects Under Attack, with Enterprises as the Ultimate Targets.* Retrieved 11 9, 2022, from HelpNet: https://www.helpnetsecurity.com/2022/09/27/open-source-projects-cyberattacks/.

Microsoft. (2022). *Microsoft Digital Defense Report 2022*. Retrieved 11 15, 2022, from Microsoft: https://query.prod.cms.rt.microsoft.com/cms/api/am/binary/RE5bUvv? culture=en-us&country=us.

Rashid, H. (2022). *95.6% of New Malware in 2022 Targeted Windows*. Retrieved 12 14, 2022, from HackRead: https://www.hackread.com/malware-targeted-windows-2022/?web_view=true.

Rech, M. (2022). *Ransomware Turns Cobalt Strike Into an Attack Vector*. Retrieved from Techguard Security: https://blog.techguard.com/ransomware-turns-cobalt-strike-into-an-attack-vector.

StatCounter. (2023). *Desktop Operating System Market Share Worldwide*. Retrieved from StatCounter: https://gs.statcounter.com/os-market-share/desktop/worldwide/.

Statistica. (2023). *Enterprise Network Infrastructure Vendor Market Share Worldwide in 2022*. Retrieved from Statistica: https://www.statista.com/statistics/1253345/enterprise-network-infrastructure-vendor-market-share-worldwide/#:~:text=Global%20enterprise%20network%20infrastructure%20market%20share%202022&text=In%202022%2C%20Cisco%20Systems%20made,the%20enterprise%20netwo.

Veracode. (2022). *State of Software Security*. Retrieved 12 14, 2022, from Veracode: https://www.veracode.com/state-of-software-security-report.

Wales, A. (2023). *Security Alert: Social Engineering Campaign Targets Technology Industry Employees*. Retrieved from GitHub.blng: https://github.blog/2023-07-18-security-alert-social-engineering-campaign-targets-technology-industry-employees/.

14

Criminal Cyber Operations and Tools

14.1 Criminal Cyber Operations and Tools

> A world where private sector companies create and sell cyberweapons is more dangerous for consumers, businesses of all sizes, and governments. These offensive tools can be used in ways that are inconsistent with the norms and values of good governance and democracy …
>
> *(Microsoft, 2022)*

In the mid-2010s, Hal Martin and Joshua Schulte leaked a large number of nation-state-developed tools (Chapter 3). These tools, initially called out by the Shadow Brokers, quietly preceded the outbreak of ransomware, and the Ransomware as a Service (RaaS) subindustry that became an over $20 Billion problem (Table 13.3) for business and government systems during the 2020–2022 pandemic.

14.1.1 Shadow Brokers' Tools

Among the Shadow Brokers' tools was a Microsoft protocol exploit that effectively provided a skeleton key to unpatched systems. The Server Message Block (SMB) is a proprietary Microsoft protocol that is used to share files and printers within a network. One of the convenient items provided by SMB is putting files in one location. However, without proper security, this also creates a vulnerability.

> In 2017, EternalBlue, an exploit used against a vulnerability in SMB v1.0, set the stage for some of the most intrusive and impactful malware in cybersecurity history. Among the malware that used the EternalBlue

Cyber Operations: A Case Study Approach, First Edition. Jerry M. Couretas.
© 2024 John Wiley & Sons, Inc. Published 2024 by John Wiley & Sons, Inc.

exploit are WannaCry (ransomware) and Emotet (Trojan), both of which can self-propagate throughout a network, causing widespread damage.

(CIS, 2020)

SMB exploits provide the initial access that cyber operators use to access a system. This access is then managed via the attacker's command and control (C2) applications, sometimes performed via penetration testing frameworks (e.g., Cobalt Strike).

14.1.1.1 Criminals Continue to Misuse Cobalt Strike

Cobalt Strike was used by the Darkside ransomware group in the Colonial Pipeline attack, discussed in Chapter 3, for compromising the entire U.S. East Coast fuel supply (Sherstobitoff, 2021). Due to this widespread abuse of the Cobalt Strike platform by hackers, Microsoft formed a partnership with Fortra, the Cobalt Strike developer, to take technical and legal actions against "cracked" versions of Cobalt Strike that are currently in the hands of criminals (Hogan-Burney, 2023).

14.1.2 Malware Loaders

Secure connectivity is a key step to ensure that cyber criminals and attackers cannot get access to a network of interest. When a nefarious cyber actor gets access to a network, one of the first things that they do is to plant a loader onto a target system for future exploitation. These loaders are then used to implant malware.

Malware loaders are used to provide an initial toehold onto the targeted system/network. Loaders can be associated with an Initial Access Broker (IAB), or a team that provides initial system penetration. The team then trades this access to a team that exploits the target. Exotic Lily (Arghire, 2022), for example, is an IAB that is known to use BazarLoader for initial access, with the CONTI team performing the follow-on exploit with BumbleBee malware (Table 14.1)

Table 14.1 Example Malware Loaders.

Loader	Famous For	Associated Malware
BazarLoader	Tailored development for use by Initial Access Broker (IAB) Exotic Lily	BumbleBee malware; Conti/Diavol ransomware
Raindrop/Teardrop	SolarWinds Attack	
TrickBot	Banking attacks	Emotet, Ryuk malware

Of the three examples, BumbleBee seems to be the most updated of the loaders, sometimes associated with Exotic Lily, and is often a precursor to CONTI and Diavol ransomware operations (Toulas, 2022).

14.1.2.1 EMOTET

EMOTET is known to be one of the most expensive banking malware examples. Operating with a "wormable" capability, EMOTET has the ability to move laterally, once in a system, making the cleanup a challenge.

EMOTET Exploitation Example An example of EMOTET's operation is provided in Figure 14.1.

As shown in Figure 14.1, Emotet uses SMB (Table 14.1) (Step 2) to find writable share drives and then creates a registry autostart in order to inject itself into a running process and thereby establish persistence. Once established, Emotet reports back, receives instructions, and then propagates through a network (step 4).

EMOTET Evolution Timeline Emotet has gone through multiple iterations since it was first spotted in 2014 (Figure 14.3).

As shown in Figure 14.2, EMOTET has adapted multiple times during its lifetime. EMOTET operations are usually associated with dropping other tools and malware onto a target for future exploitation. For example, as recently as 2022, EMOTET was observed dropping Cobalt Strike beacons for future pwning of a target of interest. EMOTET has also been observed dropping Ryuk ransomware for financial target exploitation.

As shown in Table 14.2, Ryuk ransomware, one of the more famous exploit kits for financial attacks derives from Hermes ransomware. Performing a ransomware attack using Trickbot/Emotet/Ryuk in a few steps is described in Table 14.3.

As shown in Table 14.3, Trickbot/Emotet/Ryuk operates together for a criminal attack example (Figure 14.3).

In addition to the Trickbot/Emotet/Ryuk tools shown in Figure 14.3, the Trickbot gang also started spreading the BazarLoader backdoor since at least April 2020 through spear phishing campaigns (Ilascu, 2020). Unlike the highly detected Trickbot malware, the BazarLoader backdoor was likely reserved for valuable victims at first, to deploy a Cobalt Strike beacon that provides remote access to the operators.

14.1.2.2 HIVE Ransomware Group use of Cobalt Strike Example

As discussed in Section 14.1.1.1, Cobalt Strike was used in the Colonial Pipeline attack. The use of pirated versions of Cobalt Strike is unfortunately common in ransomware attacks.

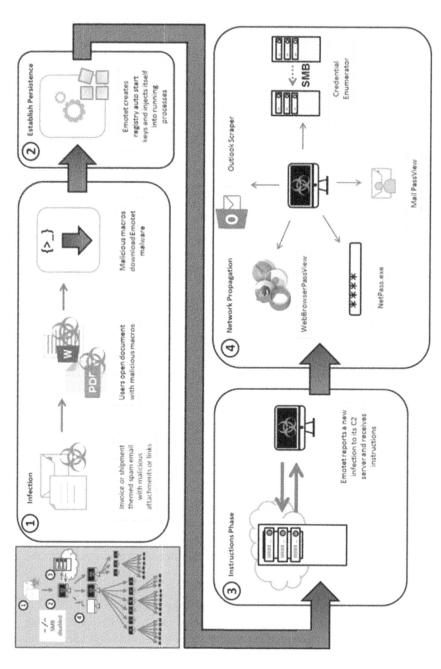

Figure 14.1 EMOTET Dropper Example. *Source*: Adapted from DHS CISA (2020).

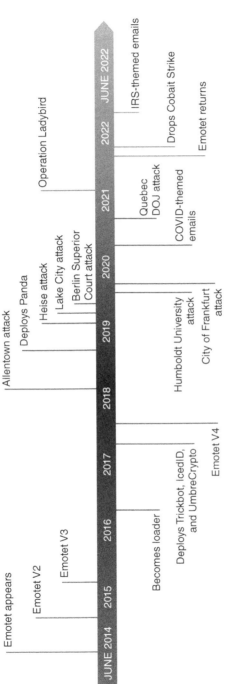

Figure 14.2 EMOTET Timeline of Activity. *Source:* "Lakshmanan, New Report Uncovers Emotet's Delivery and Evasion Techniques Used in Recent Attacks, 2022"/VMare.

Table 14.2 Ryuk Ransomware Development from Hermes.

Time Frame	Ransomware	Famous For	Associated Threat Actor
>2017	Hermes	Commodity ransomware code used by multiple actors – Base code for Ryuk	
>2018	Ryuk	Believed to be preceded by TrickBot compromise of target	Wizard Spider (eCrime group). Responsible for netting over $3.7 million from over 52 transactions (Hanel, 2019)

Source: Adapted from Hanel (2019).

Table 14.3 Trickbot/Emotet/Ryuk Cyber Attack.

Step	Description
1	Trickbot/Emotet are used for initial access into vulnerable systems
2	Using access (1), probe for damaging information to steal
3	With success at step (2), use business intelligence system (e.g., ZoomInfo, Owler, etc.) to assess organization's revenues and thereby determine how much to set the ransom demand
4	Use Ryuk malware in an attack, usually occurring in the middle of the night in the respective time zone, so as to inflict maximum damage
5	Negotiate ransom and collect

Source: "Renee Dudley (2022)"/Farrar, Straus and Giroux.

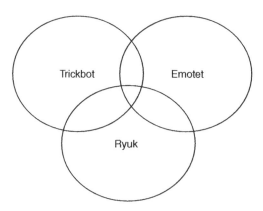

Figure 14.3 Emotet/Trickbot/Ryuk.

HIVE malware used by cyber criminals (Chapter 3) to perform ransomware operations against healthcare facilities, nonprofits, retailers, energy providers, and other sectors worldwide (Ovadia, 2022). HIVE malware uses multiple tools covered in this chapter (Table 14.4).

The HIVE malware example in Table 14.4 starts with initial access via a proxy-shell and then moves through several manual steps that use existing tools (e.g., Cobalt Strike) to exploit the network. Botnets attempt to automate some of these steps, as discussed in the Emotet example (Figure 14.1).

Table 14.4   HIVE Malware Attack Stages.

Stage	Tool	Application
1	ProxyShell/WebShell	Persistent Access
2	Cobalt Strike	The malicious PowerShell code downloaded additional stagers from a remote C2 (Command and Control) server associated with the Cobalt Strike framework. The stagers were not written to the file system but executed in memory.
3	Mimikatz and Pass-the-Hash	Leveraging the SYSTEM permissions, the threat actor created a new system administrator user named "user" and advanced to the credential dumping stage, invoking Mimikatz. By stealing the domain Administrator NTLM hash and without needing to crack the password, the operator managed to reuse it via Pass-The-Hash attack and take control of the domain admin account.
4	Scanning for Sensitive Information	Next, the threat actor performed extensive discovery activities across the network. In addition to searching for files containing "password" in their names, observed activities included dropping network scanners and collecting the networks' IP addresses and device names, followed by RDPs to the backup servers and other critical assets.
5	Ransomware Deployment	Finally, a custom-crafted malware payload named Windows.exe was delivered and executed on various devices, leading to wide encryption and denial of access to files within the organization.
		The payload created a plain text ransomware demand note during the encryption phase.
		The Forensics team observed that the actor managed to achieve its malicious goals and encrypt the environment in less than 72 hours from the initial compromise. First, the attacker exploited multiple Exchange security vulnerabilities, referred to as ProxyShell. Next, the attack placed a malicious backdoor script, referred to as webshell, in a publicly accessible directory on the Exchange server. These web scripts could then execute malicious PowerShell code over the compromised server with SYSTEM privileges.

Source: Adapted from Ovadia (2023).

14.1.3 Botnets

Botnets are estimated to be responsible for 1/2 of the current Internet traffic (Cuthbertson, 2023). In addition to using cyber to leak information, an estimated one third of botnets are used for political operations.

Bots and botnets are a security threat due to their persistent presence and ability to manipulate their host, including data extraction. An early example of a botnet designed for theft was Conficker (Chapter 9), believed to be one of the first Internet worm-based cyber attacks used to scam people into buying fake anti-virus products at scale (i.e., $72 million dollars worth) (Bowden, 2011).

14.1.3.1 Mirai Botnet

While Conficker might be considered a common criminal among botnets, simply robbing banks, Mirai is next generation in that it attacks Internet-of-Things (IoT) devices. Home cameras, vacuums, appliances, and other mundane devices that we take for granted are exploited and controlled by Mirai in order to create a botnet. Mirai is believed to spread at 3250 infections/hour and has been observed at over 600,000 infections in a single botnet composition (Mirai Botnet (Antonakakis, 2017)).

> Mirai evolved to infect a wide range of IoT devices including internet protocol cameras, security camera digital video recorders, and routers. The attack vector bypassed legacy security controls and poses a risk for endpoints within the network by exploiting additional vulnerabilities and moving laterally. Mirai has been redesigned multiple times, with variants adapting to different architectures and exploiting both known and zero-day vulnerabilities to compromise new attack vectors. The use of Mirai grew among both 32- and 64-bit x86 CPU architectures over the past year, and the malware was given new capabilities that were rapidly adopted by nation state and criminal groups. Nation state attacks now leverage new variants of existing botnets in distributed denial of service (DDoS) attacks on foreign adversaries.
>
> *(Microsoft, 2022)*

As discussed, Mirai provides the potential to rapidly construct a DDoS botnet from the rapidly expanding number of IoT devices.

As shown in Table 14.5, Conficker, Emotet, and Trickbot are used for bank theft. Cobra, the DPRK botnet, fits with this grouping due to the use of crime that the DPRK employs to fund its weapons programs (Chapter 7). Each of the botnets is used in conjunction with other tools covered in this chapter.

14.1.4 Criminal Cyber Tools' Wrap-up

Criminal cyber tools leverage botnets to deploy loaders (e.g., Trickbot/Emotet/ Ryuk). While ransomware is often approached through standard compromise

Table 14.5 Criminal BOTNETs.

Time Frame	Botnet	Famous For	Associated Threat Actor
2009–2011	Conficker	Bank theft ($71 million)	Ukrainian bank hackers (Bowden, 2011)
>2014	Emotet	Banking malware	Various Criminals
>2016	TrickBot (CISA, 2022)	Banking malware (NCSC, 2020)	Wizard Spider (eCrime group) (Hanel, 2019)
>2016	Cobra	Espionage	DPRK Lazarus Group (Chapter 7)
>2016	Mirai	DDoS	Various Criminals

(e.g., phishing e-mail), these operations are sometimes managed through pirated penetration tools (e.g., Cobalt Strike). An example set of these different tools are provided in Table 14.6.

Table 14.6 Criminal Cyber Tool Examples.

Tool Type	Description
Remote Access Tools (RATs)	A Remote Access Tool (RAT) is a program, which, once installed on a victim's machine, allows remote administrative control. In a malicious context, they can provide the ability for an actor to upload and download files, execute commands, log keystrokes, and/or record a user's screen.
Web Shells	Web shells are malicious scripts that are uploaded to a target host after an initial compromise and grant an actor remote access into a network. Once this access is established, web shells can facilitate lateral movement within a network.
Credential Stealers	Credential stealers are tools used for obtaining credentials from memory. A credential stealer's main purpose is to allow an actor to collect credentials of other users who are logged in to a targeted machine by accessing them in memory within the Local Security Authority Subsystem Service (LSASS) system process. These credentials can be reused to give access to other machines on a network.
Lateral Movement Frameworks	Lateral movement tools are designed to allow an actor (or penetration tester) to move around a network after gaining initial access. Another well-known and open-source framework is the Metasploit Project.
Command and Control Obfuscators	Actors will often want to disguise their location when compromising a target. They may use generic privacy tools such as The Onion Router (TOR), or more specific tools to obfuscate their location. Cyber actors can use this technique to redirect their packets through multiple compromised hosts to gain greater access to hosts in a network.

Bibliography

Antonakakis, M. (2017). *Understanding the Mirai Botnet*. Retrieved from Usenix: https://www.usenix.org/system/files/conference/usenixsecurity17/sec17-antonakakis.pdf.

Arghire, I. (2022). *Google Analyzes Activity of 'Exotic Lily' Initial Access Broker*. Retrieved from Security Week: https://www.securityweek.com/google-analyzes-activity-exotic-lily-initial-access-broker/.

Bing, C. (2017). *Leaked NSA Hacking Tools are a Hit on the Dark Web*. Retrieved 4 10, 2023, from CyberScoop: https://cyberscoop.com/nsa-hacking-tools-shadow-brokers-dark-web-microsoft-smb/.

Bowden, M. (2011). *Worm – The First Digital World War*. New York: Atlantic Monthly Press.

CIS. (2020). *Commonly Exploited Protocols: Server Message Block (SMB)*. Retrieved from Center for Internet Security (CIS): https://www.cisecurity.org/insights/blog/commonly-exploited-protocols-server-message-block-smb.

CISA. (2022). *Fact Sheet: TrickBot Malware*. Retrieved from CISA: https://www.cisa.gov/uscert/sites/default/files/publications/TrickBot_Fact_Sheet_508.pdf.

Cuthbertson, A. (2023). *Nearly Half of all Internet Traffic is Now Bots, Study Reveals*. Retrieved from Independent: https://www.independent.co.uk/tech/internet-bots-web-traffic-imperva-b2339153.html#.

DHS CISA. (2020). *Emotet Malware*. Retrieved 9 28, 2022, from Alert (TA18-201A): https://www.cisa.gov/uscert/ncas/alerts/TA18-201A.

Hanel, A. (2019). *Big Game Hunting with Ryuk: Another Lucrative Targeted Ransomware*. Retrieved from Crowdstrike: https://www.crowdstrike.com/blog/big-game-hunting-with-ryuk-another-lucrative-targeted-ransomware/.

Hogan-Burney, A. (2023). *Stopping Cybercriminals from Abusing Security Tools*. Retrieved 4 10, 2023, from Microsoft: https://blogs.microsoft.com/on-the-issues/2023/04/06/stopping-cybercriminals-from-abusing-security-tools/.

Ilascu, I. (2020). *How Ryuk Ransomware Operators made $34 Million from One Victim*. Retrieved 9 20, 2022, from Bleeping Computer: https://www.bleepingcomputer.com/news/security/how-ryuk-ransomware-operators-made-34-million-from-one-victim/.

Lakshmanan, R. (2022). *New Report Uncovers Emotet's Delivery and Evasion Techniques Used in Recent Attacks*. Retrieved 11 7, 2022, from The Hacker News: https://thehackernews.com/2022/10/new-report-uncovers-emotets-delivery.html.

Microsoft. (2022). *Microsoft Digital Defense Report 2022*. Retrieved 11 15, 2022, from Microsoft: https://query.prod.cms.rt.microsoft.com/cms/api/am/binary/RE5bUvv?culture=en-us&country=us.

NCSC. (2020). *Advisory: Trickbot.* Retrieved from National Cyber Security Centre: https://www.ncsc.gov.uk/news/trickbot-advisory.

Ovadia, N. (2022). *Hive Ransomware Analysis.* Retrieved from Varonis: https://www.varonis.com/blog/hive-ransomware-analysis.

Ovadia, N. (2023). *Hive Ransomware Analysis.* Retrieved 4 12, 2023, from Varonis: https://www.varonis.com/blog/hive-ransomware-analysis.

Renee Dudley, D.G. (2022). *The Ransomware Hunting Team – A Band of Misfits' Improbable Crusade to Save the World from Cybercrime.* New York: Farrar, Straus and Giroux.

Sherstobitoff, R. (2021). *New Evidence Supports Assessment that DarkSide Likely Responsible for Colonial Pipeline Ransomware Attack; Others Targeted.* Retrieved 9 27, 2022, from SecurityScorecard: https://securityscorecard.com/blog/new-evidence-supports-assessment-that-darkside-likely-responsible-for-colonial-pipeline-ransomware-attack-others-targeted.

Toulas, B. (2022). *Google Exposes Tactics of a Conti Ransomware Access Broker.* Retrieved from Bleeping Computer: https://www.bleepingcomputer.com/news/security/google-exposes-tactics-of-a-conti-ransomware-access-broker/.

15

Russian Cyber Operations and Tools

15.1 Russian Cyber Operations and Tools

As discussed in Chapter 5, Russia deploys a full spectrum of cyber operations, from IO to system-level manipulation. From a technical standpoint, as discussed in Section I, the Russian Federation monitors its Internet and telecommunications through SORM (e.g., SORM-3 (Lewis, 2014)). Additional cyber operations infrastructure is provided by contractors, from cyber tool developers to networking gear.

15.1.1 Example Operations' Attack Paths

Due to the long history of Russian cyber operations, we have attack paths for both the attempted penetration of the U.S. Star Wars' missile defense program in the 1980s and Operation Moonlight Maze in the 1990s. The Star Wars' attack was documented in detail by Clifford Stoll in his book "The Cuckoo's Egg" (Stoll, 2005).

15.1.1.1 U.S. Star Wars Missile Defense

In the late 1980s, German hackers, working on behalf of the Former Soviet Union's KGB, penetrated the Lawrence Berkeley Lab's computer network in an attempt to get information on the U.S. Star Wars missile defense program portfolio (Section 9.1.1.1). This is an excellent description of how an international hack works, with technical information that includes

- keystroke logging to monitor attacker behavior
- honey files to deceive and track a cyber attacker
- honey tokens to track a cyber attacker
- network diagrams to show the attacker's path

Cyber Operations: A Case Study Approach, First Edition. Jerry M. Couretas.
© 2024 John Wiley & Sons, Inc. Published 2024 by John Wiley & Sons, Inc.

As shown in Figure 15.1, "The Cuckoo's Egg" also provides an early example of an International cyber attack path that leverages satellite links and multiple logical/physical server locations in order to probe U.S. Government sites for Star Wars data. This includes multiple hop points and the use of the ARPANET to access U.S. bases and the Pentagon.

"The Cuckoo's Egg" also provides an example of how the KGB used a hacker community for nefarious purposes. For example, each of the "Hanover Gang" perpetrators in Dr. Stoll's investigation was Chaos Computer Club members (Section 9.1.1), an organization that currently has over 7700 registered members that share hacking information and hold an annual conference (Toulas, 2022a). And, while the KGB and its hackers did not succeed in Dr. Stoll's book, only a few

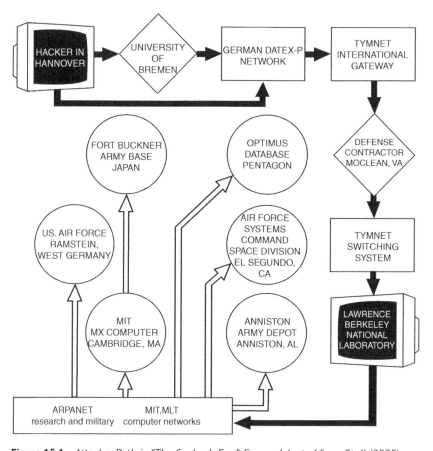

Figure 15.1 Attacker Path in "The Cuckoo's Egg". *Source:* Adapted from Stoll (2005).

years later Russian intelligence performed a large collection campaign against U.S. military sites called Operation Moonlight Maze (Chapter 5).

15.1.1.2 Moonlight Maze (1990s)

Within 10 years of Clifford Stoll foiling the KGB effort to pilfer U.S. Star Wars secrets, Russian hackers were at it again, using cyber to grab as much data as possible from U.S. military sites. With the Soviet Union gone and Russia seen as neutral, even friendly, it came as a surprise that a hack was coming from the new Russian Federation. However, this hack turned out to be government sponsored as well.

As described by Chris Doman (Doman, 2016), Operation Moonlight Maze consisted of a probe on the Air Force Institute of Technology (AFIT) and the Air Force Research Labs (AFRL) through Internet accounts at multiple universities (Figure 15.2).

As shown in Figure 15.2, Operation Moonlight Maze was similar to the attack profiled in the Cuckoo's Egg in that Russian hackers used multiple locations (i.e., university networks) to probe U.S. Government research sites. Operation Moonlight Maze was traced back to the Russians due to time (Doman, 2016)

- 3 a.m. login time on a Sunday (i.e., time zone anomaly)
- conspicuous lack of activity during Russian Orthodox holidays

While the goal of Operation Moonlight Maze was information collection, relying on a team with conspicuous human errors ended up compromising the

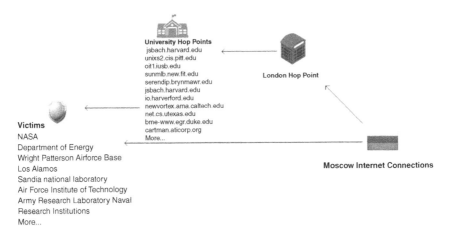

Figure 15.2 Operation Moonlight Maze Attack Connections. *Source:* Doman (2016)/ Chris Doman.

operation. Building a new covert cyber architecture, via "Snake," was the next tool development for the Russian Federation after Operation Moonlight Maze.

15.1.1.3 Snake Botnet (>2000)

As discussed in Chapter 5, the Russian FSB is a strong player in cyber, implicated in scanning U.S. critical infrastructure using HAVEX malware in Operation Dragonfly (2012–2017). A key tool used by the FSB includes the "Snake" toolset, which includes a specially encrypted network for communicating information securely (Braken, 2023).

The Snake botnet consisted of a set of peer-to-peer nodes built out in domains in over 50 countries. Snake disguised traffic to collect information from exploited nodes within NATO, small businesses, universities, and critical infrastructure sites (CISA, 2023).

Operation MEDUSA, a cooperative effort between the U.S. FBI and multiple foreign governments, neutralized the Snake malware that was used to spy on NATO, among other organizations (DoJ, 2023). More recently, Russian operators were observed developing new domain names in what is believed to be preparation for future attacks (Greig, 2023).

SOLARDEFLECTION Command and Control Architecture In addition to clearly documented cyber operational attack paths, the SolarWinds attack included command and control infrastructure, SolarDeflection, that used typosquats for domain name construction

> ... these typosquats have included the misuse of brands across multiple industry verticals, particularly in the news and media industries. This same group of actors (i.e., Nobelium) has made extensive use of typosquat domains in SSL certificates and will likely continue to use deceptive techniques, including typosquat redirection, when using Cobalt Strike tooling.
> *(Insikt Group, 2022)*

A novel element of the SolarWinds exploit was the attacker's ability to access the code development process, identify components used to develop the Orion software package, and insert a back door into the development (Crowdstrike, 2021). SOLARDEFLECTION is one example of the dynamic nature of cyber attack path development. Developing a peer-to-peer network (e.g., Snake botnet) is more sophisticated than the simpler multiple hop attack paths used for Operation Moonlight Maze or the early Star Wars attack and is likely to only get more complex with future cyber operations tools.

15.1.2   Russian Cyber Operations and Tools

In building cyber operations tools, Russia uses contractors. Vulkan, for example, provides scanning and training tools for Russia's cyber operators.

15.1.2.1   Vulkan – Russian Cyber Tools Developer

Russian intelligence organizations perform cyber operations in order to meet their mission objectives. These missions include traditional counter intelligence, along with espionage and tactical use of cyber. In support of these missions, the respective Russian intelligence organizations are supported by a defense contractor, Vulkan (Eddy, 2023), an IT government contractor in St Petersburg, Russia. In Figure 4.1, we introduced the idea that a nation-state capability includes research, development, and clandestine service elements. Vulkan is an example of a development capability. A disaffected employee at Vulkan provided a glimpse into the types of tools that are developed for Russia's intelligence agencies and military (Table 15.1).

As shown in Table 15.1, Vulkan tools provide for developing new operational infrastructure (Amezit), scanning candidate targets for vulnerabilities (Scan V), and training of cyber operators for the takedown of critical transportation capabilities (Crystal 2V).

15.1.2.2   FSB

The FSB has a broad portfolio of cyber operations and one of the more famous tools used by the FSB was HAVEX (Paganini, 2014), a malware that used Microsoft's Object Linking and Embedding (OLE) for Process Control (OPC)

Table 15.1   Russian Cyber Tools.

Name	Example Function
Amezit	Used to surveil and control the Internet in regions under Russia's command. Amezit also enables persona development for fake social media profiles that is used for the propagation of disinformation.
Crystal 2V	Training program for cyber operatives in the methods required to bring down rail, air, and sea infrastructure.
Scan V	Scans the Internet for vulnerabilities that are then stored for use in future cyber attacks.

Source: Alden and Gabby (2023), Luke Harding (2023).

servers controlling U.S. natural gas pipelines (i.e., Operation Dragonfly (DoJ, 2022; Symantec, 2017), as discussed in Chapter 5. The HAVEX (CRS, 2022) campaign included

> In the first phase of the campaign, which took place between 2012 and 2015, the DOJ said the attackers "engaged in a supply chain attack, compromising the computer networks of ICS/SCADA system manufacturers and software providers and then hiding malware – known publicly as "Havex" – inside legitimate software updates for such systems."
>
> *(Lennon, 2022)*

While the FSB may have pioneered Russian cyber supply chain attacks, the Foreign Intelligence Service (SVR) Sluzhba Vneshney Razvedki may have taken supply chain exploitation to a new level with the SolarWinds attack.

15.1.2.3 SVR

SVR is likely most famous for the supply chain attack against SolarWinds using a pirated copy of Cobalt Strike, a penetration testing tool. With a target set believed to be approximately 200 organizations, the SolarWinds attack compromised 30,000 organizations (Chapter 5), as discussed by Microsoft

> SVR cyber operators are capable adversaries.... FBI investigations have revealed infrastructure used in the intrusions is frequently obtained using false identities and crypto currencies. VPS infrastructure is often procured from a network of VPS resellers. These false identities are usually supported by low reputation infrastructure including temporary e-mail accounts and temporary voice over Internet protocol (VoIP) telephone numbers. While not exclusively used by SVR cyber actors, a number of SVR cyber personas use e-mail services hosted on cock[.]li or related domains.
>
> *(CISA, 2021)*

The FBI also notes that SVR cyber operators have used open source or commercially available tools continuously, including Mimikatz – an open source credential-dumping too – and Cobalt Strike – a commercially available exploitation tool (CISA, 2021).

As shown in Figure 15.3, the SolarWinds attack used a novel loader (i.e., raindrop, teardrop) to deliver beacons from a standard penetration testing toolkit (i.e., Cobalt Strike) and then proceeded to exploit the targeted machine (Microsoft, 2021).

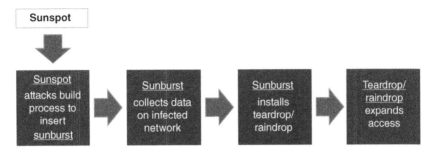

Figure 15.3 SolarWinds Attack Cycle. *Source:* Adapted from Microsoft, (2021).

15.1.2.4 Russian Cyber Operations and the Ukraine

One example of monitoring Russian information operations is the Russian Propaganda Index (RPI), developed by Microsoft

> The Russian Propaganda Index (RPI) monitors the flow of news from Russian state-controlled and sponsored news outlets and amplifiers as a proportion of overall news traffic on the Internet. The RPI can be used to chart the consumption of Russian propaganda across the Internet and in different geographies on a precise timeline. Microsoft notes, however, that we can only observe the Russian propaganda posted to previously identified websites. We do not have insight into propaganda on other types of websites, including authoritative news websites, unidentified websites, and social network groups.
>
> *(Microsoft, 2022)*

As shown in Figure 15.4, when the Ukraine war began, we saw a 216 percent increase in Russian propaganda, peaking on March 2, 2022. In addition, Figure 15.4 shows how this sudden increase coincided with the invasion (Microsoft, 2022).

15.1.2.5 Bot Farm Example

During the Russo-Ukraine war of 2022, Ukrainian law enforcement eliminated five bot-farms with approximately 100,000 fake social media accounts and 10,000 sim cards (Toulas, 2022b). One use of these accounts was to run fake ammunition fundraisers for Ukrainian troops.

15.1.2.6 Russian uses of Wipers against Ukrainian Targets (2022 Invasion)

As noted by Microsoft (Microsoft, 2022), the Foxblade wiper was one of the first weapons deployed prior to Russian troops crossing into the Ukraine in February

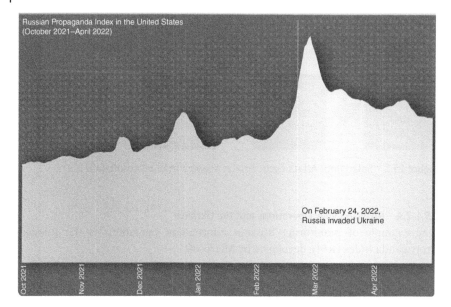

Figure 15.4 Russian Propaganda Index. *Source:* Microsoft (2022)/Microsoft.

of 2022. Foxblade was eventually complimented by a broad set of other wipers (e.g., Caddy, Hermetic, Isaac, etc.) to attack computer systems from the master boot record to various file deletions (Faife, 2022; Threat Intelligence Team, 2022).

15.1.3 Russian Cyber Tools' Wrap-up

Russian cyber operations span from physical system manipulation to information operations. This includes support by both government operators (e.g., FSB, GRU, SVR) and tool developers/contractors (e.g., Vulkan). Russia has been performing cyber operations since the beginning of networked operations. For example, the cyber attack on the U.S. Star Wars missile defense system (1980s) and Operation Moonlight Maze (1990s) are some of the first cyber operations.

We also reviewed cyber operations support. Vulkan, for example, provides cyber scanning and training tools. This is in addition to the legacy SORM system, traditionally supported by multiple telecommunications contractors (e.g., Nokia, Ericsson, etc.). Maintaining these support contracts, and associated capabilities, is a challenge due to boycotts and sanctions of Russia following the 2/2022 invasion of the Ukraine (Smalley, 2023).

Bibliography

Alden, W, Gabby, R. (2023). *Contracts Identify Cyber Operations Projects from Russian Company NTC Vulkan.* Retrieved from Mandiant: https://www.mandiant.com/resources/blog/cyber-operations-russian-vulkan.

Braken, B. (2023). *FBI Disarms Russian FSB 'Snake' Malware Network.* Retrieved from Dark Reading: https://www.darkreading.com/attacks-breaches/fbi-disarms-russian-fsb-snake-malware-network.

CISA. (2021). *Russian Foreign Intelligence Service (SVR) Cyber Operations: Trends and Best Practices for Network Defenders.* Retrieved from CISA: https://www.cisa.gov/news-events/cybersecurity-advisories/aa21-116a.

CISA. (2022). *Tactics, Techniques, and Procedures of Indicted State-Sponsored Russian Cyber Actors Targeting the Energy Sector.* Retrieved from CISA: https://www.cisa.gov/news-events/cybersecurity-advisories/aa22-083a#:~:text=Beginning%20in%202013%20and%20continuing,on%20multiple%20ICS%20vendor%20websites.

CISA. (2023). *Hunting Russian Intelligence "Snake" Malware.* Retrieved from CISA: https://www.cisa.gov/news-events/cybersecurity-advisories/aa23-129a.

Crowdstrike. (2021). *SUNSPOT: An Implant in the Build Process.* Retrieved 9 20, 2022, from Crowdstrike: https://www.crowdstrike.com/blog/sunspot-malware-technical-analysis/.

CRS. (2022). *Russian Cyber Units.* Retrieved from Congressional Research Service: https://crsreports.congress.gov/product/pdf/IF/IF11718.

DoJ. (2022). *Four Russian Government Employees Charged in Two Historical Hacking Campaigns Targeting Critical Infrastructure Worldwide.* Retrieved from U.S. Department of Justice: https://www.justice.gov/opa/pr/four-russian-government-employees-charged-two-historical-hacking-campaigns-targeting-critical.

DoJ. (2023). *Justice Department Announces Court-Authorized Disruption of Snake Malware Network Controlled by Russia's Federal Security Service.* Retrieved from DoJ: https://www.justice.gov/opa/pr/justice-department-announces-court-authorized-disruption-snake-malware-network-controlled.

Doman, C. (2016). *The First Cyber Espionage Attacks: How Operation Moonlight Maze made History.* Retrieved 8 4, 2019, from Medium: https://medium.com/@chris_doman/the-first-sophistiated-cyber-attacks-how-operation-moonlight-maze-made-history-2adb12cc43f7.

Eddy, N. (2023). *Vulkan Playbook Leak Exposes Russia's Plans for Worldwide Cyberwar.* Retrieved from Dark Reading: https://www.darkreading.com/vulnerabilities-threats/vulkan-playbook-leak-exposes-russia-plans-worldwide-cyber-war.

Faife, C. (2022). *Researchers Find New Destructive Wiper Malware in Ukraine.* Retrieved 4 8, 2022, from The Verge: https://www.theverge.com/2022/3/14/22977873/ukraine-new-destructive-caddywiper-malware-eset.

Greig, J. (2023). *Russia-based Hackers Building New Attack Infrastructure to Stay Ahead of Public Reporting*. Retrieved from The Record: https://therecord.media/ russian-hackers-building-new-infrastructure.

Insikt Group. (2022). *SOLARDEFLECTION C2 Infrastructure Used by NOBELIUM in Company Brand Misuse*. Retrieved from Recorded Future: https://www. recordedfuture.com/solardeflection-c2-infrastructure-used-by-nobelium-in-company-brand-misuse.

Lennon, M. (2022). *US Charges Russian Hackers Over Infamous Triton, Havex Cyberattacks on Energy Sector*. Retrieved from Security Week: https://www. securityweek.com/us-charges-russian-hackers-over-infamous-triton-havex-cyberattacks-energy-sector.

Lewis, J. A. (2014). *Reference Note on Russian Communications Surveillance*. Retrieved from CSIS: https://www.csis.org/analysis/reference-note-russian-communications-surveillance.

Luke Harding, S. S. (2023). *'Vulkan files' Leak Reveals Putin's Global and Domestic Cyberwarfare Tactics*. Retrieved 4 3, 2023, from Guardian: https://www. theguardian.com/technology/2023/mar/30/vulkan-files-leak-reveals-putins-global-and-domestic-cyberwarfare-tactics?mc_cid=7359a027e7&mc_eid=e840f8b673.

Microsoft. (2021). *Deep Dive into the Solorigate Second-stage Activation: From SUNBURST to TEARDROP and Raindrop*. Retrieved from Microsoft Threat Intelligence: https://www.microsoft.com/en-us/security/blog/2021/01/20/ deep-dive-into-the-solorigate-second-stage-activation-from-sunburst-to-teardrop-and-raindrop/.

Microsoft. (2022). *Microsoft Digital Defense Report 2022*. Retrieved 11 15, 2022, from Microsoft: https://query.prod.cms.rt.microsoft.com/cms/api/am/binary/ RE5bUvv?culture=en-us&country=us.

Paganini, P. (2014). *Researchers at FireEye have Detected a New Variant of Havex RAT, Which Scans SCADA Network via Object Linking and Embedding for Process Control (OPC)*. Retrieved from Security Affairs: https://securityaffairs.com/26778/ cyber-crime/havex-variant-opc.html.

Smalley, S. (2023). *Russia's Vast Telecom Surveillance System Crippled by Withdrawal of Western Tech, Report Says*. Retrieved from The Record: https://therecord.media/ russia-telecommunications-sorm-surveillance-western-technology.

Stoll, C. (2005). *The Cuckoo's Egg: Tracking a Spy Through the Maze of Computer Espionage*. Pocket Books.

Symantec. (2017). *Dragonfly: Western Energy Sector Targeted by Sophisticated Attack Group*. Retrieved from Symantec: https://symantec-enterprise-blogs.security.com/ blogs/threat-intelligence/dragonfly-energy-sector-cyber-attacks.

Temple-Raston, D. (2021). *A 'Worst Nightmare' Cyberattack: The Untold Story Of The SolarWinds Hack*. Retrieved from NPR: https://www.npr.org/2021/04/16/985439655/a-worst-nightmare-cyberattack-the-untold-story-of-the-solarwinds-hack.

Threat Intelligence Team. (2022). *Double Header: IsaacWiper and CaddyWiper*. Retrieved from MalwareBytes: https://www.malwarebytes.com/blog/threat-intelligence/2022/03/double-header-isaacwiper-and-caddywiper#:~:text=IsaacWiper%20was%20one%20of%20the,)%20and%20HermeticRansom%20(ransomware).

Toulas, B. (2022a). *Maui Ransomware Operation Linked to North Korean 'Andariel' Hackers*. Retrieved from Bleeping Computer: https://www.bleepingcomputer.com/news/security/maui-ransomware-operation-linked-to-north-korean-andariel-hackers/.

Toulas, B. (2022b). *Ukraine Dismantles 5 Disinformation Bot Farms, Seizes 10,000 SIM Cards*. Retrieved 4 7, 2022, from Bleeping Computer: https://www.bleepingcomputer.com/news/security/ukraine-dismantles-5-disinformation-bot-farms-seizes-10-000-sim-cards/.

16

Iran, China, and DPRK Cyber Operations and Tools

16.1 China, DPRK, and Iran Cyber Operations and Tools

China, the DPRK, and Iran are known to perform cyber operations, often with an economic or espionage focus. For example, in Section I, we looked at the development of Chinese cyber operations from patriotic hacktivists to strategic espionage collections. Similarly, Iran attempted to shut down international finance and oil production in the wake of STUXNET. The DPRK, however, is more focused on money, said to fund up to 1/3 of their nuclear weapons program through cyber theft. While the impact of each of these cyber operations is unprecedented in the pre-cyber age, each player's methods and tools have parallels in a focus on tradecraft with limited technical development.

16.1.1 Chinese Cyber Operations

Chinese cyber operations include a heavy reliance on tradecraft. For example, Operation Night Dragon (2011–2013), a probing of U.S. critical infrastructure systems, was an unexpected cyber surveillance operation that relied heavily on social engineering for system access.

16.1.1.1 2011–2013 Operation Night Dragon (CISA, 2021) (China)
While technical tools are important, especially when keeping track of the most recent vulnerability exploits (e.g., zero days), a lot of cyber targeting still focuses on the people running the networks and their system-level access. For example, with the U.S. announcing a "pivot to Asia" in 2011, Chinese cyber actors stepped up their attacks, probing U.S. gas pipelines for possible vulnerabilities.

Cyber Operations: A Case Study Approach, First Edition. Jerry M. Couretas.
© 2024 John Wiley & Sons, Inc. Published 2024 by John Wiley & Sons, Inc.

> CISA and the FBI provided incident response and remediation support to a number of victims of this activity. Overall, the U.S. Government identified and tracked 23 U.S. natural gas pipeline operators targeted from 2011 to 2013 in this spear phishing and intrusion campaign. Of the known targeted entities, 13 were confirmed compromises, 3 were near misses, and 7 had an unknown depth of intrusion. The U.S. Government has attributed this activity to Chinese state-sponsored actors. CISA and the FBI assess that these actors were specifically targeting U.S. pipeline infrastructure for the purpose of holding U.S. pipeline infrastructure at risk. Additionally, CISA and the FBI assess that this activity was ultimately intended to help China develop cyberattack capabilities against U.S. pipelines to physically damage pipelines or disrupt pipeline operations. (CISA, 2021)

During the gas pipeline intrusion campaign, Chinese operators attempted to exploit, sometimes successfully, the people, processes, and technologies of the targeted companies. For example, Operation Night Dragon used spear phishing to compromise key personnel at select natural gas pipeline operations.

In addition to spear phishing, CISA and the FBI were made aware of social engineering attempts by malicious actors believed to be associated with this campaign. The apparent goal was to gain sensitive information from asset owners. One asset owner reported that individuals in their network engineering department, including managers, received multiple phone calls requesting information about their recent network security practices. Asset owners reported that these calls began immediately after they had identified and removed the malicious intruder from their network and performed a system-wide credential reset. The caller identified himself as an employee of a large computer security firm performing a national survey about network cyber security practices. He inquired about the organization's policy and practices for firewall use and settings, types of software used to protect their network, and the use and type of intrusion detection and/or prevention systems. The caller was blocking his caller ID, and when the targeted organization tried to return the call, they reached a number that was not in service.

During the investigation of these compromises, CISA and FBI personnel discovered that Chinese state-sponsored actors specifically collected and exfiltrated ICS-related information. The Chinese state-sponsored actors searched document repositories for the following data types:

- Document searches: "SCAD*"
- Personnel lists
- Usernames/passwords
- Dial-up access information
- System manuals

Chinese cyber operators were able to penetrate natural gas pipeline systems and probe internal networks and their connected control systems. For example,

> Based on incident data, CISA and FBI assessed that Chinese state-sponsored actors also compromised various authorized remote access channels, including systems designed to transfer data and/or allow access between corporate and ICS networks. Though designed for legitimate business purposes, these systems have the potential to be manipulated by malicious cyber actors if unmitigated. With this access, the Chinese state-sponsored actors could have impersonated legitimate system operators to conduct unauthorized operations. According to the evidence obtained by CISA and FBI, the Chinese state-sponsored actors made no attempts to modify the pipeline operations of systems they accessed. (CISA, 2021)

These sophisticated actors may have "covered their tracks" and erased log data, preventing forensics operators from discerning attack paths. These cyber operators, due to their skill in accessing targeted systems and exfiltrating data, likely contributed to other aspects of Chinese industry and operations.

16.1.1.2   2019 Great Cannon

Throughout the summer and fall of 2019, the "Great Cannon" denial of service was used to jam messaging (e.g., Telegram), web for a, and protestor coordination of electoral reforms in Hong Kong. Since the handover of Hong Kong from the United Kingdom to the PRC, there have been multiple protests and demonstrations by Hong Kongers to attempt to maintain the civil rights that they inherited from the British. With the protestors taking some of these activities online, the PRC has similarly used cyber means to suppress this movement (Booz Allen Hamilton, 2022). While China uses cyber for political repression, this is in addition to the more traditional cyber collections that China is famous for. In one cyber attack, China used a web shell (e.g., China Chopper) to gain a foothold into systems for follow-on exploitation operations.

16.1.1.3   2021 China Chopper

Web shell attacks are becoming increasingly popular due to their effectiveness. For example, "China Chopper," deployed by APT 41 (Figure 6.4), has been used to attack MSSPs in order to extract data from the F-35 program office (Security Week, 2017). In addition, Chinese cyber operators were prominent in the 2021 Microsoft Exchange Server attacks (Mathieu Faoue, 2021).

In one example, "China Chopper" (DHS CISA, 2021) was used to exploit zero days in Microsoft Exchange Server, installing web shells for backdoor and follow on exploitation operations. This included over 60,000 compromised web-facing servers before Microsoft became aware of this exploit on March 2, 2021 (Kost, 2021); the attack was estimated to be two months old when Microsoft first became aware of it. Along with compromising web-facing servers, China also finds vulnerabilities through the National Disclosure Law.

16.1.1.4   2022 China and Zero-Day Development Based on National Disclosure Law

China is part of security agreements that are designed to ensure Chinese national security, and international supply chain security, due to China's role as a manufacturing center. Unfortunately, China uses this positioning to convert threat alerts into zero days in order to attack its commercial allies.

> China-based nation state threat actors are particularly proficient at discovering and developing zero-day exploits. China's vulnerability reporting regulation went into effect September 2021, marking a first in the world for a government to require the reporting of vulnerabilities into a government authority for review prior to the vulnerability being shared with the product or service owner. This new regulation might enable elements in the Chinese government to stockpile reported vulnerabilities toward weaponizing them. The increased use of zero days over the last year from China-based actors likely reflects the first full year of China's vulnerability disclosure requirements for the Chinese security community and a major step in the use of zero-day exploits as a state priority. (Microsoft, 2022)

In addition to developing zero days via an agreed upon National Disclosure Law, China's APT 41 is responsible for stealing tens of millions of dollars in U.S. COVID relief benefits since 2020 (Reuters, 2022). This is similar to the DPRK focus on using cyber for online theft.

16.1.2   DPRK Cyber Operations

WannaCry was one of the more famous attacks by the Lazarus Group. WannaCry also may have been the first ransomware operation to use the Shadow Broker's tools (Khandelwal, Shadow Brokers, Who Leaked WannaCry SMB Exploit, Are Back With More 0-Days, 2017) (Chapter 3). WannaCry was propagated through EternalBlue and DoublePulsar, exceptionally capable access tools for exploiting the Microsoft Server Message Block (SMB) for remote code execution (Khandelwal, Turns Out Microsoft Has Already Patched Exploits Leaked By Shadow Brokers, 2017). While Microsoft had already provided a patch, many users had not updated their systems. It is estimated that over 300,000 computers in 160 countries were affected by WannaCry (Newman, 2017), causing $4–$8 billion in damages (White, 2022).

The components of the WannaCry attack were relatively simple (White, 2022). Using EternalBlue/DoublePulsar (i.e., Shadow Broker's Tools (Chapter 3)), the attacker accessed a machine through Port 445, a sometimes Internet-facing doorway to a computer. The code would land on each new computer through Port 445, send a signal to an abstract URL name, a web address, and determine whether to continue. Unless the signal was negative, the hack would continue, using standard Windows file encryption "WINCRY" (aka WannaCry) (White, 2022) to encrypt the files with a unique password. The ransom was paid to get access to this unique password.

In addition to DPRK prowess in successfully extracting funds from banks, they are now expanding their use ransomware against medical targets, to extort cash. For example, Maui ransomware is one of the key tools that Andariel uses to disrupt electronic health records services, diagnostics services, imaging services, and intranet services (DHS CISA, 2022; Toulas, 2022).

As shown in Section I's Table 7.2, the DPRK's limited number of attacks is memorable due to their being bold. The DPRK also employs multiple attack paths in its cyber operations (Figure 16.1).

As shown in Figure 16.1, Mr. Park uses multiple e-mail addresses to access over a dozen operational attack paths to maneuver on high-profile targets that span from Defense contractors (e.g., Lockheed Martin), banks (e.g., Bangladesh), and movie provides (e.g., Sony Pictures, AMC theaters). The DPRK's Cobra Botnet is a peer-to-peer network that the DPRK often uses for these cyber operations (CISA, 2017).

16.1.3   Iranian Operations

In contrast to the DPRK, Iranian cyber operations include cases of population monitoring and retribution. Iran is also known to exchange both technology and training with China and Russia (Chapter 8).

16.1.3.1   2012 Iran and False Flag Operations

One of Iran's first documented cyber operations included using "false flag" deception, pretending to be a criminal or terrorist group, in order to deceive the target into thinking that the attacker was someone else. Collecting on other countries requires both additional skills and a desire to refute the claim that the surveillance was performed by Tehran.

> Conducting offensive cyber operations through covert organizations provides Tehran plausible deniability for any attacks, thereby protecting its claim to victimhood while also allowing the state to signal its intentions to its opponents. (Carnegie Endowment for International Peace, 2018)

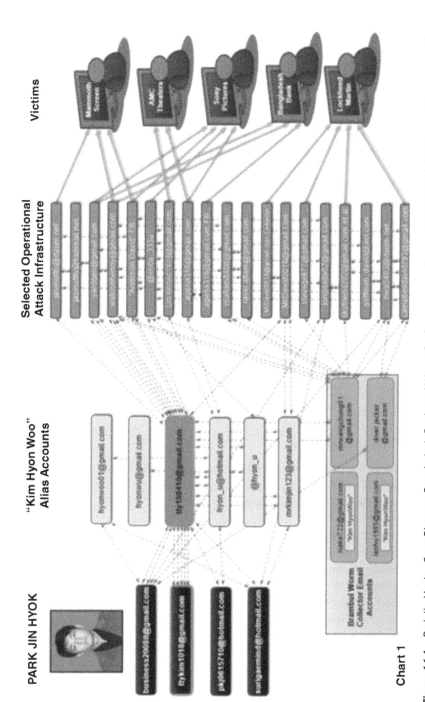

Figure 16.1 Park Jin Hyok – Sony Pictures, Bangladesh Bank, and WannaCry Ransomware. *Source:* DoJ (2018)/United States Department of Justice / Public domain.

Along with using deception during Al Ababil, or the 2012 attack on the U.S. financial system, Iran simultaneously performed Al Shamoon, an attack on Saudi Aramco's oil production facilities, using disttrack malware. Disttrack malware wiped the master boot record on over 30,000 disk drives in the Saudi Aramco IT systems (Clark, 2012).

Iran also used a retribution attack to destroy the Sands Casino IT system in 2014. This attack was performed by relatively simple pieces of code (e.g., 160 lines of Visual Basic used to cause $40 million in damages to the Sands Casino (Gallagher, 2014) (Chapter 8)).

16.1.3.2 2020 Monitoring Dissidents through Fake Game Apps
Iran develops novel spyware. For example, Iran has been known to put spyware in wallpaper, restaurant, and game apps used to target dissidents and perceived regime opponents (Corera, 2021).

16.1.3.3 2020 Iranian Domain Names for Information Operations Campaigns
Iran attempted to influence the 2020 U.S. Presidential Election (Chapter 8). This, along with ongoing support for terrorist organizations, resulted in 92 domains being impounded in order to limit the Iran Revolutionary Guard Corps' (IRGC) ability to conduct information operations (Department of Justice, 2020).

16.1.3.4 2022 Hyperscrape – Iranian E-mail Extraction Tool
In a continuation of early (2009) Iranian cyber operations against DigiNotar to extract certificates in order to read their citizens' Gmail accounts (Chapter 8), the IRGC extended this capability to a tool that can read entire e-mail inboxes. For example, APT 35, sometimes called Charming Kitten, developed a tool where a user can download the contents of an inbox (e.g., Gmail, Yahoo, etc.) from their own machine, using compromised credentials. This tool, called Hyperscrape, was developed for Charming Kitten operations and is profiled by the Google Threat Analysis Group (TAG) for indicators of compromise (Bash, 2022).

16.1.3.5 2022 Multi-Persona Operations – "Social Proof" for Implied Validity
APT 42 (Table 8.2) has been observed, in the collection of strategic intelligence, to use multiple personas, each allegedly from U.S. and W. European policy think tanks, in order to fool middle-eastern researchers into responding (Lakshmanan, Iranian Hackers Target High-Value Targets in Nuclear Security and Genomic Research, 2022). The idea is to leverage the psychology principle of "social proof" in order to increase the authenticity of the threat actor's correspondence so as to make the target buy into the scheme, a tactic that demonstrates the adversary's continued ability to step up its game.

Multi-persona operations are resource-intensive, hinting at the support of an organization that can afford the cultivation of multiple personas for the compromise of a single target. We looked at one of the signatures of a nation-state operator (Figure 4.1) as having resources from a research institution, engineering development, and a mature clandestine service. Target development via multi-personas is a candidate for this broad level of technical and operational support. Using multi-persona operations for their cyber operations marks the IRGC as a well-developed cyber actor.

16.1.4 Tactical Cyber Tools' Wrap-up

Iran's cyber operations span from false flag operations to the employment of destructive malware (e.g., use of Disttrack against Saudi Aramco in 2012). This is different from the theft operations that characterize DPRK and PRC cyber operations. The DPRK, having stolen over $1 billion via crypto theft (Chapter 7), is the current leader in cyber theft operations, all with the Cobra Botnet and tradecraft attributable to just a few cyber operators (Figure 16.1). China is similar in using theft as espionage to gather data, with the additional twist of using the National Disclosure Law to manufacture zero-day exploits on an unprecedented scale (Section 16.1.1.4).

Bibliography

Bash, A. (2022). *New Iranian APT Data Extraction Tool.* Retrieved 8 29, 2022, from Google Threat Analysis Group: https://blog.google/threat-analysis-group/new-iranian-apt-data-extraction-tool/.

Booz Allen Hamilton. (2022). *Same Cloak, More Dagger: Decoding How the People's Republic Of China Uses Cyberattacks.* Retrieved 11 8, 2022, from Booz Allen.

Carnegie Endowment for International Peace. (2018). *Iran's Cyber Ecosystem: Who Are the Threat Actors?* Retrieved 8 20, 2022, from Carnegie Endowment for International Peace: https://carnegieendowment.org/2018/01/04/iran-s-cyber-ecosystem-who-are-threat-actors-pub-75140.

CISA. (2017). *HIDDEN COBRA – North Korea's DDoS Botnet Infrastructure.* Retrieved from CISA: https://www.cisa.gov/news-events/alerts/2017/06/13/hidden-cobra-north-koreas-ddos-botnet-infrastructure.

CISA. (2021). *Chinese Gas Pipeline Intrusion Campaign, 2011 to 2013.* Retrieved 11 10, 2022, from CISA: https://www.cisa.gov/uscert/ncas/alerts/aa21-201a.

Clark, J. (2012). *Shamoon Malware Infects Computers, Steals Data, then Wipes them.* Retrieved from ZDNet: https://www.zdnet.com/article/shamoon-malware-infects-computers-steals-data-then-wipes-them/.

Corera, G. (2021). *Iran 'Hides Spyware in Wallpaper, Restaurant and Games Apps'.* Retrieved 9 19, 2022, from BBC: https://www.bbc.com/news/technology-55977537.

Department of Justice. (2020). *United States Seizes Domain Names Used by Iran's Islamic Revolutionary Guard Corps.* Retrieved 9 22, 2022, from Department of Justice: https://www.justice.gov/opa/pr/united-states-seizes-domain-names-used-by-iran-s-islamic-revolutionary-guard-corps.

DHS CISA. (2021). *Mitigate Microsoft Exchange Server Vulnerabilities.* Retrieved 9 15, 2022, from Alert (AA21-062A): https://www.cisa.gov/uscert/ncas/alerts/aa21-062a.

DHS CISA. (2022). *More Alerts Alert (AA22-187A) North Korean State-Sponsored Cyber Actors Use Maui Ransomware to Target the Healthcare and Public Health Sector.* Retrieved 7 16, 2022, from CISA: https://www.cisa.gov/uscert/ncas/alerts/aa22-187a.

DoJ. (2018). *North Korean Regime-Backed Programmer Charged With Conspiracy to Conduct Multiple Cyber Attacks and Intrusions.* Retrieved from DoJ: https://www.justice.gov/opa/pr/north-korean-regime-backed-programmer-charged-conspiracy-conduct-multiple-cyber-attacks-and.

Gallagher, S. (2014). *Iranian Hackers used Visual Basic Malware to Wipe Vegas Casino's Network.* Retrieved from Arstechnica: https://arstechnica.com/information-technology/2014/12/iranian-hackers-used-visual-basic-malware-to-wipe-vegas-casinos-network/.

Khandelwal, S. (2017a). *Shadow Brokers, Who Leaked WannaCry SMB Exploit, Are Back With More 0-Days.* Retrieved from The Hacker News: https://thehackernews.com/2017/05/shodow-brokers-wannacry-hacking.html.

Khandelwal, S. (2017b). *Turns Out Microsoft Has Already Patched Exploits Leaked By Shadow Brokers.* Retrieved from The Hacker News: https://thehackernews.com/2017/04/window-zero-day-patch.html.

Kost, E. (2021). *Critical Microsoft Exchange flaw: What is CVE-2021-26855?* Retrieved 9 11, 2022, from Upguard: https://www.upguard.com/blog/cve-2021-26855.

Lakshmanan, R. (2022). *Iranian Hackers Target High-Value Targets in Nuclear Security and Genomic Research.* Retrieved 9 16, 2022, from The Hacker News: https://thehackernews.com/2022/09/iranian-hackers-target-high-value.html.

Mathieu Faoue, M. T. (2021). *Exchange Servers Under Siege from at Least 10 APT Groups.* Retrieved 9 10, 2022, from ESET: https://www.welivesecurity.com/2021/03/10/exchange-servers-under-siege-10-apt-groups/.

Microsoft. (2022). *Microsoft Digital Defense Report 2022.* Retrieved 11 15, 2022, from Microsoft: https://query.prod.cms.rt.microsoft.com/cms/api/am/binary/RE5bUvv?culture=en-us&country=us.

Newman, L. H. (2017). *How an Accidental 'Kill Switch' Slowed Friday's Massive Ransomware Attack.* Retrieved 4 12, 2023, from Wired Magazine: https://www.wired.com/2017/05/accidental-kill-switch-slowed-fridays-massive-ransomware-attack/.

Reuters. (2022). *Chinese Hacking Team 'Winnti' Stole US Covid Relief Worth Millions.* Retrieved 1 27, 2023, from Reuters: https://www.reuters.com/technology/chinese-hackers-stole-millions-worth-us-covid-relief-money-secret-service-says-2022-12-05/.

Security Week. (2017). *F-35 Stealth Fighter Data Stolen in Australia Defence Hack.* Retrieved from Security Week: https://www.securityweek.com/f-35-stealth-fighter-data-stolen-australia-defence-hack/.

Toulas, B. (2022). *Maui Ransomware Operation Linked to North Korean 'Andariel' Hackers.* Retrieved from Bleeping Computer: https://www.bleepingcomputer.com/news/security/maui-ransomware-operation-linked-to-north-korean-andariel-hackers/.

White, G. (2022). *The Lazarus Heist – From Hollywood to High Finance: Inside North Korea's Global Cyber War.* New York: Penguin.

17

Strategic Cyber Technologies – ICS/SCADA, Election Machines, and Crypto Currencies

17.1 Strategic Cyber Technologies

Strategic cyber technologies include critical infrastructure, election machines, and currency whose manipulation or denial can result in a nation-state changing is way of life. As discussed in Chapters 10 and 11, strategic cyber effects include affecting a national defense program (e.g., STUXNET), denying critical infrastructure, or influencing elections. Due to the breadth of strategic cyber technologies, it is a challenge to defend them. In addition, due to the widespread use of computing technology, the supporting supply chains are only becoming larger and more complicated.

17.1.1 Software Supply Chain

Along with the physical supply chain, we have a software supply chain that is used to provide software components for increased application functionality. And adversaries are adept at attacking the software supply chain. In Chapter 5, we saw an example of the Russian SVR using a supply chain attack on SolarWinds, infecting over 30,000 users across government and industry.

Similarly, mobile apps for the U.S. Army were recently using "PushWhoosh" software that ultimately comes from a Russian company. The PushWhoosh code is for software developers to profile smartphone app users based on their online activity. In penetrating the supply chain, several towns across Illinois used the PushWhoosh code in the development of their "Gov 311" code to help them access general information about their local communities and officials (KrebsonSecurity, 2022).

Cyber Operations: A Case Study Approach, First Edition. Jerry M. Couretas.
© 2024 John Wiley & Sons, Inc. Published 2024 by John Wiley & Sons, Inc.

17.1.1.1 Software Bill of Materials

An additional development that will help in mitigate malware in commercial code is the introduction of a software bill of materials (SBOM) (Stevens, 2023). While the open-source movement showed promise for getting good programmers, and code, to make "free" applications for the masses, there are cases where foreign intelligence agencies exploited these good intentions. This includes inserting backdoors into open-source code to develop future accesses (Goodin, 2022). For example, the Winnti group leveraged Linux to access cloud platforms in the Cloud Hopper Campaign (Rob Barry, 2019). In addition, PushWhoosh, a Russian monitoring application, was found to be inadvertently included in several U.S. Army and local government applications. The use of an SBOM per current memoranda (Young, 2022) and developing policy (CISA, 2022a) will further increase the understanding of the code included in many of the open-source tools.

17.1.2 Election Machines

As a result of 2017 election system uncertainty, Harri Hursti did an independent study on election systems, finding that companies were resistant to technical criticism, the machines were indeed hackable, and that there was little in the way of formal policies and procedures to guarantee the fidelity of technical election systems (Hursti, 2020). This work included House Testimony by University of Michigan Professor J. Alex Halderman on the vulnerability of voting machines (CSE, 2017).

While policy is developing for protecting the software supply chain and critical infrastructure applications, there are already reported voting system penetrations via cyber. For example, during the 2023 RSA conference, General William Hartman described how USCYBERCOM hunt forward teams found the Iranian cyber operator, "Pioneer Kitten," penetrating a U.S. election results website during the 2020 U.S. Presidential Election (Menn, 2023).

Election machines are known to have technical vulnerabilities in terms of the voter registration system, the recording of voter rolls (i.e., who is registered to vote), and the counts of actual ballots. As separate systems, each of these elements might be compromised to falsify the electorate and/or mis-count the ballots, showing a false victory for the candidate preferred by the cyber operations team.

It is a challenge to track the jurisdictions served by each of the voting machine manufacturers due to the procurements being made at the county level. From available data, Table 17.1 provides a snapshot of the usage and known vulnerabilities by voting machine manufacturer.

As shown in Table 17.1, each of the most popular election machines has vulnerabilities that a determined hacker might take advantage of. In addition, due to the over 230,000 polling places in the United States, alone, the cost of ensuring secure

Table 17.1 Election Machine Types.

Manufacturer Name	Usage	System Security Information
Dominion voting systems	Dominion reported serving 19 states and 133 local jurisdictions to Dun and Bradstreet (Andrzejewski, 2020)	Dominion Voting Systems Democracy Suite ImageCast X has multiple vulnerabilities that might be exploited by a determined attacker (CISA, 2022b)
ES&S	ES&S is the largest voting machine company in the United States, with an estimated half of the market (Huseman, 2019)	Actively working with a security company (Synack) to find vulnerabilities before fielding (Newman, 2020)
Hart InterCivic	Hart InterCivic is the smallest of the voting machine providers	Partnered with Microsoft to provide end-to-end verifiability of a ballot (Microsoft, 2020)

voting machines, and subsequent election results are high (Polling Places, 2022). For example, the Brennan Center estimates a cost of approximately $1.8 billion in order to upgrade aging voting machines and replace vulnerable ones in the United States (Brennan Center, 2022).

The key election system manufacturers, ES&S, Dominion Voting Systems Corp., and Hart InterCivic Inc. are becoming more open to testing by "hackers" to ensure the systems are not compromised (Robert McMillan, 2020). For example, ES&S opened its system to hackers in order to find vulnerabilities before nefarious actors do. And at DefCon 2020, ES&S revealed that it is working with a security firm (Synack) to provide their voting machines to red teams in order to find bugs and make the fixes before the products are sent to polling places (Newman, 2020).

17.1.3 Industrial Control Systems/Supervisory Control and Data Acquisition

While voting systems are using the hacker community to test their security, critical infrastructure is still sometimes visible by attackers via the Internet from web-facing industrial control ports. These ICS/SCADA systems can also be accessed via the business computer network that interfaces to the control system. Therefore, in the majority of cases, if the overall business network is vulnerable, able hackers can maneuver through the network and find the control system interface in order to compromise physical machinery.

HAVEX malware was observed in the 2014 time frame to be used against Microsoft Object Linking and Embedding (OLE) for Process Control (PC)

(Khandelwal, 2014). OLE-PC was added to industrial control systems in order to provide a standard, modern, interface to the traditionally crude interfaces used to view and program control systems. However, the addition of OLE-PC now made industrial controls vulnerable to the same type of exploits as any other desktop machine running the Microsoft Windows operating system.

Operational technology has multiple protocols for communicating within their system. However, as shown in Figure 17.1, EtherNet remains one of the top communications protocols.

EtherNet is the predominant ICS protocol, as shown in Figure 17.1. Cyber attacks are also occurring, via specialized tools, against the lesser known protocols. For example, similar to the development of Triton malware for Triconex Safety Instrumented System (SIS) controllers on middle-eastern systems

> ... custom-made tools are specifically designed to single out Schneider Electric programmable logic controllers (PLCs), OMRON Sysmac NEX PLCs, and Open Platform Communications Unified Architecture (OPC UA) servers.
>
> *(Lakshmanan, 2022)*

And, in an echo back to STUXNET, Mandiant recently identified malware specifically targeting Siemens controllers, with extra stealth capability (Mandiant, 2016). Along with this Siemens-specific threat, ICS/SCADA systems

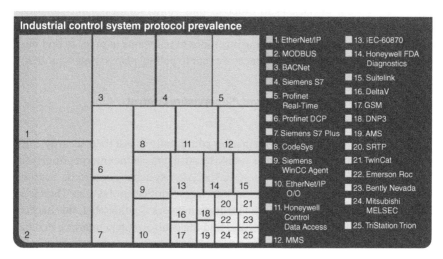

Figure 17.1 Industrial Control System Protocols and Frequency of Use. *Source:* Adapted from Microsoft (2022).

more generally have a large number of protocols that compose a widely scoped attack surface.

17.1.4 Crypto Currency and Sanctions Avoidance

While crypto currencies started as a hobby, mining Bitcoin, Ethereum, and other crypto currencies are now a multibillion-dollar industry. For example, over 400,000 Bitcoin trade per day (YCharts, 2023). And, at an early 2023 average of $25,000 per Bitcoin, this amounts to approximately $10 billion in daily trading.

In order to mine Bitcoin, or one of the other crypto currencies, the overall capability of an organization, or pool of organizations, is called hashpower.

Hashpower: The computational capability in a machine that is used for crypto mining. Hash power may also refer to the total computing power of a miner or mining pool (PCMag, n.d.)

Using this metric, we can then look at who has the greatest capability to produce crypto currency. For example, looking at Figure 17.2, we can see how the hash rate for commercial organizations changed in early 2022.

As shown in Figure 17.2, hash rates can change in the tens of percent in a matter of months. The units on the y-axis, EH/s, stand for

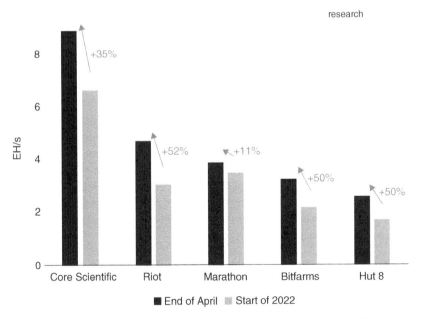

Figure 17.2 Commercial Organization Hash Rates and Changes (early 2022). *Source:* Adapted from Kyouma (2022).

Table 17.2   Bitcoin Mining by Country.

Country	Bitcoin Mining (%)
United States	35
Kazakhstan	18
Russia	11
Canada	10
Ireland	5
Malaysia	5
Germany	4
Iran	3

Source: Adapted from World Population Review (2023).

Exahashes per second (EH/s) that are equivalent to one quintillion hashes are used to express the hash rate of BTC. By comparing the average time between mined blocks with the network difficulty at a particular time, the overall network hash rate may be roughly calculated (SINGH, 2022)

We can also use these units to discuss which countries have the highest hash rate (Table 17.2).

As shown in Table 17.2, less than 10 countries account for over 90% of the global Bitcoin mining. This includes the use of crypto currency capability to defeat sanctions. For example, both Iran and Russia convert oil and gas assets into cryptocoin via crypto mining.

Iran is subject to a number of sanctions due to differences that the current regime has with the International community. These sanctions restrict the movement of technology, services, and funding that would otherwise be available. One way to circumvent financial restrictions includes the use of crypto currency as a means to exchange value. A recent report estimated that Iran is moving $8 billion through crypto currency to get around current sanctions. It is estimated that Iran uses approximately 10 million barrels of oil, or 4% of its annual production, to produce Bitcoin (Reuters, 2021). The sanctioned oil is converted into Bitcoin in order to circumvent sanctions.

17.1.5   Strategic Cyber Technologies' Wrap-up

The use of Bitcoin to avoid sanctions is the latest twist in the use of crypto currencies. The Silk Road (2012) settled its online drug trades in Bitcoin. Similarly, the Hydra market helped ransomware operators wash Bitcoin into convertible currency. This is similar to what the DPRK currently does with mixers in converting stolen crypto currencies for weapon system procurements.

While crypto currencies are used to directly convert energy to "new" money, critical infrastructure and election system attacks are more like traditional cyber effects. For example, tailoring access tools to penetrate ICS/SCADA protocols or an election system interface are common cyber manipulation operations.

Bibliography

Andrzejewski, A. (2020). *Dominion Voting Systems Received $120 Million From 19 States And 133 Local Governments To Provide Election Services (2017-2019).* (Forbes, Producer) Retrieved 10 25, 2022, from Forbes: https://www.forbes.com/sites/adamandrzejewski/2020/12/08/dominion-voting-systems-received-120-million-from-19-states-and-133-local-governments-to-provide-election-services-2017-2019/?sh=3fb3c0dd620f.

Blake, J., Dan, C. (2017). *Attackers Deploy New ICS Attack Framework "TRITON" and Cause Operational Disruption to Critical Infrastructure.* Retrieved from Mandiant: https://www.mandiant.com/resources/blog/attackers-deploy-new-ics-attack-framework-triton.

Brennan Center. (2022). *Voting Machines at Risk in 2022.* Retrieved 10 25, 2022, from Brennan Center for Justice: https://www.brennancenter.org/our-work/research-reports/voting-machines-risk-2022.

CISA. (2022a). *BOD 23-01: Improving Asset Visibility and Vulnerability Detection on Federal Networks.* Retrieved from CISA: https://www.cisa.gov/binding-operational-directive-23-01.

CISA. (2022b). *ICS Advisory (ICSA-22-154-01).* (D. C. (CISA), Producer) Retrieved 10 25, 2022, from DHS Cybersecurity and Infrastructure Security Agency (CISA): https://www.cisa.gov/uscert/ics/advisories/icsa-22-154-01.

CSE. (2017). *Prof. J. Alex Halderman Testifies in Front of Senate Intelligence Committee on Secure Elections.* Retrieved from U of M Computer Science and Engineering: https://cse.engin.umich.edu/stories/prof-j-alex-halderman-testifies-in-front-of-senate-intelligence-committee-on-secure-elections.

Goodin, D. (2022). *Backdoor in Public Repository Used New form of Attack to Target Big Firms.* Retrieved from ArsTechnica: https://arstechnica.com/information-technology/2022/05/backdoor-in-public-repository-used-new-form-of-attack-to-target-big-firms/.

Hursti, H. (2020). *Kill Chain: The Cyber War on America's Elections.* Retrieved 7 16, 2022, from HBO.

Huseman, J. (2019). *The Market for Voting Machines Is Broken. This Company Has Thrived in It.* Retrieved 10 25, 2022, from ProPublica: https://www.propublica.org/article/the-market-for-voting-machines-is-broken-this-company-has-thrived-in-it.

Khandelwal, S. (2014). *New Variant of Havex Malware Scans for OPC Servers at SCADA Systems.* Retrieved 11 9, 2022, from The Hacker News: https://thehackernews.com/2014/07/new-variant-of-havex-malware-scans-for.html.

KrebsonSecurity. (2022). *U.S. Govt. Apps Bundled Russian Code With Ties to Mobile Malware Developer.* Retrieved 1 27, 2023, from KrebsonSecurity.

Kyouma, H. (2022). *Which Mining Company Contributed Most To Bitcoin's Hashrate Growth In 2022?* Retrieved from Bitcoinist: https://bitcoinist.com/which-mining-company-bitcoins-hashrate-growth-2022/.

Lakshmanan, R. (2022). *U.S. Warns of APT Hackers Targeting ICS/SCADA Systems with Specialized Malware.* Retrieved from The Hacker News: https://thehackernews.com/2022/04/us-warns-of-apt-hackers-targeting.html.

Mandiant. (2016). *IRONGATE ICS Malware: Nothing to See Here...Masking Malicious Activity on SCADA Systems.* Retrieved from Mandiant: https://www.mandiant.com/resources/blog/irongate-ics-malware.

Menn, J. (2023). *Iran Gained Access to Election Results Website in 2020, Military Reveals.* Retrieved from The Washington Post: https://www.washingtonpost.com/technology/2023/04/24/election-2020-iran-hacking/.

Microsoft. (2020). *Hart and Microsoft Announce Partnership to Incorporate ElectionGuard.* Retrieved 10 25, 2022, from Microsoft Security Team: https://www.microsoft.com/en-us/security/blog/2021/06/03/hart-and-microsoft-announce-partnership-to-incorporate-electionguard/.

Microsoft. (2022). *Microsoft Digital Defense Report 2022.* Retrieved 11 15, 2022, from Microsoft: https://query.prod.cms.rt.microsoft.com/cms/api/am/binary/RE5bUvv?culture=en-us&country=us.

Newman, L. H. (2020). *Voting Machine Makers Are Finally Playing Nice With Hackers.* Retrieved 10 25, 2022, from Wired: https://www.wired.com/story/voting-machine-makers-hackers-ess/.

PCMag. (n.d.). *Hash Power.* Retrieved from PCMag: https://www.pcmag.com/encyclopedia/term/hash-power.

Polling Places. (2022). Retrieved from National Conference of State Legislatures: https://www.ncsl.org/research/elections-and-campaigns/polling-places.aspx.

Reuters. (2021). *Iran Uses Crypto Mining to Lessen Impact of Sanctions, Study Finds.* Retrieved from Reuters: https://www.reuters.com/technology/iran-uses-crypto-mining-lessen-impact-sanctions-study-finds-2021-05-21/.

Rob Barry, D. V. (2019). *Ghosts in the Clouds: Inside China's Major Corporate Hack A Journal investigation finds the Cloud Hopper attack was much bigger than previously known.* Retrieved 6 8, 2020, from Wall Street Journal: https://www.wsj.com/articles/ghosts-in-the-clouds-inside-chinas-major-corporate-hack-11577729061.

Robert McMillan, A. C. (2020). *Hackers Get Green Light to Test Election Voting Systems.* Retrieved 9 22, 2022, from Wall Street Journal: https://www.wsj.com/articles/hackers-get-green-light-to-test-u-s-voting-systems-11596628099?mod=djemCybersecruityPro&tpl=cy.

Singh, O. (2022). *What is Bitcoin Hash Rate and Why does it Matter?* Retrieved from Cointelegraph: https://cointelegraph.com/explained/what-is-bitcoin-hash-rate-and-why-does-it-matter.

Stevens, B. (2023). *Software Bill of Materials is the Key to Cybersecurity Compliance.* Retrieved from C4ISRNet: https://www.c4isrnet.com/thought-leadership/2023/01/30/software-bill-of-materials-is-the-key-to-cybersecurity-compliance/?utm_source=sailthru&utm_medium=email&utm_campaign=c4-cyber.

World Population Review. (2023). *Bitcoin Mining by Country 2023.* Retrieved from World Population Review: https://worldpopulationreview.com/country-rankings/bitcoin-mining-by-country.

YCharts. (2023). *Bitcoin Transactions Per Day (I:BTPD).* Retrieved from YCharts: https://ycharts.com/indicators/bitcoin_transactions_per_day#:~:text=Bitcoin%20Transactions%20Per%20Day%20is,79.69%25%20from%20one%20year%20ago.

Young, S. (2022). *Enhancing the Security of the Software Supply Chain through Secure Software Development Practices.* Retrieved from White House: https://www.whitehouse.gov/wp-content/uploads/2022/09/M-22-18.pdf

18

Cyber Case Studies Conclusion

The goal of this book is to help the reader understand cyber operations. And discussing cyber attacks is one way to untangle the teams, targets, and tools that compose a cyber operation. While current cyber operations' reporting can be a challenge to "unpack," this book defines the terms, describes the operations, and profiles some of the key players that scan our critical infrastructure, broadcast fake news, and influence our elections.

Section I started with tactical operations' examples (e.g., ISIS, Russia) (Chapter 1). We then reviewed web use for insurgent maneuver. For example, AQI/ISIL/ISIS dynamics roughly map to the classic Mao model in transitioning between insurgency phases (Chapter 2).

Chapter 3 was a background on cyber-crime. This included a review of the Shadow Brokers and the subsequent proliferation of ransomware. Chapters 4 through 8 described nation-state cyber operations, including Russia, China, the DPRK, and Iran. And Chapter 9 reviewed independent cyber operators, including the development from hactivists, with simple criminal effects, to the global effects felt from Wikileaks in 2010.

Throughout Section I, we reviewed the development timeline for each of the respective actors. Russia performed nearly continuous cyber operations from the initial use of West German hackers to attempt to penetrate the U.S. Star Wars missile defense program in the 1980s. One thread that became apparent in this review was the prominent role of the Russian Federation's FSB. For example, in Chapter 5, we saw how Turla, an FSB team, conducted Operation Moonlight Maze in the 1990s. In addition, the FSB conducted Operation Dragonfly, a probing of U.S. energy systems in the 2012–2014 time frame. And, more recently, the outed snake malware was an FSB tool used to monitor diplomatic targets.

In Chapter 6, we found a similar phenomenon in China. APT 41 features prominently in key cyber attacks. For example, APT 41 conducts cyber operations that

Cyber Operations: A Case Study Approach, First Edition. Jerry M. Couretas.
© 2024 John Wiley & Sons, Inc. Published 2024 by John Wiley & Sons, Inc.

span from theft to critical infrastructure and are said to be protected by the Ministry of State Security. We also saw a similar key team in Chapter 7, with the DPRK's Lazarus performing cyber operations that span from the 2014 Sony denial/outing attack, to the 2016 Bank of Bangladesh heist, to the more recent rash of digital wallet thefts that are said to fund up to 1/3 of the DPRK nuclear program.

Iran (Chapter 8) focuses more on using the Internet for population monitoring and control due to the heavy influence of the MOIS. Developing and controlling the National Information Network (NIN) is one way to ensure access to personal communications over the Internet. In addition, Iran penetrated DigiNotar, a Dutch certificate authority, in 2011 in order to spy on Iranian nationals' e-mail communications. And, in the aftermath of STUXNET (2010), Iranian cyber teams seemingly came out of nowhere to attempt to create a global energy and financial crisis in 2012 through attacks on Saudi oil operations (Operation Al Shamoon I) and U.S. financial institutions (Operation Ababil). More recently, Iran's focus on regime threats turned to a ransomware like attack on Albanian government systems, due to Albania's harboring MeK, an Iranian resistance group.

While Iran, the DPRK, China, and Russia perform nation-state cyber operations, independent cyber operators also produced strategic cyber effects (Chapter 9). For example, the Wikileaks' release of U.S. State Department cables is said to have influenced the toppling of governments across North Africa in the 2011 Arab Spring.

Section II discusses cyber effects in terms of strategic, tactical, and criminal. Strategic effects, with the ability to cause a nation-state enough duress to invoke a major change of plans, were found to come from both nation-state operations and hackers/criminals. As discussed in Chapter 10, STUXNET is a good example of a strategic cyber effect, delaying Iran's nuclear program by two to three years. In addition, comparing STUXNET to a conventional air campaign (i.e., Operation Desert Fox) resulted in an estimated 18:1 cost advantage due to the use of cyber.

We also saw how this cyber advantage works for an adversary in Chapter 11. A back-of-the-envelope estimate for the Chinese advantage accrued from F-35 design theft is a development reduction time of up to 1/2 for the J-31. Quantifying espionage, or the value of deception, is a challenge. Barton Whaley's historical loss exchange ratio (LER) study is one example of an attempt to estimate deception as an independent variable in military engagement. And cyber collection, similar to espionage, depends on stealth, a form of deception.

Similar to Chapter 10's STUXNET analysis, in Chapter 12, we compared Operation Orchard (2007) to the Al Sharyat airfield strike (2017). For this tactical cyber attack, we estimated a 7:1 cost benefit due to cyber. More challenging to describe are Russian denial operations in Estonia (2007), combined cyber denial and manipulation operations starting with Georgia (2008), and continuous cyber operations in the Ukraine since 2014. Russia deployed wiper attacks early on in the February 2022 attack on the Ukraine, with the idea of denying key government, military, and communication systems. This, however, was after eight years of continuous cyber attacks, leading some to believe that lack of cyber effectiveness led to a resort to kinetic attack.

In Chapter 12, we also reviewed how cyber was used for longer-term tactical suppression, via Operation Glowing Symphony (2016), and compared this to the estimated costs for an aerial intelligence, surveillance, and reconnaissance (ISR) campaign. While challenging to compare directly, the advantages in using cyber over an aerial ISR portfolio include cost reductions associated with forward basing. And, while tactical cyber effects are a challenge to assess, criminal cyber effects have remediation or ransom costs, making quantification much easier in some cases.

Chapter 13 included a review of criminal cyber effects. Some criminal effects overlap with the strategic, due to the target being classified as critical infrastructure. For example, in 2021 alone, the Darkside ransomware group caused fuel shortages that shut down the U.S. East Coast (Colonial Pipeline) and locked the Costa Rican government out of its computer systems. As discussed in Chapters 10 and 11, quantifying these strategic effects, even though they are due to a criminal operation, are more challenging than simply using reconstitution or ransom costs for the criminal effect.

Section III was a review of cyber terrain, designed to discuss the current composition of the Internet and the systems whose compromise have the ability to change our way of life (e.g., voting machines, critical infrastructure, developing crypto currencies).

In Chapter 14, we looked at tools used in example cyber crimes, from operational command and control frameworks (e.g., Cobalt Strike) to example botnet/team combinations (e.g., Emotet/Trickbot/Ryuk) currently used to compromise financial institutions. We followed this up in Chapter 15 with Russian cyber attack paths used for both the Former Soviet Union's attempted to penetrate the U.S. Star Wars missile defense system (1980s) and Operation Moonlight Maze (1990s).

We also discussed the Russian Federation's current use of the cyber tool contractor Vulkan, which supplies both scanning software and cyber operator training to exploit rail, aircraft, and sea infrastructure. This was a follow on from a discussion of the FSB's HAVEX industrial control supply chain compromise (2012), preceding the SVR's SolarWinds software supply chain compromise by almost 10 years (2019–2020).

The Russian Federation's (i.e., FSB) surveilling of U.S. energy pipelines (i.e., HAVEX), starting in 2012, was also the same time frame that China started its own reconnaissance of U.S. energy infrastructure with Operation Night Dragon (Chapter 16). Chapter 16 also reviews the multiple techniques of Iran's cyber operations, including false flag and multi-persona operations. These social engineering techniques are used to deceive a human target in order to gain trust. Similarly, DPRK digital theft operations are almost always performed via an initial social engineering engagement in order to gain access to systems of interest, accounting for an over $1 billion extraction from digital wallets from the late 2010s to early 2020s, and said to fund 1/3 of the DPRK's current nuclear development program (Chapters 7 and 16).

While nation-states now have a mature cyber capability, complete with the ability to deliver strategic, tactical, and criminal effects, Chapter 17 reviews the key cyber terrain that a functioning democracy will want to defend in order to maintain government, critical infrastructure, and business processes. We therefore looked at example election machines, ICS/SCADA systems, and crypto currency developments.

Election machines, while initially vulnerable, seem to have taken security measures seriously. Similarly, ICS/SCADA have been attacked (e.g., HAVEX, Industroyer) for over a decade with limited flickering of the lights. This is not to minimize the threat. The current cyber environment includes cyber-attack tools from the Shadow Brokers and Vulkan, along with near-continuous criminal and nation-state-level attacks.

Section III

Cyberspace Environment and Tools Conclusion

Election machines and industrial control systems (ICS) use technologies, and supporting supply chains, that are vulnerable to cyber-attack. IT gear suppliers, formerly commodity gadget makers, are now stakeholders in our collective security. In a recent example, Microsoft is playing a developing role in the cyber thread of the Ukraine war.

Being a twenty-first-century war, the Russian invasion of the Ukraine, while still relying on planes, tanks, and other kinetic weapons, now has a cyber element from beginning to end. Because of this cyber footprint, Microsoft is now a key observer and participant in the campaign, publishing a survey that includes key insights

> The Russian invasion relies in part on a cyber strategy that includes at least three distinct and sometimes coordinated efforts – destructive cyberattacks within Ukraine, network penetration and espionage outside Ukraine, and cyber influence operations targeting people around the world. (Smith, 2022)

As recently as the wars in Iraq and Afghanistan, strategic and tactical assessments were pretty exclusively products of think tanks (e.g., Institute for Defense Analysis (IDA), RAND, etc.); limited insight or input from traditional defense contractors. However, due to the scope and scale of cyber operations, operating system, and networking companies, "outsiders" with deep technical specialties, the folks who designed and developed this new domain of conflict, are now also providing their tactical insights as to the course of the engagements, missions, and campaigns, from a cyber perspective. This insight is leading some to consider what a software-focused acquisition system might look like (Fox and Probasco, 2022).

Cyber Operations: A Case Study Approach, First Edition. Jerry M. Couretas.
© 2024 John Wiley & Sons, Inc. Published 2024 by John Wiley & Sons, Inc.

Due to the heavy online footprint of the Russo-Ukraine war, technology companies (e.g., Microsoft) are playing a more active role in providing both analysis and insight regarding cyber activities that are related to the war. For example, in 2022 Microsoft acquired Miburo, a company specializing in detecting and attributing cyber influence campaigns across 16 languages (Burt, 2022). Advanced IO and IT analysis capabilities are important for understanding the developing cyber terrain that includes advanced firing platform development (Section 14.1) and the False Flag/Multi-Persona operations (Section 15.3). While the (mis) use of Cobalt Strike, a commercial penetration testing tool, made up approximately 2/3 of cyber attacks in 2022 (Rech, 2022), there are always new capabilities developing from the likes of Vulkan (Section 15.2.1).

As discussed in Chapter 3, crypto currency is a key method for criminals to take their payment for ransomware attacks. In Chapter 7, we discussed how the DPRK actively targets digital wallets and has garnered hundreds of millions of dollars by stealing from online gamers and other crypto currency enthusiasts. And in Chapter 17, we looked at how Russia and Iran circumvent sanctions by mining Bitcoin for exchangeable currency.

Iran has been using crypto currency to circumvent sanctions, with estimates as high as $8 billion worth of trades since 2018 (Chapter 8) (Angus Berwick, 2022). Similarly, Russian citizens are estimated to trade eight billion rubles per month, via crypto currency, in order to move money abroad (Angus Berwick, 2023). This is in addition to the Siberian crypto mining, the process of converting its oil and gas reserves into crypto currency, as discussed in Chapter 5.

We started looking at the cross pollination of cyber skills in Chapter 8, where we learned that China was training Iranian cyber operators in operational technology exploitation as early as 2013 through their 863 program (Perlroth, 2020). Similarly, Iran and Hezbollah, their proxy in Lebanon, sometimes use the same tool sets (i.e., Magic Kitten), implying a supportive cyber operations relationship between them (Colin Anderson, 2018).

The cyber tool release of 2016–2017, described in Chapter 3, resulted in the Shadow Brokers/Equation Group making the tools available on the Darknet. By 2017, Shadow Brokers' tools were key topics in Russian and Chinese darknet forums (Bing, 2017). Shortly thereafter, the DPRK was observed using EternalBlue for WannaCry ransomware attack (2017). And ransomware has been with us every since.

With software relying on persistent code libraries, one method to reduce future vulnerabilities will be to automate source code quality updates. The recent resurgence of artificial intelligence (AI) provides a security promise for automating the verification of open source and legacy code libraries based on known and developing vulnerabilities. For example, Anne Neuberger provided a comment on potential AI contributions.

> As Neuberger sees it, generative AI could conceivably be used to clean up old code bases, identify vulnerabilities in open-source repositories that lack dedicated maintainers, and even be used to produce provably secure code in formal languages that are hard for people to write. Companies that run extensive end-point security systems – and have access to the data they generate – are in a good position to train effective security models, she believes. (Elias Groll, 2023)

As shown, AI may be promising to ensure the code that we rely on for every day applications is secure in its sources. This helps ensure that each of our end points can be trusted to carry on day-to-day operations. There is precedent for this approach. For example, in the early 2000s Microsoft provided governments with the ability to review their operating system code on a limited basis (Bekker, 2003). This resulted in the ability of about 1/3 of the 193 registered governments getting access to Microsoft source code through visits to Microsoft for one to two weeks in order to assess the technical approach and offer criticism, where warranted.

While recent experience with China (Chapter 15 (Microsoft, 2022)) might argue against a peer review approach, another method might be to use standards, tested by an independent authority. Standards have helped in other areas (e.g., food, transportation, etc.) and can have a positive impact on cyber security. One development along these lines is that Underwriter's Lab, famous for ensuring the fire safety of electrical equipment, is also providing services for cyber gear (UL, 2023). This has the potential to be very helpful in the age of the Internet of Things (IoT).

Due to the human factor in each major cyber security failure, a culture of security, similar to the culture of quality introduced in manufacturing a generation ago, is increasingly seen as an answer to cyber security problems (Keman Huang, 2019). In the absence of voluntary approaches to cyber security, the Government may force a solution. For example, over two decades ago, as a result of Operation Moonlight Maze (circa, 2000), testimony (U.S. Senate, 2000) included the introduction of an Office of Business Assurance. However, this organization was never stood up.

> The Office of Business Assurance was never created. As you have already discovered, the idea for the creation of the Office of Business Assurance was suggested by James Adams, CEO of Infrastructure Defense Inc., in a hearing before the Senate Committee on Government Affairs, March 2, 2000. However, I have found no evidence that Congress took any additional steps in creating such an office. (Couretas, 2022)

A new government office might add focus to cyber defense. However, this office would also need to be complemented by improved technology. For example, looking at Table A.1, we see an over $1 million dollar savings, and one month cut in remediation time, for organizations that employ extended detection and response. Investments in advanced detection may therefore be the fastest route to cyber security.

III.A   Appendix I – Tool Examples

Table A.1   Tool Uses by Respective Actors.

Chapter Examples	Preparation	Engagement	Presence	Effect
S1C1, S1C2				• Facebook • Twitter
S1C3, S1C4	• Shadow Brokers	• PowerShell • DNS Tunneling • ToR • Spear Phishing	• RATS • Web Shells • Credential Stealers • Lateral Movement Frameworks • Command and Control Obfuscators	• Wiper(s) • Crypto Currency • PasteBin • Facebook • Twitter • RPI
S1C5	• Ryuk (?)	• Emotet • TrickBot • Cobalt Strike	• HAVEX/OPC • SolarWinds (?)	• BlackEnergy • Industroyer • Wiper(s)
S1C6	• Zero Day Production		• China Chopper • Cloud Hopper	• Great Cannon
S1C7		• Watering holes • H0lyGh0st	• Hidden Cobra	• WannaCry • Maui Ransomware
S1C8		• Log4J • SilverHawk (SEA)		• Wiper(s)
S1C9				• Wikileaks

Bibliography

Angus Berwick, P. K. (2023). *Binance, the Biggest Player in Crypto, Is Facing Legal Risks Over Russia*. Retrieved from Wall Street Journal: https://www.wsj.com/finance/binance-cryptocurrency-russia-sanctions-ddb948c3.

Angus Berwick, T. W. (2022). *Crypto Exchange Binance Helped Iranian Firms Trade $8 Billion Despite Sanctions*. Retrieved from Reuters: https://www.reuters.com/

business/finance/exclusive-crypto-exchange-binance-helped-iranian-firms-trade-8-billion-despite-2022-11-04/.

Bekker, S. (2003). *Microsoft Opens Source Code to Some Governments.* Retrieved 8 30, 2022, from Redmond Channel Partner: https://rcpmag.com/articles/2003/01/15/microsoft-opens-source-code-to-some-governments.aspx?m=1.

Bing, C. (2017). *Leaked NSA Hacking Tools are a Hit on the Dark Web.* Retrieved from Cyberscoop: https://cyberscoop.com/nsa-hacking-tools-shadow-brokers-dark-web-microsoft-smb/.

Burt, T. (2022). *In 2022 Microsoft Acquired Miburo, a Company Specializing in Detecting and Attributing Cyber Influence Campaigns Across 16 Languages.* Retrieved from Microsoft: https://blogs.microsoft.com/blog/2022/06/14/microsoft-to-acquire-miburo/.

Christine H. Fox, Emelia S. Probasco. (2022). *Big Tech Goes to War to Help Ukraine, Washington and Silicon Valley Must Work Together.* Retrieved from Foreign Affairs: https://www.foreignaffairs.com/ukraine/big-tech-goes-war.

Colin Anderson, K. S. (2018). *Iran's Cyber Ecosystem: Who Are the Threat Actors?* Retrieved from Carnegie Endowment for International Peace: https://carnegieendowment.org/2018/01/04/iran-s-cyber-ecosystem-who-are-threat-actors-pub-75140.

Couretas, J. (2022). Library of Congress Inquiry.

Elias Groll, C. V. (2023). *Reality Check: What will Generative AI Really do for Cybersecurity?* Retrieved from CyberScoop: https://cyberscoop.com/generative-ai-chatbots-cybersecurity/.

Keman Huang, K. P. (2019). *For What Technology Can't Fix: Building a Model of Organizational Cybersecurity Culture.* Retrieved 5 2, 2022, from MIT Sloan School of Management: https://web.mit.edu/smadnick/www/wp/2019-02.pdf.

Microsoft. (2022). *Microsoft Digital Defense Report 2022.* Retrieved 11 15, 2022, from Microsoft: https://query.prod.cms.rt.microsoft.com/cms/api/am/binary/RE5bUvv?culture=en-us&country=us.

Perlroth, N. (2020). *This is How they Tell me the World Ends.* New York: Bloomsbury.

Rech, M. (2022). *Ransomware Turns Cobalt Strike Into an Attack Vector.* Retrieved from Techguard Security: https://blog.techguard.com/ransomware-turns-cobalt-strike-into-an-attack-vector.

Smith, B. (2022). *Defending Ukraine: Early Lessons from the Cyber War.* Retrieved from Microsoft: https://blogs.microsoft.com/on-the-issues/2022/06/22/defending-ukraine-early-lessons-from-the-cyber-war/.

U.S. Senate. (2000). *Testimony of James Adams Chief Executive Officer Infrastructure Defense, Inc.* Retrieved from COMMITTEE ON GOVERNMENTAL AFFAIRS: https://www.hsgac.senate.gov/wp-content/uploads/imo/media/doc/adams.pdf.

UL. (2023). *Cybersecurity.* Retrieved from UL: https://www.ul.com/services/portfolios/cybersecurity.

Vanderlee, K. (2020). *They Come in the Night: Ransomware Deployment Trends.* Retrieved 5 2, 2022, from Mandiant Threat Research: https://www.mandiant.com/resources/they-come-in-the-night-ransomware-deployment-trends.

Verizon. (2021). *2022 Data Breach Investigations Report (DBIR).* Retrieved 10 20, 2021, from Verizon: https://enterprise.verizon.com/resources/reports/2021/2021-data-breach-investigations-report.pdf?_ga=2.104515456.1203943201.1634719020-1809100645.1633781925.

CCS Glossary

911 Centers Cyber attacks, in the form of denial of service, or even ransomware, are used to incapacitate emergency response systems.

Abu Sayyaf Abu Sayyaf was an ISIS leader with intimate understanding of the finance and demographic makeup of ISIS.

Al Ababil Iranian cyber operation against U.S. financial firms (2012).

Al-Qaeda Logistical support network started to support Muslims fighting the Soviet Union in the late 1980s. Later, Al-Qaeda attacked the United States in the 9–11 attack on New York's world trade towers, and multiple attack attempts since that time.

Al-Qaeda in Iraq (AQI) Al-Qaeda in Iraq first appeared in 2004, when Abū Muṣʿab al-Zarqāwī, a Jordanian-born militant already leading insurgent attacks in Iraq, formed an alliance with al-Qaeda, pledging his group's allegiance to Osama bin Laden in return for bin Laden's endorsement as the leader of al-Qaeda's franchise in Iraq. Al-Zarqāwī, who quickly came to be regarded as one of the most destructive militants in Iraq, organized a wave of attacks, often suicide bombings, that targeted security forces, government institutions, and Iraqi civilians. Predecessor of ISIS.

Al Quds Force (IRGC) The IRGC-QF is one of the Iranian regime's primary organizations responsible for conducting covert lethal activities outside of Iran, including asymmetric and terrorist operations. Iran views terrorism as a tool that it can use to support its efforts to deter and counter its perceived foes, assert leadership over Shia Muslims worldwide, and project power in the Middle East.

Al Shamoon Iranian cyber operation against Saudi Aramco. Consisted of two phases in 2012 and 2017.

Al Sharyat Air Field Attack (2017) U.S. bombardment of Syria's Al Sharyat airfield, from which Syria launched nerve gas attacks on its own citizens on April 4, 2017.

Andariel Part of DPRK Lazarus (APT 38) financial operations team.

Anonymous Anonymous, decentralized international movement of digital activists known for generating high-profile cyber attacks against governments, companies, and other institutions.

Cyber Operations: A Case Study Approach, First Edition. Jerry M. Couretas.
© 2024 John Wiley & Sons, Inc. Published 2024 by John Wiley & Sons, Inc.

Anthem Breach Anthem Blue Cross Blue Shield announced that approximately 78.8 million former and current policyholders nationwide had personal information stolen in a cyber attack of the company's IT system.

Arab Spring Wave of pro-democracy protests and uprisings that took place in the Middle East and North Africa beginning in 2010 and 2011, challenging some of the region's entrenched authoritarian regimes. The wave began when protests in Tunisia and Egypt toppled their regimes in quick succession, inspiring similar attempts in other Arab countries.

Artificial Intelligence/Machine Learning (AI/ML) AI is the broader concept of enabling a machine or system to sense, reason, act, or adapt like a human and ML is an application of AI that allows machines to extract knowledge from data and learn from it autonomously.

Attack the Network (AtN) the development of initiatives in support of anticipatory analysis and effective planning for lethal/non-lethal engagement of networks including the understanding of the complex nature of threat networks and their interaction with neutral/friendly ones;

Axie Infinity Axie Infinity is a Pokemon-inspired play-to-earn metaverse game created on the Ethereum blockchain. Lunacia, the Axie homeland, is made up of 90,601 land plots. Players can gather, grow, breed, and battle digital creatures known as Axies.

Bangladesh bank National bank of Bangladesh.

BazarCall BazarCall malware uses malicious call centers to infect victims.

Beacon BEACON is the name for Cobalt Strike's default malware payload used to create a connection to the team server. Active callback sessions from a target are also called "beacons." (This is where the malware family got its name.) There are two types of BEACON: (1) The Stager is an optional BEACON payload. Operators can "stage" their malware by sending an initial small BEACON shellcode payload that only does some basic checks and then queries the configured C2 for the fully featured backdoor. (2) The Full backdoor can either be executed through a BEACON stager, by a "loader" malware family, or by directly executing the default DLL export "ReflectiveLoader." This backdoor runs in memory and can establish a connection to the team server through several methods.

Belt and Road Initiative (BRI) The Belt and Road Initiative is a massive China-led infrastructure project that aims to stretch around the globe.

Bitcoin a type of digital currency in which a record of transactions is maintained and new units of currency are generated by the computational solution of mathematical problems, and which operates independently of a central bank.

Blender See Mixer.

Blockchain A system in which a record of transactions made in Bitcoin or another cryptocurrency are maintained across several computers that are linked in a peer-to-peer network. Blockchain is a shared, immutable ledger, and forms the basis for developing crypto currencies.

Bluenoroff Part of DPRK Lazarus (APT 38) financial operations team.

Botnet A botnet, a blend of "robot" and "network," is a network of computers infected by malware and under the control of a single attacking party known as the "bot-herder." Each infected machine, referred to as a bot, works in unison with others within the botnet.

Byzantine Hades Intrusion set by Chinese cyber operators in the mid-1990s.

Chaos Computer Club The Chaos Computer Club e. V. (CCC) is Europe's largest association of hackers. For more than 30 years, we are providing information about technical and societal issues, such as surveillance, privacy, freedom of information, hacktivism, data security, and many other interesting things around technology and hacking issues. As the most influential hacker collective in Europe, we organize campaigns, events, lobbying, and publications as well as anonymizing services and communication infrastructure. There are many hackerspaces in and around Germany which belong to or share a common bond to the CCC as stated in our hacker ethics.

China Chopper China Chopper is a web shell that allows attackers to retain access to an infected system using a client-side application, which contains all the logic required to control the target.

China Message (Information Operations (IO)) The Chinese Communist Party (CCP) relies on an extensive influence apparatus that spans a range of print and broadcast media, with varying degrees of attributability, to advance both its domestic monopoly on power and its claims to global leadership. This apparatus draws on nearly a century of experience running information operations.

CI0P CI0p ransomware group – first identified in February 2019 – has been confirmed as the perpetrator behind the MOVEit Transfer exploitation. The group follows the common tactic of "naming and shaming" victims by posting company profiles on their leak site to coerce them into paying the ransom.

Cobalt Strike Cobalt Strike is a commercial adversary simulation software that is marketed to red teams but is also stolen and actively used by a wide range of threat actors from ransomware operators to espionage-focused Advanced Persistent Threats (APTs).

Cold War the state of political hostility that existed between the Soviet bloc countries and the U.S.-led Western powers from 1945 to 1990.

Colonial Pipeline The Colonial Pipeline hack is the largest publicly disclosed cyber attack against critical infrastructure in the United States. The attack involved multiple stages against Colonial Pipeline IT systems. The pipeline's operational technology systems that actually move oil were not directly compromised during the attack. The attack began when a hacker group identified as DarkSide accessed the Colonial Pipeline network. The attackers stole 100 GB of data within a two-hour window. Following the data theft, the attackers infected the Colonial Pipeline IT network with ransomware that affected many computer systems, including billing and accounting.

Command and Control (C2) Command and control (C2) is often used by attackers to retain communications with compromised systems within a target network. They then issue commands and controls to compromised systems (as simple as a timed beacon, or as involved as remote control or data mining). It is usually the compromised system/host that initiates communication from inside a network to a command and control server on the public Internet. Establishing a command and control link is often the primary objective of malware.

CONTI Gang Conti was an extremely damaging ransomware due to the speed with which encrypts data and spreads to other systems. It was first observed in 2020, and it is thought to be led by a Russia-based cybercrime group that goes under the Wizard Spider pseudonym.

Costa Rican Ransomware Operation On April 11, 2022, Conti began their last incursion under this brand after gaining initial access to the Costa Rica government's network and engaging in reconnaissance activity. More than 10 Cobalt Strike beacon sessions were set up in the early stages of the attack. According to a note on the Conti leak site, the ransom demand was initially $10 million and then increased to $20 million when Costa Rica refused to pay. Following this crippling attack, Costa Rica was forced on May 8 to declare a national emergency as the intrusion had extended to multiple government bodies, with some agencies resuming activity in early June.

Counter-Improvised Explosive Device (C-IED) A broad set of efforts used to counter-improvised explosive devices used to attack coalition troops in Iraq and Afghanistan.

Counter-Insurgency (COIN) a program or an act of combating guerrilla warfare and subversion.

Counterfeiting Copying an object and portraying it as an original.

Crypto heist Theft of crypto currency.

Crypto jacking Use of another organization's resources to mine crypto currency.

Crypto currency A digital currency in which encryption techniques are used to regulate the generation of units of currency and verify the transfer of funds, operating independently of a central bank. A digital currency that is stored and recorded on an immutable ledger (i.e., blockchain).

Cuckoo's Egg Book, written as a detective story, that follows a system administrator's journey to determine who is cracking into U.S. national systems in the 1980s.

Cut Out A mechanism or person used to create a compartment between the members of an operation to allow them to pass material or messages securely; also an agent who functions as an intermediary between a spymaster and other subagents.

Cyber Attack Path An attack path is a path a malicious actor may take after exploiting a vulnerability or weakness within your attack surface. The attack path is a visual representation of possible paths an attacker could take to compromise an asset from any entry point.

Cyber Operations Tracker Council on Foreign Relations list of reported cyber operations going back to 2005 (https://www.cfr.org/cyber-operations/).

Darkside DarkSide Hacker Group is a cybercriminal organization that extorts organizations worldwide with ransomware. Among "big game hunter" cybercriminals, DarkSide Hacker Group is one of the most selective, allegedly refusing to target any sort of medical, educational, or government targets.

Denial of Service (DoS) Computer system is denied the ability to perform legitimate services due to the actions of a malicious cyber actor.

DigiNotar Formerly a Dutch certificate authority – destroyed by an Iranian compromise that the IRGC used to access gmail inboxes of Iranian citizens.

Digital Wallet Digital wallets are financial applications that allow you to store funds, make transactions, and track payment histories on devices like phones and tablets.

Domain Name A domain name is a string of text that maps to an alphanumeric IP address, used to access a website from client software. In plain English, a domain name is the text that a user types into a browser window to reach a particular website. For instance, the domain name for Google is 'google.com'.

Emmanet Pasargad Iranian contractor that supported information operations discrediting the 2020 U.S. presidential election.

EMOTET The Emotet banking Trojan was first identified by security researchers in 2014. Emotet was originally designed as a banking malware that attempted to sneak onto your computer and steal sensitive and private information. Later versions of the software saw the addition of spamming and malware delivery services – including other banking Trojans. Emotet uses functionality that helps the software evade detection by some anti-malware products.

Emotet uses worm-like capabilities to help spread to other connected computers. This helps in distribution of the malware. This functionality has led the Department of Homeland Security to conclude that Emotet is one of the most costly and destructive malware, affecting government and private sectors, individuals, and organizations, and costing upwards of $1M per incident to clean up.

Equifax Breach In September of 2017, Equifax announced a data breach that exposed the personal information of 147 million people. The company has agreed to a global settlement with the Federal Trade Commission, the Consumer Financial Protection Bureau, and 50 U.S. states and territories. The settlement includes up to $425 million to help people affected by the data breach.

EternalBlue EternalBlue is an exploit that allows cyber threat actors to remotely execute arbitrary code and gain access to a network by sending specially crafted packets. It exploits a software vulnerability. in Microsoft's Windows operating systems (OS) Server Message Block (SMB) version 1 (SMBv1).

EternalRomance EternalRomance is one of the handful of "exploitation tools" leaked by a group called The Shadow Brokers (TSB) that take advantage of weaknesses in how Windows implemented the Server Message Block (SMB) protocol. Successful exploitation results in a remote code execution (RCE) attack.

F-35 The F-35A is the U.S. Air Force's latest fifth-generation fighter. It will replace the U.S. Air Force's aging fleet of F-16 Fighting Falcons and A-10 Thunderbolt II's, which have been the primary fighter aircraft for more than 20 years, and bring with it an enhanced capability to survive in the advanced threat environment in which it was designed to operate.

Facebook Facebook is a social networking website that was founded in February 2004 to provide an online book of faces for Harvard university students to connect and share information.

False Flag operations (Al Qassem Brigade) False Flag is a form of deception where the perpetrator masquerades as another entity when performing a crime.

Five-Year Plans Economic planning system often used in Stalinist/Communist command driven economies (especially in the former Soviet Union) a government plan for economic development over five years. The first such plan in the Soviet Union was inaugurated in 1928.

Foxblade FoxBlade is a malicious trojan installed on systems to enable Distributed Denial of Service (DDoS) attacks, which means that the malware is not deployed within the target environments, but instead installed on as many targets as possible. Once enough systems are compromised, the infected machines can be collectively controlled to knock the actual target off the Internet by flooding their public network connections with more traffic than they can handle.

Ghostwriter The Ghostwriter campaign is a cyber-enabled influence campaign that integrates information, manipulation tactics, and techniques and has triggered multiple social control responses from across several European countries.

GRU – Russian Foreign Intelligence Agency (Glavnoye razvedyvatel'noye – GRU) It is the Russian acronym for Main Intelligence Directorate of the armed forces.

Guccifer 2.0 "Guccifer 2.0" is a persona which claimed to be the hacker(s) that hacked into the Democratic National Committee (DNC) computer network and then leaked its documents to the media, the website WikiLeaks, and a conference event. Some of the documents "Guccifer 2.0" released to the media appear to be forgeries cobbled together from public information and previous hacks, which had been mixed with disinformation. According to indictments in February 2018, the persona is operated by Russian military intelligence agency GRU. On July 13, 2018, Special Counsel Robert Mueller indicted 12 GRU agents for allegedly perpetrating the cyber attacks.

Hacktivist a person who gains unauthorized access to computer files or networks in order to further social or political ends.

Hash power Hash power or hashing power is the power that your computer or hardware uses to run and solve different hashing algorithms. These algorithms are used for generating new crypto currencies and allowing transactions between them. This process is also called mining.

HAVEX Havex is a Remote Access Trojan (RAT) that communicates with a command and control (C&C) server. The C&C server can deploy payloads that provide additional functionality. ICS-CERT has identified and analyzed one payload that enumerates all connected network resources, such as computers or shared resources, and uses the classic DCOM-based (Distributed Component Object Model) version of the Open Platform Communications (OPC) standard to gather information about connected control system devices and resources within the network. The known components of the identified Havex payload do not appear to target devices using the newer OPC Unified Architecture (UA) standard.

HermeticWiper Malware HermeticWiper is a new form of destructive malware designed to infiltrate Windows devices and render them inoperable by destroying files, corrupting Master Boot Record (MBR), and afflicting physical drives belonging to Ukraine organizations.

Hezballah (Lebanon) Lebanese proxy of the Iranian IRGC that includes cyber and military units.

Industrial Control Systems (ICS) An information system used to control industrial processes such as manufacturing, product handling, production, and distribution. Industrial control systems include supervisory control and data acquisition systems used to control geographically dispersed assets, as well as distributed control systems and smaller control systems using programmable logic controllers to control localized processes.

Industroyer Malware Industroyer is a malware framework considered to have been used in the cyber attack on Ukraine's power grid on December 17, 2016. The attack cut a fifth of Kiev, the capital, off power for one hour. It is the first ever known malware specifically designed to attack electrical grids.

Information Operations (IO) The integrated employment, during military operations, of information-related capabilities in concert with other lines of operation to influence, disrupt, corrupt, or usurp the decision-making of adversaries and potential adversaries while protecting our own. Also called IO.

Information-Related Capabilities (IRCs) IRCs are the tools, techniques, or activities that affect any of the three dimensions of the information environment. They affect the ability of the target audience (TA) to collect, process, or disseminate information before and after decisions are made.

Initial Access Broker (IAB) Initial access brokers are threat actors that sell cybercriminals access to corporate networks. They are highly skilled in their field and possess a specialized set of skills honed over a long period of black hat hacking that they utilize to access secure networks.

Intrusion Set

Iowa Food Cooperative (NEW) On September 20, 2021, an Iowa grain co-op said it was hit with a cyber attack that security researchers are linking to newly launched ransomware group BlackMatter, which the researchers said demanded $5.9 million to unlock the organization's data.

Irhabi007 One of the initial online jihadists disseminating propaganda and tactical military training via the Internet.

ISIS the Islamic State of Iraq and Syria (ISIS).

J-31 The Shenyang J-31 (F-60) is a fifth-generation, multi-role, twin-engine stealth fighter aircraft being manufactured for the People's Liberation Army Air Force (PLAAF) by Shenyang Aircraft Corporation, an affiliate of Aviation Industry Corporation of China (AVIC).

JBS Foods JBS Foods paid an $11 million ransom to cybercriminals after it was forced to halt cattle-slaughtering operations at 13 of its meat processing plants. JBS confirmed the payment in a statement following a cyber attack attributed to the Russian-speaking ransomware gang "REvil." The company paid the ransom in Bitcoin cryptocurrency to prevent further disruptions of the meat plants, mitigating potential damage to the food supply – including restaurants, grocery stores and farmers that rely on JBS production.

Julian Assange Australian computer programmer who founded the media organization WikiLeaks. Practicing what he called "scientific journalism" – i.e., providing primary source materials with a minimum of editorial commentary – Assange, through WikiLeaks, released thousands of internal or classified documents from an assortment of government and corporate entities.

Kata'ib Hizballah (Iraq) Founded in 2007, KH seeks to establish an Iran-aligned government in Iraq, expel U.S. and coalition forces from the country, and advance Iranian interests throughout the Middle East.

Killnet KillNet is a Russia-aligned hacktivist group that gained notoriety during the first month of the Russian–Ukraine conflict when they began a widespread – although relatively unsophisticated – campaign of Distributed Denial of Service (DDoS) attacks, political rhetoric, and misinformation. KillNet's self-proclaimed anti-war axiom states that their primary targets are supporters of Ukraine, including NATO countries and their allies.

Kimsuky DPRK information operations group focused on South Korea.

Korea Computing Center The Korea Computer Center (KCC), the leading IT R& D base of the DPRK, was founded on October 24, 1990, under the careful guidance of President Kim Il Sung and leader Kim Jong Il.

Lazarus DPRK Lazarus financial operations team (APT 38).

Letter of Marque A letter of marque authorizes private parties to engage in conduct that, absent the letter, would legally be piracy. Used extensively during the War of 1812, these letters allowed privateers to capture British merchant ships, leveraging private sector efforts in a controlled manner.

Lin Yong Chinese Patriotic hactivist, leader of the Honker Union, active in the late 1990s (Henderson).

Malware software that is specifically designed to disrupt, damage, or gain unauthorized access to a computer system.

Mandiant Mandiant is one of the leaders in cyber threat intelligence.

Mao's Three Phase Insurgency Model It is a doctrine to capture State power through a combination of armed insurgency, mass mobilization, and strategic alliances. The Maoists also use propaganda and disinformation against state institutions as other components of their insurgency doctrine. Mao called this process, the "Protracted Peoples War," where the emphasis is on "military line" to capture power.

Maroochy Shire In November 2001, 49-year-old Vitek Boden was sentenced to 2 years in prison for using stolen wireless radio, SCADA controller and control software to release up to one million liters of sewage into the river and coastal waters of Maroochydore in Queensland, Australia.

Metasploit The Metasploit framework is a very powerful tool, which can be used by cybercriminals as well as ethical hackers to probe systematic vulnerabilities on networks and servers. Because it is an open-source framework, it can be easily customized and used with most operating systems.

Ministry of Intelligence and Security (MOIS) The primary mission of Iran's intelligence agencies is to keep the Islamic regime in power. The Ministry of Intelligence and Security (MOIS) and the Islamic Revolutionary Guard Corps (IRGC) Intelligence Organization are the main intelligence agencies. Their missions overlap extensively because their agendas are broad.

Ministry of State Security (DPRK) DPRK national police organization that reports directly to the Supreme Leader.

Mirim College Advanced training institute for cyber adept DPRK cadre.

Mixer A crypto mixer is a service that blends the crypto currencies of many users together to obfuscate the origins and owners of the funds. Because Bitcoin, Ethereum, and most other public blockchains are transparent, this level of privacy is otherwise hard to achieve.

Morris Worm The Morris Worm was a self-replicating computer program (worm) written by Robert Tappan Morris, a student at Cornell University, and released from MIT on November 2, 1988. According to Morris, the purpose of the worm was to gauge the size of the precursor "Internet" of the time – ARPANET – although it unintentionally caused Denial of Service (DoS) for around 10% of the 60,000 machines connected to ARPANET in 1988. The worm spread by exploiting vulnerabilities in UNIX send mail, finger, and rsh/rexec as well as by guessing weak passwords. Before spreading to a new machine, the Morris Worm checked if the machine had already been infected and was running a Morris Worm process. If a target machine had already been infected, the Morris Worm would re-infect it one in seven times. This practice of "1-in-7 re-infection" ensured that a user could not completely avoid a Morris Worm infection by creating a fake Morris Worm process to pretend his or her machine was already infected. It also caused some users' machines to be infected many times – once too many Morris Worm processes were running on a target machine it would run out of computing resources and begin to malfunction.

Mossack Fonseca Due to outdated, unpatched, software, the Mossack Fonseca exfiltration included 11.5 million confidential documents dating from the 1970s through late 2015. The 2.6 terabytes of leaked data include 4.8 million emails, 3 million database format files, 2.2 million PDFs, 1.1 million images, and 320,000 text documents.

Muddy Water Targets governments, primarily in the Middle East and South Asia, for espionage purposes.

Mujihideen e Kalq (MEK) The Mujahedeen-e-Khalq or MEK is a controversial Iranian resistance group; it was once listed as a Foreign Terrorist Organization (FTO) by the United States for its alleged killing of U.S. personnel in Iran during the 1970s, and for its ties to former Iraqi leader Saddam Hussein.

Natanz Nuclear Facility One of the targets of the STUXNET worm whose centrifuges reportedly spun out of control, destroying the Uranium enrichment process, and delaying the Iranian nuclear program.

National Fraud and Cyber Crime Reporting CISA call center for reporting cyber crimes.

National Information Network (NIN) The Iranian government has undertaken a massive project named the National Information Network NIN to provide better connectivity to their populace and to better control communication – both inside and leaving Iran.

Navy Marine Corps Internet (NMCI) The Navy Marine Corps Intranet (NMCI) is the second-largest network in the world; only the Internet is larger.

Network Battalion 65 (NB65) Network Battalion 65, a pro-Ukrainian outfit, appeared on Twitter in February 2022 and almost immediately started compromising high-profile Russian targets with alarming regularity, under the #OpRussia banner.

NotPetya The NotPetya malware was spread by a centralized update to the MeDoc tax accounting software used by many Ukrainian businesses. The malware was using the EternalBlue exploit, possibly developed by the NSA, leaked by a hacker group calling itself the Shadow Brokers, and repurposed by the GRU.

Office of Personnel Management (OPM) (U.S.) The U.S. Office of Personnel Management (OPM) serves as the chief human resources agency and personnel policy manager for the Federal Government. OPM provides human resources leadership and support to federal agencies and helps the federal workforce achieve their aspirations as they serve the American people.

Open-Source Software Open-source software (OSS) is software that is distributed with its source code, making it available for use, modification, and distribution with its original rights.

Operation Aurora Operation Aurora was a series of cyber attacks from China that targeted U.S. private sector companies in 2010. The threat actors conducted a phishing campaign that compromised the networks of Yahoo, Adobe, Dow Chemical, Morgan Stanley, Google, and more than two dozen other companies to steal their trade secrets.

Operation Cleaver This threat actor targets governments and private sector entities for espionage and sabotage purposes. It is believed to be responsible for compromising U.S. Navy computers at the Navy Marine Corps Intranet in San Diego, the U.S. energy company Calpine Corporation, Saudi Aramco, Pemex, Qatar Airways, and Korean Air.

Operation Desert Fox In response to Saddam Hussein's continued refusal to cooperate with U.N. weapons inspectors, the United States Government planned Operation DESERT FOX in the fall of 1998. The primary mission of DESERT FOX was to strike military targets in Iraq that contributed to its ability to produce, store, maintain, and deliver weapons of mass destruction (WMD).

Operation Ghostnet GhostNet was a large-scale electronic espionage program used to spy on individuals, organizations, and governments. The threat actors breached 1295 computers in 103 countries over a two-year period, predominately focusing on governments in Southeast Asia.

Operation Newscaster Iranian threat actors used more than a dozen fake personas on popular social networking sites, to run a wide-spanning cyber espionage operation (2011–2014).

Operation Night Dragon Chinese cyber operation that included in-depth probing of U.S. natural gas infrastructure (CISA).

Operation Orchard (2007) In Operation Orchard, Israel secretly destroys a reactor at Al Kibar, a Syrian military facility thought to be a nuclear site constructed with the help of North Koreans.

Operation Titan Rain Titan Rain was a string of cyber operations that compromised a number of agencies within the U.S. and U.K. governments.

Chinese state-sponsored actors are suspected of breaching the unclassified networks of the U.S. Departments of State, Homeland Security, and Energy, and U.K. defense and foreign ministries.

Patriotic Hackers Hackers, often vigilantes, working on behalf of their perception of what their country needs in protesting the actions of another organization/ country.

Phishing the fraudulent practice of sending emails or other messages purporting to be from reputable companies in order to induce individuals to reveal personal information, such as passwords and credit card numbers.

Ransomware Ransomware is a malware designed to deny a user or organization access to files on their computer. By encrypting these files and demanding a ransom payment for the decryption key, cyber attackers place organizations in a position where paying the ransom is the easiest and cheapest way to regain access to their files.

Raqqa City in Syria where ISIS established a headquarters from 2013 to 2017.

Reconnaissance General Bureau (DPRK) DPRK military organization where APT 38 and APT 43 are manned and supported.

ReVIL Gang REVIL, also known as Sodinokibi, was a notorious ransomware gang that was active from at least April 2019 until (officially) it was dismantled in January 2022. Leading up to its demise, REvil became one of the most successful and damaging cybercrime syndicates in the world.

Room 39 Cell in the Worker's Party of Korea chartered with generating revenue by extra legal means.

Rye Dam Iranian cyber attack on a small dam outside of New York City. Mersad was the contractor that performed the attack.

RYUK Ryuk ransomware is a type of malware that hackers aim at high-value targets to infect systems and encrypt files until a ransom is paid.

Sands Casino Iranian cyber retribution attack that destroyed the IT systems of a casino company – $40 million in estimated damages.

Sandworm Sandworm, also known as Unit 74,455, is allegedly a Russian cyber military unit of the GRU, the organization in charge of Russian military intelligence.

Server Message Block (SMB) SMB (Server Message Block) is a Windows communication protocol that allows users to share files, access print services, and browse across a local area network (LAN).

Shadow Brokers The Shadow Brokers is a cyber threat actor group that became visible for their disclosures relating to the U.S. government's National Security Agency's hacking tools. To gain notoriety, they published hacking tools, which they attributed to the Equation Group.

Silk Road Silk Road was a notorious cyber black market for illicit goods, and the first dark web market of the Internet era. Launched in 2011 and shut down by the FBI in 2013, Silk Road paved the way for today's underground world of dark web marketplaces.

Social Engineering Social engineering is the tactic of manipulating, influencing, or deceiving a victim in order to gain control over a computer system, or to steal personal and financial information. It uses psychological manipulation to trick users into making security mistakes or giving away sensitive information.

Social Network Analysis (SNA) Social network analysis (SNA) is the broad general term used for representing connections among people and using graph analytic techniques to explore characteristics of that network.

SolarWinds A hacker group believed to be affiliated with the Russian government gained access to computer systems belonging to multiple U.S. government departments including the U.S. Treasury and Commerce in a long campaign that is believed to have started in March. The attack involved hackers compromising the infrastructure of SolarWinds, a company that produces a network and applications monitoring platform called Orion, and then using that access to produce and distribute trojanized updates to the software's users. On a page on its website that was taken down after news broke out, SolarWinds stated that its customers included 425 of the U.S. Fortune 500, the top ten U.S. telecommunications companies, the top five U.S. accounting firms, all branches of the U.S. Military, the Pentagon, the State Department, as well as hundreds of universities and colleges worldwide. The SolarWinds software supply chain attack was performed by APT29 or Cozy Bear, the hacking arm of Russia's foreign intelligence service, the SVR.

Sony Hack Denial of Service attack in 2014 on Sony Pictures for producing a film parodying Kim Jong Un, Supreme Leader of the DPRK.

Spam Spam is any kind of unwanted, unsolicited digital communication that gets sent out in bulk. Often spam is sent via email, but it can also be distributed via text messages, phone calls, or social media.

Star Wars U.S. defense program during the 1980s with the goal of providing a shield for the United States from intercontinental ballistic missiles (ICBMs).

Strategic Effect "A strategic effect occurs if and only if an action disrupts an adversary's strategy." (Thomas Tighe).

STUXNET Stuxnet is a computer worm that was originally aimed at Iran's nuclear facilities and has since mutated and spread to other industrial and energy-producing facilities. The original Stuxnet malware attack targeted the programmable logic controllers (PLCs) used to automate machine processes.

Supervisory Control and Data Acquisition (SCADA) A generic name for a computerized system that is capable of gathering and processing data and applying operational controls over long distances. Typical uses include power transmission and distribution and pipeline systems. SCADA was designed for the unique communication challenges (e.g., delays, data integrity) posed by the various media that must be used, such as phone lines, microwave, and satellite. Usually shared rather than dedicated.

Supply Chain The software supply chain consists of code, configurations, proprietary and open-source binaries, libraries, plugins, and container dependencies. It also includes building orchestrators and tools such as assemblers, compilers, code analyzers and repositories, security, monitoring, and logging ops tools. The software supply chain also encompasses the people, organizations, and processes involved in software development.

Swatting the action or practice of making a prank call to emergency services in an attempt to bring about the dispatch of a large number of armed police officers to a particular address.

Syrian Electronic Army A loosely organized collective of Syrian government–affiliated threat actors that have targeted a wide range of entities since 2011.

Tan Dailin Key Chinese hacker (APT 40, APT 41) on FBI's most wanted list (FBI ref).

Task Force Ares Joint Task Force Ares was created in 2016 to combat the militant organization online as a compliment to the global coalition fighting against the group's grip on power in Iraq and Syria.

TeaMp0isoN TeaMp0isoN was a small threat actor group that reached prominence and garnered publicity in 2012 for its black hat hacking activities. These hacking activities included attacks on the United Nations, Facebook, Minecraft Forums, NATO, NASA, and several government and commercial organizations. In 2012, TeaMp0isoN was disbanded following the arrest of two founders, Trick (actual name withheld) and MLT. Trick was purported to have hacked into the email account of a staffer of former U.K. Prime Minister Tony Blair and then exposed that information online. In addition, Trick published email addresses and phone numbers of Tony Blair's family, key contacts, and members of the U.K. government. Trick also admitted to deluging the U.K.'s national anti-terrorism hotline with automated phone calls. This attack was considered a denial-of-service attack. Trick's involvement in the U.K. hacking resulted in him being jailed for six months. Trick was expected to get a university education but instead failed to attend and ultimately relocated to the Middle East in support of ISIS activities.

The Onion Router (ToR) The Onion Router (Tor) is an open-source software program that allows users to protect their privacy and security against a common form of Internet surveillance known as traffic analysis. Tor was originally developed for the U.S. Navy in an effort to protect government communications. The name of the software originated as an acronym for the Onion Router, but Tor is now the official name of the program.

Tomahawk Land Attack Missile (TLAM) The Tomahawk Land Attack Missile (TLAM) is a long range cruise missile used for deep land attack warfare, launched from U.S. Navy surface ships and U.S. Navy and United Kingdom Royal Navy submarines.

TriCk see TeaMp0isoN.

Trickbot TrickBot (or "TrickLoader") is a recognized banking Trojan that targets both businesses and consumers for their data, such as banking information, account credentials, personally identifiable information (PII), and even Bitcoins. As a highly modular malware, it can adapt to any environment or network it finds itself in. The many tricks this Trojan has done since its discovery in 2016 are attributed to the creativity and agility of its developers. On top of stealing, TrickBot has been given capabilities to move laterally and gain a foothold within an affected network using exploits, propagate copies of itself via Server Message Block (SMB) shares, drop other malware like Ryuk ransomware, and scout for documents and media files on infected host machines.

TRITON TRITON is one of a limited number of publicly identified malicious software families targeted at industrial control systems (ICS). It follows Stuxnet, which was used against Iran in 2010 and Industroyer which was believed to be deployed by Sandworm Team against the Ukraine in 2016. TRITON is consistent with these attacks, in that it could prevent safety mechanisms from executing their intended function, resulting in a physical consequence.

Typosquat Typosquatting is what we call it when people – often criminals – register a common misspelling of another organization's domain as their own. For example: tailspintoy.com instead of tailspintoys.com (note the missing "s").

Voting Machines A machine for the automatic registering of votes.

WannaCry Ransomware attack in 2017 that caused $4–$8 billion in damage; U.K. National Health Service was estimated to require $100 million for remediation from the attack.

White House Home of sitting U.S. President and usually associated as the seat of executive power.

Wikileaks WikiLeaks is a whistleblowing platform founded by Julian Assange. It was established to obtain and disseminate classified documents and data sets from anonymous sources and leakers.

Wiper A wiper is malware that deletes or destroys an organization's access to files and data. This type of malware is commonly used as a tool for destruction and disruption since the loss of critical information could make it impossible for an organization to maintain business operations or carry out certain actions.

Worker's Party of Korea Reporting directly to the Supreme Leader, the Worker's Party of Korea, this is the sole ruling party in North Korea.

Xi Jinpin Leader of the Chinese Communist Party (CCP) (2013 –).

Yara Rules YARA rules are like a piece of programming language, they work by defining a number of variables that contain patterns found in a sample of malware. If some or all of the conditions are met, depending on the rule, then it can be used to successfully identify a piece of malware.

Yemen Cyber Army Alleged Yemeni cyber contingent to parallel fighting against Saudi Arabia in cyberspace.

Zero Trust Zero Trust is a security framework requiring all users, whether in or outside the organization's network, to be authenticated, authorized, and continuously validated for security configuration and posture before being granted or keeping access to applications and data. Zero Trust assumes that there is no traditional network edge; networks can be local, in the cloud, or a combination or hybrid with resources anywhere as well as workers in any location.

Index

Cyber Operations: A Case Study Approach, First Edition. Jerry M. Couretas.
© 2024 John Wiley & Sons, Inc. Published 2024 by John Wiley & Sons, Inc.

Printed and bound by CPI Group (UK) Ltd, Croydon, CR0 4YY

27/10/2024

14580268-0001